Legitimacy and Effectiveness of ESMA's Soft Law

ELGAR STUDIES IN LAW AND REGULATION

Series Editor: Roger Brownsword, *Professor of Law, King's College London, UK*

Regulation is a ubiquitous concept in today's world. The proliferation of new technologies necessitates continual re-appraisal of the rules that govern them, whilst globalization increases the complexity of interaction between governance systems on a national, regional and international level. As a field of study, regulation continues to grow and evolve, both in consideration of specific sectors, and at a conceptual level, as the rationale and motivation for regulation are scrutinized.

This new and exciting series is an important forum for original works of scholarship that explore regulation and its interaction with the law. It favours work that has a critical, innovative or analytical perspective and, whilst having a primary focus on legal writing, welcomes approaches that draw on other disciplines. The scope of the series encompasses a wide range of regulatory fields, from biotechnology and ICT to machine learning and AI, from security, food, and environment to health, leisure, and employment. At the same time the series plays host to broader discussions on the nature of risk, governance models, the role of democracy, regulatory theory and many others.

The primary mission of the series is to stimulate the development of original thinking across law and regulation and to foster the best theoretical and empirical scholarship in the field.

Titles in the series include:

Regulatory Stewardship of Health Research
Navigating Participant Protection and Research Promotion
Edward S. Dove

Competition and Regulation in the Data Economy
Does Artificial Intelligence Demand a New Balance?
Gintarė Surblytė-Namavičienė

The Structure of Regulation
Explaining Why Regulation Succeeds and Fails
David Williamson and Gary Lynch-Wood

Legitimacy and Effectiveness of ESMA's Soft Law
Marloes van Rijsbergen

Legitimacy and Effectiveness of ESMA's Soft Law

Marloes van Rijsbergen

Currently works as Senior Policy Advisor at the Dutch Authority for the Financial Markets in the Netherlands

ELGAR STUDIES IN LAW AND REGULATION

Edward Elgar
PUBLISHING

Cheltenham, UK • Northampton, MA, USA

All thoughts and opinions expressed in this book are personal and do not necessarily reflect the view of the Dutch Authority for the Financial Markets in the Netherlands to which Marloes van Rijsbergen is affiliated.

Published by
Edward Elgar Publishing Limited
The Lypiatts
15 Lansdown Road
Cheltenham
Glos GL50 2JA
UK

Edward Elgar Publishing, Inc.
William Pratt House
9 Dewey Court
Northampton
Massachusetts 01060
USA

A catalogue record for this book
is available from the British Library

Library of Congress Control Number: 2021945176

This book is available electronically in the **Elgar**online
Law subject collection
http://dx.doi.org/10.4337/9781839109713

Printed on elemental chlorine free (ECF)
recycled paper containing 30% Post-Consumer Waste

ISBN 978 1 83910 970 6 (cased)
ISBN 978 1 83910 971 3 (eBook)

Printed and bound in the USA

To my parents

Contents

Tables

Abbreviations

ACER	Agency for the Cooperation of Energy Regulators
AFM	*Autoriteit Financiële Markten* (Netherlands)
AG	Advocate General
AIF	Alternative Investment Fund
AIFM	Alternative Investment Fund Manager
AIFMD	Directive on Alternative Investment Fund Managers
AMF	*Autorité des Marchés Financiers* (France)
APM	Alternative Performance Measure
BaFin	*Bundesanstalt für Finanzdienstleistungsaufsicht* (Germany)
BEREC	Office of the Body of European Regulators for Electronic Communications
BoS	Board of Supervisors
CBoI	Bank of Ireland (Ireland)
CCP	Central counterparty
CdT	Translation Centre for the Bodies of the European Union
CEBS	Committee of European Banking Supervisors
Cedefop	European Centre for the Development of Vocational Training
CEIOPS	Committee of European Insurance and Occupational Pensions Supervisors
CEPOL	European Union Agency for Law Enforcement Training
CESR	Committee of European Securities Regulators
CJEU	Court of Justice of the European Union
CMU	Capital Markets Union
Consob	*Commissione Nazionale per le Società e la Borsa* (Italy)
CPVO	Community Plant Variety Office
CRA	Credit Rating Agency
CRD	Capital Requirements Directive

CSDR	Central Securities Depositories Regulation
CWG	Consultative Working Group
EAMP	Emission Allowance Market Participant
EASA	European Aviation Safety Agency
EASO	European Asylum Support Office
EBA	European Banking Authority
ECDC	European Centre for Disease Prevention and Control
ECHA	European Chemicals Agency
ECSC	European Coal and Steel Community
EEA	European Economic Area
EEA	European Environment Agency
E(E)C	European (Economic) Community
EFCA	European Fisheries Control Agency
EFSA	European Food Safety Authority
EIGE	European Institute for Gender Equality
EIOPA	European Insurance and Occupational Pensions Authority
EMA	European Medicines Agency
EMCDDA	European Monitoring Centre for Drugs and Drug Addiction
EMIR	European Market Infrastructure Regulation
EMSA	European Maritime Safety Agency
ENISA	European Union Agency for Network and Information Security
EPPO	European Public Prosecutor's Office (in preparation)
ERA	European Union Agency for Railways
ESA	European Supervisory Authority
ESFS	European System of Financial Supervision
ESG	Environmental, Social and Governance
ESMA	European Securities and Markets Authority
ESRB	European Supervisory Structure comprises the European Systemic Risk Board
ETF	European Training Foundation
EU	European Union
EUIPO	European Union Intellectual Property Office

EU-OSHA	European Agency for Safety and Health at Work
Eurofound	European Foundation for the Improvement of Living and Working Conditions
Eurojust	European Union's Judicial Cooperation Unit
Europol	European Police Office
FAQs	Frequently Asked Questions
FCA	Financial Conduct Authority (United Kingdom)
FI	*Finansinspektionen* (Sweden)
FRA	European Union Agency for Fundamental Rights
Frontex	European Border and Coast Guard Agency
GSA	European GNSS Agency
HCMC	*Ελληνική Επιτροπή Κεφαλαιαγοράς* (Greece)
IMD	Insurance Mediation Directive
IMSC	Investment Management Standing Committee
IPISC	Investor Protection & Intermediaries Standing Committee
ITS	Implementing Technical Standard
MAR	Market Abuse Regulation
MEP	Member of European Parliament
MiFID	Markets in Financial Instruments Directive
MiFIR	Markets in Financial Instruments Regulation
MNB	*Magyar Nemzeti Bank* (Hungary)
NCAs	National Competent Authorities
OJ	Official Journal of the European Union
Q&As	Questions and Answers
REMIT	Regulation on Wholesale Energy Market Integrity and Transparency
RTS	Regulatory Technical Standard
SMEs	Small and Medium-sized Enterprises
SMSG	Securities and Markets Stakeholder Group
SRB	Single Resolution Board
SSR	Short Selling Regulation
TEU	Treaty on the European Union
TFEU	Treaty on the Functioning of the European Union

TR	Trade repository
UCITS	Undertaking for Collective Investment in Transferable Securities
UK	United Kingdom

Table of EU legislation

Table of cases

Court of Justice of the European Union

General Court

Opinions

ESA Board of Appeal

Table of ESMA soft law acts and other relevant documents

This table is not exhaustive, as it contains in particular those acts that are mentioned throughout the book.

ESMA's Draft Technical and Implementing Technical Standards

ESMA's Guidelines and Recommendations

ESMA's Guidelines Compliance Tables

ESMA's Non-binding Instruments

Summary of Conclusions of ESMA's Board of Supervisors

Decisions of ESMA's Management Board

ESMA Peer Reviews

ESMA Rules of Procedure

Other

Documents of Other EU Institutions, Offices, Bodies and Agencies

1. Setting the scene

1. INTRODUCTION

> *Guidelines and recommendations* adopted by the European Supervisory Authorities (ESAs) pursuant to Article 16 of the ESAs Regulations are of *non-binding nature* but have specific characteristics ('comply or explain' effect). They proved to be a flexible instrument for convergence however stakeholders pointed to some *uncertainties*[1] *relating to the concrete scope and nature of these measures.*[2]
>
> *Source:* European Commission, 8 August 2014, Review of the European System of Financial Supervision (ESFS)

The above example from the first report of the European Commission on the review of the European System of Financial Supervision exemplifies the intertwined nature of two trends in the EU institutional framework that are becoming increasingly important, that is, the establishment of EU agencies and the use of soft law. However, both 'agencification' and soft law-making go beyond the realm of the EU Treaties. Despite the close relationship between EU agencies and soft law, these two subjects have so far been studied separately.[3] This book fills this gap in the sense that it systematically studies these two modes of governance together. It focuses on an EU agency with a variety of soft law-making powers, that is, the European Securities and Markets Authority (ESMA), which is responsible for the improvement of the functioning of the financial markets in Europe. It was established to deal with the lack of effectiveness of its predecessor, the Committee of European Securities

---

[1] For instance, clarity was requested from many stakeholders on the possibility of challenging guidelines and recommendations under EU law and the ESAs were urged to enhance the transparency of the regulatory process, including by setting an adequate time frame for responding to public consultations and by providing more detailed feedback on the input received on this occasion.

[2] Commission, 'Report from the Commission to the European Parliament and the Council on the operation of the European Supervisory Authorities (ESAs) and the European System of Financial Supervision (ESFS)' COM(2014) 509 final, 5.

[3] On EU agencies, see Busuioc 2013a, Chamon 2016 and Scholten 2014a. On EU soft law, see Georgieva 2017, Senden 2004, Stefan 2012a and Van Dam 2020.

Regulators (CESR), and has for this reason been entrusted with stronger powers, including soft law-making powers. The textbox above however shows the tension between ensuring the effectiveness of Union law, on the one hand, and its legitimacy, on the other. This book investigates from an EU perspective *whether ESMA's soft law instruments are effective in achieving the Union's objectives* and *whether a sufficient level of legitimacy is provided for at the same time*. This includes the significant changes to the amended ESMA Regulation[4] brought about by the ESA review, which have an impact on the agency's soft law-making powers and bring to light new legitimacy and effectiveness concerns.

The book addresses the question of what procedural and institutional safeguards regarding ESMA's soft law would reflect an adequate balancing of both legitimacy and effectiveness concerns. It develops and tests an *assessment framework* of eight stages in which the possible links and tensions between legitimacy and effectiveness come to the fore.[5] The book offers recommendations to ESMA and to the Union legislature. It also proposes to parties involved in the establishment of other EU agencies, authorities and institutions with similar powers that they too apply this assessment framework.[6]

The following subsections explain ESMA's origins and the recent changes to its legal framework; describe ESMA's objectives, tasks, powers and governance structure; present the concepts of EU agencies and soft law; provide an initial overview of the main legitimacy and effectiveness concerns regarding EU agencies' soft law; and set out the book's underlying question, purpose and method.

2. ESMA'S ORIGINS

The current architecture of financial market regulation has its origins in the so-called Lamfalussy process, which resulted in the Final Report of the Committee of Wise Men on the Regulation of European Securities Markets.[7] One of the major conclusions of the report was that the regulatory system in existence at that time was too slow, too rigid and too ambiguous.[8] Therefore, 'a higher degree of convergence and greater Community presence in the field of enforcement' was thought to be necessary.[9] The proposals in the Report

---

[4] Regulation (EU) No 2019/2175 amending the ESA Regulations.

[5] See Chapter 2.

[6] See Chapter 11.

[7] Final report of the Committee of Wise Men on the regulation of European Securities Markets, 15 February 2001. See also Scholten & Ottow 2014.

[8] Tridimas 2011, p. 786.

[9] Ibid., p. 783.

aimed at 'ensuring that Community legislation on financial services represents a fast and flexible response to developments in the financial markets'.[10] To this end, the Lamfalussy process introduced a new four-level law-making model in the area of financial services.[11]

The first level was with the European Parliament and Council, which adopted framework principles in specific areas of substantive law by Directives or Regulations under the ordinary legislative procedure of Article 294 TFEU. At the second level, the European Commission concretised these framework principles by means of implementing measures adopted under Comitology procedures. At the third level, the so-called level 3 committees – the Committee of European Securities Regulators (CESR), Committee of European Banking Supervisors (CEBS) and Committee of European Insurance and Occupational Pensions Supervisors (CEIOPS) – were responsible for advising the Commission on the feasibility of measures proposed at level 2. Finally, level 4 consisted of envisaging timely and correct transposition of EU legislation into national law and taking action against Member States if transposition was not in compliance with EU law.

While the Lamfalussy system has enhanced cooperation between EU Member States, the 2008 financial crisis challenged its foundations and revealed the necessity to reform the system by furthering integration. The De Larosière report, issued by a group of experts mandated by the Commission under the chairmanship of Jacques de Larosière, demonstrated the weaknesses of the Lamfalussy architecture.[12] Among other things, implementation practices varied enormously within the different Member States and the European Commission did not sufficiently enforce timely and correct transposition in cases of negligent Member States.[13]

The level 3 committees' lack of binding power was seen as a pressing problem in this regard, since stronger powers were considered to be necessary to address the inconsistencies and enforcement deficits at the national level.[14] This in turn led to the transformation of the level 3 committees, with their non-binding powers, into EU agencies with legally binding decision-making

---

[10] Ottow 2012.

[11] Final report of the Committee of Wise Men on the regulation of European Securities Markets, 15 February 2001.

[12] Report by The High-Level Group on Financial Supervision in the EU chaired by Jacques de Larosière, 25 February 2009.

[13] C di Noia and M C Furlo, 'The new structure of financial supervision in Europe: what's next?' in E Wymeersch, K J Hopt and G Ferrarini (eds), *Financial Regulation and Supervision: A Post-Crisis Analysis* (Oxford University Press 2012) 174.

[14] Ottow 2012.

and supervisory powers.[15] The three European Supervisory Authorities – the European Securities and Markets Authority (ESMA), the European Banking Authority (EBA) and the European Insurance and Occupational Pensions Authority (EIOPA) – were thus established to tackle their predecessors' lack of effectiveness.

The current European Supervisory Structure comprises the European Systemic Risk Board (ESRB) and the European System of Financial Supervision (ESFS). The ESRB identifies, monitors and assesses potential threats to financial stability arising from macroeconomic developments and from developments within the financial system as a whole ('macro-prudential supervision').[16] It is an independent body without legal personality or legally binding powers.[17] However, it does enjoy soft law powers through its warnings and recommendations.[18] The ESFS safeguards financial soundness at the level of individual financial institutions and protects consumers of financial services ('micro-prudential supervision').[19] It consists of the three ESAs, a Joint Committee and the national supervisory authorities. The ESAs have been established on the legal basis of Article 114 of the Treaty on the Functioning of the European Union (hereafter TFEU).[20] Although in Article 5(1) of their establishing Regulations the ESAs are described as a 'Union body with legal personality' and elsewhere the term 'Authorities' is used, they do have the status of an EU agency.[21]

3. RECENT CHANGES TO ESMA'S LEGAL FRAMEWORK

Important changes to the legislative framework of the three ESAs, including ESMA, have recently entered into force. In September 2017, as part of the so-called ESA review,[22] the Commission put forward a series of proposals to

---

15 Report by The High-Level Group on Financial Supervision in the EU chaired by Jacques de Larosière, 25 February 2009, 49.

16 Ottow 2012.

17 Commission, 'Communication on European financial supervision' COM(2009) 252 final, 5.

18 Moloney 2011b, p. 529.

19 Ottow 2012.

20 Kost de Sevres & Sasso 2011, p. 34.

21 European Union, 'The European Securities and Markets Authority (ESMA)' <https://europa.eu/european-union/about-eu/agencies/esma_en> accessed 22 February 2021. See also Wymeersch 2012, pp. 240–41 and Moloney 2011a, pp. 61–63.

22 Commission, 'Public consultation on the operations of the European Supervisory Authorities' <https://ec.europa.eu/info/consultations/public-consultation-operations-european-supervisory-authorities_en> accessed 22 February 2020.

improve the mandates, governance and funding of the three authorities in order to reinforce their coordination role. The Commission took as a basis its 2014 report on the operation of the ESAs and the ESFS as a whole,[23] its evaluation of the ESA Regulations[24] and the feedback it received during public consultation periods launched in 2013, 2016 and 2017.[25] The purpose of the last of these consultations was to gather evidence on the operations of the ESAs to evaluate whether they are delivering as expected, considering their objectives, and to build a clearer overview of areas where, going forward, the effectiveness and efficiency of the ESAs could be strengthened and improved.[26] An important part of this public consultation related to the ESA's use of soft law.

> The vast majority of respondents identify weaknesses in the definition and application of ESAs' tasks and powers on guidelines and recommendations. Recommendations include the introduction of scrutiny of guidelines and recommendations by legislators, adopting guidelines only when strictly necessary, increased openness and transparency by consulting stakeholders or conducting impact analyses (especially for costs of compliance).
>
> Many respondents, especially from industry, explicitly welcome other tools such as common interpretation of rules, Questions & Answers, supervisory briefings and supervisory handbooks. Some call for them to be made more effective, e.g. by publicly consulting on them, publishing the results or setting a deadline for ESAs to respond. However, some industry representatives feel guidelines and Questions & Answers are used too ex-

---

[23] Commission, 'Report from the Commission to the European Parliament and the Council on the operation of the European Supervisory Authorities (ESAs) and the European System of Financial Supervision (ESFS)' COM(2014) 509 final.

[24] In accordance with Article 81 of the ESA Regulations an evaluation was carried out in combination with an impact assessment during the spring of 2017, see Annex 11.5 of Commission Staff Working Document, 'Impact assessment accompanying the document proposal for a Regulation amending the Regulations establishing EBA, ESMA, and EIOPA' SWD(2017) 308 final.

[25] Commission, 'European system of financial supervision' <https://ec.europa.eu/info/business-economy-euro/banking-and-finance/financial-supervision-and-risk-management/european-system-financial-supervision_en> accessed 23 February 2021. Commission, 'Feedback statement on the public consultation on the operations of the European Supervisory Authorities having taken place from 21 March to 16 May 2017' (20 June 2017) <https://ec.europa.eu/info/sites/info/files/2017-esas-operations-summary-of-responses_en.pdf> accessed 23 February 2021.

[26] Commission, 'Public consultation on the operations of the European Supervisory Authorities' <https://ec.europa.eu/info/consultations/public-consultation-operations-european-supervisory-authorities_en> accessed 22 February 2021.

tensively by ESAs.

Source: European Commission, 20 June 2017, Feedback statement on the public consultation on the operations of the ESAs[27]

Based on the abovementioned input and sources, the Commission proposed – among other things – amendments to the ESAs' procedures in relation to their soft law instruments. On 21 March 2019, the European Parliament and Member States agreed on the core elements of reforming European supervision in the area of EU financial markets.[28] This agreement, which is regarded as an important step to ensure a fully functioning Capital Markets Union, reinforces the role and powers of the ESAs: it seeks to ensure convergence of supervisory outcomes, a level playing field for financial institutions and investors and financial integration generally within the Single Market.[29] On 18 April 2019, the European Parliament endorsed the legislation.[30] The new ESA Regulations entered into force on 1 January 2020.

4. ESMA'S OBJECTIVES, TASKS AND POWERS

Article 1(2) ESMA Regulation empowers the agency to act within the *scope* of the listed EU financial market regulations and directives, including all directives, regulations and decisions based on those acts, as well as any further legally binding Union act which confers tasks on ESMA.[31] In exercising its powers, ESMA must always operate within these scope restrictions. The *overarching objective* of ESMA is 'to protect the public interest by contributing to the short-, medium- and long-term stability and effectiveness of the financial system, for the Union economy, its citizens and businesses'.[32] This objective is further broken down into *seven more specific objectives* to which ESMA

---

[27] Commission, 'Feedback statement on the public consultation on the operations of the European Supervisory Authorities having taken place from 21 March to 16 May 2017' (20 June 2017) <https://ec.europa.eu/info/sites/info/files/2017-esas-operations-summary-of-responses_en.pdf> accessed 23 February 2021.

[28] Commission, 'Press release Capital Markets Union: Political agreement on a stronger and more integrated European supervisory architecture, including on anti-money laundering' (21 March 2019) <https://ec.europa.eu/commission/presscorner/detail/en/IP_19_1655> accessed 22 February 2021.

[29] Ibid.

[30] Ibid.

[31] An interesting example of such acts are the CRA Regulation and EMIR, which provide ESMA with a full arsenal of direct enforcement powers: see CRAR II, EMIR and Short Selling Regulation.

[32] ESMA Regulation, Art 1(5).

has to contribute.[33] In order to achieve its objectives, ESMA has been given a number of *tasks*, such as contributing to the establishment of high-quality common regulatory and supervisory standards and practices, and contributing to the consistent application of legally binding Union acts.[34] In order to achieve these tasks, ESMA has supervisory, individual decision-making and general rule-making *powers*.[35]

While national supervisors remain predominantly responsible for day-to-day supervision of individual entities,[36] ESMA has a range of supervisory coordination powers.[37] Furthermore, ESMA's founding Regulation provides for the procedural framework for a set of individual binding decision-making powers either vis-à-vis national authorities or directly vis-à-vis financial institutions.[38] Finally, ESMA's rule-making powers include assisting the European

---

[33] Ibid. These are: (a) improving the functioning of the internal market, including in particular a sound, effective and consistent level of regulation and supervision; (b) ensuring the integrity, transparency, efficiency and orderly functioning of financial markets; (c) strengthening international supervisory coordination; (d) preventing regulatory arbitrage and promoting equal conditions of competition; (e) ensuring that the taking of investment and other risks are appropriately regulated and supervised; (f) enhancing customer and investor protection; (g) enhancing supervisory convergence across the internal market.

[34] See ESMA Regulation, Art 8(1) for an overview of all ESMA's tasks.

[35] ESMA Regulation, Art 8(2).

[36] Commission, 'Communication on European Financial Supervision' COM(2009) 252 final, 9.

[37] These powers include the participation in and coordination of colleges of supervisors (ESMA Regulation, Art 21); the identification and management of systemic risk and the development of resolution structures, in cooperation with the ESRB (ESMA Regulation, Arts 22–27); the promotion of a common supervisory culture (ESMA Regulation, Art 29); the identification of Union strategic supervisory priorities (ESMA Regulation, Art 29a); peer review of competent authorities (ESMA Regulation, Art 30); supervisory coordination (ESMA Regulation, Arts 31 and 31b); information exchange on fitness and propriety (ESMA Regulation, Art 31a); market assessment, including stress tests (ESMA Regulation, Art 32); and information-gathering (ESMA Regulation, Art 35). Moreover, CRAR II and EMIR have delegated very important exclusive supervisory powers over credit rating agencies (CRAs) and trade repositories (TRs) to ESMA. These include the powers to examine and take copies of any relevant records and material, to ask for oral explanation, to summon and hear persons, to require telephone and data traffic records and to interview persons (CRA Regulation II, Art 23c). These powers are not available even to the European Parliament in its investigatory capacity: see Scholten & Van Rijsbergen 2014b, p. 1243. See for critical reviews on ESMA's direct enforcement powers Van Rijsbergen & Scholten 2016, Van Rijsbergen & Foster 2017 and Simoncini & Van Rijsbergen 2020.

[38] ESMA has the right to issue binding decisions in three horizontal fields of action which concern the breach of Union law (ESMA Regulation, Art 17), action in emergency situations (ESMA Regulation, Art 18) and settlement of disagreements between

Commission in formulating and adopting a single rulebook applicable to all EU financial institutions.[39] To this end, ESMA is entitled to propose drafts of binding regulatory and implementing technical standards in specific areas which acquire legal effect after endorsement by the European Commission.[40] It may also issue interpretative guidelines and recommendations, with which competent authorities and financial market participants should make every effort to comply.[41] Furthermore, ESMA may develop and issue non-binding instruments, such as opinions, Q&As and other practical instruments and convergence tools.[42]

All in all, the supervisory, decision-making and rule-making powers of ESMA are far-reaching, especially in comparison with the competences of all the other EU agencies. The accumulation of its different tasks results in synergy effects that greatly strengthen the role of this EU agency vis-à-vis the national authorities.[43] The focus of this book is on ESMA's rule-making powers. However, in the following section, ESMA's governance structure will first be explained.

5. ESMA'S GOVERNANCE STRUCTURE

ESMA comprises a Board of Supervisors, a Management Board, a Chairperson and an Executive Director. In addition, the agency is assisted by the Securities and Markets Stakeholder Group in order to facilitate consultation with stakeholders in areas which are relevant to its tasks, supported by Standing Committees which all have Consultative Working Groups made up of external stakeholder representatives, and scrutinised by the ESA Board of Appeal in the case that a decision of the Board of Supervisors is appealed.[44]

---

competent authorities in cross-border situations (ESMA Regulation, Art 19). The real empowerment to take such binding decisions can only be found in other legislation that refers to the ESMA Regulation. These powers allow ESMA to intervene in the relationship between competent authorities, or in the relationship between competent authorities and market actors: see Schammo 2011, p. 1885. In some instances, ESMA's decisions may prevail over the previous decisions of national authorities.

[39] Moloney 2013.

[40] These drafts and standards follow the procedural framework as established in ESMA Regulation, Arts 10–14 and 15. See Section 6.4.

[41] ESMA Regulation, Art 16(3). See Section 6.4.

[42] ESMA Regulation, Arts 16a, 29a, 16b and 29b. See Section 6.4.

[43] Chamon 2012, p. 89.

[44] See Chapter 5 for more on the SMSG, SCs and CWGs. See Chapter 10 for more on the ESA Board of Appeal.

The *Board of Supervisors* is the ultimate decision-making organ of ESMA.[45] An important part of this consists of the heads of the national public authorities competent for the supervision of financial market participants in each Member State. Together with the Chairperson, they are the only voting members. The non-voting members are one representative of the European Commission, one representative of the ESRB and one representative of each of the other two European Supervisory Authorities, that is, EIOPA and EBA.[46] In practice, ESMA's Executive Director also attends the meetings of the Board of Supervisors. Representatives of the countries of the European Economic Area (EEA) may also be permitted to attend as observers.[47] The Board of Supervisors operates under a simple majority vote for the most part, with each of its members having one vote.[48] This means that all Member States and ESMA's Chairperson are on an equal footing, with the same voting power. However, ESMA's powers relating to its draft regulatory and implementing technical standards as well as its guidelines and recommendations require a qualified majority vote (QMV).[49] With regard to such decisions, the Chairperson is not allowed to vote.[50] Notwithstanding the above, the Board of Supervisors is specifically asked to strive for consensus when taking its decisions.[51]

The *Management Board* provides operational management and ensures that ESMA carries out its mission and performs its tasks.[52] It is composed of ESMA's Chairperson and six members of the Board of Supervisors, elected by and from the voting members of the Board of Supervisors.[53] Decisions are taken based on a simple majority of the members, while striving for consensus.[54] In addition, a representative of the European Commission and ESMA's

---

45 ESMA, 'Board of Supervisors and NCAs' <www.esma.europa.eu/about-esma/governance/board-supervisors-and-ncas> accessed 22 February 2021.

46 ESMA Regulation, Art 40(1).

47 Ferran 2012, p. 134. Iceland, Liechtenstein and Norway currently attend as permanent observers.

48 ESMA Regulation, Art 44(1).

49 Ibid.

50 Ibid.

51 Ibid., Art 44(5).

52 Ibid., Art 47(1). The tasks of the Management Board relate to preparing the annual and multi-annual work programme as well as the annual report for approval to the Board of Supervisors; exercising its budgetary powers; adopting the staff policy plan and the implementing measures of the Staff Regulations; adopting rules regarding the internal organisation of ESMA, such as the rules on access to documents and the rules of procedure; and appointing and removing the members of the Board of Appeal.

53 ESMA Regulation, Art 45(1).

54 Ibid., Art 45a(1).

Executive Director participate as non-voting members at the meetings, although the Commission does have a right to vote on budgetary matters.[55]

ESMA is represented by a *Chairperson* whose task is essentially to lead and represent the organisation, especially in contact with the other EU bodies.[56] (S)he thus has high visibility to the outside world. The Chairperson is in charge of preparing the work of the Board of Supervisors and chairing the meetings of both the Board of Supervisors and the Management Board.[57] (S)he has the right to vote in both the Management Board and Board of Supervisors. The agency also has an *Executive Director* who oversees the daily management of the agency, the preparation of the work of the Management Board and the implementation of ESMA's work programmes.[58] (S)he has no voting rights.

6. CONCEPTS

We now turn to an explanation of the two main concepts of this book: EU agencies and soft law. Pursuant to the White Paper on European Governance in 2001, the use of new modes of governance by the EU was relaunched in order to develop and implement its policies.[59] The interaction between these two new methods forms the main focus of this book.

6.1 Introducing EU Agencies

The first important concept addressed by this book is EU agencies. 'Agencification' is a process that reflects the increasing importance of agencies in the EU administration both quantitatively and qualitatively.[60] Quantitatively, one can observe that the number of EU agencies established

---

[55] Ibid., Art 45a(2).

[56] Wymeersch 2012, p. 307 and Moloney 2011a, pp. 61–63.

[57] ESMA Regulation, Art 48.

[58] ESMA Regulation, Art 51(1). Next to his/her general tasks relating to the management of ESMA and the preparation of the work of the Management Board, his/her specific tasks have been described in ESMA Regulation, Art 53. These tasks involve the preparation of the multi-annual work programme, the work programme for the following year and a draft report on the regulatory and supervisory activities as well as financial and administrative matters. (S)he is responsible for the internal organisation and the working of ESMA and adopts internal administrative instructions and publishes notices for this purpose. In addition, (s)he draws up a preliminary draft budget which (s)he also implements. Finally, (s)he manages the staff in accordance with EU staff regulations and the decisions of the Management Board. See also Moloney 2011a, pp. 61–63.

[59] Commission, 'European governance: A White Paper' COM(2001) 428 final. See also Senden 2004, p. 21 and Chamon 2013, p. 153.

[60] Chamon 2013, p. 153 and Scholten & Van Rijsbergen 2014b. On the enforcement powers of EU authorities, see Scholten & Luchtman 2017.

by the EU legislature has been growing rapidly.[61] At the time of writing, there are 35 EU agencies.[62] Qualitatively, the legislature has gradually stretched the limits of what is (perceived to be) permissible regarding the delegation of powers to EU agencies.[63] Whereas the first agencies merely provided information and, at most, had the authority to make recommendations, the more recently established agencies may impose individually binding decisions upon national authorities and market operators.[64] Because of this process of agencification, EU agencies today are no longer 'an institutional curiosity'.[65]

Although it is not easy to provide a definition of what an 'EU agency' actually is,[66] generally speaking EU agencies can be divided into *regulatory* agencies and *executive* agencies.[67] The latter are easy to identify, because they have all been created on the basis of Council Regulation (EC) No. 58/2003.[68] They have been set up by the Commission on a temporary basis in order to implement and manage certain programmes and are therefore the so-to-speak 'assistant' agencies of the Commission.[69] For instance, the Executive Agency for Small and Medium-sized Enterprises was created to manage several EU programmes in the fields of support and innovation, environment, climate action, energy and maritime affairs, with a particular focus on SMEs.[70] While having autonomous legal personality, they nevertheless remain subject to a review by the Commission's Directorate General from which they originate.[71] The Commission thus supervises these agencies and may dissolve them.[72] At the time of writing, six executive agencies currently exist.[73] Since

---

[61] Scholten & Van Rijsbergen 2014b.

[62] European Union, 'Decentralised agencies' <https://europa.eu/european-union/about-eu/agencies/decentralised-agencies_en> accessed 23 February 2021: 34 EU agencies are already established, and there are ongoing discussions on the need to establish an EU agency on anti-money laundering and terrorism financing. There is a debate on how many EU agencies there actually are, see Scholten 2014a, p. 48.

[63] Scholten & Van Rijsbergen 2014b.

[64] Ibid. and Chamon 2013, p. 153.

[65] Ibid.

[66] Scholten 2014a, p. 47.

[67] Alberti 2014, p. 162; Scholten & Van Rijsbergen 2014b, p. 1229; Chamon 2013, p. 153.

[68] Council Regulation (EC) No. 58/2003.

[69] Scholten & Van Rijsbergen 2014b, p. 1229.

[70] Commission, 'Executive agency for small and medium-sized enterprises' <https://ec.europa.eu/info/departments/small-and-medium-sized-enterprises_en> accessed 23 February 2021.

[71] Alberti 2014, p. 162.

[72] Scholten 2014a, p. 51.

[73] These are: Consumers, Health, Agriculture and Food Executive Agency (CHAFEA); Research Executive Agency (REA); Executive Agency for Small and

there is no evidence of soft law instruments emanating from these bodies, they will be excluded from the analysis in this book.

The focus of this book is on those agencies designated as regulatory agencies.[74] They have been established by the EU under secondary law on the basis of provision(s) of the Treaties in order 'to perform technical and scientific tasks that help the Union institutions implement policies and take decisions'.[75] Regulatory agencies are not purely assistants of the Commission. On the contrary, they rather represent a new level of governance between the Commission and national administrations.[76] In fact, their independence or autonomy is the most distinctive feature of these agencies.[77] This implies that they have 'to be free of both political and industry interests'.[78] In the Union context, this also refers to national interests.[79] Regulatory agencies do indeed enjoy a certain degree of autonomy from the Commission, but are not fully isolated from the Commission's influence.[80]

Besides these general common characteristics, it should be noted that regulatory agencies are in reality very different from each other, given the fact that the powers entrusted to them and the dynamics by which they interact with the Commission and national authorities vary from agency to agency.[81] This is due to the fact that the establishment of agencies within the Union legal order has never been based on one single legal basis that specifically provides for

---

Medium-sized Enterprises (EASME); European Research Council Executive Agency (ERCEA); Innovation & Networks Executive Agency (INEA); Education, Audiovisual and Culture Executive Agency (EACEA). See European Union, 'Agencies and other EU bodies' <https://europa.eu/european-union/about-eu/agencies_en> accessed 23 February 2021.

[74] Both in scholarly works and in political documents, regulatory agencies are also known as decentralised agencies. The terms regulatory and decentralised are used synonymously. The term 'decentralised' has also been used to indicate the spread of EU agencies across the Union: see Curtin 2009, p. 161.

[75] European Union, 'Decentralised agencies' <https://europa.eu/european-union/about-eu/agencies/decentralised-agencies_en> accessed 23 February 2021. See also Griller & Orator, pp. 7–10; Vos 2015, pp. 120 and 122; Scholten & Van Rijsbergen 2014b, p. 1227.

[76] Scholten 2014a.

[77] Groenleer 2009, p. 29. See also Scholten 2011 (arguing that the term 'independent' is misleading).

[78] Vos 2015, p. 123. See also European Parliament, Resolution of 21 October 2008 on a strategy for the future settlement of the institutional aspects of regulatory agencies (2008) 2008/2103(INI), para 28.

[79] Ibid. See also European Union, 'Decentralised agencies' <https://europa.eu/european-union/about-eu/agencies/decentralised-agencies_en> accessed 23 February 2021.

[80] Chiti 2019, p. 1397.

[81] Alberti 2014, p. 163.

the creation of EU agencies.[82] Therefore, with a few exceptions, each organisation is the result of a unique and independent political compromise, mainly influenced by the importance of the agency's policy sector and the sentiments of the Member States towards the European integration process at the time of the creation of the agency at stake. This *heterogeneity* of EU agencies also underlies the diversity of the acts which they are able to adopt.[83]

There are two main types of rule-making through which 'EU agencies seem to provide a substantial regulatory contribution to the smooth functioning of their policy sectors'.[84] First, EU agencies may participate, as technical actors, in procedures leading to the adoption of binding implementing rules, either assisting the Commission or directly adopting technical rules.[85] Second, EU agencies are often formally or *de facto* granted the power to issue soft law instruments, either to the regulatees or to other administrations participating in the sectoral network they coordinate.[86] Taken together, these two represent the main contribution of EU agencies to administrative rule-making.

6.2 Introducing Soft Law

EU soft law is the second concept that is relevant for this book. It appears in almost all policy areas in which the EU institutions operate and has many different manifestations in practice. The most comprehensive and accepted scholarly definition of 'soft law' is given by Snyder.[87] He deems soft law to encompass 'rules of conduct which in principle have no legally binding force but which nevertheless may have practical effects'.[88] Senden further delineates this definition by adding that soft law may also produce 'legal effects':

> Rules of conduct that are laid down in instruments which have not been attributed legally binding force as such, but nevertheless may have certain (indirect) legal effects, and that are aimed at and may produce practical effects.[89]

---

82 Ibid.
83 Ibid.
84 Chiti 2013, p. 100.
85 Ibid., p. 99.
86 Ibid.
87 Snyder 1993.
88 Ibid.
89 Senden 2004, p. 112.

This conceptualisation of soft law was later used by Stefan[90] and Georgieva.[91] It will be retained for the purposes of this book as well.[92]

Generally speaking, soft law is said to have three main functions: pre-law, post-law and para-law.[93] The *pre-law function* of soft law can be understood in two different ways. First, a particular soft law act[94] may be adopted with a view to elaborating and preparing future Union legislation and policy. The aim is to assess the desirability or necessity and the possible contents thereof. Second, soft law instruments may pave the way for the adoption of legislation in the future by providing or increasing the basis of support for the rules contained therein. The *post-law function* is fulfilled by soft law instruments that are adopted subsequent to existing Union law in order to supplement and support both primary and secondary EU law. This may relate to the effectuation or further implementation of legislation or to the facilitation of the correct interpretation and (uniform) application thereof. In this respect, the existing rules may simply be restated, but new rules may also be established in line with these. The *para-law function* of Union soft law refers to its use instead of legislation. Soft law may be intended to serve as either a temporary or a permanent alternative to legislation. It will in any event be replaced by legislation in case of a temporary solution, whereas legislation is merely held out as a prospect in the event of non-compliance with the soft law act in case of a permanent solution.

Soft law-making is not recognised in the EU Treaties as a general institutional phenomenon of the EU. Its instruments and processes, and partly also the actors involved (EU agencies and networks), have therefore remained largely unregulated at the level of primary EU law.[95] The new hierarchy of norms in Articles 288 to 291 TFEU does not recognise many other instruments than the legislative, delegated and implementing acts, to be laid down in the form of regulations, directives or decisions.[96] Apart from the very limited observation in Article 288 TFEU that recommendations and opinions have no binding force, it is completely silent on the nature, function and status of other

---

90 Stefan 2012a.

91 Georgieva 2017, p. 3 (although she replaced 'rules of conduct' with 'acts of administrative guidance', arguing that Commission-issued competition soft law acts are not a transitory legal form paving the way to legislation).

92 Other definitions of soft law also exist, such as that in Terpan 2015, which explains three meanings of soft law in the doctrinal debate.

93 Senden 2004, pp. 119–20.

94 A deliberate distinction has been made between 'instruments' and 'acts'. The former term refers to a certain type of instrument in general, the latter to a specific individual act.

95 Senden & Van den Brink 2012, p. 65.

96 Senden 2013.

soft law instruments that have appeared in the Union's institutional practice over time.[97] New initiatives have never materialised or covered soft law instruments other than the recommendation and the opinion.[98]

It is true that there do exist some specific secondary legislative provisions which provide for the (mandatory) adoption of soft law, and as such for a legal basis thereof, but for most soft law instruments this is not the case.[99] Besides, soft law often emerges outside the realm of the conventional democratic decision-making procedures as the Treaties do not lay down any adoption procedures for this type of legislation. This means that the involvement of the European Parliament and the Council is not always required in the development of soft law by the Commission. With regard to Council recommendations, only in cases where the Treaties provide for such a requirement does the Council adopt recommendations on a proposal from the Commission.[100] It acts unanimously in those areas in which unanimity is required for the adoption of a Union act. As a result, soft law is only democratically legitimated to a very limited extent and it therefore derives its persuasion rather from its intended contribution to the efficiency and effectiveness of law and policy-making.[101] Indeed, the flexibility of soft law instruments allows for easy anticipation of new or urgent problems.

For a long time, soft law-making has been the prerogative of the Commission and the Council, but EU agencies are gaining general rule-making powers.[102] In fact, increasing delegation of soft law-making powers to EU agencies is being seen in a growing number of policy areas, for example in the field of aviation, pharmaceuticals and financial services,[103] in order to increase the effectiveness of EU action.[104] This trend connects with the expectations of Majone, who predicted that it would only be a matter of time before EU agencies would transform into full-fledged regulatory bodies.[105] Yet, both 'agencification' and soft law-making are outside the realm of the EU Treaties.

---

97 Senden 2004, p. 24.

98 Soft law is not mentioned in initiatives such as ReNEUAL, 'ReNEUAL model rules on EU administrative procedure' (2014) <www.reneual.eu/index.php/projects-and-publications/reneual-1-0> accessed 23 February 2021 or the Better Regulation package: see Commission, 'Better regulation: why and how' <https://ec.europa.eu/info/law/law-making-process/planning-and-proposing-law/better-regulation-why-and-how_en> accessed 23 February 2021.

99 Van Rijsbergen 2014, p. 121 and Senden 2015.

100 TFEU, Art 292.

101 Georgieva 2017.

102 Senden & Van den Brink 2012, p. 8.

103 Shapiro 2011, p. 112.

104 Van Rijsbergen 2014, p. 116.

105 Majone 1996, p. 276.

Studying them together leads to a dangerous combination in which legitimacy and effectiveness concerns arise. These concerns will be introduced in Section 7 of this chapter.

6.3 Soft Law Instruments Emanating from EU Agencies: Three Categories

Here we will first consider what types of soft law instruments EU agencies may adopt. They vary greatly and have different titles, such as opinions, guidelines, recommendations, communications, advice, and so on. However, since the denomination has no precise legal value, it is not helpful in understanding to what extent the act in question may have a *de facto* binding scope.[106] It is in fact the margin of appreciation left to the recipient that makes soft law instruments more or less 'hard'.[107] In particular, the greater the discretion afforded to the addressee of the instrument to decide whether to comply with the prescribed behaviour, the softer the legal instrument. And vice versa, the more prescriptive the scope of the act, the harder the legal instrument will be.[108] This book therefore follows a division of EU agencies' soft law instruments on the basis of their *de facto* binding scope in order to grasp the overall picture.[109] This results in a classification of three categories, starting with the 'hardest' instruments and ending with the 'softest'; that is to say, from the instruments that prescribe in the most incisive manner certain means of conduct, to those with a less detailed prescriptive scope.[110] It should nevertheless be noted that, in reality, all the soft instruments that will be introduced here may have significant effects on the decision-making processes of the Union, and even more so on national authorities and economic operators. As Table 1.1 visualises, these are: quasi-binding preparatory acts; 'comply or explain' guidelines; and non-binding instruments.[111]

---

[106] Alberti 2014, p. 164.

[107] Ibid.

[108] Ibid.

[109] This division is to a great extent inspired by the division made by Alberti 2014, p. 166. He distinguishes a fourth category: that of 'information and good practices', which are developed by a number of agencies operating in several social sectors and finally shared with the Union institutions and national administrations with the aim of improving the implementation of Union law. This category is excluded from this book, because in many cases such acts cannot be considered as rules of conduct. Furthermore, there is no evidence that these acts alone have any regulatory effect.

[110] Alberti 2014, p. 164.

[111] The EU agencies covered in this table correspond to those agencies that are being dealt with in the subsections below. Not all EU agencies are thus engaged in rule-making: ECDC, Cedefop, EEA, EFCA, EPPO, Eurofound, GSA, EIGE,

Table 1.1 *Overview of EU agencies' soft law categories*

Category of EU agencies' soft law	Corresponding agencies
Quasi-binding preparatory acts	ESMA, EBA, EIOPA, EMA, EFSA, EASA, ACER, BEREC, ECHA
'Comply or explain' guidelines	ESMA, EBA, EIOPA, EASA, EMA, ECHA
Non-binding instruments	ESMA, EBA, EIOPA, ACER, BEREC, Eurojust, ERA, EMSA, ENISA, FRA, CPVO, EUIPO

6.3.1 Category 1: quasi-binding preparatory acts

The first category consists of a series of acts which are not formally binding, but become binding after the adoption of a legally binding act by the Commission which endorses their contents. These preparatory acts are 'quasi-binding', since the secondary act conferring decision-making power on the Commission obliges the Commission to take its decision in accordance with the act prepared by the agency.[112] It is possible that this secondary act also provides that the draft of the agency can only be rejected by the Commission in very restricted and extraordinary circumstances, that the Commission is required to explicitly state the reasons which lead to a deviation from the agency's draft or that the agency has the opportunity to issue a new draft which meets the reasons invoked by the Commission. Concerning these acts, the discretion of the Commission is very narrow.

The most relevant example of such preparatory acts consists of the draft technical standards issued by the three ESAs for the adoption of delegated and implementing acts by the Commission.[113] Likewise, the European Medicines Agency (EMA) issues scientific opinions regarding the authorisation procedure for pharmaceutical products.[114] In almost all cases the Commission simply confirms the drafts of this agency,[115] and transposes the content in its

---

EMCDDA, CdT, CEPOL, Europol, EU-OSHA, EASO, IT-agency and ETF have no soft law-making powers at all.

112 Alberti 2014, p. 164.

113 ESA Regulations, Arts 10 and 15. Article 10(1) states that '*The Commission may not change the content of a draft regulatory technical standard prepared by the Authority without prior coordination with the Authority*, as set out in this Article'. Article 15(1) provides the same with regard to implementing technical standards.

114 The margin of appreciation granted to the Commission is slightly greater than in the case of draft technical standards of the ESAs. EMA Regulation, Art 10(1) entails that 'within 15 days after receipt of the agency's opinion, the Commission shall prepare a draft of the decision to be taken in respect of an application. […] *Where the draft decision differs from the opinion of the Agency, the Commission shall attach a detailed explanation of the reasons for the differences.*'

115 Senden & Van den Brink 2012.

decisions without adding any new elements.[116] The practice with regard to the financial supervisory authorities is still fairly new, but so far demonstrates similar dynamics.

Other examples of preparatory acts also fall within the scope of this category.[117] In the authorisation procedures for smoke flavourings used or intended for use in or on foods and, especially, for genetically modified organisms, the European Food Safety Authority (EFSA) provides scientific evaluations of the risk to human health.[118] In the field of the construction and design of materials for air transport, the European Aviation Safety Agency (EASA) issues opinions.[119] In the definition of the so-called gas and electricity network code, the opinions of the Agency for the Cooperation of Energy Regulators (ACER) are important.[120] And finally, with regard to the implementation of the secondary legislation on telecommunications, the Body of European Regulators for Electronic Communications (BEREC) issues opinions.[121]

Exceptionally, two types of opinions adopted by BEREC and by the European Chemicals Agency (ECHA) could be included in this category.[122] The first assists the Commission in the process of the identification, definition and harmonisation of the electronic communications markets. In this case,

---

[116] Alberti 2014, p. 164 and Gehring & Krapohl 2007.

[117] The examples come from Alberti 2014, p. 164.

[118] Regulation (EC) No. 2065/2003, Art 9: 'Within three months of receiving the opinion of the Authority, the Commission shall prepare a draft of the measure to be taken in respect of the application for inclusion of a primary product in the list referred to in Article 6(1), taking into account the requirements of Article 4(1), Community law and other legitimate factors relevant to the matter under consideration. *Where the draft measure is not in accordance with the opinion of the Authority, the Commission shall provide an explanation for the reasons for the differences.*' See also Regulation (EC) No. 1829/2003, Art 7(1): 'Within three months after receiving the opinion of the Authority, the Commission shall submit to the Committee referred in Article 35 a draft of the decision to be taken in respect of the application, taking into account the opinion of the Authority, any relevant provisions of Community law and other legitimate factors relevant to the matter under consideration. *Where the draft decision is not in accordance with the opinion of the Authority, the Commission shall provide an explanation for the differences.*' See also Case T-13/99 *Pfizer Animal Health v Council* [2002] ECR II-3305, paras 197–99.

[119] EASA Regulation, Arts 75(2)(b) and 115. Pursuant to Article 75(2)(b), EASA shall 'assist the Commission by preparing measures to be taken under this Regulation. Where those measures comprise technical rules, *the Commission may not change their content without prior coordination with the Agency.*'

[120] ACER Regulation, Art 5 and Regulation (EU) No. 2019/943, Art 59(11): '[...] ACER shall submit a draft network code prepared under this paragraph to the Commission and may recommend that it be adopted.'

[121] Framework Directive, Arts 7 and 9.

[122] Alberti 2014, p. 164.

although the opinions of BEREC should always be taken into account 'to the highest degree', they will not lead to the adoption of a binding act by the Commission, but rather to the adoption of a recommendation.[123] ECHA, in turn, adopts opinions within the framework of the authorisation procedure for the marketing of chemicals.[124] These lead to the adoption of a binding act by the Commission, but the latter enjoys a considerably greater discretion compared to the examples mentioned above.

6.3.2 Category 2: 'comply or explain' guidelines

The second category consists of so-called comply or explain guidelines. As the name suggests, the recipients of these acts (normally national authorities or economic operators) are obliged to make every effort to comply with the behaviour suggested by the agency or to expressly state the reasons for a refusal so to do. Such acts are issued by ESMA, EBA, EIOPA,[125] EASA[126] and EMA.[127] In addition, the technical and scientific guidance documents adopted by ECHA in order to facilitate the implementation of the Regulation on Registration, Evaluation, Authorisation and Restriction of Chemicals (REACH) through a description of best practices could be mentioned here.[128] On the one hand, these acts are less binding than 'comply or explain' guidelines, since they are essentially a guide for companies which intend to submit an application for the authorisation of a new chemical substance.[129] On the other hand, they are potentially more coercive than 'comply or explain' guidelines, because they in fact constitute interpretations by the agency on how the obligations of the REACH Regulation must be respected.[130] These acts seem to have a normative scope. At least, they are taken seriously, given the fact that some guidance documents have been withdrawn due to interpretation problems.[131]

---

[123] Framework Directive, Arts 15 and 19.

[124] ECHA Regulation, Arts 60 and 64.

[125] EBA Regulation, Art 16; EIOPA Regulation, Art 16; ESMA Regulation, Art 16.

[126] EASA Regulation, Arts 76(3) and 115.

[127] An overview of the different guidelines adopted by the European Medicines Agency and of the relevant legal bases (disseminated in the various legal instruments of secondary legislation in the pharmaceutical sector) is available at EMA, Procedure for European Union Guidelines and Related Documents within the Pharmaceutical Legislative Framework (2009) Doc. Ref. EMEA/P/24143/2004 Rev. 1 corr.

[128] ECHA Regulation, Art 77(2)(g).

[129] Alberti 2014, p. 165.

[130] Ibid.

[131] For example, ECHA has withdrawn Practical Guide 11: how to address specific substance identification issues: evaluation of different crystalline forms: see ECHA, 'News alert: ECHA withdraws Practical Guide 11' (21 July 2010) <https://echa.europa.eu/-/echa-withdraws-practical-guide-11> accessed 23 February 2021.

6.3.3 Category 3: non-binding instruments

The third category of instruments, being the softest type, comprises a rather heterogeneous series of opinions, recommendations, advice, and so on, through which EU agencies provide scientific and technical assistance to the EU institutions and national authorities.[132] Unlike the acts of the first category, the adoption of these soft law instruments is not necessary for the adoption of a binding instrument. Unlike the acts of the second category, they do not involve a 'comply or explain' mechanism. Therefore, these acts leave a much broader discretion to their addressees than the acts described above.

For instance, at the request of the national authorities, ACER,[133] BEREC[134] and the European Union's Judicial Cooperation Unit (Eurojust)[135] adopt opinions to assist these authorities in the implementation of EU law and in resolving transnational issues (in the case of Eurojust it concerns conflicts of jurisdiction).[136] The European Union Agency for Railways (ERA) adopts opinions and recommendations addressed to the Commission for the implementation and actualisation of secondary legislation in the area of rail transport.[137] The European Maritime Safety Agency (EMSA) adopts recommendations and opinions in the field of maritime transport;[138] the European Union Agency for Network and Information Security (ENISA) issues guidelines, conclusions, best practices and advice on cyber security issues;[139] and the European Union Agency for Fundamental Rights (FRA) publishes conclusions and opinions regarding the protection of fundamental rights in the EU decision-making process.[140] ESMA, EBA and EIOPA also issue soft law instruments such as opinions and Q&As.

6.4 Soft Law Instruments Emanating from ESMA: Three Categories

Now specifically zooming in on the soft law instruments that ESMA may adopt, we can observe that the agency has the possibility to use a wide range of regulatory and guidance tools which are directly provided for in its founding

---

132 Alberti 2014, p. 165.

133 ACER Regulation, Art 7(2–5).

134 Framework Directive, Arts 16 and 21.

135 Council Decision of 28 February 2002 setting up Eurojust with a view to reinforcing the fight against serious crime [2002] (2002/187/JHA) OJ L 063, Arts 7(2) and 8.

136 The examples come from Alberti 2014, p. 165.

137 ERA Regulation.

138 EMSA Regulation, Art 2(2)(a).

139 ENISA Regulation, Arts 4 and 5.

140 FRA Regulation, Art 4(1)(d).

Table 1.2 Overview of ESMA's soft law categories

Category of EU agencies' soft law	ESMA's soft law instruments
Quasi-binding preparatory acts	- Draft implementing acts - Draft regulatory acts
'Comply or explain' guidelines	- ESMA Guidelines
Non-binding instruments	- Opinions - Q&As - Other new practical instruments and convergence tools, such as supervisory briefings

Regulation. The instruments can be said to fall within the scope of all three categories of EU agencies' soft law instruments as identified in the section above. ESMA's draft technical standards belong to the first category of quasi-binding preparatory acts. The agency's guidelines and recommendations are part of the second category of 'comply or explain' guidelines. ESMA's opinions, Q&As and other practical instruments and convergence tools fall within the scope of the third category of non-binding instruments. The categorisation of ESMA's soft law instruments may be visualised as in Table 1.2.

6.4.1 Category 1: quasi-binding draft regulatory and implementing technical standards

ESMA's draft technical standards fall within the scope of the first category of EU agencies' soft law instruments. They are a relatively new form of measure in EU financial market regulation.[141] ESMA is empowered to develop two kinds of formally non-binding draft technical standards in the areas specifically set out in the legislative acts referred to in Article 1(2) of the ESMA Regulation: *regulatory technical standards* and *implementing technical standards.*[142] The first type concerns measures representing a delegation of quasi-rulemaking power from the institutions and having a quasi-rule quality.[143] They are adopted by the Commission by means of *delegated acts* under Article 290 TFEU. The second type concerns measures representing a delegation of implementing authority from the Member States and having a more operational, implementing quality.[144] They are adopted by the Commission by means of *implementing acts* under Article 291 TFEU. Since ESMA's draft

141 Moloney 2011a, p. 66.
142 ESMA Regulation, Arts 10–15.
143 Moloney 2011a, p. 66 and Moloney 2011b, p. 530.
144 Moloney 2011b, p. 530.

technical standards are adopted with a view to elaborate and prepare future Union legislation and policy, they fulfil a *pre-law function.*[145]

6.4.2 Category 2: 'comply or explain' guidelines and recommendations

ESMA's *guidelines and recommendations* fall within the scope of the second category of EU agencies' soft law instruments. These instruments are addressed to national supervisory authorities or financial market participants with a view to establishing consistent, efficient and effective supervisory practices within the ESFS, and to ensuring the common, uniform and consistent application of Union law.[146] They aim to influence the action of the addressees without being strictly binding under the law, but are not merely voluntary, nor are they without legal effect.[147] They are so-called comply or explain instruments, since the national supervisory authorities and financial market participants are obliged to make every effort to comply.[148] ESMA's guidelines fulfil a *post-law function*, because they are adopted subsequent to existing Union law in order to supplement and support secondary Union law as well as to ensure proper implementation thereof in the Member States. Guidelines relate to the correct interpretation and uniform application thereof.

6.4.3 Category 3: non-binding instruments

Regarding the third category of EU agencies' soft law instruments, ESMA may issue a variety of non-binding instruments through which it provides scientific and technical assistance to the national authorities and financial market participants in their daily practice. These include *opinions* directed towards national supervisory authorities (Article 29(1)(a) ESMA Regulation), *Q&As* (Article 16b ESMA Regulation)[149] and *new practical instruments and convergence tools* to promote common supervisory approaches and practices

---

[145] See Section 6.2 for the three functions of Union soft law.

[146] ESMA Regulation, Art 16(1).

[147] Fischer-Appelt 2011, p. 25; Schammo 2011, p. 1881; Wymeersch 2012, p. 276. See Chapter 8, Sections 3.2, 4.2 and 4.3 for an analysis of the legal nature of ESMA's guidelines.

[148] ESMA Regulation, Art 16(3).

[149] This abbreviation stands for Questions & Answers. These enable ESMA to publish frequently asked questions which it receives from supervised entities and to provide clarifications on matters within its competence in a quick and efficient way where a more articulate explanation such as the one used in the guidelines is not required. Given the fact that Q&As provide guidance, they always need to be approved and adopted by the Board of Supervisors. For a list of all Q&As, see ESMA, 'Questions and Answers' <www.esma.europa.eu/questions-and-answers> accessed 22 February 2021.

(Article 29(2) ESMA Regulation).[150] Such non-binding instruments leave a wide discretion to their addressees, although they contain interpretations that ESMA and the national authorities use in their supervisory practices. ESMA's non-binding instruments also fulfil a *post-law function*, because they are adopted subsequent to existing Union law in order to supplement and support secondary Union law. They relate to the further implementation of legislation and the correct interpretation thereof in the Member States.

7. THE CHALLENGE: LEGITIMACY AND EFFECTIVENESS CONCERNS REGARDING EU AGENCIES' SOFT LAW

The above sections have shown that there are several EU agencies, alongside ESMA, that adopt similar types of soft law instruments. Some of these acts are geared towards the Commission in assisting it in its administrative/executive function; others are geared towards national authorities. As such, they also share uncertainties relating to the concrete scope and nature of their soft law measures. Indeed, while being an increasingly important part of the Union's institutional framework, EU agencies and their exercise of soft law-making powers raise four legitimacy and effectiveness concerns in theory and in practice.

The first concern in relation to EU agencies' soft law-making is that the establishment of EU agencies and the delegation of regulatory powers thereto are matters that are not explicitly regulated in the EU Treaties or in general secondary legislation. As a consequence, agencies are established by secondary law instruments, often regulations, on the basis of a specific Treaty provision such as Articles 114 and 352 TFEU.[151] These provisions confer powers on the EU to develop certain (substantive) laws and policies, but the EU legislature has interpreted them so as to include also the power to establish Union organs to supervise or facilitate the implementation of the (substantive) laws and policies at issue.[152] There is also no *ex ante* regulation in primary law of what

[150] ESMA may also issue advice to the European Parliament, Council and the Commission (Article 9(4) ESMA Regulation) and opinions to the same Union Institutions (Article 16a ESMA Regulation), but both are outside the of scope of this book because they do not directly affect national competent authorities and financial market participants.

[151] Senden & Van den Brink 2012, p. 23. See Van Cleynenbreugel 2014b specifically criticising the legal basis. See Scholten 2014a for an overview of the legal bases of all EU agencies.

[152] Senden & Van den Brink 2012, p. 23. See also Case C-217/04 *United Kingdom v Parliament and Council* [2006] ECR I-3789.

powers EU agencies may or may not have, this type of rule-making not being foreseen in the hierarchy of norms as laid down in Articles 288–291 TFEU, while the Treaty of Lisbon merely introduced *ex post* review in Article 263 TFEU.[153] This means that the lawfulness of the acts of EU agencies can only be subsequently controlled. However, such control becomes very difficult without prior regulation of what EU agencies can or cannot do.[154] This non-regulation gives rise to uncertainty as to the actual competence of agencies to engage in rule-making. Because of the absence of a general legal framework on the possibility to delegate general implementing powers to entities other than the Commission and the Council, the powers of EU agencies are still subject to the constitutional limits formulated by the Court in its case-law. In the famous *Meroni*, *Romano* and *Short-Selling* judgments,[155] the CJEU established that powers may be delegated to such organs, but this must be confined to clearly defined executive powers and does not extend to powers involving a wide margin of discretion.[156] As a result, the delegation of general regulatory powers to agencies is excluded. Yet, the delegation of *soft* regulatory powers to EU agencies seems to provide a means for circumventing the properly competent legislative and executive bodies in the decision-making process. In addition, such delegation appears to bypass the case-law restrictions, because they are not considered to stand in the way of allocating soft law-making powers to EU agencies.[157] Indeed, institutional practice demonstrates that certain EU agencies have developed policy-making activity that comes close to full regulatory powers and 'while these general rule-making powers are soft by the label, they are often hard in practice'.[158]

A second concern is that EU agencies' regulation by soft law involves 'an extremely low degree of proceduralisation'.[159] This means that soft law often emerges outside the realm of the conventional democratic decision-making procedures. There is no overall tendency to formalise the procedures through which EU agencies' soft law measures are adopted, no common framework for agencies' governance, and the attempts of the Commission to conclude an inter-institutional agreement on regulatory agencies so far have not led to any

---

[153] Notwithstanding the difficulties regarding *ex post* review of soft law instruments, see Chapter 10.

[154] See Scholten 2014a on the necessity for an assessment framework.

[155] Case 9-56 *Meroni v High Authority* [1958] ECR 133. Case 98/80 *Romano* [1981] ECR 1241. Case C-270/12 *United Kingdom v Parliament and Council* [2014]. On this case in the literature, see Bergström 2015; Chamon 2014, p. 380; Marjosola 2014; Scholten & Van Rijsbergen 2014a; Van Gestel 2014.

[156] Case 9-56 *Meroni v High Authority* [1958] ECR 133.

[157] Senden & Van den Brink 2012, p. 65.

[158] Ibid., p. 23.

[159] Chiti 2013, p. 102.

concrete results.[160] In most cases, the establishing regulations and the agencies' rules of procedure do not 'envisage any kind of procedural provision concerning the elaboration and adoption of soft law measures',[161] and 'the information available on the websites does not suggest the existence of consolidated administrative practices' either.[162] In fact, the current procedural framing of soft law-making is of 'a very *ad hoc* nature'[163] and resembles a patchwork quilt, where some agencies may have put into place far more sophisticated procedural rules than others. Such a practice 'does not contribute to the predictability, consistency and coherence of EU action'[164] and the 'reasons behind the differences in approach in this regard are not always evident'.[165]

A third concern in relation to EU agencies' soft law instruments is that such instruments are not legally binding by definition, but may generate both legal and *de facto* effects. The EU Treaties do not grant any form of legally binding force to soft law documents and EU soft law cannot by itself create any rights or impose any obligations. However, soft law obtains an important authoritative function in legal practice and it appears from the case-law of the CJEU that it is definitely not devoid of legal effects.[166] Soft law measures are thus not 'harmless', especially when they are simply 'rubber stamped' by the Commission into legally binding acts.[167] Given their lack of (inherent) legally binding force, it is uncertain to what extent soft law instruments are an adequate and sufficient means to realise the regulatory goals laid down therein, and thus to what extent they can be effective. The purpose of a particular instrument is, namely, not always clearly stated by its maker or emitter.[168] The question remains, therefore, whether agencies' soft law instruments put enough pressure on the Member States and other possible addressees to transpose and to comply with them. Those concerned must be at least willing to give effect to them.

---

160 Ibid. See also Commission, 'Proposal for an inter-institutional agreement on the operating framework for the European regulatory agencies' COM(2005) 59 final; Commission, 'Communication on European agencies – the way forward' COM(2008) 135 final; Joint statement and common approach of the European Parliament, the Council of the EU and the European Commission on decentralised agencies (2012) <https://europa.eu/european-union/sites/europaeu/files/docs/body/joint_statement_and_common_approach_2012_en.pdf> accessed 23 February 2021.

161 Chiti 2013, p. 102.

162 Ibid.

163 Senden 2013.

164 Ibid., p. 72.

165 Senden & Van den Brink 2012, p. 67.

166 Georgieva 2017; Luijendijk & Senden 2011, p. 313; Stefan 2012a.

167 Dehousse 2008, pp. 790 and 799; Senden 2004; Senden & Van den Brink 2012.

168 Allott 1981, p. 233.

A fourth concern is that, given their non-binding nature, it is unclear whether EU agencies' soft law instruments can be enforced and to what extent third parties may challenge the rules that EU agencies impose on them by means of soft law instruments. The Treaties remain silent on the enforcement of soft law and do not clearly specify the extent to which EU agencies' soft law instruments are susceptible to judicial review; that is, do such acts fall within the scope of the provisions concerning judicial review? The Court's case-law is also largely silent on this point and national judicial practices differ due to the diverse ways in which national authorities deal with such instruments. As a consequence, the extent to which EU agencies' soft law instruments can be effectuated or challenged remains to be seen.

All in all, EU agencies, 'which on the basis of the law and for reasons of lack of democratic legitimacy should not have far-reaching general rule-making powers, increasingly obtain them *de facto*'.[169] Consequently, the current non-regulation of the above-mentioned concerns in the Treaties and the restrictions in the case-law of the CJEU 'appear out of step with the daily institutional and legal reality'.[170] The enhancement of both the legitimacy and effectiveness of rule-making through EU agencies by having recourse to soft law instruments is difficult to achieve under these circumstances. Hence, this book aims to find an adequate procedural and institutional response to the rule-making activity of EU agencies, taking into account the requirements stemming from both legitimacy and effectiveness-related general principles of EU law.

8. MEETING THE CHALLENGE: ENHANCING THE LEGITIMACY AND EFFECTIVENESS OF EU AGENCIES' SOFT LAW-MAKING

8.1 The Central Question, Purpose and Method

This book addresses the lack of previous systematic research on EU agencies' (soft) rule-making.[171] The Treaties only regulate small bits and pieces – some principles on agencies, some aspects of soft law – and an orderly approach to both modes of governance is lacking. The field has not yet been mapped out, and a set of clear procedural and institutional safeguards is required in order to adequately balance the legitimacy and effectiveness of EU agencies' soft law-making powers. It is precisely the aim of this book to map the ground of the soft law-making powers of EU agencies, and in particular those of ESMA,

[169] Senden & Van den Brink 2012, p. 65.
[170] Ibid.
[171] Hofmann, Rowe & Türk 2011, p. 579.

from the perspectives of legitimacy and effectiveness. Importantly, the book does not concern a measurement of the legitimacy and effectiveness of the rules as such (are the regulatory objectives actually attained?), a measurement of the effects of rule-making, a measurement of the use of soft law as an effective instrument for good supervision, or an assessment of the effectiveness of supervision.[172] Instead, the main question this book aims to answer is the following:

What procedural and institutional safeguards regarding ESMA's soft law instruments would reflect an adequate balancing of both legitimacy and effectiveness concerns?

The book first presents the assessment framework underlying this research.[173] It determines which general principles of EU law are essential in operationalising legitimacy and effectiveness and establishes the relevant stages of the policy cycle in which legitimacy and effectiveness concerns may arise. The assessment framework also explains the importance of the selected legal principles for legitimacy and effectiveness and describes to what extent they already apply in the context of soft law-making by EU agencies.

The subsequent chapters entail an investigation and assessment of the extent to which ESMA already meets the expectations stemming from the general principles of EU law in each stage of the policy cycle as set out in the assessment framework. This entails a *de iure* analysis of the legitimacy and effectiveness of ESMA's soft law-making activity on the basis of what is formally provided for by the agency's founding Regulation as well as a *de facto* analysis of what happens in practice at each stage of the policy cycle. In this sense, the book entails a confrontation of the law in the books with law in practice. Both the *de iure* and the *de facto* dimensions aim at identifying the legitimacy and effectiveness gaps in the current framework.

In order to address the identified legitimacy and effectiveness gaps, the book concludes with solutions for ESMA and presents proposals for change in terms of procedural and institutional safeguards with a view to using ESMA's soft law in a manner that is effective in achieving the Union's objectives while at the same time providing a sufficient level of legitimacy.[174] More generally, it also offers the rules of the game for the Union legislature in establishing EU agencies with soft law powers that would reflect an adequate balancing of both legitimacy and effectiveness concerns.[175]

---

172 This book does not use effectiveness as a good agency principle; see for such an approach Ottow 2015. Instead, it approaches effectiveness from an EU perspective within the EU legal framework: see Chapter 2, Section 3.

173 See Chapter 2.

174 See Chapter 11, Section 2.

175 See Chapter 11, Section 4.

The book is based on desk research (literature research and case-law research) and heavily builds upon the author's experiences during a six-month traineeship at ESMA's premises in Paris (including semi-structured interviews with ESMA officials)[176] and her current participation in one of ESMA's Standing Committees.[177]

9. STRUCTURE OF THE BOOK

This book consists of 11 chapters. Chapter 1, which comes to its end with this section, has introduced the field of study, the relevant concepts and the related research problems. It has also set out the research questions, its aim and methodological aspects. Chapter 2 develops the assessment framework underlying the analysis in this book and identifies eight stages of the policy cycle in which possible links and tensions between legitimacy and effectiveness may come to the fore. To enable a systematic investigation of the entire policy cycle, the structure of the book is based on these eight stages.

Chapter 3 deals with the issues in relation to the legal basis for ESMA's soft law instruments and thus handles specifically the power for ESMA to engage in rule-making. Chapter 4 then looks at the initiation of the agency's competence in a concrete case. Chapter 5 deals with the characteristics of the decision-making process of ESMA's soft law instruments and Chapter 6 with transparency regarding its soft law. Chapter 7 focuses on transposition and Chapter 8 on the duty of compliance for national competent authorities. Chapter 9 handles the general means of enforcing compliance (enforcement vis-à-vis national authorities) and Chapter 10 the possibilities for individual judicial protection (judicial review). Each chapter investigates and assesses the related issues on the basis of what is already regulated in the agency's founding Regulation (*de iure*) and what happens in practice (*de facto*). Chapter 11 concludes this book and makes recommendations as to the changes in terms of institutional and procedural safeguards that would be required with a view to reflecting an adequate balancing of both legitimacy and effectiveness concerns in the eight stages of the EU policy cycle concerning both ESMA's and other EU agencies' soft law.

Throughout each chapter, where relevant, a distinction is made between the three categories of ESMA's soft law instruments as identified in Section 6.4 of this chapter. These are: quasi-binding draft regulatory and implementing technical standards; 'comply or explain' guidelines and recommendations; and

---

[176] From January until June 2015 at the Legal, Convergence and Enforcement Department at ESMA's premises in Paris, France.

[177] Since July 2018.

non-binding instruments. The differences between these three types bring with them that the legitimacy and effectiveness trade-offs will be different and that the requirements stemming from the general principles of EU law identified in the assessment framework apply in practice in a different way. The reader will find highlighted text boxes throughout the book to acquaint herself with practical examples that are relevant to the theoretical issues dealt with in the respective chapters.

The book has been written on the basis of the law as it stood on 1 February 2021. Major developments after that date have, where necessary, been considered and reflected upon sporadically throughout.

2. Guiding principles for EU agencies' soft law-making

1. INTRODUCTION

This book aims to answer the question as to what procedural and institutional safeguards regarding ESMA's soft law instruments are relevant in determining an adequate balancing of both legitimacy and effectiveness concerns. This chapter presents the assessment framework which underlies the entire book. It draws on legal doctrine and EU law. As a whole, it will form the basis for assessing the legitimacy and effectiveness of soft law-making by ESMA.

To begin, Sections 2 and 3 introduce the legitimacy and effectiveness conundrum. They establish what is meant by legitimacy and effectiveness for the purposes of this book and explain the importance of balancing both notions together. Section 4 establishes the relevant stages of the policy cycle in which legitimacy and effectiveness concerns may arise, and operationalises the *ex ante* and *ex post* dimensions of the policy cycle by means of general principles of EU law.[1] It also reflects on how the selected principles generally apply in the context of soft law-making by EU agencies. Sections 5 to 13 present the core of the relevant general principles, their relevance for legitimacy and effectiveness and how they can be used to guide the analysis in this book. The chapter concludes with an explanation, in Section 14, of how the assessment framework will be used in the following chapters of this book.

2. BALANCING BETWEEN THE LEGITIMACY AND EFFECTIVENESS OF EU ACTION

In democratic nation states, legitimacy and effectiveness coexist side by side, reinforcing, complementing and supplementing each other.[2] The EU is funda-

[1] 'An established authoritative catalogue of general principles of EU administrative procedural law does not exist – neither as an instrument of primary or secondary EU law, nor in the jurisprudence of the CJEU, nor is there a minimum consensus in scholarship about such a list': see Galetta and others 2015, p. 6.

[2] Scharpf 1999, pp. 6 and 13.

mentally different from national democracies, since it predominantly aspires to effectiveness.[3] The processes of EU decision-making have continued as if legitimacy did not matter. Consequently, the Union is often said to be facing a crisis of democratic legitimacy.[4] It is therefore confronted with the difficult task of making itself more acceptable to its citizens. In essence, any exercise of public power requires democratic legitimacy and accountability in order to prevent the government from abusing the power that has been given to it by the people. This is all the more pressing in the context of the EU, given the fact that the centre of power has shifted even further away from the citizen and the state.

However, more recently, the Union has considered legitimacy increasingly important. The Commission in particular has consciously sought to remedy the democratic deficit by finding ways to make policy-making 'more inclusive and accountable' to 'civil society' as well as more transparent, as per the EU Commission's White Paper on European Governance.[5] Not only do the Treaties now mirror the Member States' desire for stronger mechanisms of control over the Union's rule-making powers, but participation also remains high on the political agenda, as is demonstrated by the Interinstitutional Agreement on Better Law-making.[6] As regards soft law, the general legal framework is still not geared towards enhancing the legal position or empowerment of the citizen in the Union's decision-making process – and, with that, enhancing legitimacy – but rather towards enhancing the effectiveness of EU action.[7]

Nevertheless, 'given the increasing welfare gap and inequality between different European countries and different classes of citizens, insufficient citizen participation in policymaking cannot be excused with the promise of economic welfare'.[8] In other words, the Union's legitimacy deficit can no longer be justified with the promise of effectiveness.[9] As Beetham has stated, 'it is never

---

[3] Ibid., p. 13 and Armstrong 2014, p. 257.

[4] For instance, citizens' limited concern with Europe is expressed in the low turnouts at European Parliament elections. Likewise, the Brexit referendum in 2016 demonstrated how citizens' votes to leave the EU were able to shake the foundations of the organisation of the European Union as a whole.

[5] Commission, 'European governance: a White Paper' COM(2001) 428 final. See also Schmidt 2013, p. 15.

[6] Interinstitutional Agreement between the European Parliament, the Council of the European Union and the European Commission on Better Law-Making (2016) OJ L 123.

[7] 'For, in and of themselves soft governance modes are very much connected with features of informality so that they can be used in a rather flexible way to address new or urgent problems. Such governance modes are therefore often linked to the efficiency and effectiveness of law and policy making': see Senden 2013, p. 59.

[8] Cengiz 2016.

[9] Ibid.

a good idea for a political system to build its relationship with citizens solely on the promise of performance, because this would leave the relationship vulnerable to a crisis when the promised performance cannot be delivered'.[10] Hence, a more holistic understanding of rule-making is required in which legitimacy and effectiveness have to be seen as playing mutually reinforcing roles, and not alternative ones.[11]

3. EXPLAINING LEGITIMACY AND EFFECTIVENESS

So, generally speaking, when exercising its rule-making powers, the Union has to fulfil both legitimacy *and* effectiveness demands.[12] Now, there are various opinions on what legitimacy[13] and effectiveness[14] mean and how they should be analysed. These demands are often said to follow from the traditional distinctions between procedural and substantive legitimacy as understood by Majone,[15] as well as 'input' and 'output' legitimacy as understood by Scharpf.[16] Schmidt adds to this the notion of 'throughput' legitimacy.[17] This book follows these three normative criteria for the evaluation of legitimacy.

According to Majone, the first dimension of legitimacy is that of *procedural legitimacy*. This implies that regulatory authorities are created by democratically enacted statutes which define their legal authority and objectives, that the regulators are appointed by representative bodies, that decisions are justified and open to judicial review and that regulatory decision-making follows formal rules, which often require public participation.[18] As such, procedural

---

[10] Ibid. and Beetham 2013.

[11] Cengiz 2016.

[12] This is not an easy task, though. As Scharpf explains, at present Europe is caught in the intersection of multiple crises, all of which – Brexit, the euro crisis, the refugee crisis, the Covid crisis – are challenging the effectiveness as well as the democratic legitimacy of government on European and national levels: see Scharpf 2017, p. 315.

[13] Bovens, Curtin & 't Hart 2010, pp. 9–30; De Búrca 1996; Majone 1999; Scott 1998.

[14] Effectiveness is an ambiguous term, which does not allow for an easy definition. The literature dealing with the notion of effectiveness paints a very extensive and varied picture indeed: see Acceto and Zleptnig 2005; Allott 1981; De Benedetto 2018; Blanc 2018; Mousmouti 2018; Ottow 2015; Piris 1994; Rangone 2018; Snyder 1993; Van den Broek 2015; Xanthaki 2018; Zamboni 2018.

[15] Majone distinguished these two dimensions in relation to the legitimacy of the regulatory branch in the context of the EU institutions. His perspective considers legitimacy and effectiveness as strongly connected notions, see Majone 1996, p. 291.

[16] Scharpf 1999.

[17] Schmidt 2013.

[18] Majone 1996, p. 291.

legitimacy links with the notion of *input legitimacy*, as it demands that those being affected by a norm have somehow been included in the process of its formulation and that they have a fair chance to scrutinise the results. According to Scharpf, input-oriented democratic thought thus emphasises 'government *by the people*'.[19] Political choices are legitimate if and because they reflect the 'will of the people'.[20]

Majone distinguishes the second dimension of legitimacy as *substantive legitimacy*. This relates to such features of the regulatory process as policy consistency, the expertise and problem-solving capacity of the regulators, the precision of the limits within which regulators are expected to operate and their ability to protect diffuse interests.[21] As such, substantive legitimacy links with the notion of *output legitimacy*, as these features emphasise the importance of effective policy outcomes. According to Scharpf, output-oriented democratic thought thus emphasises 'government *for the people*'.[22] Continuing along this line of thought, political choices are legitimate if and because they effectively promote the common welfare of the population in question.[23] Regulation is output legitimate when the regulatory outcomes are satisfactory. Furthermore, output legitimacy requires the prevention of abuse of political power by holding a regime accountable for its decisions *ex post*.[24] Whether output legitimacy is in competition or conflict with the values of input legitimacy, or the two types of legitimacy are in fact mutually reinforcing, is an ongoing debate.[25]

---

[19] Scharpf 1999, p. 6.
[20] Ibid.
[21] Majone 1996, pp. 291–92.
[22] Scharpf 1999, p. 6.
[23] Ibid.
[24] Ibid., p. 13.
[25] See, for instance, Lindgren & Persson 2010. Scharpf argues that the challenges of input and output legitimacy are at least connected: democratic legitimacy presupposes effective governing and problem-solving capacity. Hence the failure of output legitimacy may undermine or even destroy the possibility of input legitimacy. At the same time, however, the lack of input legitimacy in the present European context will constrain and may ultimately destroy the effectiveness of measures based on non-accountable supranational authority: see Scharpf 2017, p. 315. Schmidt argues that input and output can indeed involve trade-offs, where more of one may make up for less of the other, whereas more (and better) throughput does not make up for problems with either input or output while less (and worse) throughput can delegitimate both input and output: see Schmidt 2013, p. 19. In more recent work, Schmidt and Wood argue that the concept of throughput might be better seen as an 'umbrella concept' accompanying the other two such umbrella concepts of input and output legitimacy, as criteria for dynamic and 'multi-centric' processes of policy formulation and implementation: see Schmidt & Wood 2019, p. 737.

As Schmidt explains, the quality of the governance processes is also an important criterion for the evaluation of a polity's overall democratic legitimacy.[26] So-called *throughput legitimacy* involves first of all the efficacy of the many different forms of EU governance processes and the adequacy of the rules they follow in policy-making.[27] It also encompasses the accountability and transparency of the governance processes.[28] Accountability is generally taken to mean that EU actors are judged on their responsiveness to participatory input demands and can be held responsible for their output decisions,[29] as well as that policy-making processes meet standards of ethical governance, whether with regard to lobbyists or to civil servants.[30] Transparency is generally taken to mean that citizens have access to information about the processes[31] and that decisions as well as decision-making processes in formal EU institutions are public. Finally, throughput additionally concerns the quality and quantity of EU governance processes' inclusiveness and the openness of the EU's various institutional bodies to 'civil society'.[32]

In the literature, 'output legitimacy' is closely associated with 'effectiveness'.[33] Effectiveness is a precondition and guarantee for the success of any legal system.[34] This is particularly true in relation to Union law, which is largely dependent on effective implementation in the Member States.[35] The overall effectiveness of the Union regulatory regime, including the rights and benefits it is intended to confer, may in practice however be obstructed in various ways.[36] For instance, Member States may refuse or fail to implement Union law instruments[37] and substantive and procedural hurdles at the national and the Union level may erode effectiveness.[38] An exploration of the scope of

26 Schmidt 2013, p. 2.
27 Ibid., p. 6.
28 Ibid.
29 Harlow & Rawlings 2007.
30 Schmidt 2013, p. 6.
31 Héritier 2003.
32 This kind of interest-based throughput is categorically different from interest group-based 'input', in which demands are articulated through interest group pressures, protests, demonstrations, letter-writing campaigns, social movement activism and the like in efforts to influence elected representatives, and which does not capture the ways in which interest articulation has become an integral part of the very throughput process of EU governance: see Schmidt 2013, pp. 6–7.
33 Scharpf 1999 and Scharpf 2017.
34 Acceto & Zleptnig 2005, p. 375.
35 Ibid.
36 Ibid., pp. 376 and 380.
37 Ibid., p. 376.
38 Such as procedural rules, administrative practices adopted by national authorities or failures in the institutional set-up of authorities responsible for the proper application of Union law: see Acceto & Zleptnig 2005, p. 376.

the notion of effectiveness is therefore not only of theoretical interest, but also of the utmost practical importance for the daily functioning of the European Union.[39] This book consciously takes an EU approach towards the notion of effectiveness by investigating from an EU perspective *whether ESMA's soft law instruments are effective in achieving the Union's objectives* and *whether a sufficient level of legitimacy is provided for at the same time.*

The aims of legitimacy and effectiveness may overlap, but may sometimes also be at odds with each other. That is to say, gains in terms of legitimacy may come at a price in terms of effectiveness or vice versa. The demands stemming from both notions therefore require constant balancing.[40] This may mean that, although legitimacy requires a certain level of citizen involvement, effectiveness may implicate that only technical stakeholders will be involved in the rule-making procedure. The tension between legitimacy and effectiveness is also a dividing line within the different principles identified below. Weakening or strengthening one will have an effect on the other.[41] For instance, participation may increase the legitimacy of EU rule-making as it safeguards the position of individuals by bringing them closer to Union action. People are more likely to comply with the law if their concerns are being heard, thus contributing to the effectiveness of rule-making. At the same time, it is important to keep in mind that the rules and requirements stemming from the general principles of EU law may also negatively influence either legitimacy or effectiveness. Participation could slow the decision-making process by making it more timely and costly. In this way, it may actually hinder the effectiveness of rule-making.

4. ASSESSMENT FRAMEWORK

The operationalisation of legitimacy and effectiveness in the following two subsections results in the establishment of an assessment framework. It will be used for the evaluation of ESMA's soft law-making in order to demonstrate where possible links and tensions come to the fore when both legitimacy and effectiveness need to be balanced in each stage of the policy cycle. The assessment framework is composed of two dimensions, namely an *ex ante* and an *ex post* dimension of the policy cycle.

---

39 Ibid.

40 Ottow 2015, Ottow 2009 and Ottow 2006.

41 Ibid. The criteria under the 'umbrella' concept of throughput legitimacy (efficacy, accountability, transparency, inclusiveness and openness) can also work in contradictory ways, or at cross-purposes. For instance, increasing transparency may uncover a lack of inclusiveness and openness in stakeholder engagement, see Schmidt & Wood 2019, p. 730.

The *ex ante* dimension relates to the first stage of the policy cycle – that is, the definition of a legal basis, in which it has to be decided whether there is competence to take regulatory action – and to the second stage – that is, initiation, in which it has to be decided what the most appropriate level of action and type of instrument would be. The *ex ante* dimension also includes the decision-making process of the regulatory acts, which concerns the third stage of the policy cycle, as well as transparency in relation to the legal instruments, which concerns the fourth stage.

The *ex post* dimension in fact entails the effectuation of the rules. It relates to the fifth stage of the policy cycle, which involves the transposition duties for the national authorities, and the sixth stage, which relates to compliance with EU law by national authorities. The *ex post* dimension also includes the seventh stage of enforcement vis-à-vis the national authorities and, finally, the eighth stage of judicial review by the EU and national courts as an ultimate mechanism for the legitimation and effectuation of rule-making activity. This book's point of departure is that the tension between legitimacy and effectiveness occurs at all stages of the policy cycle. Both legitimacy and effectiveness concerns therefore need to be adequately balanced in each stage of the process.

4.1 Operationalising the *Ex Ante* Dimension of the Policy Cycle

Both legitimacy and effectiveness play a large role in the *ex ante* dimension of the policy cycle. In general, it can be held that the existence, division and exercise of Union power must be acceptable to citizens in order to be legitimate. The acceptability of power and the exercise thereof relies on the rule of law.[42] It guarantees that the EU can only have powers with regard to citizens on the basis of the law, and it is subject to this law when it acts.[43] This does not only mean governing on the basis of the law, that is, that there is a competence-conferring legal basis (conferral). It also means governing within the boundaries of the law, in conformity with certain principles which indicate the limits to the powers to be exercised (subsidiarity and proportionality). As will be explained in Section 6, the principle of *conferral* is important for the first stage of the policy cycle, that is, defining the legal basis, whereas Section 7 explains that the principles of *subsidiarity* and *proportionality* play a key role at the second stage, that is, the initiation stage. Effectiveness also plays an important role at both stages, because it is related to the exercise of Union competences. Such a competence may only be exercised when Union

---

[42] Burkens and others 2001, p. 9.

[43] Verhoeven & Widdershoven 2010, pp. 56–57. This can be said to require governing *sub lege* and governing *per lege*: see Senden 2004, p. 64.

action is more effective and efficient than action by the Member States, which also follows from the principle of subsidiarity.

In addition, 'legitimacy is understood in the sense of democratic legitimacy or rather of democratic legitimation of the EU decision-making process, which is often said to be weak because of the democratic deficit'.[44] That is, the citizen has only limited influence and control over this process. Although the legitimacy thereof has certainly improved over the years and now provides at least for certain democratic guarantees,[45] EU citizens still feel very alienated from the Union, and the level of openness of decision-making and decisions may not yet be sufficient.[46] Enhancing legitimacy is thus understood as an effort to increase the influence, control and participation of both the citizen and the European Parliament in the EU decision-making process and, more generally, to bring the Union closer to the citizen (input legitimacy). This conception of legitimation presupposes that legislation is adopted in conformity with democratic procedures (throughput legitimacy). As will be explained in Sections 8 and 9, the principles of *participation* and *transparency* are of crucial importance in relation to ESMA's decision-making process (stage 3) and for transparency regarding the agency's soft law instruments (stage 4), respectively. Efficiency also plays a significant role at the decision-making stage, a process which ideally evolves in a timely and efficient way.[47] When designing rule-making procedures and practices, it is consequently important to think

Table 2.1 *Principles operationalising the* ex ante *dimension of the policy cycle*

Policy cycle		***Ex ante* dimension**		
Stages	Legal basis	Initiation	Decision-making	Transparency
Principles	Conferral	Proportionality Subsidiarity	Participation	Transparency

[44] Senden 2004, p. 63.

[45] For instance, by means of the participation of those concerned in the process of law-making or through the provision of more legal, procedural guarantees (such as access to documents) in this process.

[46] This is again witnessed by the Brexit referendum in 2016, in which 51.9 per cent of the participating UK electorate voted to leave the EU.

[47] However, generally speaking, the level of detail in EU legislation often results in a lack of flexibility: see Commission, 'European governance: A White Paper', COM(2001) 428 final, 18.

about the impact of procedural steps and controls on the legal instruments.[48] Too many hurdles may result in a loss of flexibility and thus in decreased efficiency or a completely ineffective rule-making process.

The stages and relevant principles operationalizing the *ex ante* dimension of the policy cycle may be visualised as in Table 2.1.

4.2 Operationalising the *Ex Post* Dimension of the Policy Cycle

Legitimacy and effectiveness also play a large role in the *ex post* dimension of the policy cycle. Effectiveness is measured against the achievement of regulatory objectives.[49] Simply put, a given regulatory policy is effective when it realises its objectives, that is, fulfils its purposes.[50] For this, it is required that EU legislative action is capable of, or at least contributes to, achieving the objectives of the Union as spelt out in the Treaties. This implies that regulatory objectives as well as the regulatory instruments to achieve them are well defined.[51] It should not be confused with 'cost-effectiveness' or 'efficiency', which is about achieving a certain policy goal at the lowest cost. Effectiveness also connects to the ways in which regulation is effectuated after it has been adopted.[52] This has been said to include transposition, compliance, enforcement and *ex post* control.[53]

To begin with, the effectiveness of any Union measure depends on whether the Member States adequately transpose the measure into their national legal systems without leaving too many opportunities for evasion.[54] In this regard, effectiveness requires that Union law is transposed and applied correctly and in a uniform manner across the European Union.[55] Given the fact that the Member States have the expertise at the national level, their involvement also leads to enhanced output legitimacy. What concrete actions from Member States are required, and the extent to which they enjoy freedom to choose the necessary forms and methods to obtain the objective of the Union act, is dependent on the

48 The question is to what extent procedures may affect the achievement of policy objectives – that is, what happens to effectiveness if there is too much proceduralisation?

49 Majone 2007, p. 75.

50 Allott 1981, p. 233.

51 Majone 2007, p. 75.

52 Acceto & Zleptnig 2005, p. 381.

53 This connects with the normative framework as developed by Acceto and Zleptnig: they identified the implementation and execution aspect of the principle of effectiveness, the enforcement and compliance aspect, and the control aspect of effectiveness. See Acceto & Zleptnig 2005, p. 387. See also Snyder 1993, p. 26.

54 Neyer 2004, p. 27.

55 Acceto & Zleptnig 2005, pp. 379 and 390.

act at stake.[56] In this respect, the institutional and procedural autonomy of the Member States needs to be taken into account as well. Section 10 will explain the importance of the principles of *institutional and procedural autonomy* in the transposition stage.

Moreover, effectiveness focuses on compliance with the rules.[57] Indeed, in order to be fully effective, Union law needs the compliance of those to whom it is addressed. This means that differences in compliance can hamper the effectiveness of rules, because they hinder the achievement of the rules' main objective. It is therefore important to establish what the compliance duties are for national authorities and market operators. This very much depends on the (legal) effects an act may produce. The principles of *sincere cooperation* and *legitimate expectations* are helpful in establishing such effects. As will be explained in Section 11, the principles of sincere cooperation and legitimate expectations are of crucial importance in the compliance stage.

For cases where national authorities try to escape their compliance duties, appropriate enforcement mechanisms are necessary in order to enhance compliance with Union acts. This also links with effectiveness, in the sense that it is generally associated with strategies that influence the incentives to comply or deviate.[58] These strategies may operate by reducing the benefits of violations, increasing the benefits of compliance and increasing the sanctions for non-compliance.[59] It is important to distinguish between indirect and direct enforcement of EU law.[60] The latter concerns enforcement action taken by Union or Member State authorities directly against Union citizens and economic actors.[61] It does not form part of this book, because the analysis mainly concerns the relationship between ESMA and national authorities. Indirect enforcement 'involves the supervision of the application of the law by

---

56 For instance, *directives* have to be translated into national law. The Member States in principle enjoy freedom to choose the necessary forms and methods in order to obtain the directive's objective, but the Court requires the adoption of binding rules of national law as regards the 'form' of the transposition of directives. On the other hand, *regulations* do not require transposition. As a matter of principle, it is not even permitted to transpose regulations into national law. In practice, it nonetheless appears that there is often a need for the Member States to adopt implementing measures in order to grant full effect to a regulation. See Polak 2015, p. 47 and Prechal, Widdershoven & Jans 2015, p. 13.

57 It is often said that the effectiveness of a law is measured by the degree of compliance: see Allott 1981, p. 235 and Majone 2007, p. 75.

58 Majone 2007, p. 75.

59 Ibid.

60 See for a distinction Scholten, Luchtman & Schmidt 2017 and Vervaele 1999.

61 For a complete study on direct enforcement by EU authorities, see Scholten & Luchtman 2017. On ESMA's direct enforcement powers specifically, see Van Rijsbergen & Foster 2017, pp. 43–64 and Van Rijsbergen & Scholten 2016.

Table 2.2 *Principles operationalising the* ex post *dimension of the policy cycle*

Policy cycle	***Ex post* dimension**			
Stages	Transposition	Compliance	Enforcement	Judicial review
Principles	Institutional and procedural autonomy	Sincere cooperation Legitimate expectations	Proportionality	Effective judicial protection

public authorities – and foremost of the Member States – but not directly over whether citizens as such obey it'.[62] Although national authorities are significant actors in ensuring compliance with Union legal instruments, mechanisms for enforcement are increasingly put in place at the Union level, including at the EU agencies' level.[63] The choice of the most appropriate indirect enforcement mechanism may be induced by proportionality considerations. Hence, as will be explained in Section 12, the principle of *proportionality* is important for the enforcement stage.

Finally, as an ultimate mechanism for the legitimation and effectuation of rule-making activity, judicial review belongs to the *ex post* dimension of the policy cycle. It falls under the heading of effectiveness, since it relates to the ways in which regulation is effectuated and is of crucial importance for the achievement of regulatory objectives. Moreover, the adequacy of judicial protection influences the attitude of the market towards compliance with the relevant legal rules and cooperation with the actors that apply them, and in that manner also has a direct relation with the effectiveness of these rules.[64] In order to provide third parties individually with effective judicial protection and to ensure the legal certainty of the system as a whole, there is thus a need to establish opportunities for Union acts to be judicially challenged.[65] This is also the result of considerations of output legitimacy which require that decisions are open to judicial review. The Union court thus plays an important role in ensuring the legitimacy and effectiveness of Union law. National courts also have to ensure that EU law is effectively enforced whenever a conflict arises. As will be explained in Section 13, the principle of *effective judicial protection* is important for the review stage.

The stages and relevant principles operationalising the *ex post* dimension of the policy cycle may be visualised as in Table 2.2.

[62] Hofmann & Türk 2009, p. 188; Prechal, Widdershoven & Jans 2015, p. 18; Scholten, Luchtman & Schmidt 2017.

[63] See Chapter 5.

[64] De Visser 2009, p. 329.

[65] Acceto & Zleptnig 2005, p. 387.

4.3 The Applicability of the General Principles of EU Law to EU Agencies, National Authorities and Soft Law

The general principles of EU law are developed by the CJEU in its case-law and are increasingly anchored in the EU Treaties. However, many of these Treaty provisions do not mention soft law or EU agencies at all. This highlights that these subjects are not regulated in the Treaties, but by means of secondary legislation only.

As follows from *Goed Wonen*, the general principles of EU law form part of the Union legal order and are thus binding upon the EU institutions.[66] This does not necessarily entail a duty for EU agencies to observe all principles, since they are not explicitly mentioned by the Court in this case. The Treaties themselves are also ambiguous on this point. When a provision directly refers to '*the Union's bodies, offices and agencies*',[67] the principle laid down therein unambiguously applies to EU agencies. However, when a provision explicitly mentions '*the institutions of the Union*',[68] it is not entirely certain whether or not this also includes EU agencies, and thus ESMA. It seems, however, that this is logically applicable to all bodies that are engaged in regulatory action, thus including EU agencies.[69] At the same time, it does seem odd that such provisions would also apply to the CJEU, this being an institution that is mentioned in Article 13 TEU. When a provision uses broad terms like '*Union action*' and '*Union competences*',[70] the principles embedded therein may be regarded as Union principles. This means that they are addressed to the Union, that is, to all institutions in the sense of Article 13 TEU, but also to all bodies, offices and agencies as they are *all* entrusted with the 'use of Union competences'.[71] Likewise, there is no reason to assume that '*Union action*' does not encompass soft law-making by EU agencies.

---

[66] Case C-376/02 *'Goed Wonen'* [2005] ECR I-3445, para 32. See also Van den Brink 2012, p. 145.

[67] Such as the access to documents aspect of the principle of transparency as laid down in TFEU, Art 15.

[68] For instance, TEU, Arts 11(1) and 11(2) laying down the principle of participation refer to *the institutions* and to *Union action.*

[69] For instance, by virtue of TEU, Art 11, the principle of participation applies to *the institutions*. This means that EU agencies are not explicitly mentioned. Interestingly, as follows from the analysis in Chapter 5, stakeholders are nonetheless enabled to participate in ESMA's decision-making procedures resulting in the adoption of guidelines and draft technical standards. This example shows that although not explicitly mentioned in a Treaty provision, EU agencies can still be obliged to observe general principles of Union law.

[70] Such as TEU, Arts 5(1) and 5(2) laying down the principle of conferral.

[71] Weber 2010, p. 262.

Another argument for supporting the application of general principles of EU law in the context of EU agencies' soft law-making is that EU agencies are only a fragmentary part of the institutional framework. Indeed, the Union Treaties are very fragmented. It seems that the drafters did not think about creating a consistent whole or consider how the provisions might work for EU agencies. Given the impact that EU agencies have in practice, a functional and teleological interpretation of the EU Treaties does however allow for the conclusion that EU agencies such as ESMA are also bound by the general principles of EU law. Such a conclusion could also be drawn from the *Meroni* case, in which the Court set out a number of legal limitations on the power to delegate.[72] One of these constraints is that *the exercise of the powers conferred on an agency must be subject to the same conditions as those to which it would be subject if the delegating authority was exercising them directly.*[73] The Court in *Meroni* annulled the contested decision because, among other things, the exercise of the powers conferred on the private agencies was not subject to the conditions to which it would have been subject if the High Authority had exercised them directly.[74] It concluded that if the delegating authority had exercised the delegated powers itself, it would have been bound by certain principles established by the Treaty, such as the principles to state reasons and to publish an annual report.[75] Hence, when the Union legislature delegates soft law powers to EU agencies, it could be said that the latter, as the recipients of the delegated tasks, should also fulfil the duties stemming from the relevant general principles of EU law.

National implementing authorities are bound by the general principles of Union law when they act within the scope of EU law.[76] This is in line with Article 51(1) of the Charter of Fundamental Rights, which proclaims that the provisions of the Charter are also addressed to the Member States when they are implementing Union law.[77] They shall therefore respect the rights, *observe the principles* and promote the application thereof in accordance with their respective powers.[78] In such a case, the national authorities operate as 'agents' of the EU.[79] It is irrelevant whether, or to what extent, national implementing authorities are vested with discretion, that is, must also exercise their discretion

---

72 See Chapter 3 for more on the *Meroni* case.

73 Case 9-56 *Meroni v High Authority* [1958] ECR 133, paras 149–50.

74 Ibid.

75 Ibid., para. 149.

76 This is *inter alia* the case when they implement EU law: see Van den Brink 2012, p. 147.

77 Charter of Fundamental Rights of the European Union.

78 Ibid., Art 51(1).

79 Prechal 2009, p. 8.

in compliance with the relevant general principles of EU law.[80] The obligation for national implementing bodies to adhere to the general principles of Union law has its basis in the principle of sincere cooperation.[81]

5. PRINCIPLES FOR ANALYSING THE LEGITIMACY AND EFFECTIVENESS OF EU AGENCIES' SOFT LAW-MAKING

When exercising rule-making powers in the EU, the legislature has to go through the eight stages of the policy cycle as identified in the previous sections, while continuously balancing the demands stemming from both legitimacy and effectiveness. The following sections present the core contents of the relevant general principles of EU law, explain whether they are applicable in the context of EU agencies' soft law-making and elaborate on how the principles have a bearing on legitimacy and effectiveness.

6. STAGE 1: DEFINING A LEGAL BASIS FOR UNION LEGISLATION

In the first stage of the policy cycle, it is required to determine *if* the EU is competent to act. It thus concerns the determination of the presence of the competence, that is, defining the legal basis. The principle of *conferral* plays a crucial role in this regard. It marks the first step, in the sense of identifying whether there exists a legal basis for the Union to act. If no powers have been conferred upon the EU, the competences remain with the Member States.

6.1 The Principle of Conferral

Although the Union's values and objectives are listed widely and ambitiously in Articles 2 and 3 TEU, the Union is not entitled to take any measure whatsoever in order to realise its goals. This clearly follows from Article 5(2) TEU, which provides that 'the Union shall act only within the limits of the competences conferred upon it by the Member States in the Treaties to attain the objectives set out therein. Competences not conferred upon the Union in the Treaties remain with the Member States.' The limits of the Union's competences are thus governed by the principle of conferral.[82]

---

[80] Ibid.

[81] Van den Brink 2012.

[82] References to conferral are also found in TEU, Arts 1, 3(6), 4(1), 13(2) and TFEU, Art 7.

The principle of conferral entails that at least all legally binding actions by the EU institutions need a legal basis in the Treaties, either directly or indirectly in the case of delegation.[83] It means, in particular, that no legally binding rights and obligations are created and imposed without there being such a foundation.[84] Besides, EU competences can be inferred from individual Treaty provisions which, as such, provide for a legal basis for the Union's competence to act in a particular case. Since Article 5(2) TEU is broadly formulated – 'the Union shall act' – the principle of conferral also applies to soft law-making by EU agencies,[85] and thus by ESMA.

Identifying the legal basis serves the goal of establishing the existence of a competence *ex ante*. It therefore contributes to the effectiveness of Union action, because it allows the Union to legislate in the first place.[86] The legal basis indicates, to a large extent, the boundaries within which the Union may exercise its competence. In particular, it prescribes the subject that may be regulated and the scope thereof; the decision-making procedure; the nature, form and intensity of Union action (regulation, directive or otherwise, binding or non-binding); and the competent institution.[87] It thereby not only demarcates Union competences from those of the Member States, but also distributes the tasks and competences between the Union institutions. Indeed, each institution has its own defined powers in the decision-making process, which it exercises with due regard for the powers of the others. In this way, conferral plays a key role in enhancing the legitimacy of Union action as it relates to both the horizontal and vertical division and exercise of powers. The vertical division of powers aims at the demarcation of EU competences from those of the Member States. The horizontal division of powers underlines the inter-institutional relations and thus relates to the way in which tasks and competences are distributed between the EU institutions by the Treaty on European Union.

Identification of the legal basis also enables the *ex post* assessment of whether this competence has been exercised in conformity with the powers actually conferred upon the EU. As such, the legal basis provides for legal protection against the unlawful exercise of competences by the EU and its institutions.[88] It requires that the choice of the legal basis may only be founded

---

83 Verhoeven 2011, pp. 155–6.
84 Schwarze 2006, p. 238.
85 See Section 4.3.
86 Barents 1993, p. 92.
87 Senden 2004, p. 72.
88 Case 294/83, *Parti écologiste 'Les Verts' v European Parliament* [1986] ECR 1339. See also Barents 1993, p. 92.

on objective elements which are susceptible to judicial review.[89] Subjective choices based on political interests and institutional positions are therefore unlawful.[90] The legal basis thus guarantees more legal certainty for those affected by Union legislation by making it more predictable and foreseeable. In this way, it also enables supervised entities to know which rules they have to comply with. Indeed, the better the chances of compliance, the more likely it is that the policy objectives are achieved.

7. STAGE 2: INITIATING UNION LEGISLATION

If the EU is competent to act in general, it is required to determine *how* this competence should be exercised when initiating it. This concerns the determination of what the most appropriate level of action and type of instrument would be in a concrete case. Subsidiarity marks the second step after conferral, in the sense of determining whether a competence may be exercised in a given instance, or whether the appropriate level remains the national one. The proportionality element may be regarded as the third step. Once it has been established that the Union is competent to act and that the EU is the appropriate level to exercise this competence in a given instance, the next question is indeed *how* this competence should be exercised. This is exactly what the *proportionality* principle is about.

7.1 The Principle of Subsidiarity

The principle of subsidiarity is also considered to be fundamental to the functioning of the EU, and more specifically to EU decision-making. It is laid down as a general principle of EU law in Article 5(3) TEU, which reads:

> Under the principle of subsidiarity, in areas which do not fall within its exclusive competence, the Union shall act only if and in so far as the objectives of the proposed action cannot be sufficiently achieved by the Member States, either at central level or at regional and local level, but can rather, by reason of the scale or effects of the proposed action, be better achieved at Union level.

---

[89] This is the standard formula of the Court in cases on conflicts about legal bases. It means that the limits of the powers conferred by a specific provision of the Treaty are to be inferred from an interpretation of the particular wording of the provision in question which is analysed in the light of its purpose and place in the scheme of the Treaty, see Joined Cases 188 to 190/80 *France, Italy and United Kingdom v Commission* [1982] ECR 2545, para. 6.

[90] Barents 1993, p. 92.

Protocol No. 2 on the Application of the Principles of Subsidiarity and Proportionality, which is annexed to the Treaties and should be read in tandem with the Protocol on the Role of National Parliaments in the EU, defines the implementation of the principle of subsidiarity.[91] The Protocol does not foresee that subsidiarity is also applied at the level of EU agencies. Yet, Article 5(3) TEU is broadly formulated – 'the Union shall act' – which means that it also encompasses soft law-making by EU agencies,[92] including ESMA.

In the EU law context, the subsidiarity principle concerns the relationship between the Union and the Member States, that is, between two levels of government. It thus plays a key role in enhancing the legitimacy of Union action, because it helps to determine the right level of action and mainly contributes to an appropriate vertical exercise of powers between the Union and the Member States. In practical terms, this means that consideration needs to be given to whether the Union or the national level is the appropriate level for exercising competence. It is logical that the principle does not apply to areas which fall within the exclusive competence of the Union, since in those areas the Union is the only authority to act, thus the choice of the appropriate level of action has already been made.

Article 5(3) TEU contains two further elements for making this choice.[93] First, the objectives of the proposed action cannot be *sufficiently* achieved by the Member States. This element can be said to entail '*an effectiveness test*, meaning that if action at national level (including financial resources, legal instruments, potential and existing measures) is capable of producing the desired result, this level should be preferred'.[94] Second, the objectives can be *better* achieved by the Union by reason of the scale or effects of the proposed action. This element can be said to entail '*an efficiency test*, which requires a comparative evaluation of the costs and benefits of action at Union and national level'.[95] Subsidiarity thus has a link with effectiveness as well, because Union competences may only be exercised when Union action is more effective and efficient than action by the Member States. In this way, subsidiarity aims at achieving the objectives of the proposed action.

---

91 Non-binding measures were explicitly referred to in the first version of the Subsidiarity and Proportionality Protocol attached to the Treaty of Amsterdam, but the current version of the Protocol no longer does this.

92 See Section 4.3.

93 The two tests are a novelty introduced by the Treaty of Lisbon, since pre-Lisbon national insufficiency automatically resulted in (greater) comparative efficiency, whereas today a proposed action should cumulatively pass the two tests before the Union may act: see Chamon 2016, p. 158.

94 Senden 2004, p. 83.

95 Ibid.

7.2 The Principle of Proportionality

Proportionality is well established as a general principle of Union law.[96] Its requirements are also further fleshed out in Protocol No. 2. Unlike the principle of subsidiarity, proportionality applies to areas in which the EU is exclusively competent as well. It plays a key role in enhancing the legitimacy of Union action on the basis of the rule of law, because it is to a certain extent related to the horizontal division of powers between the Union institutions. The role of each institution in the process depends on the form and intensity of the action that is undertaken. In addition, proportionality has a bearing on the vertical division of powers, since the choice of either a hard or soft law instrument is decisive for the obligations being imposed on the Member States. In principle, soft law is less intrusive than hard law instruments.

To begin with, proportionality is an *ex ante* legislative doctrine for the political institutions to observe in the exercise of their decision-making functions.[97] It thus entails an assessment of the proportionality of Union action at the stage of its initiation. According to Article 5(4) TEU, 'the content and form of Union action shall not exceed what is necessary to achieve the objectives of the Treaties'. Given the broad formulation of this provision, that is, 'Union action', the principle of proportionality also encompasses soft law-making by EU agencies, and thus by ESMA.[98] Proportionality concerns both the intensity and the form or method of Union action. The former relates to the actual contents, whereas the latter refers to the means and instruments and their (legal) nature. As such, the principle entails that every exercise of competence – be it rule-making or enforcement action – by the Union has to be performed with reservation.[99] This implies that 'whenever equally effective options are available, the EU must choose the forms of action and measures which leave the Member States, individuals and businesses the greatest degree of freedom'.[100] Consequently, consideration must be given to the question of whether legislative action is actually required or whether other types of action, possibly of a non-binding nature, may suffice. Legislation should only be resorted to when this is necessary and essential. Where possible, preference has to be given to non-binding measures. Yet, the choice of instrument may already be limited as a result of the provision(s) upon which a particular act is based. However, the

---

96 Craig & De Búrca 2008, p. 545.

97 Emiliou distinguishes the *ex ante* and *ex post* dimensions of proportionality: see Emiliou 1996, p. 142.

98 See Section 4.3.

99 See Section 12 for the applicability of the principle of proportionality in the context of enforcement vis-à-vis national authorities.

100 Senden 2004, p. 83.

Treaty leaves the choice of instrument open in most cases, giving the institutions quite a lot of discretion in this regard.

Proportionality contributes to effective rule-making as it involves the choice of the most appropriate legal instrument for achieving the intended regulatory objectives. The main question is: which instrument is most fit for purpose? In reality, the principle of proportionality has an impact on the effectiveness of Union action in both the *ex ante* and *ex post* dimensions of the policy cycle. On the one hand, the legislature could opt for the least formal act, which involves less procedural steps to go through and is therefore quicker to adopt. On the other hand, it could choose a more formal act which requires, for example, consultations, adoption of which would therefore be less flexible. Effectiveness in the *ex ante* dimension of the policy cycle is then lower. Yet, a more formal act can also contribute to better implementation, and in that sense it can usefully contribute to effectiveness in the *ex post* dimension of the policy cycle.

Proportionality is also an *ex post* judicial doctrine for an assessment of the behaviour of both national and Union authorities by the national and Union courts.[101] Proportionality can thus be used to challenge Union action as well as the legality of state action which falls within the sphere of application of Union law.[102] In this manner, it constitutes a means to protect individuals from excessive interference by the Member States and the EU. This also contributes to legitimacy, because it enables that decisions are justified and may be open to judicial review.[103]

8. STAGE 3: THE DECISION-MAKING PROCESS OF UNION LEGISLATION

When the legislator has established that it is competent to act in a given instance and how it is going to act, the decision-making process begins. Decision-making starts with the actual drafting of Union acts and ends with the adoption thereof. This entails the third stage of the policy cycle. During the decision-making process, several procedural requirements should be adhered to. These are given by the principles of *participation* and *transparency*, although the latter will play a more dominant role in stage 4.

---

[101] Emiliou 1996, p. 142. This dimension of the proportionality principle lies in the *Internationale Handelgesellschaft* case where the Court examined whether the measure in question was necessary and appropriate to achieve its objective, see Case 11/70 *Internationale Handelsgesellschaft GmbH v Einfuhr- und Vorratsstelle für Getreide und Futtermittel* [1970] ECR 1125, paras 12–18.

[102] Craig & De Búrca 2008, p. 545.

[103] Majone 1996, p. 291.

8.1 The Principle of Participation

The principle of participation is directly connected with the decision-making processes of the European Union.[104] Article 11(1) TEU places the Union citizen as an active, direct participant in the European integration process and introduces participatory democracy as a post-parliamentary basis for democratic EU decision-making.[105] It stipulates that 'the institutions shall, by appropriate means, give citizens and representative associations the opportunity to make known and publicly exchange their views in all areas of Union action'.[106] Article 11(2) TEU further requires that 'the institutions shall maintain an open, transparent and regular dialogue with representative associations and civil society'. There is thus a clear link between the enhancement of the possibilities for participation and consultation, and an open and transparent rule-making procedure.[107] Article 11(3) TEU additionally states that the European Commission has to carry out consultations with the parties concerned in order to ensure that the Union's actions are coherent and transparent. Open consultations also contribute to the transparency of the decision-making process, since the public is informed about planned policies at an early stage and stakeholders are allowed to influence the design of such policies.[108] It enables critique, public debate and control over EU bodies' activities,[109] thus enhancing their legitimacy by providing those affected by the norms with a fair chance to scrutinise the results. As this obligation only relates to the Commission, none of the other Union institutions – including EU agencies – have a general Treaty-based duty to consult. With its introduction into the framework of the Treaty of Lisbon, participation was legally embedded in a more general way.[110] However, participation has not yet been recognised as a full-fledged general principle of EU law in the Treaties or as a formal right

---

[104] Curtin & Dekker 2005, pp. 5 and 10.

[105] TEU, Art 10 confirms that the Union is founded on representative democracy. This provision underlines the political role of the Union citizen as a voter or as an elected Member of the European Parliament: see Senden 2011, pp. 27–48.

[106] TEU, Art 11(1). Given the fact that this provision falls within the scope of Title II, which contains the provisions on democratic principles, participation is thus earmarked as a democratic principle.

[107] This follows from the cross-references in TEU, Art 11 and TFEU, Art 15.

[108] In this way, the open consultation of stakeholders also increases the legitimacy of decisions: see Marxsen 2015, p. 261.

[109] Ibid.

[110] The first three paragraphs of TEU, Art 11 can be seen as the constitutional embedding of an already existing informal, institutional practice, in particular of the open consultations by the Commission: see Alemanno 2014.

for individuals,[111] so there is no legal basis to claim that stakeholders indeed have a *right* to participate on the basis of the Treaties.

The principle of participation plays a key role in enhancing legitimacy by making the EU decision-making process more accessible and acceptable to those who are affected and by bringing individuals closer to Union action. Indeed, the will of citizens and stakeholders can be determined via their direct participation in the decision-making process, or indirectly via their representation through elected delegates.[112] Citizen participation fosters an element of democratic input from the 'bottom' into the making of legislation as it permits individuals to raise their voices within the decision-making and rule-making processes.[113] Democratic legitimacy is required for legislative rule-making.[114] Hence, executive rule-making does not have the democratic legitimacy of legislative procedures.[115] Fostering stakeholder participation can therefore be particularly helpful in legitimating the role of unelected bodies, such as the Commission and EU agencies, in the democratic process. This might already be sufficient for executive rule-making.[116]

Indeed, the criticism that legal norms are emanating from an unelected body is alleviated, to some extent at least, by the promise of throughput legitimacy, that is, the fact that these norms have themselves been the subject of consultation with affected parties. There is a risk, however, that consultation particularly 'involves those that have the technical and financial resources to do so and those having a particular interest'.[117] The delegation of rule-making powers to EU agencies calls into question how legitimacy is and should be ensured. This book therefore inquires into the extent to which *democratic* legitimacy is required concerning EU agencies' soft law-making and the extent

---

[111] Alemanno 2009 and Mendes 2011.

[112] Ehnert 2015, p. 50.

[113] Alemanno 2009, p. 387; Craig 1997a, p. 123; Marxsen 2015, p. 261. Public consultation can only be considered to be an aid to the legislator. Indeed, the consultation of interested parties can only ever supplement and never replace the procedures and decisions of the legislative bodies (the Council and the Parliament) which possess democratic legitimacy: see Commission, 'European governance: A White Paper' COM(2001) 428 final.

[114] This concerns rule-making by the Union legislature on the basis of TFEU, Art 289.

[115] Curtin, Hofmann & Mendes 2013, p. 11.

[116] This concerns rule-making by the Commission which results in the adoption of legally binding acts – in particular delegated and implementing acts on the basis of TFEU, Arts 290–291 – and administrative soft law acts, such as communications, notices, guidelines, codes and circulars: see Senden & Scott 2015. Standards set by EU agencies or private or semi-private actors are also part of the panorama of executive rule-making: see Curtin, Hofmann & Mendes 2013, pp. 2–3.

[117] Senden & Van den Brink 2012, pp. 67–68.

to which there is a need, stemming both from practice and from politics, for other mechanisms for control.[118]

The principle of participation also has an impact on the effectiveness of Union action in the *ex post* dimension of the policy cycle, because consultations are likely to increase the chances of compliance with the legal instrument at hand.[119] The input of stakeholders in particular allows EU bodies to make use of external expertise, and thus contributes greatly to the quality of legal acts.[120] The measures that are finally enacted will have taken better account of the views of those who are affected.[121] This makes it easier for people to accept that the resulting norms and enforcement costs will be lowered.[122] It is much more likely that the rules' addressees will follow up on them if they find open channels for voicing their concerns,[123] rather than simply having acts thrust upon them.[124] At the same time, the legislator has to pay attention to efficiency in the *ex ante* dimension of the policy stage. This means that a certain degree of flexibility needs to be ensured in the decision-making process. Yet, fulfilling the requirements stemming from participation can slow the decision-making process by making it more time-consuming and costly.

9. STAGE 4: TRANSPARENCY WITH REGARD TO UNION LEGISLATION

Similar to participation, transparency is also a significant attribute of public decision-making, and is thus also directly connected with the public decision-making processes of the European Union.[125] Transparency plays a prominent role in relation to the EU's legal instruments.[126]

---

[118] Interinstitutional Agreement between the European Parliament, the Council of the European Union and the European Commission on Better Law-Making (2016) OJ L 123.

[119] Majone 2007, p. 75.

[120] Commission, 'European governance: A White Paper' COM(2001) 428 final, 10 and 15. See also Buijze 2013, p. 46; Craig 2012, p. 231; Marxsen 2015, p. 261.

[121] Craig 1997a, p. 123.

[122] Buijze 2013, p. 42. According to Piris 1994, p. 461: 'In order to be effective, the actions of the institutions must be accepted by the citizens.'

[123] Neyer 2004, p. 33.

[124] Craig 1997a, p. 122 and Craig 2012, p. 39.

[125] Curtin & Dekker 2005, pp. 5 and 10; Craig 2012, p. 165. In the EU agency context, the concerns about participation and transparency in the procedure are broader than just for ESMA. For instance, in the case of ECHA, Vaughan argues that 'the procedures for guidance production and amendment lack full participation and transparency. These are causes for concern': see Vaughan 2015a, p. 1010.

[126] One should be aware of the risks of providing too much transparency – for example, transparency may have a negative impact on the trust the public has in the

9.1 The Principle of Transparency

Transparency is regarded as an important attribute of public decision-making.[127] It means that citizens and political representatives have access to information about governance processes and that the processes, along with the resulting decisions, are public.[128] The Treaties contain several references to the openness and transparency of the European Union.[129] Article 15 TFEU is a key Treaty provision with respect to access to documents and freedom of information.[130] The first paragraph provides that 'in order to promote good governance and ensure the participation of civil society, the Union institutions, bodies, offices and agencies shall conduct their work as openly as possible'.[131] This provision thus establishes a link between transparency and participation, which also applies to EU agencies, as they are explicitly mentioned therein. Indeed, the rule-making procedure needs to be open and transparent in and of itself in order to enable citizens and stakeholders to participate in the first place. In this way, transparency is a prerequisite for the participation and consultation process.[132]

The transparency of rule-making processes has a significant role to play in enhancing legitimacy, because it is linked to elements that serve to render the decision-making process more accessible and acceptable to those who are affected.[133] It safeguards a better position for individuals in the rule-making process. EU legislation has to be clear, precise, simple, understandable, consolidated, codified, of good quality, coherent and consistent as a body

Union itself and, as a result, may be less instrumental in realising the Union's objectives: see Frissen 2016 and De Vries 2016.

127 Commission, 'European governance: A White Paper' COM(2001) 428 final. See also Craig 2012, p. 165.

128 Héritier 2003 and Novak 2013.

129 Openness is enshrined in TEU, Art 1: 'decisions are taken as openly as possible.' While there are no single definitions of the principles of openness and transparency in EU law, these terms are often used interchangeably to convey a common idea: the 'opposite of opaqueness, complexity or even secretiveness'. See Alemanno 2014.

130 TFEU, Art 15 includes not only passive transparency (access to information upon request) but also active transparency, thus requiring the EU institutions to proactively safeguard the transparency of their proceedings (before, during, and after) and output: see Alemanno 2014; see also Hofmann, Rowe & Türk, 2011, p. 171.

131 Both TEU, Arts 1 and 10(3) reiterate that decisions are taken as openly and as closely as possible to the citizen. Given the fact that the latter provision falls within the scope of Title II, which contains the provisions on democratic principles, transparency is thus earmarked as a democratic principle.

132 This is even mentioned as such in TFEU, Art 15(1). See also Marxsen 2015, p. 272.

133 Craig 1997a, p. 120. See also Schmidt 2013.

of law.[134] Transparency also contributes to legal certainty for those affected by Union legislation by making it more predictable and foreseeable, and by allowing people to factor in the legal consequences their actions will have.[135] It enables individuals to understand the relevant norms and to know, without ambiguity, what rights and obligations ensue from the rules, and from what date.[136] This gives them an extra incentive to comply with the rules. In this way, the principle of transparency also has an impact on the effectiveness of Union action in the *ex post* dimension of the policy cycle as it relates to compliance with the rules.[137] At the same time, transparency may have a negative impact on the trust the public has in the Union itself[138] and, as a result, may be less instrumental in realising the Union's objectives. Transparency does however also capture the extent to which documentation is required throughout the process of policy-making, for example in documentation about the criteria civil servants use to structure their decision-making procedures.[139] This is where throughput legitimacy is centred.

Both the meaning and the scope of the principle of transparency include several procedural aspects. It concerns a right of *access to documents* and as such more open government. In addition, it entails the possibility of knowing the reasons behind the adoption of a certain piece of legislation as a result of the *requirement of giving reasons*. Besides, it encompasses the opportunity to take notice of EU legislation stemming from the *publication and notification requirement*.[140]

9.1.1 Access to documents

Access to all the relevant information and documents in respect of the Union organs' rule-making activity is a prerequisite for understanding the policy that is being conducted and the background of certain – legislative – measures.[141] People must be able to understand the relevant norms if they are to be able to plan their lives with knowledge of the legal consequences flowing from their actions.[142] The satisfactory resolution of this procedural issue is, therefore, a necessary precondition for the legitimacy of the EU.[143]

---

134 Tridimas 2007, p. 244.
135 Buijze 2013, p. 271.
136 Craig 1997a, p. 120.
137 Majone 2007, p. 75.
138 Frissen 2016 and De Vries 2016.
139 Schmidt & Wood 2019, p. 733.
140 Hofmann, Rowe & Türk, 2011, pp. 170–72.
141 Senden 2004, p. 99.
142 Craig 1997a, p. 120 and Tridimas 2007, p. 242.
143 Craig 1997a, p. 120.

Article 15(3) TFEU offers a formal legal basis for the right of access to documents by proclaiming that 'any citizen of the Union, and any natural or legal person residing or having its registered office in a Member State, shall have a right of access to documents of the Union institutions, bodies, offices and agencies, whatever their medium'. This provision thus demands the disclosure not only of formal legislative texts, but also of a very wide range of other documents.[144] In this way, the Treaty of Lisbon has declared the right of access to documents to be applicable to all Union organs and all Union documents, thus including EU agencies and soft law.

Access to documents is also established as a fundamental principle of Union law and administration through Article 42 of the Charter of Fundamental Rights.[145] Besides, it has been elaborated in secondary law, in particular in the Regulation on public access to documents. Article 3(1) clarifies that a 'document' shall mean 'any content whatever its medium (written on paper or stored in electronic form or as a sound, visual or audio-visual recording) concerning a matter relating to the policies, activities and decisions falling within the institution's sphere of responsibility'. This broad definition clearly also encompasses soft law instruments. Although the regulation stipulates the right of access to documents only vis-à-vis the Council, Commission and European Parliament, it has in practice been uniformly applied to EU agencies – including ESMA – as well.[146]

9.1.2 The duty to give reasons

The principle of transparency also includes the requirement to give reasons.[147] The second subparagraph of Article 296 TFEU provides that 'legal acts shall state the reasons on which they are based and have to refer to any proposals, initiatives, recommendations, requests or opinions required by the Treaties'. This provision obliges public authorities to communicate the reasons for their

---

144 Hofmann, Rowe & Türk 2011, p. 171.

145 Charter of Fundamental Rights of the European Union, Art 42: 'Any citizen of the Union, and any natural or legal person residing or having its registered office in a Member State, has a right of access to European Parliament, Council and Commission documents.'

146 Craig 2012, p. 165.

147 Shapiro 1992, pp. 180–81: 'Giving reasons requirements are a form of internal improvement for administrators. A decisionmaker required to give reasons will be more likely to weigh pros and cons carefully before reaching a decision than will a decision-maker able to proceed by simple fiat. [...] Such requirements are a mild self-enforcing mechanism for controlling discretion', and also p. 220: 'giving reasons requirements are an obvious vehicle for transparency.'

decisions, and can be seen as a specification or sub-principle of the principle of transparency.[148]

The duty to give reasons applies to almost all acts having legal effects.[149] This means it concerns soft law as soon as it produces legal effects. Since the provision does not mention anything regarding to whom the duty applies, it could be said to be relevant for any actor with the ability to draft legal acts, at times including EU agencies.[150]

The giving reasons requirement further enhances the transparency of the decision-making process and of the decisions themselves. It follows from case-law that the scope of the giving reasons requirement varies with the nature of the act or instrument at issue.[151] For instance, a decision entails a more profound statement of reasons than a regulation, for which it suffices to show its essential objectives without explaining each technical choice that has been made. The giving reasons requirement is important from different perspectives and for different parties. It provides the Member States and the parties concerned with a better understanding of the motives behind the decisions of EU institutions, which increases their possibilities of influencing or challenging them.[152] At the same time, the institutions are forced to consider carefully the purpose and lawfulness of their measures *ex ante* and the Court is put in a better position to review their lawfulness *ex post.*[153]

9.1.3 The publication and translation requirements

The principle of transparency also imposes a duty on the legislature to publish and/or notify all legislative measures and decisions.[154] Article 297 TFEU explicitly requires that *legislative acts*, and *non-legislative acts* adopted in the form of regulations and directives which are addressed to all Member States, as well as decisions which do not specify to whom they are addressed, are published in the Official Journal of the European Union. These acts enter into force on the date specified in them or, in the absence thereof, on the twentieth day following that of their publication. Other directives, as well as decisions which specify to whom they are addressed, have to be notified to those to whom they are addressed. They take effect upon such notification. Publication and notification are not considered to be constitutive requirements, hence

---

148 Buijze 2013, pp. 275–76.
149 Hartley 1998, p. 124.
150 Chapter 6 analyses whether and to what extent the duty to give reasons applies to each category of ESMA's soft law instruments.
151 Case 5/67 *Beus GmbH v Hauptzollamt München* [1968] ECR 83, p. 95.
152 Shapiro 1992.
153 Craig & De Búrca 1998, pp. 119–20.
154 Hofmann, Rowe & Türk 2011, p. 172.

belated publication or notification does not affect the validity of an act.[155] Article 15(3) TFEU moreover mentions that the European Parliament and the Council have to publish the documents relating to the legislative procedures, subject to limits on grounds of public or private interest laid down by means of regulations. Articles 15(3) TFEU and 297 TFEU remain silent on EU agencies and soft law, but the publication requirement may be said to apply to EU agencies' soft law on the basis of the reasons set out in Section 4.3, such as a functional and teleological interpretation of the Treaty provisions.

The publication aspect of the principle of transparency also necessitates the availability of documents in all official languages of the EU, because multilingualism is an indispensable component of the effective operation of the rule of law in the Union legal order.[156] Indeed, 'the rule of law requires that major normative sources should be available in the languages of those subject to them'.[157] Regulation No. 1[158] therefore determines in Article 4 that regulations and *other documents of general application* have to be drafted in the Union's official languages. It is not entirely clear whether the latter entails soft law documents.[159] Yet, given the fact that the Regulation dates from 1958, a logical explanation anno 2021 would be to apply it to soft law as well. Although the Regulation refers to the institutions of the European Union only, most EU agencies' establishing regulations – including that of ESMA – contain a provision that explicitly applies it to the agency at stake.[160]

10. STAGE 5: TRANSPOSITION OF UNION LEGISLATION

Once Union legislation has been drafted and finally adopted, it needs to be effectuated. It is therefore important that legislation is transposed[161] so that

155 Hartley 1998, pp. 128–29.

156 Case C-361/01 P *Kik v OHIM* [2003] ECR I-8283, para 60.

157 Kilpatrick 2005, p. 344 and Vaughan 2015b, p. 84.

158 Council Regulation No. 1.

159 Vaughan regards soft law documents as 'major normative sources' as they are significant both in length and in number, and often effectively operationalise the underlying legislation, see Vaughan 2015b, p. 84. In the case of ECHA, its guidance documents effectively operationalise the REACH Regulation in a number of different areas, see Vaughan 2015a.

160 See for instance ESMA Regulation, Art 73; EFCA Regulation, Art 22; EMSA Regulation, Art 9; FRA Regulation, Art 25.

161 Complying with obligations arising under Union law and, in particular, under regulations and directives is often referred to as 'implementation'. According to Prechal, Widdershoven and Jans, the process of the implementation of Union law can be distinguished in four different stages – transposition, operationalisation, application

national authorities can give proper follow-up to it. This entails the fifth stage of the policy cycle. In this stage, a shift takes place from a 'collegiate inter-authority relationship' to a 'hierarchical EU–national level relationship'.[162] It thus mostly concerns the vertical division and exercise of powers. The principles of *institutional and procedural autonomy* are the general principles of EU law that need to be adhered to.

10.1 The Principles of Institutional and Procedural Autonomy

With regard to establishing transposition duties, the national discretion of the Member States has to be respected wherever possible. Indeed, it is assumed in the literature that the transposition of Union law is governed by the *principle of institutional autonomy*.[163] This principle entails that it is up to the Member States to designate the national authorities that are responsible for the transposition of the relevant EU law, because the Member States themselves are in the best position to determine which specific body is equipped for this purpose.[164]

---

and enforcement: see Prechal, Widdershoven & Jans 2015, pp. 13–18. In her research on EU directives, Prechal distinguished only three different stages: transposition, application and enforcement. In her view, operationalisation is part of the transposition stage, because the latter may involve the empowerment of certain bodies for application of the transposed rules: see Prechal 2005, pp. 5–6.

[162] De Visser uses this terminology in the context of networks: see De Visser 2009, p. 498.

[163] The Court of Justice has never explicitly recognised the principle of institutional autonomy as such. Instead, the principle is derived from the case-law, which has determined that 'when provisions of the Treaty or of regulations confer power or impose obligations upon the States for the purposes of the implementation of Community law, the question of how the exercise of such powers and the fulfilment of such obligations may be entrusted by Member States to specific national bodies is solely a matter for the constitutional system of each State': see Joined Cases 51/71 to 54/71 *International Fruit Company and Others v Produktschap voor Groenten en Fruit* [1971] ECR 1107, para 4. There is no legal basis in the Treaties either. See also Van den Brink 2012, p. 122.

[164] Prechal, Widdershoven and Jans call this the operationalisation stage: see Prechal, Widdershoven & Jans 2015, p. 15. Prechal does not distinguish the operationalisation stage, but states that transposition may also involve the empowerment of certain bodies for the application of the transposed rules: see Prechal 2005, p. 6. In this view, operationalisation is part of the transposition stage. Hence, EU rules are generally addressed to the Member State or the 'competent authorities' and not to a specific national body. However, Member States remain responsible towards the EU. This means that if a national authority is in the process of implementing Union law and it transpires that it has acted contrary to Union law, the Member State is responsible, and the European Commission may start an infringement procedure against the Member State based on TFEU, Arts 258 and 260. See also Van den Brink 2012, pp. 125–26.

This may be done by means of primary legislation, such as an act of parliament, or by delegated or secondary legislation such as orders, decrees and ordonnances, depending entirely on the instruments available in the Member State concerned.[165] Institutional autonomy entails an effort to bring the Union closer to the citizen. In this regard, the legislature should balance the need to harmonise at the Union level with the autonomy of the Member States, to ensure that the cooperation between the EU and national levels works without excessively restricting the autonomy of any one particular actor.[166] In this way, the principle contributes to legitimacy.

Procedural rules are also necessary for the transposition of EU law by national implementing bodies. To the extent that such rules are not enshrined in EU law itself or that EU law contains explicit references to national law, the application of such national procedural rules is a matter for the internal legal order of the Member State.[167] This is referred to as the *principle of procedural autonomy*[168] and is regarded by some authors as a species of the principle of institutional autonomy.[169] Harmonisation at the European level must not illegitimately and unnecessarily intrude into domestic procedures.[170] A balance therefore has to be struck between national procedural rules and Union law requirements.[171]

Consequently, Member States are subject to the requirements formulated in *Rewe*.[172] This means that their autonomy is limited by (a) the principle of equivalence or non-discrimination, meaning that the remedies and forms of action available to ensure the observance of national law must be made available in the same way to ensure observance of EU law, and (b) the principle of effectiveness, which requires that the national conditions and procedures should not make the exercise of the rights conferred by the Union legal order

---

165 Prechal, Widdershoven & Jans 2015, p. 14.

166 Acceto & Zleptnig 2005, pp. 379, 383 and 400–01.

167 Case C-40/08 *Asturcom Telecomunicaciones* [2009] ECR I-09579, para 38. The principles of institutional and procedural autonomy thus have no absolute value. They do not preclude that it is decided in Union law itself which specific national body has to exercise the competence concerned or which common procedural rules have to be adhered to. In such a case, Member States obviously have to follow the choice of the Union legislature. This follows from Case 240/78 *Atalanta* [1979] ECR 2137, paras 4–5. See also Van den Brink 2012, pp. 124 and 127.

168 The principle of procedural autonomy was first formulated in Case 39/70 *Norddeutsches Vieh- und Fleischkontor v Hauptzollamt Hamburg St. Annen* [1971] ECR 49, para 4.

169 Prechal, Widdershoven & Jans 2015, p. 40.

170 Acceto & Zleptnig 2005, pp. 379 and 396.

171 Ibid., pp. 379 and 400–01.

172 These requirements were first formulated in Case 33/76 *Rewe v Landwirtschaftskammer für das Saarland* [1976] ECR I-1989.

virtually impossible or excessively difficult in practice.[173] These principles were originally developed in the context of the judicial process, but they are further elaborated in later case-law. Among other things, it has been established that the principles of equivalence and effectiveness also apply when it comes to effectuating obligations arising from EU law.[174]

In line with the logic that both principles apply when EU law neither appoints specific existing national bodies nor sets out any procedural rules, Member States' authorities have the freedom to decide upon these matters themselves when transposing EU agencies' soft law as well. Institutional and procedural hurdles at the national level could however also obstruct the transposition of Union law. This could have a negative impact on effectiveness, because it could make the achievement of regulatory objectives unattainable.[175]

11. STAGE 6: COMPLIANCE WITH UNION LEGISLATION

In order to give further effect to Union legislation, national authorities have to comply with it. This entails the sixth stage of the policy cycle. As in the case of transposition, a shift takes place from a 'collegiate inter-authority relationship' to a 'hierarchical EU–national level relationship'.[176] In this stage, the principles of *legitimate expectations* and *sincere cooperation* need to be taken into account.

11.1 The Principle of the Protection of Legitimate Expectations

The principle of legitimate expectations aims to protect individuals against arbitrary actions on the part of states or public authorities by requiring them to act in conformity with legitimate expectations to which they have given rise as far as possible.[177] In this way, the principle protects the position of individuals against unlimited government action. At the same time, the principle has a bearing on effectiveness, because regulatory objectives cannot be achieved if authorities suddenly no longer follow the rules. However, for a claim to be

173 Ibid.

174 Van den Brink 2012, p. 130.

175 Acceto & Zleptnig 2005, pp. 395–96 and Van den Brink 2012, p. 129.

176 De Visser uses this terminology in the context of networks, see De Visser 2009, p. 498.

177 Van den Brink & others 2015, pp. 207–08.

successful it is required that precise, unconditional and consistent assurances have been given[178] and that reliance on an expectation is legitimate.[179]

The principle has no legal foundation in the EU Treaties, but is accepted by the Court as a general principle of EU law.[180] After its first application in Union law in *Commission v Council*,[181] the Court explicitly determined in *Töpfer* in 1978 that the principle forms 'part of the Community legal order' and that any failure to comply with it forms an infringement of Union law.[182] Later on, the Court has stressed that the right to rely on the principle 'applies to any individual in a situation in which an institution, body or *agency of the European Union*, by giving that person precise assurances, has led him to entertain well-founded expectations'.[183] Besides, it clarified that various acts by public authorities may in principle give rise to a legitimate expectation,[184] such acts being legislation, administrative decisions and *soft law*.[185] Legitimate expectations can even arise in the absence of legislation.[186] So far, individuals have rarely been successful in pleading legitimate expectations before the Court, because they often lose the battle when legitimate expectations are balanced against overriding Union interests.[187]

---

[178] Hofmann, Rowe & Türk 2011, p. 178.

[179] Van den Brink & others 2015, pp. 213–14.

[180] Hofmann, Rowe & Türk 2011, p. 172.

[181] Case 81/72 *Commission v Council* [1973] ECR 575.

[182] Case 112/77 *Töpfer v Commission* [1978] ECR 1019. As such, it may result in the annulment of a contested act, or give rise to an award of damages based on TFEU, Art 340. See also Van den Brink & others 2015, p. 208.

[183] Case C-526/14 *Kotnik and Others* [2016], para 62. This has also been argued by the Court in other cases. For instance, in Case T-326/07 *Cheminova and Others v Commission* [2009] ECR II-2685, paras 180 and 182, the General Court stated that both precise assurances made by the Commission and those made by EFSA, which is an EU agency, are capable of giving rise to a legitimate expectation. With such a statement, it explicitly confirmed that legitimate expectations can also arise on the part of EU agencies. The Court however concluded that there was no evidence in the Court file that EFSA or the Commission gave the applicant any assurance capable of giving rise to a legitimate expectation on the applicant's part.

[184] Van den Brink & others 2015, p. 210.

[185] Case 81/72 *Commission v Council* [1973] ECR 575; Case 148-73 *Louwage v Commission* [1974] ECR 81; Case C-464/09 P *Holland Malt v Commission* [2010] I-12443, para 46; Joined cases C-189/02 P, C-202/02 P, C-205/02 P to C-208/02 P and C-213/02 P *Dansk Rørindustri and Others v Commission* [2005] ECR I-5425, para 211.

[186] In the EU agency context, the Court also explicitly stated this in Case T-36/09 *dm-drogerie markt v OHIM* [2011] ECR 6079, para 108.

[187] Craig 2012, p. 577 and Hofmann, Rowe & Türk 2011, p. 181.

11.2 The Principle of Sincere Cooperation

The principle of sincere cooperation as set out in Article 4(3) TEU is an important principle in the relationship between national and Union law. It constitutes the basis for cooperation between the Member States and the Union institutions, and requires the Member States' authorities to do whatever is necessary to implement and execute Union law within their jurisdictions.[188] However, when implementing Union law, Member States are likely to be torn between loyalty towards their own national interests and loyalty towards the European Union.[189] The principle of sincere cooperation therefore plays an essential role in the functioning of the EU. In this way, the principle has a bearing on the effectiveness of Union legislation. It is directed at achieving the Union's objectives and may therefore be regarded as a means to the end of effectiveness.[190] The principle imposes two positive obligations and one negative obligation. In the first place, it compels Member States to 'take any appropriate measures, general or particular, to ensure fulfilment of the obligations arising out of the Treaties or resulting from the acts of the institutions of the Union'. In the second place, they must 'facilitate the achievement of the Union's tasks'[191] and in the third place, they are required to 'refrain from any measure which could jeopardize the attainment of the Union's objectives'.

As follows from the case-law of the CJEU, the principle has a very broad scope of application. The obligations apply to all authorities applying Union law within a Member State, that is, the legislative, executive and judicial authorities.[192] Additionally, the principle is relevant for the relationship between the Member States themselves or between their authorities.[193] Besides, the requirement for Member States to cooperate with the Union insti-

---

[188] Acceto & Zleptnig 2005, pp. 385 and 387; Van den Brink 2012, p. 107.

[189] Acceto & Zleptnig 2005, p. 382.

[190] This is in line with the use of TEU, Art 4(3) as a basis for the development of legal doctrines such as state liability (Joined cases C-6/90 and C-9/90 *Francovich and Bonifaci v Italy* [1991] ECR I-5357, para 36; Joined Cases C-46 and C-48/93 *Brasserie du Pêcheur v Bundesrepublik Deutschland and The Queen/Secretary of State for Transport, ex parte Factortame and Others* [1996] ECR I-1029, para 39) and the duty of consistent interpretation, see Case 14/83 *Von Colson and Kamann v Land Nordrhein-Westfalen* [1984] ECR 1891, para 26: 'national courts are required to interpret their national law in the light of the wording and the purpose of the directive in order to achieve the result referred to in the third paragraph of [TFEU, Art 288]' in order to guarantee the effectiveness of EU law.

[191] In fact, Member States are obliged to take all measures to facilitate the full implementation of Union law, see Case 48/71 *Commission v Italy* [1972] ECR 529, para 7.

[192] Prechal 2015, p. 41.

[193] Jans, Prechal & Widdershoven 2011, p. 33.

tutions applies in the opposite direction, that is, the Union institutions are also required to cooperate with the Member States.[194] Although this principle does not explicitly apply to EU agencies, the broad interpretation given by the CJEU so far suggests it is not unlikely that this principle applies to EU agencies as well.[195] The use of the term 'acts' in Article 4(3) TEU implies that sincere cooperation also relates to Union soft law. The fact remains that there is no explicit reference to legally binding acts alone, as is the case in a provision such as Article 291(1) TFEU.[196] Yet, the Court has not interpreted the principle of sincere cooperation in such a way as to entail an independent legal basis for a general obligation of compliance with Union soft law.[197]

12. STAGE 7: ENFORCING UNION LEGISLATION

When Union law is not complied with, it is necessary that appropriate enforcement mechanisms vis-à-vis national authorities (indirect enforcement) are in place in order to enhance compliance with the law. This entails the seventh stage of the policy cycle, for which the principle of proportionality is most important.

---

[194] Van den Brink 2012, p. 109. The Union institutions are also required to cooperate with each other. TEU, Art 13(2) underlines the horizontal application of the principle of sincere cooperation: 'Each institution shall act within the limits of the powers conferred on it in the Treaties, and in conformity with the procedures, conditions and objectives set out in them. The institutions shall practice mutual sincere cooperation.' The principle thus applies between the Union institutions in the shape of an institutional balance: see Klamert 2014, pp. 9 and 12.

[195] Such a conclusion could also be drawn from the *Meroni* case, see Section 4.3. The Court ruled that the exercise of the powers conferred on an agency must be subject to the same conditions as those to which it would be subject if the delegating authority was exercising them directly. Since the Commission has delegated soft law powers to EU agencies, it could be said that the latter, as the recipients of delegated tasks, should also fulfil the duties stemming from the principle of sincere cooperation.

[196] TFEU, Art 291(1) reads: 'Member States shall adopt all measures of national law necessary to implement legally binding Union acts.'

[197] Interestingly, though, Union soft law is part of the *acquis* that has to be followed by new Member States (candidate countries) before they can join the EU. This includes all treaties, all current EU legislation, all EU Court verdicts, all types of decisions arising from the Foreign and Security Policy and Justice and Home Affairs provisions of the Treaties, as well as soft law. Candidate countries have to accept the *acquis* before they can join the EU and make EU law part of their own national legislation: see Commission, 'Conditions for Membership' <https://ec.europa.eu/neighbourhood-enlargement/policy/conditions-membership_en> accessed 15 February 2021.

12.1 The Principle of Proportionality

The principle of proportionality is also relevant for enforcement.[198] Article 5(4) TEU is broadly formulated in the sense that the principle requires that the content and form of Union *action* shall not exceed what is necessary to achieve the objectives of the Treaties. This principle does not merely apply to rule-making, but may also be said to encompass enforcement. This means that indirect enforcement mechanisms should be used on the basis of proportionality considerations. The proportionality test involves the choice of the most appropriate type of enforcement action for achieving the intended regulatory objectives. In this way, proportionality contributes to effectiveness. It also contributes to legitimacy, because it has a bearing on the vertical exercise of powers within the Union. Indeed, the choice of either a soft or hard enforcement mechanism is decisive for the obligations being imposed on the national public authorities. In principle, soft enforcement is less intrusive than a hard instrument. Since Article 5(4) TEU is broadly formulated – 'the Union shall act' – it also applies in the context of EU agencies' soft law.[199]

13. STAGE 8: REVIEWING UNION LEGISLATION

The *ex post* dimension of the policy cycle finally requires that third parties are offered the appropriate extent of individual judicial protection by ensuring that Union acts can be judicially challenged. This entails the eighth stage of the policy cycle. Here, the principle of *effective judicial protection* needs to be adhered to.[200]

13.1 The Principle of Effective Judicial Protection

The principle of effective judicial protection is the guiding principle as regards judicial protection for individuals in the EU.[201] Individuals must have the opportunity to enforce all rights conferred on them by Union law before a court.[202] It is necessary that they have effective access to a court; the court must meet institutional and procedural guarantees such as impartiality and fair

---

198 Section 7.2 sets out more elaborately what the principle entails.

199 See Section 4.3.

200 See, for two elaborate studies on soft law and courts, Stefan 2012a and Georgieva 2017.

201 It has been codified in the Charter of Fundamental Rights of the European Union, Art 47; European Convention on Human Rights, Arts 6 and 13; and TEU, Art 19(1).

202 Ortlep & Widdershoven 2015, p. 333.

trial;[203] and the court must have remedies at its disposal which are effective in enforcing Union law and rectifying breaches of that law.[204] This has been said to entail the obligation to provide citizens with effective judicial protection if their Union rights are infringed.[205] Nowadays, the availability of judicial protection is even recognised as a 'base condition for any structure that claims to be founded on the rule of law'.[206] Nonetheless, the extent of obligations stemming from the principle of effective judicial protection fully depends on the legal nature of the act in question. This also applies in the context of EU agencies' soft law.[207]

The need to establish opportunities for Union acts to be judicially challenged is the result of considerations of output legitimacy which require that decisions are open to judicial review. The principle thus protects the position of individuals against unlimited government action. Indeed, judicial review enhances the accountability of the initial rule-maker which makes it an important mechanism to prevent the abuse of public powers.[208] The threat of an unfavourable ruling, even if only slight, could also function as a pre-emptive incentive for regulatory authorities to maintain and further improve the quality of their documents.[209] Moreover, the adequacy of judicial protection influences the attitude of the market towards compliance with the relevant legal rules and cooperation with the actors that apply them, and in that way also has a direct relation with the effectiveness of these rules.[210] Judicial review also contributes to effectiveness in the sense that it relates to the ways in which regulation is effectuated and is therefore of crucial importance for the achievement of regulatory objectives.

14. TOWARDS A PROCEDURAL AND INSTITUTIONAL FRAMEWORK FOR EU AGENCIES' SOFT LAW-MAKING

The *assessment framework* as developed above consists of eight stages in which the possible links and tensions between legitimacy and effectiveness

---

[203] This has been codified in the Charter of Fundamental Rights of the European Union, Art 47 and European Convention on Human Rights, Art 6.

[204] TEU, Art 19(1). See also Ortlep & Widdershoven 2015, p. 333.

[205] Acceto & Zleptnig 2005, p. 389.

[206] TEU, Art 6(1). See also Craig 1997b and De Visser 2009, pp. 329–30.

[207] See Chapter 9.

[208] Bovens calls this legal accountability: see Bovens 2010, p. 955. See also De Visser 2009, p. 52.

[209] Scott 2000 and De Visser 2009, p. 427.

[210] De Visser 2009, p. 329.

come to the fore. These are (1) the definition of the *legal basis* for an EU agency to issue a soft law act, (2) the *initiation* of the agency's competence in a concrete case, (3) the process of *decision-making* at the agency level, (4) the *transparency* regarding the legal instruments of the agency, (5) the *transposition* duties for national authorities, (6) the *compliance* duties for national authorities, (7) the possibilities of *enforcement* vis-à-vis national authorities for the agency and (8) *judicial review* by the Union and national courts.

As the Treaties do not explicitly acknowledge the establishment of EU agencies and the notion of soft law, this chapter has considered what rules and requirements may otherwise ensue from the general principles of EU law identified above that may possibly condition the phenomenon of soft law-making by EU agencies. The following chapters of this book will test the assessment framework. They will investigate the extent to which the principles of conferral, subsidiarity, proportionality, participation and transparency apply to ESMA in the first four stages and will evaluate on the basis thereof the *ex ante* dimension of the policy cycle in relation to EU agencies' soft law-making.[211] Next, they will investigate the extent to which the principles of institutional and procedural autonomy, sincere cooperation, legitimate expectations, proportionality and effective judicial protection apply to ESMA in the last four stages, and will evaluate on the basis thereof the *ex post* dimension of the policy cycle in relation to EU agencies' soft law-making.[212]

Given the benefits of respecting the above-mentioned principles, and the problems in balancing them that are still being faced by an EU agency such as ESMA, with – as it appears – very sophisticated procedural rules, a clearer procedural and institutional framework for the adoption of EU agencies' soft law becomes very important. The final chapter of this book will therefore make some recommendations as to what such a common framework of rules and guarantees should look like.[213]

---

211 See Chapters 3 to 6.
212 See Chapters 7 to 10.
213 See Chapter 11.

3. Defining the legal basis for ESMA's soft law-making powers

A main concern in relation to EU agencies' soft law-making is that EU law does not explicitly regulate the delegation of regulatory competences to EU agencies, and the Treaties remain silent on the exercise of such powers too. Because of this silence in the Treaties, EU agencies' powers are still subject to the constitutional limits that are formulated by the CJEU.[1] This non-regulation yields uncertainty as to the actual competence of agencies to engage in rule-making of the type and nature discussed in this book. The very first question for EU agencies that have been allocated (soft) rule-making powers is therefore *if* they are competent to act in general. This entails the first stage of the policy cycle. In order to answer this question, the principle of conferral as laid down in Article 5 TEU is of crucial importance.[2] Conferral means that at least all legally binding action of the EU institutions has to have a legal basis in the Treaties, either directly or indirectly in the case of delegation.

Given the importance of the legal basis for the legitimacy and effectiveness of ESMA's rule-making powers, this chapter aims to demonstrate the extent to which the principle of conferral entails obligations for EU agencies' soft law-making. Section 1 shows the practical relevance of conferral for ESMA by presenting exemplary considerations on the legal basis. Section 2 explains, on the basis of the relevant case-law, the extent to which the Union is competent to establish EU agencies with rule-making powers in the first place. Section 3 investigates the existence of mandatory, discretionary and own-initiative competences for ESMA to adopt soft law. Section 4 explains how ESMA could obtain further level 2 powers via the new 'no-action letter' process. Section 5 assesses the influence of ESMA's *de iure* mechanisms and *de facto* practice on the legitimacy and effectiveness of soft law-making by ESMA. The chapter concludes that the principle of conferral is appropriately applied by ESMA, that the legal basis affects the extent of ESMA's discretion and that the power for ESMA to issue a 'no-action letter' may result in a new legal basis for it to issue level 1 or 2 legislation.

---

1 Case 9-56 *Meroni v High Authority* [1958] ECR 133; Case C-98/80 *Romano* [1981] ECR 1241; Case C-270/12 *United Kingdom v Parliament and Council* [2014].

2 See Chapter 2, Section 6.1.

1. CONCERNS AS TO THE EXISTENCE OF ESMA'S SOFT LAW-MAKING POWERS IN PRACTICE

Concerns with regard to conferral are not merely of theoretical relevance. As follows from ESMA's practice, ESMA is faced with considerations as regards the existence of its rule-making powers in its day-to-day business. For instance, ESMA makes such considerations while writing its yearly regulatory work programme which concretises the agency's activities in order to meet demands from the Union legislature. When making such decisions, ESMA sets out which legal acts it is going to issue in the coming year. At this stage, the agency considers the legal bases that require it to act, and will think about the areas in which it wants to take action on its own initiative. For the latter purpose, ESMA obviously needs to find a legal basis (conferral) and has to reflect upon the type of legal instrument that would best achieve its objectives: guidelines, opinions, Q&As or other convergence tools (proportionality).[3] Arguments of conferral may also be invoked by senior experts of the national competent authorities while developing the soft law instruments within the framework of the Standing Committees, or at the meetings of the Board of Supervisors, where the heads of the national supervisory authorities discuss the proposed soft law acts and their final versions. At this stage, problems regarding the existence of ESMA's competences also regularly come to the fore, because the Board members are able to express their views, doubts or concerns during such meetings. The example in the box below demonstrates this.

> During the meeting of the Board of Supervisors in June 2015, ESMA's Guidelines on Alternative Performance Measures were put on the agenda for approval.[4] Before it took its decision, the Board discussed the guidelines, and in particular the legal basis thereof.[5] The members sometimes question whether there is a legal basis at all, or discuss what the appropriate legal basis for the guidelines would be. This is mainly an effect of the own-initiative guidelines that ESMA may issue, because discussions do not make sense in the case of direct empowerments for ESMA in level one or two legislation since they are out of ESMA's control.
>
> At the same meeting, new guidelines were proposed on cross-selling practices. Among other things, the Board particularly discussed the legal basis of the proposed guidelines and interaction with sectoral legislation,

---

[3] See Chapter 4 for more on proportionality.

[4] ESMA, Board of Supervisors Summary of Conclusions of 24 and 25 September 2015 (ESMA/BS/140), 9.

[5] Ibid. The Board approved the Guidelines at this meeting.

in particular the Markets in Financial Instruments Directive (MiFID), the Capital Requirements Directive (CRD) and the Insurance Mediation Directive (IMD).[6] The Board confirmed that, from ESMA's perspective, the guidelines could be based on MiFID.[7] Half a year later, the proposed guidelines on cross-selling practices were subject to approval at the Board of Supervisors' meeting in December 2015. The members again discussed the legal basis for the guidelines and the importance of cross-sectoral consistency.[8] Although the Board adopted the guidelines, it was agreed that a letter had to be sent together with the other ESAs to the European Commission highlighting the cross-sectoral nature and the need for an appropriate legal basis for future joint guidelines.[9]

Interestingly, the three ESAs initially intended to issue joint guidelines covering all cross-selling practices taking place in the banking, insurance and securities sectors given that cross-selling is often cross-sectoral, and they had previously consulted the stakeholders on this basis.[10] However, in light of legal concerns – among others concerning the legal basis – the ESAs decided not to issue joint guidelines, but agreed that ESMA should issue ESMA-only guidelines under MiFID II in order to meet the 3 January 2016 deadline which required ESMA to act.[11]

As a result of such discussions, the members of the Board may refrain from adopting a soft law instrument such as guidelines, or are potentially able to block the referral of draft technical standards to the Commission for approval. However, given the fact that decisions in relation to ESMA's quasi-rulemaking activities have to be taken on the basis of a qualified majority of the members of the Board of Supervisors,[12] it may be that such objections are overstepped if they come from a minority of the national supervisors only. In such a situ-

---

6 Ibid., 11.

7 Ibid.

8 ESMA, Board of Supervisors Summary of Conclusions of 10 December 2015 (ESMA/2016/BS/2rev1), 4.

9 Ibid. For the letter, see ESMA, 'ESAs submit a joint letter to the European Commission on cross-selling of financial products in the EU' (27 January 2016) <www.esma.europa.eu/press-news/esma-news/esas-submit-joint-letter-european-commission-cross-selling-financial-products> accessed 16 February 2021.

10 ESMA, 'Press Release ESMA publishes MiFID II guidelines on cross-selling practices' (22 December 2015) <www.esma.europa.eu/press-news/esma-news/esma-publishes-mifid-ii-guidelines-cross-selling-practices> accessed 16 February 2021.

11 Ibid. MiFID II, Art 24(11) contains a mandate that 'ESMA, in cooperation with EBA and EIOPA, shall develop by 3 January 2016, and update periodically, guidelines for the supervision and assessment of cross-selling practices […]'.

12 ESMA Regulation, Art 44(1).

ation, guidelines are adopted and draft technical standards are referred to the Commission for adoption anyway. This is less of a problem for guidelines than for draft regulatory and implementing technical standards, since the resisting national competent authorities can choose not to comply on the basis of the 'comply or explain' mechanism, but it is indeed not desirable in the case of technical standards which become legally binding after endorsement by the Commission. For this reason, ESMA always looks for a legal basis before it issues any of its soft law instruments, because this is what national competent authorities require and what they will challenge when they do not want certain things to be regulated by ESMA.

This brief account shows the day-to-day relevance of determining the legal basis of ESMA's rule-making powers. We now turn to an investigation of the extent to which the Union is competent to establish EU agencies with rule-making powers in the first place, as well as of the extent to which ESMA is subjected to the principle of conferral.

2. THE COMPETENCE TO ESTABLISH EU AGENCIES WITH RULE-MAKING POWERS

How far can the EU legislature go in empowering EU agencies? More specifically, are EU agencies allowed to have (soft) rule-making powers in the first place? In the current legal framework, only the case-law on the delegation of powers to EU agencies as set out below provides insights into this.[13] The question whether the delegation of powers to EU agencies is lawful at all is therefore addressed in the doctrine in light of the non-delegation standard that was established by the *Meroni*[14] and *Romano*[15] judgments. However, the future relevance of this jurisprudence is unclear, since it seems to have been overturned, at least in part, by the Court in its recent *ESMA – Short Selling* case.[16] This section briefly analyses these judgments and their implications for the delegation of (soft) rule-making powers to EU agencies.[17] It shows that the case-law is very strict and does not provide many possibilities for delegation

[13] See Chapter 1.7. See also Case 9-56 *Meroni v High Authority* [1958] ECR 133; Case C-98/80 *Romano* [1981] ECR 1241; Case C-270/12 *United Kingdom v Parliament and Council* [2014]; Case C-217/04 *United Kingdom v Parliament and Council* [2006] ECR I-3789.

[14] Case 9-56 *Meroni v High Authority* [1958] ECR 133.

[15] Case C-98/80 *Romano* [1981] ECR 1241.

[16] Scholten & Van Rijsbergen 2014a.

[17] The following three subsections are largely based on Scholten & Van Rijsbergen 2014b.

at all. In other words, delegation of general regulatory powers to EU agencies is excluded.

2.1 The *Meroni* and *Romano* Non-delegation Standard

The *Meroni* non-delegation standard was established in 1958 within the framework of the European Coal and Steel Community (ECSC). In short, it allowed only for the delegation of executive powers. While the Court concluded that the delegation at stake was unlawful, it addressed the possibility of delegation at the EU level. Regarding Article 53 of the ECSC Treaty, the Court stated that delegation was not excluded, and that the institutions might use assistant bodies having a distinct legal personality.[18] In *Meroni*, the power of the High Authority 'to authorize or itself make the financial arrangement mentioned in Article 53 of the Treaty' gave it the right to entrust certain powers to such bodies subject to predetermined conditions and subject to its supervision.[19] However, such delegation was only allowed if this was necessary for the performance of the tasks set out in the respective articles and was compatible with the Treaty.[20] Furthermore, the Court ruled that the delegating authority 'could not confer upon the Authority receiving the delegation powers different from those which the delegating authority itself received under the Treaty'.[21] In *Meroni*, the Court found that if the delegating authority had exercised the delegated powers itself when issuing decisions, it would have been bound by certain principles established by the Treaty, such as the principles to state reasons and to publish an annual report.[22] However, as the agencies at stake received those powers arguably without any further guidance on how they should implement the delegated tasks, they were not bound by the relevant Treaty obligations and hence received more extensive powers than the delegating authority enjoyed itself, which violated the Treaty.[23]

While the *Meroni* judgment showed that delegation was possible in principle, the Court made it clear that not all kinds of powers were delegable. It distinguished two categories: 'clearly defined executive powers the exercise of which can be subject to strict review in the light of objective criteria determined by the delegating authority' and 'discretionary powers, implying a wide margin of discretion which may, according to the use which is made of it,

---

18 Case 9-56 *Meroni v High Authority* [1958] ECR 133, para 151.
19 Ibid.
20 Ibid.
21 Ibid., para 150.
22 Ibid., para 149.
23 Ibid., para 150.

make possible the execution of actual economic policy'.[24] The Court accepted the delegation of the first kind of powers,[25] but concluded that the second kind hindered the balance of powers guaranteed by the Treaty.[26] As a consequence, general rule-making powers cannot be delegated.

The *Romano* judgment is the second important judgment concerning delegation.[27] The CJEU established an additional non-delegation criterion: the Council was not able to delegate to EU agencies the power to adopt acts 'having the force of law'.[28] The agency at issue was the Administrative Commission, which was created by a Council Regulation. One of its main tasks was to assist the Commission in dealing 'with all administrative questions and questions of interpretation' arising from its founding regulation and subsequent regulations in the area of the application of social security schemes to employed persons and their families moving within the Community.[29]

The case concerned Mr Romano, who was entitled to pensions in two Member States: Belgium and Italy.[30] The question arose in relation to the amount of pensions he would receive in the two countries.[31] The relevant Belgian institution decided to give him a reduced pension, basing its decision on – among other things – a calculation scheme issued by the Administrative Commission.[32] The question which the Court had to answer was whether the interpretative documents of this commission had binding force upon the national authorities.[33] The Court held that the agency's decision was not of such a nature as to oblige national authorities to use certain methods of calculation, but could merely be regarded as providing guidance.[34] Regarding the underlying reasoning, the Court referred in this specific case: (i) to the judicial system which, at that moment, did not provide for a remedy against the acts of bodies such as the Administrative Commission; and (ii) to Article 155,

---

24 Ibid., para 152.

25 Ibid., para 152: 'A delegation of the first kind cannot appreciably alter the consequences involved in the exercise of the powers concerned, whereas a delegation of the second kind, since it replaces the choices of the delegator by the choices of the delegate, brings about an actual transfer of responsibility.'

26 Ibid., para 151: '[T]o delegate a discretionary power, by entrusting it to bodies other than those which the Treaty has established to effect and supervise the exercise of such power each within the limits of its own authority, would render that guarantee ineffective.'

27 Case C-98/80 *Romano* [1981] ECR 1241.

28 Ibid., para 20.

29 Regulation (EEC) No. 1408/71.

30 Case C-98/80 *Romano* [1981] ECR 1241, para 3.

31 Ibid., paras 1 and 14.

32 Ibid., paras 5, 7 and 10.

33 Chamon 2013, p. 155.

34 Case C-98/80 *Romano* [1981] ECR 1241, para. 20.

paragraph 4 EEC, which prescribed that it was only for the Commission to exercise executive powers and hence to issue legally binding decisions.[35] The delegation in question was therefore considered to be unlawful because, under the EEC Treaty, agencies were not envisaged among the possible authors of legally binding decisions and no judicial review of agency decisions was possible.[36]

All in all, the *Meroni–Romano* doctrine seems to be best characterised by the word non-delegation.[37] It imposes a rather strict limitation on the nature of delegated powers within the EU, because agencies cannot exercise discretionary powers and cannot adopt binding acts; that is, the delegation of executive powers involving no discretion is allowed, but agencies cannot issue acts with the force of law. However, in practice, EU agencies have been given discretionary powers along with the power to issue legally binding decisions.[38] The most far-reaching delegation happened in the aftermath of the 2008 financial crisis, resulting in the creation of the three ESAs, with regulatory, individual decision-making and – exclusive – supervisory powers.[39] This delegation does not seem to square well with *Meroni*, because it involves discretionary powers, nor with *Romano*, because the agencies' decisions have to be respected by national competent authorities.[40] The United Kingdom therefore raised questions on the lawfulness of this delegation, although the CJEU came to a different conclusion in its *ESMA – Short Selling* judgment.

2.2 The *ESMA – Short Selling* Case

The third judgment relevant for the delegation of powers to EU agencies is *ESMA – Short Selling*.[41] The UK sought the annulment of Article 28 of the Short Selling Regulation. This provision vests ESMA with the power to intervene under certain conditions – through legally binding acts – in the financial markets of the Member States if there is a 'threat to the orderly functioning and integrity of financial markets or to the stability of the whole or part of the financial system in the Union'. In its pleadings the UK put forward four argu-

---

[35] Chamon 2013, p. 155.

[36] Ibid. There is no consensus among scholars on the interpretation of the *Romano* judgment. Chamon gave an overview of the relevant scholarship in Chamon 2011.

[37] Scholten & Van Rijsbergen 2014a.

[38] Chamon 2013, p. 155 and Scholten 2014a, pp. 3–4.

[39] Scholten & Ottow 2014.

[40] Scholten & Van Rijsbergen 2014a.

[41] Case C-270/12 *United Kingdom v Parliament and Council* [2014], para 28.

ments regarding the *Meroni* and *Romano* restrictions and Articles 290–291 and 114 TFEU.[42]

The UK argued, first of all, that there had been a breach of the principles relating to the delegation of powers laid down in *Meroni*. Among other things, it claimed that ESMA's determination as to whether the criteria set out in Article 28 are met entails 'a very large measure of discretion'.[43] However, the Court held that this provision did not confer any autonomous power on ESMA that went beyond the regulatory framework established by the ESMA Regulation. The exercise of the powers under Article 28 was – unlike the powers delegated to the bodies concerned in the *Meroni* case – circumscribed by various conditions and criteria that limit ESMA's discretion. According to the Court, ESMA's margin of discretion was limited by both the consultation requirement and the temporary nature of the measures authorised.[44] Furthermore, the powers were precisely delineated and amenable to judicial review in the light of the objectives established by the delegating authority.[45] The powers thus complied with the requirements laid down in *Meroni* and, therefore, did not imply that ESMA was vested with a 'very large measure of discretion' incompatible with the EU Treaty.

Moreover, the UK contended that there had been a breach of the *Romano* restriction. It argued that Article 28 unlawfully authorises ESMA to adopt quasi-legislative measures of general application and observed that at issue, therefore, was not an individual decision or a bundle of individual decisions, but a 'measure of general application having the force of law'.[46] The Court noted the change of the institutional framework established by the EEC and TFEU Treaties, which seemed to imply that the *Romano* restriction became irrelevant.[47] It inferred certain implied powers from Articles 263 and 277 TFEU (which explicitly establish a judicial review of EU agencies' acts) to create agencies and to delegate powers to them in order to adopt measures of general application.[48] The Court therefore overturned the UK's objection.

---

[42] For an elaborate case-note on all four pleas, see Scholten & Van Rijsbergen 2014a. Further on this case in the literature, see Bergström 2015; Chamon 2014, p. 380; Marjosola 2014; Van Gestel 2014.

[43] Case C-270/12 *United Kingdom v Parliament and Council* [2014], para 28.

[44] Ibid., para 50.

[45] Ibid., para 53.

[46] Ibid., paras 56–57.

[47] Scholten & Van Rijsbergen 2014b, p. 1246.

[48] Ibid.

2.3 The Current Delegation Doctrine: Implications for EU Agencies' Rule-making Powers

The Court concluded the *ESMA – Short Selling* case by stating that the judicial reviewability of EU agencies' decisions (Article 263 and 277 TFEU) implies the possibility to create EU agencies with powers to issue acts of general application.[49] The new delegation standard is therefore as set out in the box below.

> [T]he delegation of powers to issue legally-binding measures, which are: (1) precisely delineated, (2) subject to sufficiently delineating conditions and criteria limiting discretion, which may include a notification requirement and the temporary character of a measure, and (3) amenable to judicial review in the light of the objectives established by the delegating authority, is allowed.[50]

In this way the *ESMA – Short Selling* case has established a new delegation doctrine in the EU, because this case is based on the Treaty provisions recognising the existence of EU agencies (at least indirectly) and it overturns, at least in part, the *Meroni–Romano* non-delegation standard. *Romano*'s ban on delegating powers with 'the effect of law' is in part overturned, because the Lisbon Treaty explicitly establishes judicial review of EU agencies' acts.[51] Furthermore, while conditional, the powers that the Union legislature can give to agencies can be *discretionary* powers transferring a part of responsibility from the legislature to the agency.[52] Thus, even though the Court states that delegation to ESMA is within the limits of *Meroni*, the latter's continuing relevance in the future is unclear.[53]

Nonetheless, the delegation of general regulatory powers to agencies is still excluded. The delegation of *soft* regulatory powers to EU agencies, however, appears to bypass the case law restrictions, because they are not considered to stand in the way of allocating soft law-making powers to EU agencies.[54] Indeed, institutional practice demonstrates that certain EU agencies have developed policy-making activity that comes close to full regulatory powers and 'while these general rule-making powers are soft by the label, they are often hard in practice'.[55] The delegation of *soft* regulatory powers to EU

---

49 Scholten & Van Rijsbergen 2014a, p. 401.
50 Ibid.
51 Ibid.
52 Ibid.
53 Ibid. See also Scholten & Van Rijsbergen 2014b, pp. 1250–51.
54 Senden & Van den Brink 2012, p. 65.
55 Ibid., p. 23.

agencies therefore seems to provide a means for circumventing the properly competent legislative and executive bodies in the decision-making process.[56]

3. ESMA'S *DE IURE* POWER TO ADOPT SOFT LAW: THE PRINCIPLE OF CONFERRAL

When ESMA considers using soft law-making powers, the first step for it is to establish *if* it is competent to act (conferral). This means that it needs to be determined whether there exists a competence for the agency to exercise this type of power. For this purpose, it is necessary on each occasion to look for a specific legal basis which indicates, to a greater or lesser extent, the boundaries within which the agency may exercise its competence. The starting point for finding the legal basis for any regulatory activity by EU agencies is the founding regulation of each agency separately. ESMA has the possibility to use three types of soft law instrument: quasi-binding draft regulatory and implementing technical standards; so-called comply or explain guidelines and recommendations; or non-binding instruments such as opinions and Q&As. This section shows that the legal basis of each category is to be found in a different place; they will therefore be discussed consecutively.

3.1 Draft Regulatory and Implementing Technical Standards

According to Article 8(2)(a) and (b) ESMA Regulation, the agency has the power to develop draft regulatory and implementing technical standards in the specific cases referred to in Articles 10 and 15 respectively. Given the fact that this provision limits the development of draft technical standards to 'specific cases', there is a need for the legislature to explicitly require or invite ESMA, in securities legislation – that is, the so-called level 1 legislation – to draft such standards. As such, we can speak of *specific* competence allocation. Articles 10 to 15 ESMA Regulation only provide the procedural framework for developing this type of legal instrument, and thus do not establish the legal basis. Instead, the legal basis for this regulatory power always has to be sought in specific sectoral legislation. For instance, the Directive on Alternative Investment Fund Managers (AIFMD) provides 23 empowerments for ESMA to develop draft technical standards. A few examples include the following.

Article 4 AIFMD:

> The European Supervisory Authority (European Securities and Markets Authority) (ESMA) ***shall develop draft regulatory technical standards*** to determine types of

[56] Simoncini 2015b, p. 320.

> AIFMs, where relevant in the application of this Directive, and to ensure uniform conditions of application of this Directive. Power is delegated to the Commission to adopt the regulatory technical standards referred to in the first subparagraph in accordance with Articles 10 to 14 of Regulation (EU) No 1095/2010.

Article 7(6) AIFMD:

> In order to ensure consistent harmonisation of this Article, ESMA ***may develop draft regulatory technical standards*** to specify the information to be provided to the competent authorities in the application for the authorisation of the AIFM, including the programme of activity. Power is delegated to the Commission to adopt the regulatory technical standards referred to in the first subparagraph in accordance with Articles 10 to 14 of Regulation (EU) No 1095/2010.

Article 7(7) AIFMD:

> In order to ensure uniform conditions of application of this Article, ESMA ***may develop draft implementing technical standards*** to determine standard forms, templates and procedures for the provision of information provided for in the first subparagraph of paragraph 6. Power is conferred on the Commission to adopt the implementing technical standards referred to in the first subparagraph in accordance with Article 15 of Regulation (EU) No 1095/2010.

As may be observed, these articles either require ('shall') or invite ('may') ESMA to develop draft technical standards in specific cases. This means that the agency sometimes has a duty to exercise this rule-making competence, whereas in other circumstances it is up to ESMA's discretion whether it will use its power and develop draft technical standards or not. There is no example of an obligation for ESMA to develop draft implementing technical standards in the AIFMD, but this does not mean that ESMA is never obliged to develop this type of technical standards. For instance, Article 26(5) Benchmark Regulation provides that:

> ESMA ***shall develop draft implementing technical standards*** to develop a template for the compliance statement referred to in paragraph 3. ESMA shall submit the draft implementing technical standards referred to in the first subparagraph to the Commission by 1 April 2017. Power is conferred to the Commission to adopt the implementing technical standards referred to in the first subparagraph in accordance with Article 15 of Regulation (EU) No 1095/2010.

Hence, with regard to draft regulatory and implementing technical standards, the agency is sometimes required and sometimes free to exercise this soft law-making power. In any case, ESMA cannot act whenever it wants, but only when there is an empowerment in sectoral legislation, making it reasonably straightforward to know when ESMA can use its competence to develop this type of legal instrument. Therefore, with regard to draft technical standards, discussions on the legal basis do not really seem to happen in practice. ESMA's only possibility of giving some steer towards new legal bases on which for it to act is to provide the Commission with an opinion on any action it considers appropriate, in the form of a proposal for a new delegated or implementing act.[57]

3.2 Guidelines and Recommendations

With regard to ESMA's guidelines and recommendations, the most obvious legal basis is in Article 16 ESMA Regulation. This provision empowers the agency directly and explicitly to 'issue guidelines addressed to all competent authorities or all financial market participants and issue recommendations to one or more competent authorities or to one or more financial market participants'. This entails a power for ESMA to issue guidelines and recommendations on its own initiative. As such, we can speak of ***general*** competence allocation. Simultaneously, an amendment to Article 16(1) in the context of the ESA review entails explicitly that guidelines and recommendations should otherwise be in accordance with the empowerments conferred by the legislative acts referred to in Article 1(2). This means that the legislature may explicitly require or invite ESMA in securities legislation, that is, the so-called level 1 legislation, to issue guidelines and recommendations. As such, we can speak of *specific* competence allocation. There already exist many level 1 regulations and directives in which such empowerments can be found. These either require ('shall') or invite ('may') ESMA to elaborate guidelines and recommendations on specified matters. For instance, ESMA's Markets & Data Reporting department had to deliver guidelines in accordance with Article 7(5) of the Market Abuse Regulation (MAR) on the definition of inside information for commodities:

> ESMA ***shall issue guidelines*** to establish a non-exhaustive indicative list of information which is reasonably expected or is required to be disclosed in accordance with legal or regulatory provisions in Union or national law, market rules, contract, practice or custom, on the relevant commodity derivatives markets or spot markets as referred to in point (b) of paragraph 1. ESMA shall duly take into account specificities of those markets.

---

[57] ESMA Regulation, Arts 9a(2) and 9a(4).

Another example shows that ESMA can choose to develop guidelines on non-complex financial instruments in accordance with Article 25(11) of MiFID II:

> ESMA ***may develop guidelines***, and update them periodically, for the assessment of financial instruments being classified as non-complex for the purpose of point (a) (vi) of paragraph 4, taking into account the delegated acts adopted under paragraph 8.

There is also a more recent development in practice which means that guidelines are now sometimes adopted on the basis of empowerments in level 2 legislation. In other words, the Commission's delegated or implementing acts that are based on ESMA's draft technical standards may provide for a mandate to draft level three text. This is the case for instance for ESMA's Guidelines on the validation and review of credit rating agencies' methodologies.[58]

Besides the general empowerment in Article 16(1), the fact that ESMA may issue guidelines and recommendations on its own initiative is clear from the wording of Articles 9(2), 22(3), 26(2) and 30(3) ESMA Regulation. For instance, Article 9(2) concerning consumer protection and financial activities provides:

> The Authority shall monitor new and existing financial activities and ***may adopt guidelines and recommendations*** with a view to promoting the safety and soundness of markets, and convergence and effectiveness of regulatory and supervisory practices.

In a similar vein, Article 22(3) with regard to systemic risk states:

> Without prejudice to the acts referred to in Article 1(2), the Authority ***shall draw up, as necessary, additional guidelines and recommendations*** for key financial market participants, to take account of the systemic risk posed by them.

Notwithstanding the above, it has to be kept in mind that no matter what the exact legal basis for ESMA's guidelines is, the procedural requirements as laid down in Article 16 ESMA Regulation always apply.[59]

---

[58] ESMA, Guidelines on the validation and review of credit rating agencies' methodologies (2017) ESMA/2016/1575.

[59] See further in Chapter 5.

3.3 Non-binding Instruments

The ESMA Regulation lays down the general empowerments for the agency to issue, either upon its own initiative or upon a request, its non-binding instruments. The legislature does not establish any express legal bases in the level one legislation. As such, we can speak of *general* competence allocation. Article 16b entails an empowerment for ESMA to issue Q&As relating to the practical application or implementation of the provisions of legislative acts referred to in Article 1(2), associated delegated and implementing acts, and guidelines and recommendations, adopted pursuant to those legislative acts. Article 29(1)(a) provides the agency with a direct power to address opinions to the national supervisory authorities, since the agency is required to play an active role in building a common Union supervisory culture and consistent supervisory practices as well as in ensuring uniform procedures and consistent approaches throughout the Union. Additionally, Article 29(2) provides ESMA with the power to develop new practical instruments and convergence tools to promote common supervisory approaches and practices, such as supervisory briefings. Before becoming a separate legal instrument in the amended ESMA Regulation, Q&As were in fact also examples of such instruments and tools. They became so common in use that they now have their own legal basis in the ESMA Regulation by virtue of Article 16b.

4. ESMA'S NO-ACTION LETTERS

As has become clear, ESMA does not have the power to regulate whatever it wants whenever it wants. Nevertheless, when ESMA is of the view that a certain matter should be regulated, but that the rule-making powers it has are not sufficient, it may send an opinion to the European Commission setting out the action it considers appropriate. This is a new power that has been introduced as part of the ESA Review, and is established in Article 9a of the ESMA Regulation. The exercise of this power is however to be preceded by a so-called no-action letter.

When ESMA considers that a level 1 Directive or Regulation or a level 2 delegated or implementing act is 'liable to raise significant issues', the agency is able to send a so-called no-action letter to the national competent authorities and the Commission, in which it has to set out the issues which it considers to exist. The letter concerns an issue for the market as a whole and makes reference to the non-enforcement of a particular article within a level 1 or 2 act currently in force.[60] ESMA may use this new power in the case that a level 1 or level 2 act raises significant exceptional issues pertaining to market confidence, customer or investor protection, the orderly functioning and integrity of financial markets or commodity markets or the stability of the whole or part of the financial system in the Union (Article 9a(4) ESMA Regulation). Besides, this power may be exercised in exceptional circumstances for at least one of the following three reasons: (1) where there is a direct conflict with another relevant act; (2) if the absence of level 2 delegated or implementing acts complementing or specifying the level 1 act would raise legitimate doubts concerning the legal consequences flowing from the level 1 act or its proper application; or (3) if the absence of guidelines and recommendations would raise practical difficulties concerning the application of the relevant level 1 act (Article 9a(1) ESMA Regulation). The third situation arguably was already within ESMA's remit under Article 16 to resolve by way of developing guidelines or recommendations as soon as practicable.[61] The first and second situations, however, were previously not within the agency's powers.

In the first two situations, ESMA *must* provide the Commission with an opinion on any action it considers appropriate (Article 9a(2) ESMA Regulation). This may include proposals for new level 1 legislation, new level 2 delegated acts or new level 2 implementing acts. If necessary, ESMA must also issue opinions to ensure consistent, efficient and effective supervisory and enforcement practices, and the common, uniform and consistent application of Union law (Article 9a(3) ESMA Regulation). In the case of any of the exceptional issues as set out in Article 9a(4) ESMA Regulation, the agency *may* provide the Commission with an opinion on the action it considers appropriate. In all of its opinions, ESMA will describe the urgency of the situation to the Commission. The opinions will be made public on ESMA's website.

---

[60] This is contrary to how its US namesakes operate. Individual firms regulated by a US financial regulator such as the Securities and Exchange Commission (SEC) may request a 'no-action letter' from the SEC in respect of a course of action the firm wants to take: US Securities and Exchange Commission, 'No Action Letters', <https://www.sec.gov/fast-answers/answersnoactionhtm.html> accessed 16 February 2021. An example would be where a financial institution regulated by the SEC wants to offer a new product or service but is uncertain whether this is allowed under current regulation. In order to obtain clarity, or at least to be open and transparent towards the regulator and to avoid any issues afterwards, the financial institution can ask the SEC upfront whether they would permit offering the new product or services. In such a case the regulator can issue a 'no-action letter', indicating that they believe it is most likely allowed and that they would not take retrospective action against the institution on these matters.

[61] Van Rijsbergen & Rogge 2021.

The 'no-action letter' has already been used in practice: on 29 April 2020 ESMA sent such a letter to the Commission with regard to the new Environmental, Social, and Governance (ESG) disclosure requirements under Articles 13(1)(d) and 27(2a) of the Benchmark Regulation (EU) 2016/1011.[62] The issue here was that it was difficult for benchmark administrators to fulfil said disclosure requirements, due to apply by 30 April 2020, as a result of the absence of relevant Delegated Acts. Put simply, these Level 2 Delegated Acts contain the necessary details of what to include in the disclosure. Alongside this letter, ESMA provided two opinions: (1) under Article 9a(2) to the Commission and national competent authorities setting out its views on the issues,[63] and (2) under Article 9a(3) to the national competent authorities as regards consistent supervisory and enforcement practices.[64] ESMA's point, as stated in its letter, was that the entry into force of the disclosure requirements should coincide with the entry into force of the related Delegated Acts, and in any event not prior to this. As it cannot disapply Union law, ESMA suggested national competent authorities do not prioritise supervisory or enforcement action on the disclosure requirements in the absence of the Delegated Acts. One could argue, though, that this guidance could be interpreted as *de facto* recommending the disapplication of Union law.

5. CONCLUSION AND ASSESSMENT ON THE EXISTENCE OF SOFT LAW-MAKING POWERS

In the context of ESMA's soft law-making, the principle of conferral appears to be very important for the determination of whether a competence exists. The above analysis leads to three different situations in which the principle in fact plays the same role. The first is with regard to 'shall' provisions, regardless of the type of legal instrument, in which case conferral has been applied by the legislature. The second is with regard to 'may' provisions, regardless of the type of legal instrument, in which case conferral has also been applied by

---

62 ESMA, 'ESMA issues No Action Letter on the new ESG disclosure requirements under the Benchmarks Regulation' <www.esma.europa.eu/press-news/esma-news/esma-issues-no-action-letter-new-esg-disclosure-requirements-under-benchmarks> accessed 16 February 2021.

63 ESMA, Opinion on appropriate action in respect of the new disclosure requirements in Regulation (EU) 2016/1011 of the European Parliament and of the Council relating to the sustainability-related disclosures for benchmarks (2020) ESMA41-137-1299.

64 ESMA, No Action Letter on sustainability-related disclosures for benchmarks (2020) ESMA41-137-1300. Note that this is actually an opinion rebranded as 'no-action letter'.

the legislature. The third is with regard to actions entirely upon ESMA's own initiative, which could entail any instrument except for draft technical standards. Conferral is also considered in a general sense by the legislature. ESMA explicitly acknowledges the general legal basis upon which its own-initiative soft law act is issued.

The following sections conclude this chapter and provide an assessment of where the existence of ESMA's competences leads to tensions on the basis of legitimacy and effectiveness concerns.

5.1 Mandatory, Discretionary and Own-initiative Power to Act Affects the Extent of ESMA's Discretion

ESMA finds its legal basis to act either in the level 1 legislation, which requires (on the basis of a 'shall' provision) or invites (on the basis of a 'may' provision) the agency to develop a particular legal instrument, or in the ESMA Regulation itself, which enables the agency to issue certain soft law instruments on its own initiative. This means that the legal basis upon which ESMA is acting affects, to a great extent, the discretion of the agency to act or not.

Regardless of the type of legal instrument, in the case of an empowerment in the level 1 legislation providing ESMA either with a *mandatory or discretionary competence* in a given case – that is, a 'shall' or 'may' provision – the choice regarding the legal basis has already been legitimated. This is due to the fact that the choice has been made by the legislature, which means that conferral has been considered in any case. The level 1 legislation is adopted on the basis of the ordinary legislative procedure, which gives the same weight to the European Parliament and the Council regarding a legislative proposal by the European Commission.[65] In addition, national Parliaments have participated on the basis of the Protocol on the role of national Parliaments in the European Union and the Protocol on the application of the principles of subsidiarity and proportionality. This means that they could have raised objections if they were of the opinion that ESMA should not have the competence to develop a particular type of instrument. Although they have a high level of legitimacy, such pre-established choices by the legislature do limit ESMA's discretion. This is unfortunate, because the ability to exercise discretion is very useful from the perspective of effectiveness. ESMA can make a contribution to legal certainty, especially in cases where the agency issues soft law instruments upon its own initiative in order to interpret or clarify binding rules, as it can do with its guidelines and non-binding instruments. Luckily, as per the new no-action letter process, ESMA may provide the Commission with an opinion

---

[65] TFEU, Arts 289(1) and 294.

on any action it considers appropriate, in the form of a new legislative proposal or a proposal for a new delegated or implementing act.[66] Via this detour, it may still acquire a new legal basis to use one of its powers.

Legitimacy seems to be of more concern when it is upon ESMA's *own initiative* to exercise its soft law-making competence. In such cases, it is for ESMA itself to seek a legal basis, meaning that the legislature is in no way involved in this choice. The agency thus has discretion to take rule-making action and may consequently also choose *not* to act. In other words, the Union legislature has given ESMA own-initiative powers *in abstracto*, but is not involved *in concreto*. ESMA is however in a better position to also consider effectiveness than it is in cases of mandatory or discretionary competence, because its discretion is not compromised.

At the same time, after the ESA review, a new Article 60a is inserted in the amended ESMA Regulation which provides any natural or legal person that is directly and individually concerned with the opportunity to send reasoned advice to the Commission if that person is of the opinion that ESMA has exceeded its competence when acting under Articles 16 and 16b. This entails another mechanism of control on ESMA's use of its power to issue guidelines, recommendations and Q&As. This prevents ESMA from stretching its discretion so far that it exceeds its competence.[67]

5.2 No-action Letters: A 'Right of Initiative' for ESMA As Regards Level 1 and 2 Legislation?[68]

Under the previous ESMA Regulation, ESMA already had the power to issue guidelines and recommendations, and other non-binding instruments such as opinions and Q&As, on its own initiative. The right of initiative with regard to level 1 and 2 texts, however, is the exclusive domain of the Commission, with the usual role for the European Parliament and the Council. As per the non-delegation doctrine laid down in the *Meroni*,[69] *Romano*[70] and *Short Selling* cases,[71] EU agencies are not supposed to have general rule-making powers. Under the new ESMA Regulation, though, this appears to change slightly where the new powers of the 'no-action letter' are used.

---

66 ESMA Regulation, Arts 9a(2) and 9a(4).

67 More on this in Chapter 10 on judicial review.

68 This section is largely based on Van Rijsbergen & Rogge 2021.

69 Case 9-56 *Meroni v High Authority* [1958] ECR 133.

70 Case C-98/80 *Romano* [1981] ECR 1241.

71 Case C-270/12 *United Kingdom v Parliament and Council* [2014]; Bergström 2015, p. 219.

When using the 'no-action letters', ESMA under Article 9a(2) and (3) must, and may under (4), actively ask the European Commission by way of opinion for a change in level one or two text. Does this imply, however, that it gets a subtle grip on binding rule-making competences, including on Directives and Regulations, even if this power is to be used in very specific circumstances only? The counterargument would be that such an opinion can be regarded as merely advisory, and that the European Commission is not bound to follow it. Consider again the example of the use of the 'no-action letter' by ESMA in the case of ESG disclosure requirements under the Benchmark Regulation, as discussed earlier:[72] by ensuring its temporary non-enforcement, it could be argued to, in effect, delay the application of level 1 text for the purpose of preventing substantive issues, but without, of course, actually amending it. Although it can rightly be argued that the substantive issues are the underlying cause leading to the delay, this delay would not be realised without the issuance of the 'no-action letter'. This is an interesting development from the viewpoint of legitimacy as it may run somewhat counter to the division of competences within the EU and it could be regarded as a further entanglement between ESMA and the Commission.

The usual path for ESMA to commence drafting level 2 texts has so far been derived from a provision in the corresponding level 1 legislation, providing ESMA with top-down competence in a given case. Such choices are made by the EU legislature. In this way, the choice regarding the legal basis for ESMA to act has been legitimated as a result of the (controlling) role given to the Union institutions and the national Parliaments.[73]

'No-action letters' allow for a different path to be taken, where ESMA may advise the Commission by way of an opinion, in a bottom-up kind of way, and in specific circumstances only, to make amendments in level 1 and 2 texts. This is not to say that this different path is entirely without legitimacy, first because the power to issue a 'no-action letter' is derived from a Regulation, and second because any such proposed amendment would be subject to the usual parliamentary processes and scrutiny. Nonetheless, with its 'no-action letter' power, ESMA, in specific circumstances where issues have arisen in financial markets, may advise the Commission to amend level 1 texts, which could be regarded as an increased influence in the level 1 sphere. This path gains further force through the fact that ESMA has to make its opinions public, which means that the Commission has to explain why it would not give follow-up to one of ESMA's requests.

---

[72] See Section 4.

[73] See Section 5.1.

On the positive side, giving ESMA a specific tool to address shortcomings causing well-defined issues in financial markets might be seen as a good development, because the ability to exercise such a tool is very useful from the perspective of effectiveness. It can enhance the quality of the legislation and at the same time contribute to a better achievement of the goals which the rules aim to achieve. It appears a stronger tool than, for example, a forbearance statement, such as the one issued in the context of Covid-19, and upcoming deadlines for the publication of periodic reports by fund managers.[74] While both a forbearance statement and a 'no-action letter' may have the same impact for market participants – that is, *de facto* disapplication of EU law – the latter allows for the submission of a legislative proposal. However, one could argue that an opinion already allowed for some form of proposal for legislative changes, and in the aforementioned case of ESG disclosures ESMA in fact put their communications in the form of an opinion, the difference being that the latter opinion has become a mandatory part of the 'no-action letter' process.

[74] ESMA, 'Public Statement: Actions to mitigate the impact of Covid-19 on the deadlines for the publication of periodic reports by fund managers' (2020) ESMA34-45-896.

4. Initiation of ESMA's soft law-making powers

When it has been established that EU agencies that have been allocated (soft) rule-making powers are competent to act in general, the second question is whether and *how* they may exercise their power in a concrete case. This entails the second stage of the policy cycle. In order to answer this question, the principles of subsidiarity and proportionality as laid down in Article 5 TEU are of crucial importance.[1] Subsidiarity relates to the relationship between the Union and the Member States, which means that consideration needs to be given to whether the Union or the national level is the appropriate level for exercising competence. Proportionality deals with both the content and the form of Union action.

Given the importance of the level and the type of action (in terms of content and form) for the legitimacy and effectiveness of ESMA's rule-making powers, this chapter aims to demonstrate the extent to which the principles of proportionality and subsidiarity entail obligations for EU agencies' soft law-making. Section 1 shows the practical relevance of subsidiarity and proportionality for ESMA by presenting exemplary considerations on the appropriateness of the level of action and the type of instrument. Section 2 investigates whether ESMA makes any considerations regarding the level at which its soft law competence is to be exercised (subsidiarity). Sections 3–8 investigate how ESMA should exercise its soft law-making competence on the basis of the contents and form of action it wants to take (proportionality). Section 9 assesses the influence of ESMA's *de iure* mechanisms and *de facto* practice on the legitimacy and effectiveness of its soft law-making. The chapter concludes that the principle of proportionality is appropriately applied by ESMA, whereas subsidiarity currently does not play a role at the EU agency level itself.

---

1 See Chapter 2, Section 7.

1. CONCERNS AS TO THE DIVISION AND EXERCISE OF ESMA'S SOFT LAW-MAKING POWERS IN PRACTICE

Concerns with regard to subsidiarity and proportionality are not merely of theoretical relevance. As follows from ESMA's practice, ESMA is faced with considerations as regards the division and exercise of its rule-making powers. To begin with, the agency itself makes such considerations in its day-to-day business, for instance while writing its strategic orientation.

In its 2020–22 strategic orientation,[2] ESMA commits to being an outcome-focused supervisor and regulator. The agency claimed that mitigating risks that might endanger the fulfilment of its mission while respecting the legal requirements and processes is more important than the tool used. For this purpose, ESMA has to think about the methods and instruments which may best help to achieve its objectives, and about the choice of tools most appropriately matched to the aims and role of the organisation in general. In its strategic orientation, ESMA also states that in the years to come it will focus more and more on the actual and consistent implementation of the requirements laid down in the single rulebook. The agency claims that it will only make use of regulatory tools when the same objective could not be achieved through supervisory convergence and/or supervision. This is therefore a clear point at which ESMA is considering the proportionality of its actions.

Arguments of subsidiarity and proportionality may also be invoked by senior experts of the national competent authorities while developing the soft law instruments within the framework of the Standing Committees.

In practice, some 4–6 representatives of the national authorities are responsible for writing the first version of the instrument in question. They thus have a strong influence on which matters will actually be included or excluded from the substantive scope of the act. Hence, this is a good moment for them to argue that they want to retain the possibility to regulate a certain matter at the national level (subsidiarity) or that they prefer a legal instrument other than the one proposed by ESMA, such as an opinion instead of guidelines (proportionality).

---

[2] ESMA, Strategic Orientation 2020–2022 (2020) ESMA22-106-1942.

The next occasion for this type of discussion would be when the first draft of the act is debated during the next Working Group or Standing Committee meeting, which includes the representatives of all 27 Member States' supervisory authorities and a few ESMA staff members. The drafts are discussed paragraph by paragraph or page by page, which means that the Working Group or Standing Committee members have a number of opportunities to suggest amendments to the texts. This may result in very heated debates, especially if there are very contradictory topics on which national authorities strongly disagree. At the final Standing Committee meeting, the experts of the national competent authorities may once more exert influence when they decide to submit the draft legal instrument to ESMA's Board of Supervisors for approval. All members of the Standing Committee have to agree, more or less, to the finalised version, so national authorities can again raise objections if they are of the opinion that, for instance, the act goes beyond the scope of the mandate that has been given to ESMA or encroaches upon their national competences.

Third, at the meetings of the Board of Supervisors, the heads of the national supervisory authorities discuss the proposed soft law acts and their final versions. At this stage, problems regarding the division and exercise of ESMA's competences also regularly come to the fore, because the Board members are able to express their views, doubts or concerns. The example given in the box below demonstrates this.

At the July 2019 meeting of the Board of Supervisors, the Chair of the Investment Management Standing Committee (IMSC) presented the Final Report on Guidelines on liquidity stress testing in UCTS and AIFs.[3] The Board discussed a number of issues, among others a preference for proportionality considerations for smaller funds. Hence, the Board instructed the IMSC to adjust the proportionality language in the Guidelines and to present the revised Guidelines to the Board of Supervisors for adoption by written procedure.

This brief account shows the daily relevance of determining the scope of ESMA's rule-making powers. We now turn to an investigation of the extent to which ESMA is subjected to the principles of subsidiarity and proportionality.

---

3 ESMA, Board of Supervisors Summary of Conclusions of 11 July 2019 (ESMA22-106-1895).

2. ESMA'S EXERCISE AND DIVISION OF SOFT LAW-MAKING POWERS: THE PRINCIPLE OF SUBSIDIARITY

Closely linked to the question of the *existence* of competence is the principle of subsidiarity, which is intended to regulate the *exercise* and *division* of competence.[4] Hence, the second step for EU agencies is to determine whether the competence may actually be exercised in a given instance. In the Union law context, the subsidiarity principle concerns the relationship between the Union and the Member States. In the ESMA context, this means that consideration needs to be given to whether action should be undertaken by the EU agency or by the national competent authorities, that is, whether the Union or the national level is the appropriate level for exercising competence.[5] It thus touches upon the vertical division of powers.

Subsidiarity does not play a large part in ESMA's practice when it exercises its soft law-making powers, because it is more of a political process and therefore mostly relevant at the level of the legislature. Indeed, the legislature already applied the effectiveness and efficiency test of subsidiarity by creating ESMA in the first place, and by adopting sectoral legislation that empowers the agency to exercise soft law-making powers.[6] This legislation is adopted on the basis of the ordinary legislative procedure, which gives the same weight to the European Parliament and the Council regarding a legislative proposal of the European Commission.[7] In addition, national Parliaments have participated on the basis of the Protocol on the role of national Parliaments in the European Union and the Protocol on the application of the principles of subsidiarity and proportionality. It would not fit within the logic of the system if the Union institutions and national parliaments were then able to also interfere with all the soft law acts that ESMA issues. Rather, they can make themselves heard when ESMA's establishing regulation is being reviewed and when the sectoral

[4] Craig 2012, p. 390.

[5] TEU, Art 5(3) and Protocol on the application of the principles of subsidiarity and proportionality.

[6] For instance, ESMA explicitly refers to this fact in its cost–benefit analysis on draft technical standards: 'The main policy decisions have already been taken under the primary legislation and the impact of such policy decisions have already been analysed and published by the European Commission.' See ESMA, Annex III to the Final Report on draft Technical Standards under the Regulation No 909/2014 of the European Parliament and of the Council of 23 July 2014 on improving securities settlement in the European Union and on central securities depositories and amending Directives 98/26/EC and 2014/65/EU and Regulation (EU) No 236/2012 (2015) ESMA/2015/1457/Annex III, 4.

[7] TFEU, Arts 289(1) and 294.

legislation (regulations or directives) which empowers the agency to take soft law measures is being adopted or reviewed.[8]

This section shows that ESMA barely exercises the effectiveness test and that it applies *an* efficiency test, which is more of an economic cost–benefit analysis, instead of *the* efficiency test determining whether action is required by ESMA or the NCAs.

2.1 ESMA's Role in Relation to the Effectiveness Test

Article 5(3) TEU explains that the principle of subsidiarity is only relevant insofar as the Union's competence is not exclusive. Applying subsidiarity then involves an effectiveness and an efficiency test.[9] The first test requires that if action at the national level is capable of producing the desired result, this level should be preferred (effectiveness).[10]

When ESMA is required to use its soft law-making powers on the basis of a 'shall' provision, there is no reason to apply an effectiveness test at all. In such a case, it is beyond doubt that the competence is for ESMA, because it has been unambiguously given to the agency by means of an explicit empowerment. The choice of the appropriate level has thus already been made by the legislature. The effectiveness test can be applied only to the extent that the legal basis gives to ESMA the choice whether to act and/or a choice as to the nature and extent of the action.[11] As seen in Chapter 3, Section 3 ESMA has no such discretion when it acts pursuant to a 'shall' provision. With regard to a 'may' provision, ESMA does have the choice whether to act or not. However, it still does not become involved with an effectiveness test, because the result of its inaction is not necessarily that the power is then exercised at the national level but rather that there is no rule-making activity at all. Although ESMA's own-initiative actions give the agency the freedom to act and then the choice as to the nature and extent of the action, ESMA still does not formally apply a full subsidiarity test. Indeed, the effectiveness test has already been applied by the legislature and has resulted in the general empowerments in its founding

---

[8] In the case of ESMA, level 1 and 2 legislation empowers the agency to develop draft technical standards or to issue guidelines.

[9] See Chapter 2, Section 7.1.

[10] TEU, Art 5(3) and Protocol on the application of the principles of subsidiarity and proportionality.

[11] European Council, Conclusions of the Presidency, Edinburgh (11–12 December 1992), 17. Although these conclusions belong to a previous version of the Protocol on the application of the principles of subsidiarity and proportionality, this interpretation is still valid today.

regulation, so this test is no longer carried out by the agency.[12] In practice, however, the desirability to issue a particular soft law act at ESMA level is regularly discussed at the meetings of Standing Committees and Working Groups. Sometimes NCAs are of the view that it would be better to address the issue at the national level. If this is the majority view, the decision is taken not to work on the proposed guidance. Following from this, ESMA itself is thus involved to a limited extent in the application of the effectiveness test as mandated by the subsidiarity principle.[13]

2.2 ESMA's Role in Relation to the Efficiency Test

The principle of subsidiarity also involves a second test. The so-called efficiency test requires a cost–benefit analysis where the trade-off is between action at the Union level or at the national level.[14] Interestingly, where appropriate ESMA does apply *an* efficiency test itself, but this test is not determinative for the question of whether action is required by ESMA or by the national competent authorities.[15] ESMA's efficiency test is merely an economic cost–benefit analysis, that is to say, a limited impact assessment.[16] The rationale

---

[12] It is not excluded that such test is carried out internally, without it being made public. There could be situations in which a subsidiarity test would need to be applied, but there are no signs of this in the documents themselves. ESMA should therefore explicate its considerations: see the recommendation in Chapter 11, Section 2.1.

[13] This is good, in a way, in order to safeguard the independence of the members of the Board of Supervisors, because they cannot weigh their national interests with regard to the question whether action should be undertaken by ESMA or by the national competent authorities with which they are affiliated.

[14] The Court itself has clearly recognised in Case T-13/99 *Pfizer Animal Health v Council* [2002] ECR II-3305, para 410 that 'a cost/benefit analysis is a particular expression of the principle of proportionality'.

[15] For example, the cost–benefit analysis in relation to draft regulatory and implementing technical standards of 28 September 2015 on Central Securities Depositaries (CSD) requirements and on internalised settlement runs to 83 pages, but there is no consideration at all of whether the Union or the national level would be the most appropriate level on which to act. See ESMA, Annex III to the Final Report on draft Technical Standards under the Regulation No 909/2014 of the European Parliament and of the Council of 23 July 2014 on improving securities settlement in the European Union and on central securities depositories and amending Directives 98/26/EC and 2014/65/EU and Regulation (EU) No 236/2012 (2015) ESMA/2015/1457/Annex III, 4.

[16] See also the criticism of impact assessments in which the Commission is sometimes said to be biased towards legislative solutions: Meuwese 2008, p. 59. In fact, ESMA quite often refers to its cost–benefit analysis as impact assessments: see ESMA, Draft RTS on the content and format of ratings data periodic reporting to be requested from credit ratings agencies for the purpose of on-going supervision by ESMA (2011) ESMA/2011/464, 10.

behind such an analysis is therefore not a subsidiarity test. ESMA only carries out a cost–benefit analysis when this is required on the basis of the procedural framework for the adoption of the soft law act at hand or upon request by the Board of Supervisors in the case of Q&As.

Articles 10(1) and 15(1) ESMA Regulation require the agency to analyse the potential costs and benefits in relation to the draft technical standards it intends to submit to the Commission for adoption. ESMA may refrain from such analyses when it would be highly disproportionate in relation to the scope and impact of the draft technical standards concerned or in relation to the particular urgency of the matter. An example of a situation in which it can occur in practice that a draft technical standard is submitted to the Commission without a cost–benefit analysis is where the addressees would only be the national competent authorities of the Member States and not financial market participants.[17] In addition, Article 16(2) ESMA Regulation requires the agency to analyse the potential costs and benefits in relation to the guidelines and recommendations it intends to issue, but only if this is appropriate. Besides, such an analysis has to be proportionate in relation to the scope, nature and impact of the legal instruments. In comparison to the draft technical standards, appropriateness and nature are additional reasons which give ESMA the opportunity to explain why, on occasion, it will not carry out a cost–benefit analysis.[18] Previously, if ESMA issued any of its non-binding instruments, there was no formal procedural requirement for ESMA to make a cost–benefit analysis.[19] This changed recently as part of the ESA review, since by virtue of Article 29(2) ESMA Regulation it is now obliged to analyse potential costs and benefits where this is appropriate in the case of opinions to NCAs and new practical instruments and convergence tools. Such an analysis also has to be proportionate in relation

---

[17] According to Commission Implementing Regulation (EU) 2016/1212, recital 7, ESMA did not analyse the potential related costs and benefits of introducing the standard forms and procedures for the relevant competent authorities, as this would have been disproportionate in relation to their scope and impact, taking into account that the addressees of the implementing technical standards would only be the national competent authorities of the Member States and not market participants.

[18] For an example, see ESMA, Guidelines on Cooperation between authorities under Articles 17 and 23 of Regulation (EU) No. 909/2014 (2017) ESMA70-151-435.

[19] See Chapter 5 for more on the decision-making processes of ESMA's non-binding instruments. Interestingly, a representative of the European Commission expressed at the Board of Supervisors meeting in June 2015 that the Commission would welcome cost–benefit analyses also on technical advice. With regard to the technical advice at issue, ESMA therefore decided to provide the Commission with further qualitative cost–benefit data. ESMA was accordingly willing to accept this additional safeguard in the adoption procedure at the expense of a quick process without any procedural hurdles. The trade-off between legitimacy and effectiveness has in this case thus been made in favour of legitimacy.

to the scope, nature and impact of the instruments. In the case of Q&As there is no such obligation, but three voting members of the Board of Supervisors may request that the entire Board decides that ESMA has to analyse potential related costs and benefits.[20] The same particularities regarding proportionality would then apply. The only soft law instrument where a cost–benefit analysis is lacking altogether is an opinion to the European Parliament, the Council and the Commission.[21] Yet this is rather logical, because it is submitted to the EU institutions and does not directly affect market participants. If ESMA's opinion were to lead to a new legislative proposal or a proposal for a new delegated or implementing act, a subsidiarity test will be carried out by the Union legislature in any case. As follows from an enquiry into the rather insightful cost–benefit analyses attached to the final reports of ESMA's guidelines and draft technical standards,[22] it appears that the objective of ESMA's analysis is not to discover the most appropriate level to regulate and therefore it does not concern the relationship between the Member States and the EU. Instead, it aims to assess the costs and benefits of the various policy or technical options which were analysed during the process of drafting the instrument at issue.[23] Alongside the benefits, the agency looks at the costs for the regulator, the compliance costs, the costs for other stakeholders and the indirect costs of each possible technical option it considers.[24] Although a cost–benefit analysis does take into account the costs for the regulator at the national level, this is done only for the purpose of choosing the most appropriate option for regulating a certain matter. For instance, ESMA would only issue guidelines if it were to come to the conclusion that the benefits of issuing guidelines outweigh the costs.[25] Especially when guidelines are on ESMA's own initiative, the

---

20 ESMA Regulation, Art 16b(4).

21 Ibid., Arts 9a and 16a. Such opinions are otherwise outside the scope of this book.

22 There are no examples of cost–benefit analyses in relation to ESMA's non-binding instruments as of yet.

23 ESMA, Consultation Paper on the Guidelines on participant default rules and procedures under CSDR (2016) ESMA/2016/732, para 2; ESMA, Guidelines on the application of the definitions in Sections C6 and C7 of Annex I of Directive 2004/39/EC (2015) ESMA/2015/675, para 2; ESMA, Guidelines and Recommendations regarding written agreements between members of CCP colleges (2013) ESMA/2013/661, para 1 of the cost–benefit analysis. According to the Interinstitutional Agreement on Better Law-Making, para 12: 'Impact assessments should cover the existence, scale and consequences of a problem and the question whether or not Union action is needed.' This is not what ESMA is doing.

24 ESMA, Final Report on Draft regulatory technical standards on indirect clearing arrangements under EMIR and MiFIR (2016) ESMA/2016/725.

25 See the cost–benefit analysis belonging to ESMA, Guidelines on the application of the definitions in Sections C6 and C7 of Annex I of Directive 2004/39/EC (2015) ESMA/2015/675, para 11.

choices or options envisaged by ESMA while drafting guidelines are limited to whether or not to issue the guidelines.[26] This thus makes it a proportionality test rather than a subsidiarity test. Indeed, if the benefits do not outweigh the costs, the adoption of a legal act would exceed what is necessary to achieve the objectives of the Treaties. This is exactly what Article 5(4) TEU aims to prevent. Unnecessary regulation is not proportionate. Anyway, the subsidiarity and proportionality tests pretty much coincide. According to Schütze, subsidiarity should not be confined to the question of whether the EU should act but should also address *how* the EU should act, since reducing subsidiarity to the 'whether' question would result in a dual federalism, whereby either the EU or the Member States may exercise their competences, instead of a cooperative federalism.[27]

3. ESMA'S EXERCISE OF SOFT LAW-MAKING POWERS: THE PRINCIPLE OF PROPORTIONALITY

Once it is established that ESMA is competent to act and that it may exercise this competence in a given instance, the third step for ESMA is to determine *how* it should exercise this competence. This is exactly what the proportionality principle as laid down in Article 5(4) TEU is about. The test entails an assessment of the proportionality of Union action on the basis of two requirements: consideration of the *form* of action an agency wants to take and of the *contents* of the action. For this purpose, ESMA has to choose the most appropriate instrument to act, which thus entails '*instrument choice*'. Likewise, it has to bear in mind the *substantive scope* of the legal basis upon which it acts and it has to take into account the *technical and policy dimension* of its powers.

3.1 ESMA's Discretion Regarding the Choice of Instrument

The first requirement of the proportionality test entails consideration of the *form* of action an EU agency wants to take. For this purpose, ESMA has to choose the most appropriate instrument to act. As a general matter, there is no single universally optimal mechanism or policy instrument, because the choice is pragmatic and involves several considerations.[28] The first thing for ESMA to

---

[26] ESMA, Consultation Paper on the Guidelines on participant default rules and procedures under CSDR (2016) ESMA/2016/732, paras 3 and 4; ESMA, Guidelines on the application of the definitions in Sections C6 and C7 of Annex I of Directive 2004/39/EC (2015) ESMA/2015/675, paras 3 and 4.

[27] Chamon 2016 and Schütze 2009, p. 250.

[28] Wiener & Richman 2010.

do, therefore, is to take a look at the mandate in the legal basis and see whether it prescribes the adoption of a certain instrument or whether it is free to decide for itself what the most appropriate tool would be. In order to establish how much discretion ESMA has with regard to selecting the most appropriate type of legal instrument, it is important to distinguish between its mandatory, discretionary and own-initiative soft law-making action.

As was explained in the previous chapter, ESMA may be either required (on the basis of a 'shall' provision) or invited (on the basis of a 'may' provision) in sectoral legislation to exercise its powers to elaborate soft law instruments. Besides, it may act on its own initiative even without such empowerments. Once a legal basis is established, ESMA thus has to reflect upon whether it shall or may act, that is, whether there is a mandatory or discretionary competence for the agency to develop soft law. The legal basis upon which ESMA is acting affects to a great extent how much discretion the agency has.

With regard to the issue of discretion, it is first of all interesting to consider recital 26 of the preamble to the ESMA Regulation, which provides that 'in areas not covered by regulatory or implementing technical standards, the Authority should have the power to issue guidelines and recommendations on the application of Union law'.[29] On the one hand, this recital may imply that ESMA is free to issue guidelines and recommendations on any issue in its policy area which it deems necessary and important.[30] On the other hand, it may imply that if securities legislation provides for the power to draft regulatory or implementing technical standards, ESMA may not use its power to adopt guidelines and recommendations.[31] The interpretation of this recital followed by ESMA is as follows. In cases where a specific issue is to be covered by regulatory or implementing technical standards according to the level 1 legislation, ESMA cannot consider guidelines, but should first approach the matter via draft technical standards. ESMA cannot choose to issue guidelines on that point just because it does not want to go through the procedure of having its rules adopted by the Commission, for instance.[32] This is rather straightforward in the case of a 'shall' provision, because there is no discretion for the agency not to issue the instrument or to issue another instrument. However, the question remains as to how a 'may' provision should be understood when it invites ESMA to develop draft technical standards. Does this mean that the agency can either issue technical standards or nothing at all, or does it suggest that

---

[29] ESMA Regulation, recital 26.

[30] Van Rijsbergen 2014.

[31] Ibid.

[32] This in fact entails an unlawful proportionality consideration. For this reason, it is recommended that ESMA explicates its proportionality considerations in the soft law instruments it issues: see Chapter 11, Section 2.1.

the agency can choose not to issue technical standards but then to act upon its own initiative in that policy area by means of guidelines or another tool? If the latter were possible, this could lead to situations in which the other Union institutions could be circumvented by ESMA on purpose. This choice would then upset the institutional balance as regards the adoption procedure to be followed and the role of the other institutions therein.

In order to deal with such ambiguities, it is useful to consider the Union courts' case-law, which reveals that the CJEU has used the term discretion to cover a number of different situations.[33] Drawing on Craig's analysis of this case law, the first type of case can be termed *classic discretion*.[34] This is where the relevant Treaty provision, regulation, directive or decision states that where certain conditions exist, the Union *may* take certain action.[35] This is so when the enabling provision states: 'if X1, X2, X3 exist, you may do Y.'[36] In the case of *Westzucker*, a regulation provided that when certain conditions were present denaturing premiums might be granted, but did not have to be.[37] The CJEU characterised this as giving rise to Commission discretion in the granting of premiums.[38] Following this line of reasoning, a 'may' provision inviting ESMA to take a particular type of regulatory action could thus be seen as giving the agency the discretion either to take the action if it considers it to be necessary in that given case, or to not use the power that it has been given. This means that the agency, acting upon a 'may' provision, does have classic discretion. It can choose not to issue the instrument, but it cannot choose to issue another instrument instead.[39] This in fact entails that ESMA can no longer apply a proportionality test, since the instrument choice has already been made by the legislature and laid down in the legal basis.

Craig's account of the case-law also shows that the EU courts have used the term discretion in a second type of case, even where the enabling Treaty provision, regulation, directive or decision is cast in mandatory terms.[40] Where the relevant legislation provides 'if X, you shall do Y' and Y entails a specific measure there will be *no* room for any meaningful *discretion* once the

---

[33] Craig 2012, p. 403.

[34] Ibid., p. 404.

[35] Ibid.

[36] Ibid.

[37] Case 57/72 *Westzucker GmbH v Einfuhr- und Vorratsstelle für Zucker* [1973] ECR 321.

[38] Craig 2012, p. 404.

[39] Van Ooijk argues the opposite. He is of the opinion that it is possible to adopt non-binding measures while referring to a legal basis that mentions one or more binding legal instruments. The idea is that those who may do more, may also do less. In that case, soft law cannot establish legally binding effects: see Van Ooijk 1999, p. 276.

[40] Craig 2012, p. 404.

conditions have been met.[41] There are also other instances where the content of Y, the mandatory obligation, is cast in more general terms, thereby leaving discretion as to how it should be fulfilled.[42] The first situation applies to ESMA. A 'shall' provision always requires the agency to elaborate a particular type of soft law instrument. This means that the agency, acting upon a 'shall' provision, does not have any discretion at all. It cannot choose not to issue the instrument and it cannot choose to issue a different instrument instead. This means that, in such cases, ESMA cannot apply a proportionality test either. This is mostly the case for draft technical standards and guidelines, although in some cases the level 1 legislation prescribes that the agency 'shall issue an opinion' addressed to the national competent authorities on a given issue.[43] In this sense, the proportionality principle has already been applied by the legislature. Indeed, where ESMA is acting under a legislative obligation to adopt an act in a specific form, ESMA complies with that requirement.

Craig's examination reveals that the EU courts have in fact also used the term discretion in a third type of case, that is, where there are broadly framed conditions that have to be established before the power or duty can be exercised at all.[44] The phrase *jurisdictional discretion* can be used to capture this type of situation.[45] This is exemplified by *Philip Morris Holland*.[46] This could be the case for ESMA when it considers using one of its tools – such as guidelines, opinions or Q&As – on its own initiative, so without any 'shall' or 'may' provision in sectoral legislation. If ESMA uses its own-initiative power, there is no legislative obligation to act and the instrument to be used is not specified. It has to act within the scope of Articles 1(2) and 1(3) ESMA Regulation, but may otherwise issue such instruments whenever it can find a legal basis and can fulfil the corresponding conditions. This means that the agency, acting upon its own initiative, does have jurisdictional discretion. ESMA may in fact make two choices: whether to issue an instrument or not, and what type of instrument it wants to use. In the latter case, the agency of course needs a legal basis to act. It is therefore only in this situation that ESMA can apply a proportionality test. The choice of form is then a matter for ESMA to decide. This is also in line with Article 296 TFEU, which provides that 'where the Treaties do not specify the type of act to be adopted, the institutions shall select it on

---

41 Ibid.

42 Ibid.

43 A few examples may be found in the AIFMD. Article 25(6) states that 'ESMA shall issue advice' to competent authorities and Articles 37(5), 37(9) and 37(11) all provide that 'ESMA shall issue advice' to the relevant competent authorities.

44 Craig 2012, p. 404.

45 Ibid.

46 Case 730/79 *Philip Morris Holland BV v Commission* [1980] ECR 2671.

a case-by-case basis, in compliance with the applicable procedures and with the principle of proportionality'. Indeed, if ESMA acts on its own initiative, it does have discretion to select one type of instrument over another. The agency's instrument choice may for instance depend on whom ESMA is seeking to address with its instrument, the regulatory objective (what is the purpose of its action and what does it want to achieve with it) and the timing. Nonetheless, it is never possible to make a specific choice for technical standards without an empowerment in level 1 or level 2 legislation, because the ESMA Regulation merely provides the procedural framework for the development of this type of legal instrument and empowerments therefore always need to be sought elsewhere. ESMA's guidelines, opinions, Q&As and other convergence tools may be used more freely, also beyond any orders from sectoral legislation, because those instruments find a more general legal basis in the ESMA Regulation itself.[47]

4. ESMA'S CONSIDERATIONS ON THE CHOICE OF INSTRUMENT IN PRACTICE

The choice of instrument is a very important step in the process, because each and every legal instrument has its own procedure, own legal status and own consequences for those affected by it.[48] Indeed, a different decision-making procedure applies to each category of ESMA's soft law instruments. For instance, Q&As may be adopted without consultations on the basis of a simple majority vote, whereas consultations are required for the adoption of guidelines and draft technical standards on the basis of a qualified majority vote.[49] Likewise, the possibilities for judicial review differ: technical standards adopted by the Commission are legally challengeable under Article 263 TFEU whereas guidelines and non-binding instruments do not automatically fall within the scope of this provision and are therefore not always challengeable.[50] As a result, the legal protection of individuals becomes dependent on the form of the act in question.[51] Hence, consideration should be given in each case to the inherent characteristics of ESMA's soft law instruments in terms of the appropriateness of procedural obligations and the extent of legal effects.

---

47 See Chapter 3, Section 3.

48 See also Van Ooijk on the consequences of the choice of the legal basis: Van Ooijk 1999, pp. 209–322.

49 See Chapter 5 for more on the decision-making processes.

50 See Chapter 10.

51 This contradicts the case-law of the EU courts according to which only the contents of the act are decisive for the interpretation of the requirement of direct and individual concern: see Barents 2010, p. 725.

This means that ESMA, at this stage of the process, needs to strike a balance between legitimacy and effectiveness. If it focuses on efficiency in a given instance, it would be better to opt for an instrument with fewer procedural hurdles. If it considers legitimacy to be more important, it would need to choose an instrument where consultations and a qualified majority are required. Such consultations may also lead to effectiveness in the sense that compliance may be higher when there is support from the market. An example of the fact that ESMA is aware of the importance of such balancing in practice is presented in the textbox that follows.

> At the meeting of the Board of Supervisors in December 2016, a note on ESMA's use of Q&As and other own-initiative supervisory convergence tools was presented by the Executive Director.[52] The Board discussed a number of issues, such as the importance of stakeholder consultation on significant issues, whether introducing national consultations should be considered and the need to maintain a flexible instrument to provide market participants with swift guidance. Eventually, 'the Board endorsed the existing approach to Q&As noting that there should be sufficient need for guidance by stakeholders when deciding to issue a Q&A. *ESMA should actively consider on a case-by-case basis whether there is a need for other legal instruments on which market participants are consulted* (e.g. Guidelines) depending on the impact on market participants. ESMA will increase the presentation of both Q&As and the process leading to them on its website. ESMA will consult stakeholders on Q&As where relevant and needed through the existing Consultative Working Groups (CWGs) and the Securities and Markets Stakeholder Group (SMSG). The Board agreed not to introduce national consultations.'[53]

From a legal perspective the preferred approach would be to go for a binding instrument wherever possible, because it is much clearer and it enhances legal certainty. However, in many cases, problems only come to the fore once the level 1 and level 2 text has already been produced and people start working with this text in practice. Only then does it become obvious that something is unclear or simply does not work. In such a situation, there are in fact two choices for ESMA. The *first option* is to go back to the Commission, saying the legislation does not work and asking it to legislate further.[54] This is a fairly

---

52 ESMA, Board of Supervisors Summary of Conclusions of 14 December 2016 (ESMA22-247440098-55), 6.

53 Ibid.

54 ESMA Regulation, Art 9a.

unpopular proposition, because it takes a long time. The *second option* is to try to offer a working explanation to the market as to how it might work by issuing guidelines or non-binding instruments on the matter. Guidelines or non-binding instruments therefore have an important role to play in the interpretation of the underlying legislation and are used to make it easier to comply with the level 1 and 2 rules. Hence, guidelines and non-binding instruments cannot be seen as free-standing, as they are often produced when there is an *interpretative gap* and in this situation also partly a *regulatory gap*. From the perspective of legitimacy, it would therefore be desirable for guidelines and non-binding instruments to be used as a temporary solution whose content will be integrated in the level 1 or 2 legislation when that is updated.

One problem with the second option remains, however, that it regularly occurs that some NCAs prefer a certain interpretation whereas others favour the exact opposite understanding. They then bring it to the Board of Supervisors, which decides upon it in one way or another. It would probably be better to deal with this kind of problem through a binding instrument, because guidelines just add another level of complexity to solving the issue as the problem in the legislation is still there. The guidelines tell addressees what to do but that is not the last word on the matter, since national competent authorities may decide not to comply.

5. CONTROLLING ESMA'S USE OF DISCRETION REGARDING THE CHOICE OF INSTRUMENT

Normally, Union institutions are exposed to the danger of using proportionality considerations as a cover for not resorting to a proposal for legislation, though such a proposal might in fact be needed or desired.[55] This could enable them to circumvent other Union institutions' involvement in the decision-making process, which would clearly affect the horizontal division of powers, that is, the institutional balance. ESMA does not really face this risk, however, because it cannot choose to use draft technical standards on its own initiative[56] and otherwise must follow the legislative obligations in the level one legislation. We should however be aware of another looming risk: that of ESMA's

---

[55] Senden 2004.

[56] In the *Grimaldi* case, the Court held that recommendations 'are generally adopted by the Union institutions of the Community when they do not have the power under the Treaty to adopt binding measures or when they consider that it is not appropriate to adopt more mandatory rules': see C-322/88 *Grimaldi v Fonds des maladies professionnelles* [1989] ECR 4407, para 13. This line of reasoning seems to apply to agencies as well, since ESMA does not have the power to adopt binding measures on its own initiative and therefore resorts to soft law.

potential abuse of Q&As to the detriment of guidelines. In this way, even the safeguards specifically related to the guidelines would be curtailed, with, for example, in principle no consultations, translations and 'comply or explain'. If this were the result of an improper balancing between legitimacy and effectiveness in seeking to choose a timely and efficient process, it would amount to a form of regulation by the backdoor, in the worst sense of the term.[57]

Proportionality has been given a much more prominent role in the amended ESMA Regulation than was previously the case. Paragraph 5 of the preamble clearly states that when performing their tasks and exercising their powers the ESAs, including ESMA, should act in accordance with the principle of proportionality laid down in Article 5 of the Treaty on European Union (TEU), as well as with the better regulation policy. Besides, it stipulates that the *content* and *form* of the ESAs' actions and measures, including instruments such as guidelines, recommendations, opinions or questions and answers, should always be based on and within the boundaries of the legislative acts referred to in Article 1(2) of the founding regulations or within the scope of their powers. It concludes that the ESAs, including ESMA, should not exceed what is necessary to achieve the objectives of this Regulation and should act proportionately to the nature, scale and complexity of the risks inherent in the financial activity or business of the affected financial institution or undertaking. A concrete reflection of this increased attention to proportionality is Article 60a, which deals with a potential excess of competence by ESMA. It enables any natural or legal person to send reasoned advice to the Commission if that person is of the opinion that ESMA has exceeded its competence – including by failing to respect the principle of proportionality – when acting under Articles 16 (guidelines and recommendations) and 16b (Q&As), and when that is of direct and individual concern to that person.

In practice, ESMA's discretion is also subject to objections on the ground of proportionality from the members of Standing Committees and Working Groups during the drafting process and from the members of the Board of Supervisors when the legal instrument at stake is discussed at their meetings.

For instance, at the September 2015 meeting of the Board of Supervisors, the opinion on Deposit Guarantee Schemes was on the agenda for decision. The Board discussed various aspects, among which was the question of whether an opinion was the best legal instrument.[58]

---

[57] This can be prevented by making explicit the proportionality considerations in each soft law act.

[58] ESMA Board of Supervisors, Summary of Conclusions of 21 November 2014 (ESMA/BS/202), 12–13.

In addition, in the case of technical standards, one could say that there is an extra proportionality check by the Commission. As follows from recital 23 in the original ESMA Regulation, technical standards are only subject to amendment by the Commission in very restricted and extraordinary circumstances. As explicitly mentioned in the recital, one of these circumstances would be if the draft technical standards do not respect the principle of proportionality.[59] This is an important safeguard, because ESMA cannot make a proportionality assessment itself when it acts on the basis of a 'shall' provision. The choice it has in case of a 'may' provision is only limited to whether or not to develop draft technical standards, that is, it cannot choose a different instrument for that particular topic instead.[60] Such a safeguard does not exist with regard to its own-initiative instruments, such as guidelines and Q&As, because they come into being without any involvement of the other Union institutions. The choice of instrument thus has a bearing on the horizontal division of powers within the EU, as the role of each institution is different per instrument. For instance, the other Union institutions have no involvement in the case of guidelines, whereas in the case of draft technical standards the Commission plays a large role. The legislature apparently considers this to be desirable, because it is often the legislature itself that decides for ESMA what type of instrument it has to issue.

An additional safeguard with regard to ESMA's own-initiative action is that the CJEU has retained jurisdiction concerning the reviewability of acts adopted by the Union by ensuring in its jurisprudence that the choice of form cannot change its ability to assess the true nature of a measure.[61] In *Commission v Council*, the Court held that an action for annulment must be available in the case of 'all measures adopted by the institutions, whatever their nature or form, which are intended to have legal effects'.[62] The extent to which the CJEU might declare itself admissible to review any of ESMA's soft law instruments remains to be seen, however.[63] Additionally, the judiciary is cautious in cases where proportionality is used to challenge a discretionary

---

[59] Other grounds for amendment are if they are incompatible with Union law or run counter to the fundamental principles of the internal market for financial services as reflected in the acquis of Union financial services legislation: see ESMA Regulation, recital 23.

[60] See Chapter 3, Section 3.

[61] For example, see Case 101/76 *Koninklijke Scholten Honig v Council and Commission* [1977] ECR 1977, paras 5 and 7; Joined Cases 789/79 and 790/79 *Società Emiliana Lavorazione Frutta SpA v Commission* [1980] ECR 1949, para 7.

[62] Case 22/70 *Commission v Council (ERTA)* [1971] ECR 263, para 42.

[63] See Chapter 10.

policy choice made by the administration.[64] The administrative/political arm of government makes policy choices, and it is generally recognised that the courts should not overturn these merely because they believe that a different way of doing things would have been better.[65] They should not substitute their judgement for that of the administration.[66] The courts will therefore probably only overturn a policy choice if it is clearly or manifestly disproportionate.[67]

6. THE SUBSTANTIVE SCOPE OF ESMA'S SOFT LAW-MAKING POWERS

When ESMA has discretion and the Union level is indeed the best level at which to act, ESMA has to take into account the *substantive scope* of the legal basis upon which it acts in order to remain within its limits. The question of how the agency deals with this discretion now arises.[68] Indeed, does the agency stay within the substantive scope of the legal basis upon which it acts? This section shows that issues do not arise with regard to draft technical standards and non-binding instruments, whereas the substantive scope of ESMA's guidelines raises concerns both in theory and in practice.

6.1 Draft Regulatory and Implementing Technical Standards

Since draft technical standards can only be developed pursuant to a mandatory or discretionary empowerment in the level 1 legislation and thus not on ESMA's own initiative, they always have to remain strictly within the compass of the legal bases upon which ESMA acts. When ESMA is of the view that the rule-making powers it has are not sufficient, but that a certain matter should be

---

[64] Craig 2012, p. 591.

[65] Ibid.

[66] Ibid.

[67] Ibid. In this way, the courts would apply proportionality as an *ex post* judicial doctrine in reviewing the legality of Union action. In this manner, proportionality constitutes a means to protect individuals from excessive interference by the Member States and the EU: see Emiliou 1996, p. 142. See for an example Case 11/70 *Internationale Handelsgesellschaft GmbH v Einfuhr- und Vorratsstelle für Getreide und Futtermittel* [1970] ECR 1125, paras 12–18.

[68] 'Some argue that [...] the powers of independent agencies should be interpreted as strictly as possible. They say that discretionary powers should be as limited as possible. Research shows, however, that the distinction between policymaking and policy implementation is difficult to make in practice and may result in independent agencies having too limited legal mandates to take proper action. This in turn creates a risk of independent agencies being unable to exercise their powers adequately and to contribute effectively to the attainment of the goals of regulation.' See Ottow 2015, p. 71.

regulated by means of binding legislation, its only option is to send an opinion to the European Commission setting out the action it considers appropriate in the form of a new legislative proposal or a proposal for a new delegated or implementing act.[69]

6.2 Guidelines and Recommendations

When ESMA issues guidelines and recommendations on the basis of a 'shall' or 'may' provision in sectoral legislation, it has to remain strictly within the compass of such legal bases, because the subject matter has already been given. However, when ESMA issues guidelines and recommendations upon its own initiative, a particular issue that deserves attention is the substantive scope of Article 16 ESMA Regulation. ESMA's own-initiative power does not imply that the agency has *carte blanche* simply to adopt soft law measures in any situation. Yet, it is not entirely clear what its limits are either.[70] Article 16(1) ESMA Regulation refers to two relevant objectives for which the agency may decide to issue guidelines and recommendations: to establish consistent, efficient and effective supervisory practices and to ensure the common, uniform and consistent application of Union law. In practice, most guidelines meet both criteria. The purpose of this type of soft law is thus clearly to achieve greater effectiveness in the sense of consistency, efficiency and uniformity. This again shows the importance of the balancing exercise between the notions of both legitimacy and effectiveness.

Concerns about the scope of ESMA's guidelines are not merely of theoretical interest. During the 2017 Commission consultation on the operation of the European Supervisory Authorities, it once again became clear that industry stakeholders have raised concerns that the ESA guidelines are increasingly expansive and go beyond their originally intended function, namely to ensure the 'common, uniform and consistent application of Union law'.[71] A new paragraph 2a to Article 16 therefore imposes a further limit to the substantive scope of guidelines and recommendations, because they shall not merely refer to, or reproduce, elements of legislative acts. Before issuing a new guideline or recommendation, ESMA first has to review existing guidelines and recommendations, in order to avoid any duplication. In this way, ESMA's exercise of power remains acceptable to citizens and stakeholders, and therewith legitimate.

---

[69] ESMA Regulation, Art 9a.

[70] Van Rijsbergen 2014, p. 131.

[71] Commission, 'Public consultation on the operations of the European Supervisory Authorities' <https://ec.europa.eu/info/sites/info/files/2017-esas-operations-consultation-document_en.pdf> accessed 16 February 2021.

6.3 Non-binding Instruments

Since non-binding instruments are adopted only upon ESMA's own initiative, the agency is less limited as to what it may regulate, because it may act on the basis of rather broad provisions without fulfilling many procedural obligations. Q&As may follow after 'any questions relating to the practical application or implementation of the provisions of legislative acts referred to in Article 1(2), associated delegated and implementing acts, and guidelines and recommendations adopted pursuant to those legislative acts'.[72] The scope of ESMA's opinions to national supervisory authorities is as wide as 'providing a contribution to building a common Union supervisory culture and consistent supervisory practices as well as to ensuring uniform procedures and consistent approaches throughout the Union'.[73] New practical instruments and convergence tools may be developed by ESMA, with the very broad objective 'to promote common supervisory approaches and practices'.[74]

7. THE TECHNICAL AND POLICY DIMENSION OF ESMA'S SOFT LAW-MAKING POWERS

Besides taking into account the substantive scope of its powers, in exercising discretion ESMA also has to consider the technical and policy dimension of its powers. When is the agency limited to making technical choices and under what circumstances could it also be allowed to make policy choices? What is still lawful and when does its policy-making amount to regulation by the backdoor? This section shows that only draft technical standards are explicitly required to be technical without implying strategic decisions and policy choices. Such limitations do not apply to ESMA's guidelines and non-binding instruments.

7.1 Draft Regulatory and Implementing Technical Standards

ESMA has a large degree of discretion as to how it develops draft regulatory and implementing technical standards. Given the technical expertise of the agency in the areas where technical standards should be developed, the Commission has stated its intention to rely, as a rule, on the drafts submitted to it by ESMA.[75] The discretion of the Commission is thus very narrow. Proposed

---

[72] ESMA Regulation, Art 16b(1).
[73] Ibid., Art 29(1)(a).
[74] Ibid., Art 29(2).
[75] Ibid., recital 24.

drafts should only be amended in very restricted and extraordinary circumstances, because ESMA is the actor in close contact with, and the one that best knows about, the daily functioning of financial markets.[76] Drafts are therefore only subject to amendment if they are incompatible with Union law, do not respect the principle of proportionality or run counter to the fundamental principles of the internal market for financial services as reflected in the *acquis* of the Union's financial services legislation.[77] In any case, the Commission may not change the content of the draft technical standards prepared by ESMA without prior coordination with ESMA. This suggests that the Commission is not merely rubberstamping the draft technical standards, since the Commission may refuse them if it has problems with whatever ESMA submits, but it is not meant to review the standards from scratch.

The Commission is only likely to reject the drafts when it has really strong reasons for stating that what ESMA presents does not work, especially because the Commission has not done all the consultative work that ESMA has done and has not collaborated with the stakeholders in the same way. Legally speaking, the Commission most certainly will not hesitate to interfere if the draft technical standards have gone beyond the scope of the empowerments. This is also in line with Articles 10(1) and 15(1) ESMA Regulation, which reiterate that regulatory and implementing technical standards 'shall be technical and shall not imply strategic decisions or policy choices'. At the end of the day, it is the Commission that has to adopt the standards and it will obviously object if it believes that ESMA does not respect these limits. As the examples in the following box show, it is questionable to what extent ESMA always respects the Commission's prerogative for policy-making and whether ESMA does not in fact introduce regulation by the backdoor, since the agency itself sometimes engages in policy-making in the technical standards process.

During the Board of Supervisors meeting of 7 May 2015, an example of policy-making in the case of draft technical standards arose.[78] The Market Integrity Standing Committee presented the technical standards it drafted on the basis of an empowerment in the Market Abuse Regulation (MAR).[79] The European Commission representative who was present at this meeting

[76] Ibid., recital 23.

[77] Ibid.

[78] ESMA, Board of Supervisors Summary of Conclusions of 7 May 2015 (ESMA/BS/90rev), 4.

[79] Market Abuse Regulation, Art 17(10), which was a 'shall' empowerment that required ESMA to develop draft implementing technical standards (ITS) to determine the technical means for appropriate public disclosure of inside information and for delaying the public disclosure of inside information.

expressed strong reservations regarding the decision to apply the same requirements to Emission Allowance Market Participants (EAMPs) for the public disclosure of inside information as were applicable to other entities. The Commission representative stated that this would not be in line with the text of recital 51 of MAR, which should be read as demanding that no disclosure obligations should be imposed on top of those provided for by the Regulation on Wholesale Energy Market Integrity and Transparency (REMIT). He added that should the Commission's early legal review provide confirmation, this could lead to a rejection of the technical standards by the Commission. Interestingly, the Board took note of the concerns expressed by the Commission representative, yet still *approved the policies* embedded in the technical standards as presented. In line with the procedure as laid down in Article 15(1) ESMA Regulation, the draft technical standards were sent to the Commission for endorsement. As a response, the Commission sent a letter to inform ESMA that it intended to endorse the proposed technical standards once a number of amendments had been introduced.[80] ESMA replied by means of an Opinion and explained why it did not agree with the Commission's view.[81] Interestingly, the final version of the Commission Implementing Regulation shows that the Commission followed ESMA's approach in the end, because the draft technical standards were adopted by the Commission without the amendments it requested from ESMA.[82]

Also during the Board of Supervisors meeting of 24–25 September 2015, a clear signal of ESMA being involved with policy-making came to the fore.[83] The Market Data Reporting Working Group presented the final report on technical standards under Article 9 of the European Market Infrastructure Regulation (EMIR). After discussion among the Board members, the Board *endorsed the policy aspects* of the technical standards and decided to approve the technical standards after the legal review by the European Commission. The Board thus recognised the superiority of the

---

80 ESMA, Opinion on Draft Implementing Technical Standards on the technical means for appropriate public disclosure of inside information and for delaying the public disclosure of inside information (2016) ESMA/2016/982, para 5: in particular, the Commission requested the deletion of the reference 'in accordance with paragraph 1' in Article 2(2) of the draft ITS in order to avoid undue 'double disclosure'.

81 Ibid., paras 4–7.

82 Commission Implementing Regulation (EU) 2016/1055, Art 2(2) still contains the reference 'in accordance with paragraph 1'.

83 ESMA, Board of Supervisors Summary of Conclusions of 21 November 2014 (ESMA/BS/202), 7.

Commission Legal Service, but nonetheless openly showed that it was dealing with policy choices in these draft technical standards.

The examples just given were rather straightforward, because policy-making was signalled at the Board of Supervisors meetings, but the line between what is an actual policy choice and what is not is very unclear. Whether one could argue that ESMA is making technical choices or real policy choices very much depends on the content of the provisions in the legal text. However, drawing boundaries between technical and policy matters, especially in an area as complex as financial regulation, is notoriously difficult.[84] In practice, there are very few rules in the financial market sphere which do not have any policy implications.[85]

7.2 Guidelines and Recommendations

ESMA has even more discretion as regards the content of its guidelines and recommendations, since there is no formal role for the Commission in this process and Article 16 ESMA Regulation does not exclude strategic decisions or policy choices. The Commission has no possibility to block the adoption of ESMA's guidelines or reject them in any other way. It may express its opinion during the Standing Committee and Board of Supervisors meetings in which the draft documents are discussed or at the meetings of the Board of Supervisors, but the agency is not obliged to follow up on what the Commission says. However, even though Article 16 does not exclude strategic decisions and policy choices from ESMA's guidelines and recommendations, things are not as simple as they would seem on the basis of the legal framework alone. The question of what the substantive nature of the guidelines then can and cannot be is left open.

For example, does it amount to an acceptable policy choice if ESMA promotes guidelines on the basis that they provide a quicker way for ESMA to see whether there has been compliance or non-compliance with a provision in a technical standard, or on the basis that it is more effective for market participants to comply in a particular way with a technical standard? It is inevitable that ESMA will do that sometimes, because it is in fact inherent in the function of guidelines to clarify or interpret provisions in the underlying legislation. This evidently brings a certain degree of choice with it, because often more

---

[84] Chamon 2011, p. 1070 argues that '[i]n reality, however, such an assumed clear distinction between technical issues and policy choices does not exist, as is already well recognized in legal literature on agencies'. He refers to Griller & Orator 2010, p. 22. See also Tridimas 2011, p. 802.

[85] Moloney 2011a, p. 68.

than one interpretation is possible. These are probably not the sort of major policy choices involving 'a very large measure of discretion' which are prohibited by the relevant case-law,[86] but they nonetheless entail a degree of policy or at least technical choice. As a consequence, judicial review is important to assess whether or not ESMA has remained within the framework of its powers and has not added any new obligations to Union law that do not already result from existing EU law.[87]

Occasionally, the legislature does not make any intervention, because it cannot reach political agreement. In such cases, ESMA also sometimes issues guidelines when it considers that it would be good to have rules anyway. This may indeed be desirable from a practical perspective, even for financial market participants, but in areas where no action is taken by the legislature, ESMA's choices may come close to policy choices. In such a situation, ESMA is really taking the place of the legislature, because such guidelines are in fact of a quasi-legislative character. Given the constraints in the non-delegation case law, ESMA should not do this.[88] It can be very difficult to find a legal basis for such guidelines, so they risk legal challenge before the court. In much the same way, an undesirable situation would ensue where the legislature took a certain position in a new directive and ESMA tried to give it a different spin with its guidelines, even though the preparatory works made clear that this was not in line with the legislature's intention. Such guidelines would also contain policy choices or would be at least policy-oriented.[89] Likewise, if it was clearly decided by the legislature to leave a certain provision out of the legislative text, ESMA should not introduce such provision through its guidelines. Were this to happen, it could lead to a successful challenge to the agency at the CJEU because using soft law in such a way as to – in fact, unlawfully – circumvent the influence of the other institutions in the decision-making process is obviously problematic, being tantamount to regulating by the backdoor. For such challenges to succeed, it is necessary that ESMA's guidelines are indeed amenable to judicial review.[90]

---

[86] Case C-270/12 *United Kingdom v Parliament and Council* [2014], para 28.

[87] See Chapter 11 for more on the possibilities for judicial review.

[88] See Chapter 3, Section 2 for the case law constraints.

[89] The fact that such a situation might occur could be demonstrated by an example that is not related to guidelines: in relation to the draft MiFID II technical advice, the head of the French NCA stated that in his opinion the draft proposal on financial research goes beyond the wishes of the co-legislators. Nonetheless, the Board approved the technical advice: see ESMA, Board of Supervisors Summary of Conclusions of 21 November 2014 (ESMA/BS/202), 6.

[90] See Chapter 6 for an analysis of the possibilities for a judicial review of ESMA's guidelines.

In conclusion, it seems to be the case that the overall constraint on what ESMA could actually say and regulate in its guidelines must come back to the level 1 legislation. If a choice is totally beyond the scope of the level 1 text, it cannot be made. This means that it is possible to make technical choices – indeed, this happens all the time – but it should never be possible to make the type of policy choices within the meaning of level 1 policy choices which are reserved for the EU legislature.

7.3 Non-binding Instruments

ESMA used to have a great deal of discretion in developing its non-binding instruments. There were no procedural requirements such as consultations which would result in stakeholder views that the agency had to take account of. In addition, there was no formal role for any of the Union institutions in their adoption. This has changed somewhat as a result of the ESA review. Indeed, Article 28(2) ESMA Regulation now prescribes that ESMA is also required to conduct open public consultations in relation to its opinions and new practical instruments and convergence tools under the same conditions applicable to guidelines and recommendations. In addition, upon the instigation of three voting members of the Board of Supervisors, the Board may decide to request that ESMA conduct open public consultations in relation to Q&As. This is laid down in the ESMA Regulation in a new Article 16b(4). Particularly with regard to Q&As, there is also an important new role for the Commission, because ESMA now has to forward to it all questions that require the interpretation of Union law.[91] Yet, the legal basis for such instruments does not exclude strategic decisions or policy choices. The Commission could still express reservations during the meetings of the Standing Committees and Board of Supervisors when the draft instruments are discussed and adopted, but ESMA is not obliged to obey. In practice, this has led to a number of cases at the Board of Supervisors meetings where such acts were sent back to the Standing Committee or Working Group concerned, for them to carry out further work.

8. CONCLUSION AND ASSESSMENT ON THE DIVISION AND EXERCISE OF SOFT LAW-MAKING POWERS

In the context of ESMA's soft law-making, the principle of proportionality appears to be very important in determining how ESMA has to exercise its

---

[91] ESMA Regulation, Art 16b(5).

competence. In contrast, subsidiarity does not currently play a role at the agency level itself. The above analysis leads to three different situations in which the principles of subsidiarity and proportionality play their own role. The first is with regard to 'shall' provisions, regardless of the type of legal instrument, in which case subsidiarity and proportionality have been applied by the legislature. The second is with regard to 'may' provisions, regardless of the type of legal instrument. Subsidiarity and proportionality are applied by the legislature, but a second test of proportionality is carried out by ESMA when it assesses whether it is proportionate to deploy the instrument in the concrete case. The third is with regard to actions entirely upon ESMA's own initiative, which could be any instrument except for draft technical standards. Subsidiarity is considered in a general sense by the legislature, whereas proportionality is applied by ESMA in the concrete situation. ESMA explicitly acknowledges the general legal basis upon which its own-initiative soft law act is issued, but does not apply a subsidiarity check in the concrete case.

The following sections conclude this chapter and assess where the division and exercise of ESMA's competences lead to tensions on the basis of legitimacy and effectiveness concerns.

8.1 ESMA Does Not Apply the Correct Subsidiarity Test

Whenever ESMA has discretion, it needs to apply a subsidiarity test. The Union legislature applied the subsidiarity test by creating ESMA in the first place, and by adopting sectoral legislation that empowers the agency to exercise soft law-making powers. These are the moments during which the Union institutions and national Parliaments can make themselves heard. If ESMA acts on the basis of a *'shall' provision*, that is, when it has *mandatory competence*, there is no reason for the agency to apply a subsidiarity test, because it is beyond doubt that the competence is for ESMA and not for the national competent authorities. In fact, ESMA has no choice at all over whether to act or not, and likewise no choice with regard to the nature and extent of the action. This makes a subsidiarity test by the agency superfluous.

If ESMA acts on the basis of a *'may' provision*, subsidiarity does not play a part in ESMA's practice. This has to do with the fact that, if ESMA decides to take no action, the result of its inaction is not necessarily that the power is then exercised at the national level but rather that there is no rule-making activity at all. The lack of a subsidiarity check by ESMA is a shortcoming from the perspective of legitimacy, though. Member States can only make themselves heard during the drafting process within the framework of the Standing Committees and Working Groups in which experts of the national competent authorities take part. Subsidiarity plays virtually no role after this stage.

Nor does subsidiarity play a role when ESMA exercises its soft law-making competence *upon its own initiative*. The agency does not engage in the effectiveness and efficiency test of the principle of subsidiarity. It does apply *an* efficiency test with regard to its guidelines and recommendations, and will from now on do so with regard to its opinions and other practical instruments and convergence tools, but this is merely an economic cost–benefit analysis which is not determinative for the question of whether action has to be undertaken by ESMA or the national competent authorities. The nature of ESMA's efficiency test is thus different from that of the efficiency test as part of the principle of subsidiarity. With regard to its Q&As, ESMA does not carry out any efficiency test either, because there is no standard requirement to carry out a cost–benefit analysis.[92] Should it be requested to do so, it will most likely apply a similar efficiency test to that of its guidelines and recommendations.

This means that concerning ESMA's own-initiative action, subsidiarity only played a role *in abstracto* when the general competences for ESMA to issue soft law instruments such as guidelines and recommendations, opinions, Q&As and other convergence tools were laid down in the ESMA Regulation. In concrete cases, that is, *in concreto*, the subsidiarity check does not therefore exist. The defence could be raised that this is in fact not a problem in terms of efficiency. It is not without reason that it is generally determined that ESMA may exercise soft law-making powers at its own discretion. The Union institutions and national Parliaments apparently agreed to that when the regulation establishing ESMA was adopted. For ESMA to consider subsidiarity all over again would take some time, which would, as a result, undermine flexibility in the adoption procedure.

However, in order to respect the vertical division and exercise of powers within the EU, and to enhance legitimacy, such a test should be required.[93] One solution with regard to ESMA's *own-initiative tools* could be to add the appropriate EU–national level subsidiarity test to ESMA's efficiency test – the cost–benefit analysis – that it carries out with regard to its guidelines and recommendations. However, ESMA does not always carry out a cost–benefit analysis regarding guidelines, recommendations and non-binding instruments, and the decision-making procedure of its Q&As does not as a standard request such an analysis at all. In order to cover all of ESMA's own-initiative soft law instruments, it would therefore be best to take on board the weighing between

[92] See Chapter 5 for the decision-making processes of all three categories of ESMA's soft law instruments.

[93] This may also be said to follow from *Meroni*, which requires that the exercise of the powers conferred on an agency must be subject to the same conditions as those to which it would be subject if the delegating authority was exercising them directly: see Case 9-56 *Meroni v High Authority* [1958] ECR 133, paras 149–150.

the Union and the national dimension when ESMA applies the proportionality test. There is less necessity with regard to draft technical standards, because they can never be developed upon ESMA's own initiative and it is therefore more difficult for the agency to interfere with the sphere of competence of the Member States.

8.2 The *Content* of ESMA's Soft Law-making Action Greatly Affects Legitimacy and Effectiveness

The first requirement of the proportionality test entails a consideration of the *content* of the action that ESMA wants to take. If ESMA acts on the basis of a *'shall' or 'may' provision* in the level 1 legislation, the *substantive scope* of its power is strictly limited to the subject matter in the empowerment. This applies to all of ESMA's soft law instruments. Overstepping the scope would be illegitimate and ineffective, because the risk of legal challenges would be very high. Besides, in the case of draft technical standards, the Commission most certainly will not hesitate to interfere.[94] If ESMA acts on its *own initiative*, it is less limited as to what it may regulate. This applies especially with regard to non-binding instruments, since the scope of the legal foundations for these instruments is very broad. Little concern has been expressed as to whether the scope would in fact be too broad. The story is different with regard to ESMA's guidelines and recommendations, whose scope is limited to the two objectives set out in Article 16(1) ESMA Regulation. Concerns have been expressed by the Commission and financial market participants, plus the Board of Supervisors and lawyers at ESMA are racking their brains over the question of what the scope of guidelines and recommendations actually entails. Enlarging the scope would contribute to the effectiveness of such legal acts, because it would help to better achieve ESMA's regulatory objectives in some cases. However, it would run counter to the constitutional limits of the Treaty basis which was used to establish ESMA and to the non-delegation case-law which prohibits EU agencies from misusing their discretion. Indeed, sticking to the scope as set out in the Article 16 empowerment would be more in line with the demands stemming from legitimacy, since it would ensure that the exercise of power remains acceptable to citizens and to ESMA's stakeholders.

When ESMA considers the *technical and policy dimension* of its powers, it is important for the agency to distinguish between the different categories of soft law instruments. To begin with, ESMA has a large degree of discretion

---

[94] In accordance with the procedure as laid down in ESMA Regulation, Arts 11 and 15: the Commission may ask ESMA to amend the draft technical standards and may ultimately reject ESMA's proposals.

in how it develops its draft technical standards. The Commission may only amend the drafts in very restricted and extraordinary circumstances. In any case, the Commission may not change the content of the drafts without prior coordination with ESMA. However, ESMA's margin of appreciation is limited on the basis of the procedure set out in Articles 10 and 15 ESMA Regulation, which require the agency to develop standards of a technical nature only. Indeed, policy-making is the prerogative of the legislature. Accordingly, ESMA's drafts cannot imply any strategic decisions or policy choices at all. Yet, practice shows that ESMA sometimes engages in policy-making and therefore oversteps its discretion. This is of course not desirable from the perspective of legitimacy.

Second, ESMA has even more discretion regarding its guidelines and recommendations because there is no formal role for the Commission in the process and Article 16 ESMA Regulation does not exclude strategic decisions or policy choices. However, not every policy choice is also an *acceptable* policy choice. On the one hand, some guidelines lay down a particular form of compliance with the underlying binding legislation or a helpful interpretation or clarification of legally binding rules. These entail a degree of policy or at least technical choice, but they are not the sort of major policy choices that involve 'a very large margin of discretion' as prohibited by the relevant case-law.[95] On the other hand, some guidelines could give the impression that ESMA has taken the place of the legislature. This could happen if the legislature could not reach a political agreement and ESMA were to adopt guidelines instead, or if the legislature explicitly decided to leave a certain provision out of the legislative text and ESMA introduced such a provision by means of guidelines. Such guidelines should be challengeable before the Court, because using soft law in such a way leads to circumvention of the influence of the other Union institutions in the decision-making process.[96] This is a rule of law concern. ESMA cannot go this far. Such practice is particularly pressing in the case of guidelines, because, unlike with regard to draft technical standards, the Commission is not formally involved and therefore cannot intervene itself.

---

[95] Case C-270/12 *United Kingdom v Parliament and Council* [2014].

[96] This is in line with Case C-57/95 *France v Commission* [1997] ECR I-1627, paras 21–23. This case concerned the Commission's Interpretative Communication on an Internal Market for Pension Funds, which was published only days after the Commission had withdrawn the proposal for a directive. The Court pointed at the fact that this Communication contained measures which constituted the subject-matter of the proposal for a directive which the Commission withdrew 'because of a deadlock in the negotiations with Member States in the Council'. Consequently, the Court concluded that this Communication intended to have legal effects of its own and that the Commission was therefore lacking the necessary competence to adopt it.

This means that other legitimacy guarantees should be put in place in order to protect against such use, or even abuse, of power. This is in line with the idea that more, or different, procedural guarantees are required in the case of policy choices, as opposed to very technical choices. As a result, Article 60a has been introduced as part of the ESA review, which enables natural and legal persons to address issues of perceived excess of competence by ESMA when acting under Article 16 (guidelines and recommendations) whenever they are directly and individually concerned.

Third, ESMA used to have unlimited discretion with regard to its non-binding instruments, but this has been curtailed somewhat as a result of the ESA review. The Commission is now involved where Q&As require the interpretation of Union law; ESMA has to carry out consultations with regard to its opinions and new practical instruments and convergence tools; and the Board of Supervisors may on a case-by-case basis decide to request ESMA to conduct open public consultations in relation to Q&As. Strategic decisions and policy choices are still not explicitly excluded from its non-binding instruments. This means that ESMA can issue such acts as long as it remains within the substantive scope of the legal foundations upon which the acts are based.

From the perspective of effectiveness, such tools are very useful, as they can respond to market changes and technical developments very quickly. However, their legitimacy is in some cases more difficult to establish, particularly when there is no involvement whatsoever of any of the Union institutions and industry stakeholders. This problem is not corrected by stakeholders' views on the content that ESMA aims to regulate in such acts. In addition, as will be discussed later in Chapter 10, judicial review is impossible with regard to this type of soft law instrument. This means that the addressees of such acts are often also completely empty-handed when it comes to *ex post* review. For Q&As, a partial solution has been introduced after the ESA review with the introduction of the 'exceeding of competence by the authority' provision in the ESMA Regulation.[97]

8.3 The *Form* of ESMA's Soft Law-making Action Greatly Affects Legitimacy and Effectiveness

The second requirement of the proportionality test entails a consideration of the *form* of action ESMA wants to take. The choice of instrument has an enormous bearing on the legitimacy and effectiveness of ESMA's soft law-making. Each legal instrument has its own procedure, its own legal status and its own consequences for those who are affected by it. Likewise, the possibilities for judicial

---

[97] ESMA Regulation, Art 60a.

review differ. This means that ESMA, at this stage of the process, needs to strike a balance between legitimacy and effectiveness.[98] In the case of a *'shall'* or *'may' provision*, the proportionality principle has already been applied by the legislature, because such empowerments set out which legal instrument ESMA has to issue. With regard to technical standards, there is an additional safeguard for the Commission to amend ESMA's drafts if they have not respected the principle of proportionality.[99] With regard to a '*may*' provision, it should be noted that ESMA applies an extra proportionality check itself as it reviews whether or not it will develop the prescribed legal instrument. It may also decide not to take any action. When ESMA acts upon its *own initiative*, the agency has a great deal of freedom with regard to its instrument choice. This could be problematic, because the choice of instrument has a bearing on the horizontal division of powers within the Union and thus determines to what extent the Union institutions are involved. Therefore, proportionality was given a much more prominent role in the amended ESMA Regulation. Concretely with regard to Articles 16 (guidelines and recommendations) and 16b (Q&As), any directly and individually concerned natural or legal person may now flag issues at the Commission in order to prevent a potential excess of competence by ESMA.[100]

ESMA's choice of instrument also affects the *ex ante* procedural safeguards, the transposition and compliance duties of the national competent authorities and the *ex post* possibilities for enforcement and judicial review. For instance, Q&As are not translated and consultations are not required before they can be adopted, whereas this is the case for guidelines. Likewise, it is more likely that guidelines can be challenged at the CJEU than that Q&As can be challenged.[101] In order to ensure the effectiveness of ESMA's rule-making powers, the agency therefore has the discretion to choose the most appropriate legal instrument for achieving the intended regulatory objectives. It is apparent that all institutions and national Parliaments agreed to give the agency this liberty. ESMA itself should therefore strike a balance between legitimacy and effectiveness for each act it wants to develop, as it does by taking into account the appropriateness of procedural obligations and the extent of legal effects. Indeed, the more effects an instrument has, the more legitimacy becomes an issue, because the more guarantees are required. At the moment, ESMA does not explain its instrument choice in its soft law acts themselves. As a result, in a given case we do not know why the agency has selected, for instance, Q&As

---

98 See the example in Section 5.

99 ESMA Regulation, recital 23.

100 ESMA Regulation, Art 60a.

101 This follows from the analysis in Chapter 10.

instead of guidelines. In order to further prevent any abuse of powers, ESMA should therefore explicate the choice of instrument and the reasons for its choice in each separate soft law act.[102]

[102] See Chapter 11.

5. ESMA's decision-making process

Once EU agencies have found a legal basis to act, and where the exercise of their power remains within the boundaries of the principles of subsidiarity and proportionality, it is time to start the decision-making process, that is, the actual drafting and adoption of the soft law instruments. This entails the third stage of the policy cycle. The focus of this chapter is therefore on how ESMA's soft law instruments are elaborated and adopted and which procedural requirements have to be adhered to. Since participation is a significant attribute of public decision-making and is thus directly connected with the public decision-making processes of the European Union,[1] this chapter deals with the principle of participation. Participation relates to the involvement of citizens and stakeholders in the decision-making process.[2]

Given the importance of the decision-making process for the legitimacy and effectiveness of ESMA's rule-making powers, the aim of this chapter is to demonstrate the extent to which the principle of participation entails obligations for EU agencies' rule-making. Section 1 demonstrates the practical relevance of participation for ESMA by presenting exemplary considerations on the decision-making process. Sections 2–6 investigate the role of national competent authorities and external stakeholders in the rule-making process (participation) both from a *de iure* and a *de facto* perspective. Section 7 assesses the influence of ESMA's *de iure* and *de facto* practice on the legitimacy and effectiveness of soft law-making by ESMA. The chapter concludes that participation is important for the decision-making processes of ESMA, although risks lurk with regard to regulatory capture and imbalanced stakeholder involvement; that there is a need to officially recognise participation rights; that the involvement of national competent authorities actually exceeds mere participation; and that there is fairly limited involvement of the Union institutions.

---

1 Curtin & Dekker 2005, pp. 5 and 10; Craig 2012, p. 165. In the EU agency context, the concerns about participation and transparency in the procedure are broader than just for ESMA. For instance, in the case of ECHA, Vaughan argues that 'the procedures for guidance production and amendment lack full participation and transparency. These are causes for concern': see Vaughan 2015a, p. 101.

2 See Chapter 2, Section 8.1.

1. DECISION-MAKING CONCERNS IN RELATION TO ESMA'S SOFT LAW INSTRUMENTS IN PRACTICE

Concerns with regard to participation are not merely of theoretical relevance. As follows from ESMA's practice, there are multiple moments during which the agency considers the decision-making process. This section provides some examples of instances during which participation reflection or problems generally come to the fore. These are mainly observed during the decision-making process itself, such as when the Commission rejects ESMA's draft technical standards, or during the discussions at the meetings of the Board of Supervisors. The example in the textbox that follows shows that ESMA is certainly aware of its duty to consult stakeholders where necessary and is unwilling to take its decisions without the required input.

> During the meeting of the Board of Supervisors in June 2015, the Board discussed the Guidelines on Sound Remuneration Policies under the UCITS Directive as presented by the Investment Management Standing Committee.[3] Among other things, the Board particularly examined the *need for further data and input from market participants* in the context of establishing a Capital Markets Union (CMU). The European Commission representative suggested gathering further input from market participants on the potential implications in the context of establishing a CMU. The Board took its decision at the same meeting and agreed that market participants should be consulted in particular on the impact of the cross-reading between securities markets legislation and prudential requirements in the context of establishing a CMU.

The next example shows that ESMA aims to provide sufficient guarantees in the consultation process. Indeed, the agency deems it important to have sufficient input from stakeholders. This is to be welcomed from the perspective of legitimacy, but could have an impact on efficiency as it makes the process lengthier.

> During the Board of Supervisors meeting of 11 July 2019, the Board discussed the Market Abuse Regulation (MAR) Regulatory Technical Standards (RTS) on cooperation with third countries, in particular whether a specific clause on ESMA's coordination and facilitation role should be

---

[3] ESMA, Board of Supervisors Summary of Conclusions of 24 and 25 September 2015 (ESMA/BS/140), 9–10.

included in the RTS. The Board decided against this, but did not adopt the RTS. Instead, it was agreed that ESMA would *first seek the opinion of the Securities and Markets Stakeholder Group (SMSG)* before submitting the RTS for approval to the Board of Supervisors.

This brief account shows the daily relevance of ESMA considering potential problems in relation to its decision-making process. We now turn to an investigation of the extent to which ESMA is subjected to the principle of participation.

2. ESMA'S DECISION-MAKING PROCESS: THE PRINCIPLE OF PARTICIPATION

EU agencies present a varied picture with regard to possible forms of participation in EU decision-making processes.[4] Quite a few regulations do not contain any specific provisions on the participation and consultation of stakeholders at all, whereas others do refer to participation or consultation. For instance, the members of the Administrative Council of the Community Plant Variety Office (CPVO) may be assisted, subject to their rules of procedure, by advisers or experts.[5] Besides, the Regulation of the European Food Safety Authority (EFSA) stipulates that there shall be open and transparent public consultations during the preparation, evaluation and revision of food law, except where urgency precludes this.[6] Likewise, the European Aviation Safety Agency (EASA) is also obliged to consult interested parties and to respond to their comments in writing.[7] This variety reflects the diversity of EU agencies. They are endowed with different functions and powers in accordance with the goals of integration pursued in the fields in which they operate,[8] so it is not surprising that the possibilities regarding participation also differ.[9] Hence, whenever EU agencies start the decision-making process with regard to their soft law-making powers, it is important for them to determine what obligations they are expected to fulfil in order to involve the public sufficiently.

---

4 Mendes 2011, p. 103.

5 Council Regulation (EC) No 2100/94, Art 37(2). Senden and Van den Brink point to the fact that the involvement of advisors or experts is not entirely at the discretion of the authorities concerned, because the assistance of advisors and experts must be laid down in the rules of procedure of the Administrative Council respectively: see Senden & Van den Brink 2012, p. 46.

6 EFSA Regulation, Art 9.

7 EASA Regulation, Art 115(1)(c). See also Craig 2012, p. 169.

8 Mendes 2011, p. 103.

9 Scholten 2014a shows that the differences are not always based on good reasons.

This section reveals the different forms of participation in the structure of ESMA.[10] These are demonstrated on the basis of a structured analysis of *who* is involved in what part of the process, *how* involvement takes place and the kind of *follow-up* by ESMA to this involvement. It considers the role of national competent authorities, expert stakeholders, citizens and the other Union institutions in the various stages of the decision-making process in relation to the three categories of ESMA's soft law instruments. It will also discuss the risks of imbalanced stakeholder involvement and regulatory capture for the independence of the agency. The section not only sets out what is required on the basis of the legislation (*de iure* level), but also shows how ESMA deals with its stakeholders in practice (*de facto* level). The peculiarities with regard to the different forms of participation and the three different categories of ESMA's soft law instruments are visualised in Table 5.1 and explained in the following subsections.

3. THE INVOLVEMENT OF NATIONAL COMPETENT AUTHORITIES IN THE DRAFTING PROCESS OF ESMA'S SOFT LAW INSTRUMENTS

ESMA starts its decision-making process with the actual drafting of its legal acts. Much of this work is carried out within the framework of ESMA's Standing Committees or Working Groups,[11] which draw together senior experts from the national competent authorities and are supported by ESMA

---

[10] Mendes' analysis of participatory structures in agencies and procedures involving them clarifies that different forms of organic and procedural participation have been created, respectively, in the structure of some agencies and in the legal regime under which they operate: see Mendes 2011, pp. 30 and 102. Organic participation takes place when the persons affected by the decision-making processes are included in the institutional structures with a consultative role (e.g. advisory bodies) or as interest representatives in decisional bodies. Mendes recognises that it is also referred to as institutionalised participation, but prefers the term organic, since procedural participation, being formalised by specific decisional structures, is also institutionalised. Procedural participation implies that participants remain outside institutional structures. The universe of participants is not *a priori* delimited. Participants are defined in relation to the subject matter of the specific decision-making procedure in which they intervene. This analysis in this book shows, however, that the distinction is no longer as black and white as Mendes suggests. Procedural participation does not necessarily exclude organic participation, and vice versa.

[11] For an overview of all of ESMA's Standing Committees, see ESMA, 'Standing Committees and other bodies' <www.esma.europa.eu/about-esma/working-methods/standing-committees> accessed 17 February 2021.

Table 5.1 *Forms of participation per category of ESMA's soft law instruments*

	Who participates?	**Draft technical standards**	**Guidelines and recommendations**	**Non-binding instruments**
Drafting in Standing Committee or Working Group	- Experts of national competent authorities (NCAs) - Commission representative as observer	Yes	Yes	Yes
Seeking input from Consultative Working Group	Appointed private stakeholders	Yes, on a case-by-case basis	Yes, on a case-by-case basis	Yes, on a case-by-case basis
Conducting open public consultations	Could be anyone, but targeted at private stakeholders	Yes, mandatory	Yes, where appropriate	- Q&As: only upon request of the BoS - Opinions to NCAs: yes, where appropriate - Other practical instruments and convergence tools: yes, where appropriate
Consulting Securities and Markets Group	Appointed private stakeholders	Yes, mandatory	Yes, where appropriate	- Q&As: only upon request of the BoS - Opinions to NCAs: yes, where appropriate - Other practical instruments and convergence tools: yes, where appropriate
Decision-making by ESMA Board of Supervisors	- Heads of national competent authorities (NCAs) - ESMA Chairperson - Commission, ESRB, EIOPA, EBA representative as observer	Yes, qualified majority vote	Yes, qualified majority vote	Yes, simple majority vote

staff members who act as '*rapporteurs*'.[12] The different Standing Committees and Working Groups are established on a permanent basis. Their involvement has an enormous impact on the rule-making process. Indeed, they are in a position to exert considerable influence on the content of the soft law acts, because they are the main drafters of the acts themselves. In this way, they may even be regarded as being the *de facto* regulators.

During the Standing Committee or Working Group meetings, the Chair asks which experts are willing to draft the first version of a new legal instrument. This usually results in a small working group that does the drafting. Normally 4–6 people volunteer, especially if something is very important in their jurisdiction. Some people always volunteer; some never do. Who drafts the guidelines is very much dependent on the topic and on the resources of the national competent authorities. The largest authorities have the most resources to draft documents – this is factual rather than political. Yet, the result is that the NCAs with the most money also have the most input and influence on the contents. Concerning the topic of the legal instrument, there are Member States where certain financial services or instruments do not exist, so there is no immediate interest for the national authority of such a country to help with the drafting. All in all, the more active the role of NCAs in the drafting, the more influence they will have on the content of a soft law act. If they want to act on this advantage, they need to allocate sufficient resources for this purpose.

Interestingly, ESMA cannot deviate from the drafts of the NCAs in the drafting process of its soft law acts. The agency may only propose amendments of a legal nature. It signals to the Standing Committee or Working Group members what does not work and what would go beyond the scope of ESMA's mandate and empowerments in the level 1 legislation. However, in the end, only the Standing Committee members can decide when a draft legal act has received enough support from all the NCA representatives in the Committee and when it is ready to be submitted to the Board of Supervisors for approval. It is therefore unfortunate that the public does not know who participates in these Committees and Groups or what has been discussed during their meetings, as no minutes are made available.[13]

---

[12] Ibid.

[13] The same goes for comitology committees that are consulted in the case of implementing acts. In every committee every EU country is represented: see Regulation (EU) No 182/2011, Art 3(2). In principle, Member States are free to decide who will be sent to a comitology committee meeting. Typically, Member States are represented by policy specialists working within ministries or in agencies to which the management of a particular policy has been delegated, but it is often unknown who exactly is attending: see Brandsma 2010, p. 45.

4. PARTICIPATION OF PRIVATE STAKEHOLDERS IN THE DRAFTING PROCESS OF ESMA'S SOFT LAW INSTRUMENTS

Next, the consultation of private stakeholders is an essential procedural step in the decision-making process concerning ESMA's soft law instruments. This section shows that it may take three forms. In the initial stage of the process, when ESMA develops its consultative proposals, the Standing Committees can (1) seek input from the external stakeholder representatives sitting in the corresponding Consultative Working Groups (CWG). When a first draft is ready, where appropriate, the agency (2) organises formal public consultations with the broader public and (3) asks the institutionally embedded Securities and Markets Stakeholder Group (SMSG) for advice. Such consultations may also be targeted towards particularly affected parties, such as retail investors.[14] Whereas the first and third forms may be regarded as a form of closed consultation of stakeholders, the second takes the form of an open public consultation. In a closed consultation, specific stakeholders with potential concerns or opinions on a policy are approached in order to include their views in the decision-making process.[15] In an open public consultation, in principle every citizen and organisation is invited to participate.[16]

It is worth mentioning that ESMA staff also regularly meet external stakeholders bilaterally or multilaterally for the purposes of discussing items within ESMA's central scope of action, that is, items related to risk assessments, the single rulebook, supervisory convergence or direct supervision.[17] For this purpose, external stakeholders are defined as 'any organisation or self-employed individual having the objective of directly or indirectly influencing the formulation or implementation of ESMA policy-making and implementation'.[18] This institutional practice could be regarded as a form of informal, yet closed, stakeholder consultation. When external stakeholders attend a meeting with ESMA staff, the existence of this meeting will be recorded on ESMA's website together with a brief description of the topics

---

[14] The need to actively seek out the views of retail investors is considered critical. 'For this reason, ESMA will place high importance on liaising with retail investors' representatives, including national associations representing their interests': ESMA, Public Statement on Consultation Practices (2020) ESMA34-39-969, 1.

[15] Marxsen established this with regard to the Commission, but it is true for other Union organs as well: see Marxsen 2015, p. 261.

[16] Ibid.

[17] ESMA, Procedure on publication of ESMA staff meetings with stakeholders (2016) ESMA/2016/1525, 4.

[18] Ibid.

discussed.[19] This type of information is published at the beginning of January, April, July and October, for the previous quarter, in order to reach the highest possible standards of transparency in ESMA's interactions with stakeholders.[20]

4.1 Consultative Working Groups

During the drafting process, the Standing Committee may discuss initial thoughts with its Consultative Working Group (CWG).[21] CWGs are mainly expected to advise and assist the Standing Committee on: (a) technical standards to be submitted to the European Commission; (b) guidelines, Q&As and other relevant guidance under ESMA's supervisory convergence mandate in relation to relevant legislative provisions within the Standing Committee's field of competence and (c) any issues in the context of the implementation and application of the relevant legislation; and (d) assessment of the potential impact of any measures contemplated by the Standing Committee.[22] They therefore play an important role with regard to ESMA's regulatory activity. A CWG group consists of private stakeholders, that is, market participants – including practitioners, consumers and end-users – that are drawn from across the Member States of the EU.[23] They are not intended to represent national or institutional interests and do not replace the important process of full consultation with all market participants and other stakeholders or the specific role of the Securities and Markets Stakeholder Group as set out in the ESMA Regulation.[24] Hence, CWG consultation could be regarded as an additional form of participation which has been established by ESMA beyond

---

19 ESMA does this because the agency is committed to the Treaty principles of openness and transparency: see ESMA, 'Working methods' <www.esma.europa.eu/about-esma/working-methods> accessed 17 February 2021. When external stakeholders attend a meeting with ESMA staff, the existence of this meeting will be recorded on ESMA's website together with a brief description of the topics discussed in application of ESMA's related policy: see ESMA, Procedure on publication of ESMA staff meetings with stakeholders (2016) ESMA/2016/1525.

20 See for instance ESMA, ESMA Staff Stakeholder contacts in the First Quarter 2020 (2020) ESMA20-92-154.

21 See 'Standing Committees and other bodies' <www.esma.europa.eu/about-esma/working-methods/standing-committees> accessed 17 February 2021.

22 ESMA, 'Call for expressions of interest: Consultative Working Group of the ESMA Secondary Markets Standing Committee' (2020) ESMA70-154-1934.

23 The composition of CWGs is known to the public: see ESMA, 'Standing Committees and other bodies' <www.esma.europa.eu/about-esma/working-methods/standing-committees> accessed 17 February 2021.

24 ESMA, 'Working methods' <www.esma.europa.eu/about-esma/working-methods> accessed 17 February 2021. See more on the consultations with market participants and the role of the SMSG in the following two subsections.

the requirements of its founding regulation, that is, as a form of institutional practice. The CWGs are part of the institutional structure of the agency. This includes persons that are affected by the decision-making process.[25] They are *a priori* selected for a renewable term of two years.[26] It is important to note that whether or not to seek input from the CWG is a matter at the discretion of the Standing Committee. Hence, it is not a mandatory step in the rule-making procedure of any of the three categories of ESMA's soft law instruments. Likewise, as the idea behind the CWGs is merely to discuss initial thoughts with the private stakeholders, the Standing Committees are not bound by their input. There is thus no possibility for the CWG members to claim that they should have been consulted or that ESMA should have taken their input into account.

4.2 The *De Iure* Obligations to Conduct Open Stakeholder Consultations

After the contingent participation of the Consultative Working Group, the next step for the Standing Committee is to consider whether it is required to consult publicly with all interested parties. There is no Treaty obligation for EU agencies to consult. For the moment, each agency therefore has to look at its own founding regulation. It may be observed that the ESMA Regulation contains much more far-reaching mechanisms to consult than most of the other EU agencies.[27] For instance, EASA's Management Board is required to establish transparent procedures which must 'whenever necessary, involve experts from relevant interested parties or draw on the expertise of the relevant European standardisation bodies or other specialised bodies' and include

---

[25] Their names and affiliations are published on ESMA's website: ESMA, 'Standing Committees and other bodies' <www.esma.europa.eu/about-esma/working-methods/standing-committees> accessed 17 February 2021.

[26] Every now and then, a call for candidates appears on ESMA's website in order to renew the composition of one of its Consultative Working Groups. See for instance the call for candidates of 4 June 2019 in which the agency invited interested stakeholders with suitable backgrounds to cast their interest for the CWG which advises ESMA's Investor Protection and Intermediaries Standing Committee (IPISC), as the two-year term of the existing CWG was soon to expire: ESMA, 'Call for expression of interest Consultative Working Group of ESMA's Investor Protection and Intermediaries Standing Committee (2019) ESMA35-30-658.

[27] See the comparison in Section 2. EFSA's website features a document entitled 'EFSA's approach on Public Consultation on scientific outputs'. This could be seen as the agency's own consultation standards: see EFSA, Guidelines on EFSA Consultations <https://efsa.onlinelibrary.wiley.com/doi/pdf/10.2903/sp.efsa.2018.EN-1390> accessed 17 February 2021.

wide consultation with interested parties in accordance with a timetable and following a procedure 'which includes an obligation on the agency to give a written response to the consultation process' in the case of opinions, certification specifications and other detailed specifications, acceptable means of compliance and guidance material issued by the agency.[28] This indicates a certain degree of consideration for those affected by the agency's regulatory action and a rather consistent involvement of interested persons in the decision-making process.[29]

With regard to ESMA, Articles 10(1) and 15(1) ESMA Regulation oblige the agency to conduct open public consultations on *draft regulatory and implementing technical standards*, unless such consultations are highly disproportionate in relation to the scope and impact of the technical standards concerned or in relation to the particular urgency of the matter.[30] Likewise, Article 16(2) requires the agency to conduct, where appropriate, open public consultations regarding its *guidelines and recommendations*. Such consultations have to be proportionate in relation to the scope, *nature* and impact of the guidelines and recommendations. In contrast to draft technical standards, ESMA has somewhat more leeway with respect to its guidelines and recommendations, as consultations are to be conducted 'where appropriate'[31] and consultations with regard to draft technical standards may only be skipped when this would be highly disproportionate. As a follow-up to its *de iure* obligations, ESMA has laid down its rules for consultations in a Public Statement on Consultation Practices.[32] These rules have particular significance when ESMA provides technical advice to the European Commission and when it develops draft regulatory or implementing technical standards, guidelines and recommendations.[33] The consultation process that ESMA has to follow with

---

28 EASA Regulation, Arts 115(1)(b) and (c).

29 Mendes 2011, p. 117.

30 This is in line with the Commission's duty to consult before proposing legislative acts as laid down in TEU, Art 11(3) and as elaborated in the Protocol on the application of the principles of subsidiarity and proportionality, Art 2, which states that 'in cases of exceptional urgency, the Commission shall not conduct such consultations'.

31 Busuioc 2013b, p. 119 states: 'The difference seems to be due to the different procedural outcome; that is, whereas the former result in the adoption of binding rules, the latter amount to the adoption of guidelines and recommendation. However, given the "strong" nature of these guidelines and recommendations as outlined above, one could question whether such a differentiation is indeed warranted.'

32 ESMA, Public Statement on Consultation Practices (2020) ESMA34-39-969. The other two ESAs did the same, see EBA, Public Statement on Consultation Practices (2012) EBA BS 2012 182 (II) (EBA DC 57- Annex1) and EIOPA, Public Statement on Consultation Practices (2011) EIOPA-BOS-11-016.

33 ESMA, Public Statement on Consultation Practices (2020) ESMA34-39-969, para 1.

regard to both draft technical standards and guidelines is institutionalised by the founding regulation. In this way, it is formalised as a mandatory step in the adoption procedures of both types of act, subject to the exceptions mentioned in the relevant provisions.[34] Nevertheless, the participants remain outside the institutional structure and are not *a priori* delimited.

In practice, the starting point is that ESMA always conducts open public consultations on its *draft technical standards* and *guidelines and recommendations*. This is also in line with Article 296 TFEU, which requires the institutions to adopt their legal acts in compliance with the applicable procedures and with the principle of proportionality. However, as the boxed examples below demonstrate, ESMA occasionally decides otherwise.

For instance, ESMA wanted to issue its Guidelines on risk measurement and the calculation of global exposure for certain types of structured UCITS in April 2011,[35] but CESR had already conducted consultations for its general guidelines on risk measurement and the calculation of global exposure and counterparty risk for UCITS in April–May 2010.[36] ESMA therefore considered it inappropriate to conduct new public consultations.[37]

The draft Implementing Technical Standards on penalties and measures under Directive 2009/65/EC (UCITS Directive) provide another example of a soft law act that has been adopted without conducting open public consultations. ESMA considered that this would have been disproportionate in relation to their scope and impact, taking into account that the addressees of the implementing technical standards would only be the national competent authorities of the Member States, not market participants.[38] Since the senior experts of the NCAs draft the technical standards themselves within the framework of the Standing Committees and the heads of the NCAs are responsible for the final decision-making within the framework of the Board of Supervisors, the addressees/public stakeholders have sufficient opportunities to express their views and are even in a position to prevent the

34 This might entail a participation right: see the assessment in Section 7.2.

35 ESMA, Guidelines to competent authorities and UCITS management companies on risk measurement and the calculation of global exposure for certain types of structured UCITS (2011) ESMA/2011/112, para 1.

36 CESR, CESR's Guidelines on risk measurement and the calculation of global exposure and counterparty risk for UCITS (2010) CESR/10-788.

37 See to that effect ESMA Regulation, Art 16(2).

38 Commission Implementing Regulation (EU) 2016/1212, recital 7. A similar reasoning was applied to ESMA, Guidelines and Recommendations regarding written agreements between members of CCP colleges (2013) ESMA/2013/661, para 21. Among other things, ESMA considered that it was not appropriate to hold an open public consultation given the limited impact of these Guidelines.

adoption of the legal act at hand, that is, by voting against the proposal, so that a qualified majority cannot be reached.[39]

Previously, the legal basis for ESMA's *non-binding instruments* did not oblige the agency to consult.[40] This has changed under the revised ESMA Regulation. Indeed, Article 28(2) ESMA Regulation now prescribes that ESMA is also required to conduct open public consultations in relation to its opinions and new practical instruments and convergence tools under the same conditions applicable to guidelines and recommendations. In addition, upon the instigation of three voting members of the Board of Supervisors, the Board may decide to request ESMA to conduct open public consultations in relation to Q&As. This is laid down in the ESMA Regulation in a new Article 16b(4). With these changes, the EU legislature has thus tilted the balance between efficiency and legitimacy towards the latter in the case of opinions and new practical instruments and convergence tools. Yet, in the case of Q&As, efficiency still plays a predominant role, because consultations will only take place in exceptional circumstances.

4.3 The *De Facto* Consultation Practices

As follows from practice, when consultations take place, they happen in any case on paper. A public hearing is sometimes additionally organised when it is considered desirable to speak with the addressees in person, such as in the case of credit rating agencies (CRAs).[41] After the consultation period is over, the responses are processed. The members of the Standing Committee then meet in person or have a conference call in order to discuss the content of the draft legal acts. This is done paragraph by paragraph or page by page, which sometimes results in lengthy meetings. During these debates, the NCA representatives suggest amendments of all kinds. Some prefer another definition of a particular term in order to include or exclude certain elements from the scope of the draft text. Others want a particular text to be reformulated or redrafted

---

[39] ESMA Regulation, Art 44(1) para 2: 'with regard to the acts specified in Articles 10 to 16 of this Regulation [...], the Board of Supervisors shall take decisions on the basis of a qualified majority of its members.'

[40] ESMA Regulation, Art 29.

[41] For example, on 24 February 2020 an open hearing took place on internal controls for CRAs, see ESMA, 'Open hearing on CP on internal controls for Credit Rating Agencies' <www.esma.europa.eu/press-news/hearings/open-hearing-cp-internal-controls-credit-rating-agencies> accessed 16 February 2021. For an overview of all hearings, see ESMA, 'Hearings' <www.esma.europa.eu/press-news/hearings> accessed 16 February 2021.

and focus on the smallest details. Still others advocate the deletion of a certain provision, paragraph, phrase or term. The representatives of the NCAs respond to each other's proposed amendments and enter into (sometimes heated) debates, especially if there are very contradictory topics. The Commission representative of each Standing Committee also provides input on an informal basis. ESMA staff take all the comments into account and update the previous draft accordingly. In the end, the texts are therefore often the result of negotiations and compromises with the NCAs. A new document is eventually sent to every member and, if necessary, a new discussion will take place during yet another meeting or conference call. If in the end a revised proposal is radically different from the original proposal on which consultations were based, ESMA may consult for a second time.[42] The process is repeated until an agreement has been reached or the deadline has passed. ESMA's legal department carries out a final legal review as soon as the text is agreed upon. Once all members of the Standing Committee have more or less agreed on a finalised version of the draft guidelines or technical standards, it will be submitted to the Board of Supervisors for approval.

As follows from the above, ESMA thus follows up on the feedback from private stakeholders by using it for the refinement of its draft legal acts, as the aim of such consultations is to reach consensus where possible between all interested and affected parties on what legislation or regulatory action is appropriate and to improve the agency's decision-making process.[43] Although ESMA does not have much discretion with regard to the decision whether to carry out open public consultations or not, the agency is not strictly bound by the responses of the private stakeholders. However, as will be discussed in Chapter 6, Section 4, the duty to give reasons (as part of the principle of transparency) entails that ESMA cannot simply ignore the feedback either. It has to respond to the arguments that have been put forward and to justify why it came to a different conclusion (if this is the case), so that the parties concerned get a better understanding of the motives behind ESMA's decisions.

4.4 The Securities and Markets Stakeholder Group

At the same time as carrying out the open public consultations, ESMA is obliged to request the advice of the Securities and Markets Stakeholder Group (SMSG).[44] It has two main roles. First of all, the SMSG is consulted on actions

---

42 ESMA, Public Statement on Consultation Practices (2020) ESMA34-39-969, p. 3.

43 Ibid., p. 1.

44 Each ESA has its own stakeholder group(s). For EBA, this is the Banking Stakeholder Group (BSG): see EBA Regulation, Art 37. EIOPA has two, namely the

taken in accordance with Articles 10 to 15 concerning *regulatory and implementing technical standards* and, where appropriate and to the extent that these do not concern individual financial market participants, Article 16 concerning *guidelines and recommendations*.[45] This requirement did not apply to ESMA's *other non-binding instruments* until the revision of its founding Regulation. ESMA now also has to request advice in the case of issuing opinions and new practical instruments and convergence tools (Article 28(2) ESMA Regulation), and may be required by the Board of Supervisors to do so in the case of Q&As (Article 16b(4) ESMA Regulation).

The SMSG is institutionally embedded in ESMA's organisational structure by virtue of Article 37(1) ESMA Regulation. At the same time, consulting the SMSG is formalised as a mandatory step of the adoption procedure and is only subject to the exceptions mentioned in Articles 10, 15, 16 and 28(2) ESMA Regulation. The SMSG's 30 members are very experienced high-level private stakeholders that are affected by the decision-making process.[46] They are selected for a fixed four-year term, following which a new selection procedure takes place.[47] Of these members, 13 are bound to represent, in balanced proportions, financial market participants operating in the Union.[48] Another 13 members must represent employees' representatives of financial market participants operating in the Union, consumers, users of financial services and representatives of small and medium-sized enterprises (SMEs).[49] Four of its members have to be independent top-ranking academics.[50] The members are appointed by the Board of Supervisors of ESMA, following an open and transparent selection procedure. In making its decision, the Board of Supervisors ensures, as far as possible, an appropriate reflection of diversity of the securities and markets sector, geographical and gender balance and the representation of stakeholders across the EU.[51] The SMSG elects its own chair from among its members for a term of two years.[52] As far as is possible, the

---

Insurance & Reinsurance Stakeholder Group (IRSG) and the Occupational Pensions Stakeholder Group (OPSG): see EIOPA Regulation, Art 37.

45 ESMA Regulation, Art 37(1).

46 The composition of the SMSG is made known to the public: see ESMA, 'SMSG' <www.esma.europa.eu/about-esma/governance/smsg> accessed 16 February 2021. This includes the names and a short CV of the members.

47 ESMA Regulation, Art 37(4). The members may serve two successive terms.

48 Ibid., Art 37(2).

49 Ibid.

50 Ibid.

51 Ibid., Art 37(3).

52 Ibid., Art 37(3a).

Group takes decisions by consensus.[53] In the event that a consensus has not been reached and decisions are put to a vote, agreement among two-thirds of the members present is required (except in relation to elections for the Chairperson or Vice-Chairperson).[54]

In practice, the starting point is that the SMSG is always formally consulted in the case of new draft technical standards or guidelines. During the meetings, the stakeholders provide extensive (technical) information and elaborate on what happens in the Member States where they are based and on what the national competent authorities in their countries do. They thus often point to good and bad practices at the national level or in their sector. Such consultations take place on the basis of ESMA's own initiative.

Second, on its own initiative, the SMSG may submit advice to ESMA on any issue related to the tasks of the agency, with a particular focus on the tasks set out in Articles 10 to 16 (draft technical standards, guidelines and recommendations) and Articles 29 (common supervisory culture), 30 (peer review) and 32 (assessment of market developments).[55] Since the revision of the ESMA Regulation, where members of the Group cannot agree on advice, one third of its members or the members representing one group of stakeholders are permitted to issue separate advice with a dissenting view. ESMA publishes on its website the advice of the SMSG, the separate advice of its members, the results of the Group's consultations and information on how advice and results of consultations have been taken into account.[56]

In terms of follow-up, ESMA takes the responses of the SMSG into account when it revises its draft legal acts. Although the agency does not have much discretion with regard to the decision to request the SMSG's advice, the agency is not strictly bound by the responses of the members of this group. The duty to give reasons applies in the same way as it does with regard to the open public consultations,[57] because Article 37(7) explicitly requires ESMA to publish how the arguments put forward by the SMSG have been taken into account. In practice, ESMA staff also attend the meetings of the SMSG and explain and justify their choices there.

---

[53] ESMA, Decision of the Securities and Markets Stakeholder Group Rules of procedure (2020) ESMA22-106-2371, Art 7(1).

[54] Ibid., Art 7(2).

[55] ESMA Regulation, Art 37(5).

[56] Ibid., Art 37(7).

[57] See Chapter 6, Section 4.

5. THE INVOLVEMENT OF NATIONAL COMPETENT AUTHORITIES IN TAKING THE FINAL DECISIONS ON ESMA'S SOFT LAW INSTRUMENTS (BOARD OF SUPERVISORS)

Once the consultations with private stakeholders are over and all of the members of the Standing Committee have agreed on a finalised version of the draft legal act, it will be submitted to the Board of Supervisors. Since the Board is the ultimate decision-making body, it has to adopt the draft technical standards and guidelines with a qualified majority vote, and the non-binding instruments such as opinions and Q&As with a simple majority vote.[58] The Chairperson is allowed to vote on the adoption of the non-binding instruments, but regarding the adoption of draft technical standards and guidelines, the heads of the NCAs are the only voting members.[59] Additionally, a Commission representative participates during the meetings of the Board, but has no right to vote. The representative merely has a watchdog function. He or she flags issues when the Commission considers that ESMA is going too far, or joins the discussions when more details are required from ESMA. Decision-making at ESMA is thus dominated by representatives of the Member States. These representatives are not simply national middle-level technocrats seconded to the agency:[60] their involvement has an enormous impact on the rule-making process, in the sense that they take the final decisions to adopt the agency's soft law acts. There is no way for ESMA to deviate from the Board's decisions. That is to say, it can neither annul a decision nor adopt a decision without the required majority of votes of the Board members. The role of the heads of the NCAs therefore cannot be labelled as mere participation. Instead, they may be regarded as the ones who have the *true decision-making powers*.

Such a structure creates the potential for conflicts of interest. As Busuioc puts it, 'it is these very board members who are to vote and adopt draft technical standards and guidelines that will be addressed to the authorities they head, or financial institutions within their Member State'.[61] As such, conflicts of interest run the risk of finding their way into the very substance of ESMA's work,[62] because groups of national supervisors could thwart agency

---

[58] ESMA Regulation, Art 44(1).

[59] Ibid., Art 40(1): the non-voting representatives are one representative of the Commission, one of the European Systemic Risk Board (ESRB) and one of each of the other two ESAs.

[60] This makes its decision-making structure different from other such agencies: see Craig 2012, p. 172.

[61] Busuioc 2013b, p. 121.

[62] Ibid.

rule-making.[63] In the case of ESMA, the risks of interference are further reinforced by the fact that the agency is partially funded by obligatory contributions from the NCAs.[64]

Such involvement may indeed pose risks for the independence of the agency, notwithstanding the fact that Article 42 ESMA Regulation proclaims the independence of the Board of Supervisors very clearly: 'The members of the Board of Supervisors shall act independently and objectively in the sole interest of the Union as a whole and shall neither seek nor take instructions from Union institutions or bodies, from any government of a Member State or from any other public or private body.'[65] It remains however questionable to what extent a Board consisting of, among others, German, Italian and Danish experts pursues the common interests of a policy area instead of the members' own national interests.[66] It has therefore been argued that the rule-making set-up is strongly at odds with the agency's independent mandate and thus risks jeopardising the legitimacy of ESMA's regulatory output.[67] As part of the ESA review, the Union legislator tried to improve this situation by adding a new obligation for all members of the Board of Supervisors, the Chairperson and non-voting representatives and observers participating in the meetings of the Board. Before such meetings, they have to accurately and completely declare the absence or existence of any interest which might be considered prejudicial to their independence in relation to any items on the agenda.[68] If there is a conflict of interest, they shall abstain from participating in the discussion of, and voting upon, such points.[69] The Board of Supervisors has to lay down in its rules of procedure the practical arrangements for the prevention and management of conflict of interest, including for the rule on declaration of interest.[70]

---

63 Ibid.

64 Ibid.

65 There are numerous references to 'independence' and 'acting in the Union interest alone' or 'in the sole interest of the Union' in other specific articles of the regulation. This reflects the fact that the ESMA model is strongly premised upon independence: see Busuioc 2013b, p. 120.

66 Shapiro 2011, p. 117.

67 Busuioc 2013b, p. 121.

68 ESMA Regulation, Art 42(3).

69 Ibid.

70 This obligation derives from ESMA Regulation, Art 42(4). See also ESMA, 'Decision of the Board of Supervisors adopting a policy on independence and decision-making processes for avoiding conflicts of interest (conflict of interest policy) for non-staff' (2020) ESMA-22-328-402. A specific agenda item is included in the Summary of Conclusions of each meeting of the Board of Supervisors in which the Board has to endorse the Chair's statement not to have received any indication by

6. THE ROLE OF THE UNION INSTITUTIONS

ESMA's soft law-making practice occurs for a large part in the shadow of the other Union institutions. Most importantly, this section shows that the European Parliament is only engaged in the case of draft *regulatory* technical standards in the sense that it may object to the entry into force of the final *delegated* act. The Parliament does not play any role regarding ESMA's draft *implementing* acts, guidelines and other non-binding instruments. The section also demonstrates that the Commission merely has a watchdog function at the Standing Committees, Working Groups and Board of Supervisors meetings.

6.1 Draft Regulatory and Implementing Technical Standards

After a decision on the basis of a qualified majority of the members of the Board of Supervisors, ESMA submits its draft *regulatory* and *implementing* technical standards to the Commission for adoption in order to give them binding legal effect. They then take the form of *delegated* acts under Article 290 TFEU or *implementing* acts under Article 291 TFEU.[71]

Throughout the process, the European Parliament and the Council merely have the right to be informed. For instance, they receive a copy of the draft technical standards at the same time as the Commission, and are notified when the Commission intends not to adopt a standard or to adopt it in part or with amendments. The Commission obviously plays a much larger role, because ESMA is completely dependent on the Commission's approval. Upon receipt, the Commission decides within three months whether or not to adopt a draft technical standard.[72] Very often, the Commission adopts the draft standard in full.[73] However, it retains the right to adopt the draft in part or with amendments, or indeed not at all.[74] In such a case, the Commission sends the draft technical standard back to ESMA, explaining why it does not intend to adopt

a Board Member of any interest which might be considered prejudicial to her/his independence in relation to any items on the agenda.

[71] ESMA Regulation, Arts 10–15.

[72] Ibid., Arts 10(1) and 15(1).

[73] In some cases, the Commission does propose amendments, though. For instance, on 17 December 2015, the European Commission informed ESMA of its intention to amend the draft ITS submitted by ESMA by including two additional equity indices: see ESMA, Opinion on Draft Implementing Technical Standards on main indices and recognised exchanges under the Capital Requirements Regulation (2016) ESMA/2016/163, para 3.

[74] ESMA Regulation, Arts 10(1) and 15(1).

it or explaining the reasons for its amendments.[75] However, the Commission's discretion in this regard is very low.

If the Commission adopts a *regulatory* technical standard, it has to notify it simultaneously to the European Parliament and the Council.[76] The latter two may object to a regulatory technical standard within a period of three months from this date of notification.[77] If neither the European Parliament nor the Council has objected to the regulatory technical standard, it is published in the Official Journal of the European Union and enters into force on the date stated therein.[78] In the case of an objection, the regulatory technical standard does not enter into force.[79] In accordance with Article 296 TFEU, the institution which objects is required to state its reasons for objecting to the regulatory technical standard.[80]

If the Commission amends or does not adopt a draft *regulatory* technical standard, it has to inform ESMA, the European Parliament and the Council, stating its reasons.[81] In this way, the Commission is placed in a position in which it has to justify itself to the agency[82] and the other Union institutions. Where appropriate, the Parliament and Council may invite the responsible EU Commissioner and the Chairperson of ESMA for an *ad hoc* meeting of the competent committee of the European Parliament or the Council to present and explain their differences.[83]

Although the procedure with regard to draft *implementing* technical standards is very similar to the case of draft regulatory technical standards,[84] the implementing technical standards are not subject to the privileges of the Council or European Parliament to revoke the delegation or object against their adoption. The entire procedure is therefore faster as the matter is more technical in nature.[85] They are considered to be acts of lesser importance and can therefore be adopted by the Commission on a mere proposal by ESMA.[86] The efficiency of the decision-making process is higher, yet the level of legitimacy is much lower as there is no parliamentary control. However, one might argue

75 Ibid.
76 ESMA Regulation, Art 11(2).
77 Ibid., Art 13(1).
78 Ibid., Art 13(2).
79 Ibid., Art 13(3).
80 Ibid.
81 ESMA Regulation, Art 14(1).
82 Busuioc 2013b, p. 116.
83 ESMA Regulation, Art 14(2).
84 Di Noia & Furlo 2012, p. 179.
85 Wymeersch 2012, p. 255.
86 Ibid., p. 254.

that this is justified due to the technical character of this type of executive rule-making.

The system regarding draft *implementing* and *regulatory* acts is in fact very similar to the Articles 290–291 TFEU approach. Indeed, the Parliament and Council may decide to revoke the delegation or to object to the entry into force of *delegated* acts by virtue of Articles 290(2)(a) and(b) TFEU. The institutions do not have this role with regard to *implementing* acts under Article 291 TFEU.

6.2 Guidelines and Recommendations

The other EU institutions are in no way involved in the adoption of ESMA's guidelines and recommendations.[87] The only relation that exists is that ESMA lists the guidelines and recommendations that have been issued in its annual report to the European Parliament, the Council, the Commission, the Court of Auditors and the European Economic and Social Committee.[88] This annual reporting does not lead to the proper involvement of the Union institutions in the decision-making process, however, but rather establishes an accountability relationship. Interestingly, under the previous ESMA Regulation, there was an obligation on ESMA to state which national competent authorities have not complied with its guidelines and recommendations, and to outline how it intends to ensure that the non-complying authorities concerned follow its guidelines and recommendations in the future. This obligation has been removed after the ESA review. Article 16 now seems to better reflect the nature of ESMA's guidelines; it actually allows national competent authorities to not follow them as long as they properly explain their reasons for not doing so. Making ESMA accountable for such non-compliance by requesting it to explain in its annual report to the Union institutions how it intends to ensure compliance by non-complying authorities in the future runs counter to the idea of guidelines and recommendations being soft law instruments.

6.3 Non-binding Instruments

With regard to ESMA's non-binding instruments, there was no role for the Union institutions in the decision-making process at all. Importantly, in relation to Q&As this has changed under the revised ESMA Regulation. The agency now has to forward all questions that require the interpretation of Union

---

[87] Except for the role of the Commission as observer in the Standing Committees and in the Board of Supervisors.

[88] ESMA Regulation, Art 16(4).

law to the Commission, thus giving the latter an important new role.[89] ESMA publishes on its website an overview of the pending questions that are forwarded to the Commission[90] and will have to publish the answers provided by the Commission once finalised and agreed upon by the Board of Supervisors. In contrast to ESMA's guidelines and recommendations, there is no formal obligation for the agency to render accountability to the Union institutions. Yet, in practice ESMA mentions the opinions, Q&As and supervisory briefings that have been issued in its annual report to the European Parliament, the Council, the Commission, the Court of Auditors and the European Economic and Social Committee.[91]

7. CONCLUSION AND ASSESSMENT ON THE DECISION-MAKING PROCESS

As follows from the analysis above, concerning draft *technical standards*, *guidelines and recommendations*, and *non-binding instruments*, the NCAs play an important role in the decision-making process; that is, their experts are responsible for the actual drafting of these acts within the Standing Committees and Working Groups, and their heads take the final decisions concerning the adoption of these acts within the Board of Supervisors. In this capacity they may be regarded as the *de facto* regulators and true decision-makers. In the case of draft technical standards and guidelines, there are three different variants of participation by private stakeholders. The Consultative Working Groups may be asked by the Standing Committees to discuss initial thoughts. Once a first version of a draft legal act is ready, open public consultations are carried out. Although anyone can respond, usually only private expert stakeholders participate and not EU citizens. The participants are not *a priori* delimited. At the same time, the high-level experts of the SMSG are requested to provide advice on the proposed legal text. All in all, ESMA thus has a high level of consultation with regard to its draft technical standards, guidelines, opinions and new convergence tools. ESMA can either follow or ignore the feedback from the private stakeholders. This applies to all the stakeholders, that is, those in the CWGs, those in the SMSG and those that respond to the open public consultations. However, in the latter two cases ESMA is required to respond to the arguments that have been put forward by the respondents by virtue of the duty to give reasons; it cannot simply ignore the feedback.

---

89 ESMA Regulation, Art 16b(5).

90 ESMA, 'Questions and Answers' <www.esma.europa.eu/questions-and-answers> accessed 17 February 2021.

91 For an example, see ESMA, Annual Report 2019 (2020) ESMA20-95-1264.

The other EU institutions are not involved in the decision-making process regarding guidelines and non-binding instruments and *implementing* technical standards. The European Parliament and Council may however object to the adoption of *regulatory* technical standards. The Commission merely has a watchdog function in the meetings of the Standing Committees, Working Groups and Board of Supervisors.

With regard to ESMA's *Q&As*, the NCAs play a similar role in the Standing Committees and Working Groups as well as in the Board of Supervisors. However, private stakeholders only have a say if the Board of Supervisors requests that ESMA conducts open public consultations or asks for advice from the SMSG, or if the national experts sitting in the Standing Committees decide to discuss initial thoughts with their CWG. Since there is no obligation for the Standing Committee and Board to do so, this means that some soft law acts may be adopted with no private stakeholder involvement whatsoever. Even if the CWG has been approached, no documentation on this will be available online. Hence, in the current situation, it is unclear if and how ESMA has taken into account the views of the private stakeholders sitting in the CWG. The Union institutions have no involvement in the decision-making process regarding non-binding instruments either. These tools therefore suffer from a rather low level of legitimacy and their final quality may be said to be lower than that of any of ESMA's other soft law instruments, because experts in the field have only been heard to a limited extent, if at all. Yet, the fact that stakeholders might in some cases be consulted through public consultations is an improvement, because this was not the case before the ESA review.

The following sections conclude this chapter and provide an assessment of where ESMA's decision-making processes lead to tensions on the basis of legitimacy and effectiveness concerns.

7.1 The Risks of Imbalanced Stakeholder Involvement and Regulatory Capture Threaten Legitimacy

Notwithstanding the potential benefits of participation from the perspective of legitimacy and effectiveness, we should be aware of the risks of imbalanced stakeholder involvement and regulatory capture.

To begin with, stakeholder involvement runs the risk of imbalanced involvement by actors, since the decision-making process most of all increases the opportunities of those actors with the technical and financial resources and a particular interest in participating.[92] As such, the involvement of citizens

---

92 Senden & Van den Brink 2012, p. 47 and Shapiro 2011, p. 116.

is potentially affected by wealthy stakeholders,[93] because complexity might increase participation costs to a level afforded by only well-resourced industry players.[94] This may lead to imbalanced representation in the rule-making process, in which case it is difficult to argue that the 'will of the people' is reflected and that the demands of input legitimacy are met.[95] The strong institutional embedding of stakeholder groups may even exacerbate this problem of imbalanced involvement, if no guarantees for balanced representation are provided for at the same time.[96] In such a case, EU agencies are considered to provide at most for some form of technical accountability, rather than any democratic accountability. Indeed, accountability towards the 'epistemic community' (that is, a group of expert actors that share the same values, often know each other personally, and so on) usually plays a much bigger role than accountability towards the Member States and to the citizenry as a whole.[97]

In theory, regular citizens thus have a possibility to participate in the rule-making procedures of ESMA through the open public consultation process.[98] This relates to the promise of open consultations to increase the legitimacy of the EU, as they are supposed to allow citizens to raise their voice within decision-making processes.[99] However, the agency's discussion

---

93 Marxsen also observed in relation to consultations by the Commission that 'participating at the EU level is cost intensive: understanding and analysing the Commission's proposals and answering its questions require experts and those usually do not work for free but need to be employed'. Hence, the problem for public participation is often financial: see Marxsen 2015, p. 278.

94 Schemmel 2016, p. 478. Likewise, in the case of Commission consultations, the main finding of the research by Marxsen is that 'business and industry organisations dominate the consultative process while the participation of citizens and not-for-profit organisations is generally weak'. He concludes that 'the consultation process as one mechanism of participatory governance does not provide a functioning new way of legitimation. It allows stakeholders to participate and in that sense gives voice to them. However, this abstract possibility does not necessarily lead to an actually broader and above all more representative participation and, hence, does not automatically lead to an increased legitimacy of governing institutions.' See Marxsen 2015, p. 280.

95 Scharpf 1999, p. 6.

96 Senden & Van den Brink 2012, p. 47.

97 Ibid., pp. 47 and 68; Schapiro 2011, p. 117.

98 It is also not common for other agencies to consult regular citizens. Exceptionally, the ESA held the first Citizens' Debate on Space for Europe. During this day, citizens had the opportunity to learn, debate, have their say and participate by suggesting priorities on all aspects of current and future space programmes: see ESA, 'No 27–2016: 10 September 2016: Citizens' debate on space for Europe in all ESA Member States' (1 July 2016) <www.esa.int/For_Media/Press_Releases/10_September_2016_Citizens_debate_on_Space_for_Europe_in_all_ESA_Member_States> accessed 17 February 2021.

99 Marxsen 2015, p. 261.

and consultation papers do not attract much public attention in practice. Nonetheless, a lack of public interest and relevance is certainly not the reason for such under-representation.[100] The reason is, rather, the technical nature of ESMA's work, which makes it difficult for citizens to take any role in the conversation.[101] Indeed, participating in EU affairs is not something the average individual can do.[102] This in itself stands as proof of the fundamental democracy problems in the making of these policies.[103] People may feel that the EU decision-making process is dominated by experts, and that real democratic control is lacking.[104] To make things worse, the European Parliament is not involved, whether formally or informally, which then means that the citizen has no representation whatsoever at the EU level.[105] But ESMA's work has a significant impact on citizens' daily experiences and their welfare. The representation issue has already led to a serious clash at the EU level.[106] On the basis of an alleged breach of EU law for failing to ensure an adequate balance between the representatives of the industry and those of users and consumers,[107] a complaint against ESMA's Stakeholder Group has been filed with the Ombudsman.[108] The issue of balanced representation is thus of practical relevance to the people as well.

Two different views can be held with regard to the involvement of citizens in technical rule-making processes. Some argue that policies regulating markets and the economy are inherently technical.[109] Thus, experts should

---

[100] For instance, the consultations on the regulations for credit rating agencies had almost no participation by not-for-profit groups, although the practical relevance, especially in light of the economic crisis at that time, is evident. See also Marxsen, p. 279.

[101] Cengiz 2016.

[102] Buijze 2013, p. 44.

[103] Cengiz 2016.

[104] Buijze 2013, p. 44.

[105] This is usually the case with regard to soft law-making: see Ehnert 2015, p. 59.

[106] Schemmel 2016, p. 477.

[107] As is required on the basis of ESMA Regulation, Art 37(1), which legally guarantees a balanced representation.

[108] European Ombudsman, 'The composition of ESMA's 30-member Securities and Markets Stakeholders Group' 545/2014/LP (10 October 2016). Previously, the European Ombudsman formally opened an inquiry to investigate an alleged breach of Union law by a biased composition of the Stakeholder Groups of EBA and EIOPA. As a response, the two agencies chose to dissolve their already established groups and to reappoint them with a more balanced cast. See: European Ombudsman, 'Decision of the European Ombudsman closing her inquiries into complaints 1874/2011/(EIS)LP and 1877/2011/(EIS) LP against the European Insurance and Occupational Pensions Authority' 1874/2011/LP (26 February 2014); European Ombudsman, 'Decision of the European Ombudsman closing her inquiry into complaint 1876/2011/(EIS)LP against the European Banking Authority' 1876/2021/LP (19 December 2003).

[109] Cengiz 2016.

have the primary say in these policies, as citizens do not have as much to contribute to the discussion.[110] According to such a position, it is questionable whether citizen participation is even desirable with regard to technical decision-making.[111] Given the fact that stakeholders are generally the ones with expertise, well-organised stakeholder involvement may be far more important. However, others contend that economic policies have a significant impact on citizens' welfare, which makes citizen participation a must in policy-making[112] – but for this to happen, the currently inaccessible, overly technical discourses should be replaced with accessible, simple, citizen-friendly ones.[113]

In my view, input legitimacy in the sense of direct or indirect participation by citizens is not required for this type of executive rule-making exercised by ESMA. The feedback of stakeholders during open public consultations is a sufficient means to legitimate the soft law acts of ESMA in the decision-making process, that is, throughput legitimacy. It is however important to always ensure an appropriate balance in the Securities and Markets Stakeholder Group, including representatives of consumers and end users at all times.[114]

Another risk of involving only industry in the rule-making process is that of 'regulatory capture'. Capture refers to the situation in which a regulated industry is able to control decisions made by regulators about that industry.[115] In other words, the industry 'captures' regulatory decision-making, so that what regulators decide is what industry prefers they decide.[116] Industry is then able to use regulation to steer benefits to itself over other potential targets of those benefits.[117] Stakeholder involvement may thus be seen as a double-edged sword, contributing to agency accountability and control, but with an inevitable risk of dependence on the regulated industry.[118] But this is a risk that should be prohibited because it hampers the agency's independence.[119] It also

---

110 Ibid.

111 Ibid. Cengiz argues that citizen participation is required if both input and output legitimacy concerns have to be met.

112 Ibid.

113 Ibid.

114 Note that as part of the ESA review, the Union legislator reconsidered the composition of the stakeholder groups of the ESAs and specified that 13 members must represent employees' representatives of financial market participants operating in the Union, consumers, users of financial services and representatives of Small and Medium-sized Enterprises (SMEs): see ESMA Regulation, Art 37(2).

115 Mitnick 2011, p. 35; Ottow 2015; Aelen 2014.

116 Ibid.

117 Ibid., and Ossege 2016.

118 Arras & Braun 2017, p. 3.

119 Independence is important, since it is the most distinctive feature of EU agencies. It implies that they have to be free of both political and industry interests: see Chapter

hinders a proper implementation of Article 298 TFEU, which provides that the institutions, bodies, offices and agencies of the Union require the support of an open, efficient and independent European administration when carrying out their missions.

Since participation and independence are both important features of a legitimate and effective rule-making process, a balance needs to be struck between participation and consultation mechanisms, on the one hand, and the independence of the regulator, on the other. ESMA needs to take the views from the field into account when drafting the rules, but should be careful to retain its own opinion as well, and, in this way, its discretion to decide.[120] However, regulators should not be completely isolated from any form of control either. Independent is not supposed to mean 'unaccountable'.[121]

7.2 The Need to Recognise Participation Rights

The above analysis shows that ESMA's practice of carrying out open public consultations and consulting the SMSG regarding its draft technical standards, guidelines and new convergence tools comes close to the existence of *participation rights* for private stakeholders. Such consultations are formalised as mandatory steps in the decision-making process, so the agency does not have much discretion with regard to the choice to consult or not – although there are some exceptions, as mentioned in the relevant provisions.[122] It therefore seems likely that stakeholders would want to challenge a soft law act when open public consultations have not taken place in a case where they think they should have been consulted, or where they have not received feedback on their input, or where ESMA's consultation period is considered to be too short.[123] Likewise, a situation could arise in which the SMSG believes it should have been consulted in a case in which ESMA has decided not to involve the group.

1, Section 6.1. In the context of the European Union, it also refers to national interests: see Scholten & Van Rijsbergen 2014b.

[120] However, regulators should not be completely isolated from any form of control either. Independent is not supposed to mean 'unaccountable': see Scholten 2014b. See Chapter 10 on the possibility to hold ESMA judicially accountable.

[121] Scholten 2011 and Scholten 2014b.

[122] Concerning technical standards, consultations are mandatory, unless they are disproportionate in relation to the scope and impact of the technical standards concerned or in relation to the particular urgency of the matter: see ESMA Regulation, Arts 10(1) and 15(1). Concerning guidelines, consultations have to be proportionate in relation to the scope, *nature* and impact of the guidelines and recommendations: see ESMA Regulation, Art 16.

[123] Legally speaking, a failure to have followed the adoption procedures can result in the annulment of the measure.

An important difference is, however, that the SMSG may also submit advice to ESMA on its own initiative.

On the question whether any participation rights should be recognised at the Union level, there are differing views. Some argue that a situation in which a proposal could be challenged in the court, on the grounds that interested parties had allegedly not been consulted, must be avoided. According to the Commission, 'such an over-legalistic approach would be incompatible with the need for timely delivery of policy, and with the expectations of the citizens that the European Institutions should deliver on substance rather than concentrating on procedures'.[124] However, others are of the opinion that a duty to consult risks remaining a purely formal way of legitimising decisions if it is not paired with the possibility to seek judicial control where, for instance, an organisation feels that the feedback offered by the Commission regarding its contribution to an EU consultation is not satisfactory.[125] Indeed, we must ensure that throughput legitimacy is not viewed as a 'tick-box' exercise.[126] The recognition of any participation right thus involves a weighing of legitimacy with effectiveness. Participation rights would enhance legitimacy, but may at the same time hamper the efficiency of the process by making it more rigid and slow.

If participation rights are to be recognised, there must at least be resources that interested parties can use to control whether and how actors with rule-making powers adhere to the principle of participation. That control could be regarded as the necessary corollary of the principle. There is first of all a role to play for the European Ombudsman, who is empowered by virtue of Article 228(1) TFEU[127] to investigate complaints from EU citizens, natural and legal persons concerning instances of maladministration in the activities of the Union institutions, bodies, offices or agencies, with the exception of the CJEU acting in its judicial role.[128] Additionally, a role could be foreseen for the EU Courts. Indeed, the question is whether it would be possible to challenge the

---

[124] Commission, Communication, 'Towards a reinforced culture of consultation and dialogue: General principles and minimum standards for consultation of interested parties by the Commission' COM(2002) 704 final 10. See also Alemanno 2009, p. 392 and Obradovic & Alonso Vizcaino 2006, p. 1059.

[125] Ibid.

[126] Schmidt & Wood 2019.

[127] See also the Charter of Fundamental Rights of the EU, Art 43. This provision does not as yet explicitly mention EU agencies, though.

[128] Obradovic & Alonso Vizcaino 2006, p. 1059. The decision-making practice of the European Ombudsman shows that it will consider as maladministration a failure to act by the Commission in accordance with the consultation guidelines that it established itself: see Senden 2011, pp. 27–48.

final legislative act for an alleged lack of consultation of interested parties.[129] The answer is yes. Judicial review of the procedural requirements laid down in Articles 10, 15, 16 and 29(2) ESMA Regulation may be envisaged when a Union Court, called upon to review the legality of the final act within the context of an Article 263 or 267 TFEU procedure, has to examine an alleged violation of a procedural requirement. For instance, a Member State, an institution or even an individual – provided that that individual satisfies the locus standi conditions in the case of a direct action – could raise the issue of ESMA's non-compliance with the procedural requirements before the courts.[130] The claimant could then argue that the soft law act at issue is not legitimate, because a procedural step has been skipped.[131] In such a case, judicial review is used in order to effectuate the right to participation.[132] All in all, in the case of ESMA, *participation rights* should be acknowledged for the stakeholders participating in the open public consultations in relation to technical standards, guidelines and new convergence tools. This does not apply to Q&As, because public consultations are not a standard step in the decision-making process. Instead, ESMA is obliged to conduct such consultations merely upon request by the Board of Supervisors.[133] Only if the agency does not give follow-up to this request will stakeholders be able to invoke their right to participate.

Contrarily, there is *no right to participate* for the stakeholders in the Consultative Working Groups, because it is at the discretion of the Standing Committees whether or not to seek input from the CWGs. Hence, it does not entail a mandatory step of the rule-making procedure. Likewise, as the idea behind the CWGs is merely to discuss initial thoughts with the private stakeholders, the Standing Committees are not bound by their input. There is

---

[129] Alemanno 2009, p. 383.

[130] On this point, one has to note that, although the case-law of the EU courts is particularly restrictive in the interpretation of the locus standi requirements for private parties, a 'participation exception' has been recognised, whereby an individual enjoys standing before a Union court when it enjoys 'specific procedural guarantees conferring upon [it] a right to participate in the political process'. According to Scott and Sturm, in a new governance setting it would seem appropriate to acknowledge standing even when a party's entitlement to participate is not legally mandated: see Scott & Sturm 2007, pp. 579–80.

[131] Alemanno argued that '[t]o be successful, the plaintiff will have to prove that a consultation represents a binding step in the decision-making process, whose omission, or incorrect application, might affect the legality of the final act': see Alemanno 2009, p. 396. In this regard, it is very helpful that ESMA conforms to the giving reasons requirement of the principle of transparency, because that allows the addressees to review whether the decision was legitimate and to decide whether they want to challenge it: see Chapter 6, Section 4.

[132] See Chapter 10 on judicial review and the conclusions in Chapter 11.

[133] ESMA Regulation, Art 16b(4).

thus no possibility for the CWG members to claim that they should have been consulted or that ESMA should have taken their input into account.

7.3 Involvement of National Competent Authorities Exceeds Mere Participation

The involvement of national competent authorities in ESMA's decision-making process goes much further than mere participation. They may in fact be regarded as the *de facto* regulators and as the ones having *true decision-making powers*. ESMA cannot deviate from their drafts, nor from what they decide within the framework of the Board of Supervisors. Only the Standing Committee can decide when a soft law act is ready to be submitted to the Board of Supervisors for approval. If the Board does not reach a qualified majority, the soft law act is simply not going to be adopted. The agency itself cannot do anything about this, except for trying to convince the Standing Committee to redraft the act and to submit the proposal for approval to the Board once again.

In this regard, the investigation in this chapter shows that ESMA has an interesting position within the EU institutional structure, because it has elements of being a 'shadow Commission' as well as a 'shadow Council'. On the one hand, ESMA has the right of initiative and has to carry out the consultations, which is similar to what the Commission does in the Union legislative process. On the other hand, Member States' authorities are the key players in the drafting and decision-making of the acts, which is similar to what the Council does. Although ESMA officially has the status of an EU agency, in practice it mostly operates as a conglomerate of the national authorities.

The adoption of the Interinstitutional Agreement on Better Law-Making shows that there seems to be a greater need to involve the Member States in EU rule-making and to obtain their input. Indeed, representatives of the Member States are now also consulted with regard to delegated acts. There is political and institutional pressure on the Commission not only to consult private stakeholders, but also to engage national representatives. It is therefore not surprising that the national competent authorities have been assigned such an important role within the institutional structure of ESMA, although their involvement goes much further than consultation of Member States' experts, as intended with regard to delegated acts. Since the aim is that the rules are actually applied and complied with, it is meaningful to ensure that there is support under NCAs, as they are ultimately responsible for taking the rules into account while carrying out their supervision activities. Their involvement thus most likely results in a higher compliance rate and therefore contributes to effectiveness. Likewise, given the fact that the Member States are the ones with expertise at the national level, their involvement leads to enhanced legitimacy.

7.4 Limited Involvement of the Union Institutions

With regard to the involvement of the Union institutions, the following may be noted. In relation to all three categories of ESMA's soft law instruments, the Commission participates in the Standing Committees and Working Groups during the discussions of the draft legal acts, but it does not play a role in the actual drafting of the texts. Its representative merely has a watchdog function and signals when the agency is going too far or when more details are required from ESMA. Likewise, the Commission only has a role as an observer during the Board of Supervisors' meetings, and has no right to vote. The Commission is thus rigidly constrained, both legally and politically, in terms of any amendment to draft soft law acts.[134] The legal and political reality is therefore that ESMA is run by the Member States through top-level national officials in a manner that is very different in comparison to other EU agencies.[135]

Except for the right to be informed, the other EU institutions are in no way involved in the adoption of ESMA's guidelines and recommendations, opinions and new convergence tools.[136] This raises the question as to whether the current procedure with open public consultations is sufficiently legitimate. It merely engages expert stakeholders, thus giving the guidelines an elevated level of technocratic throughput legitimacy rather than democratic input legitimacy. A further consideration is therefore whether or not a role should be foreseen for the European Parliament in the decision-making process of ESMA's guidelines. The Parliament represents all Union citizens and it is clear that citizens cannot easily make themselves heard at EU agencies due to the highly technical nature of the soft law instruments. Nonetheless, the lack of parliamentary involvement can be justified precisely because of this technical nature. There is less of a need for democratic input legitimacy for this type of executive rule-making. Besides, with this well-organised consultation process the guidelines are legitimised in another, more appropriate way. The Commission is also of the opinion that the appointment of MEPs would be inappropriate in view of the agency's regulatory work.[137] The fear is that the European Parliament could then exercise external political supervision over their actions.[138]

---

[134] Craig 2012, p. 174.

[135] Ibid., 172.

[136] Except for the role of the Commission as observer in the Standing Committees and in the Board of Supervisors.

[137] Commission, 'Communication on the operating framework for the European Regulatory Agencies' COM(2002) 718 final 5.

[138] Ibid.

With regard to the majority of ESMA's Q&As, there is no role for any of the Union institutions here either. Legitimacy is of more concern here, because expert stakeholders are in principle not involved through open consultations either. This means that the lack of democratic input legitimacy is not evened out by technocratic throughput legitimacy. Yet, given the legal nature of this category of soft law instruments, it could be held that the demands stemming from legitimacy should not be as high. Indeed, they only produce *de facto* effects, they do not impose an extra layer of requirements and compliance is voluntary.[139] Nonetheless, given the importance Q&As have in practice, it is to be welcomed that the Union legislator took the ESA review as an opportunity to create a possibility for the Board of Supervisors to request ESMA to conduct consultations or to request advice from the SMSG. This can be done on a case-by-case basis only and should not be seen as a standard step in the decision-making process. So far, ESMA has not received any such requests from the Board of Supervisors. It therefore remains to be seen how often, and for what reasons, this will happen in practice.

Where Q&As require the interpretation of Union law, ESMA now has to forward such questions to the Commission, thus giving the latter an important new role.[140] This makes sense where it concerns the underlying legislation to which the Q&As are related, because it entails a better reflection of the horizontal division of powers. It underlines the inter-institutional relations and thus relates to the way in which tasks and competences are distributed between the EU institutions by the Treaty on European Union. Nevertheless, the Court of Justice of the EU of course has the final say on the definitive interpretation of EU law.

---

139 See further on this in Chapter 8, Sections 3.3, 4.4 and 4.5.

140 ESMA Regulation, Art 16b(5).

6. Transparency with regard to ESMA's soft law instruments

Similar to participation, transparency is a significant attribute of public decision-making and is thus also directly connected with the public decision-making processes of the European Union.[1] This chapter therefore deals with the principle of transparency in relation to ESMA's output. Transparency deals with the right of access to documents and the duty to give reasons, and entails publication and translation requirements.[2] It involves the fourth stage of the policy cycle.

Given the importance of transparency for the legitimacy and effectiveness of ESMA's rule-making powers, the aim of this chapter is to demonstrate the extent to which the principle of transparency entails obligations for EU agencies' rule-making. Section 1 demonstrates the practical relevance of transparency for ESMA by presenting exemplary considerations regarding its soft law instruments. Sections 2–5 investigate what is already regulated in the ESMA regulation regarding access to documents, the duty to give reasons and publication and translation (*de iure* level), and what happens in practice in this regard (*de facto* level). Section 6 assesses the influence of ESMA's *de iure* and *de facto* practice on the legitimacy and effectiveness of soft law-making by ESMA. The chapter concludes that transparency plays a crucial role, although the strictness of the requirements depends on the category of soft law instrument in question, hence resulting in different levels of legitimacy and effectiveness. It also concludes that the amended ESMA Regulation entails a step towards equalisation in relation to the requirement to give reasons.

---

[1] Curtin & Dekker 2005, pp. 5 and 10; Craig 2012, p. 165. In the EU agency context, the concerns about participation and transparency in the procedure are broader than just for ESMA. For instance, in the case of ECHA, Vaughan argues that 'the procedures for guidance production and amendment lack full participation and transparency. These are causes for concern': see Vaughan 2015a, p. 101.

[2] See Chapter 2, Section 9.

1. TRANSPARENCY CONCERNS IN RELATION TO ESMA'S SOFT LAW INSTRUMENTS IN PRACTICE

Concerns with regard to transparency are not merely of theoretical relevance. As follows from ESMA's practice, there are multiple points at which the agency considers transparency regarding its soft law instruments. This section provides some examples of the instances during which transparency reflections or problems generally come to the fore. These are mainly observed during the discussions at the meetings of the Board of Supervisors.

The example in the following box demonstrates the fact that the agency takes the principle of transparency seriously. In this case, it was particularly concerned about the publication requirement.

> At the January 2019 meeting of the Board of Supervisors, the Board discussed the supervisory briefing on the supervision of non-EU branches of EU firms providing investment services and activities.[3] The briefing was designed to assist NCAs in their supervision of EU firms' establishment of branches in non-EU countries. The Board had a debate on the scope of the supervisory briefing and whether further coordination was needed with prudential authorities as well as on the question *whether or not the briefing should be published.* Eventually, the Board adopted the briefing and agreed to its publication.

This brief account shows the daily relevance of ESMA considering potential problems in relation to transparency. We now turn to an investigation of the extent to which ESMA is subjected to the principle of transparency.

2. ESMA'S SOFT LAW INSTRUMENTS: THE PRINCIPLE OF TRANSPARENCY

EU agencies are required to conduct their work as openly as possible, to grant access to their documents and to ensure that their proceedings are transparent.[4] Hence, whenever EU agencies are using soft law-making powers, they have to adhere to the transparency requirements during the process. The establishing regulations of EU agencies differ considerably as to the extent to which

---

[3] ESMA, Board of Supervisors Summary of Conclusions of 30 January 2019 (23 April 2019) ESMA22-106-1676, p. 4.

[4] TFEU, Art 15.

they mention transparency.[5] In the case of newer agencies, the regulations generally include a broader and more fundamental collection of transparency obligations. For example, the ESAs are required to publish the results of public consultation processes. In contrast, the scope of the transparency policies of older agencies is often limited and more *ad hoc* in nature.[6] These agencies frequently adopt soft law on the basis of procedures that are characterised by an extreme absence of transparency; for example, the participating stakeholders are not identified, no information is provided about their views, and the measures are often poorly reasoned.[7] As a result, a wide range of obligations may be observed in the establishing regulations with a view to making their actions and decisions public.[8] This may be partly explained by the fact that 'agencies deal with different subject matters and that transparency may be relatively more or less important in some areas rather than others'.[9] This explanation is unconvincing, however, given the fact that the requirements stemming from the principle of transparency are important in all public decision-making.[10]

This section demonstrates the extent to which ESMA takes account of the right to have access to documents and the duty to give reasons, as well as the publication and translation requirements when it issues one of its soft law acts. It not only sets out where to find the *de iure* requirements that ESMA needs to take into account, but also shows how the agency deals with them in practice. The section shows that the requirements of the principle of transparency have to be fulfilled in a different way in relation to each category of soft law instrument.

3. ACCESS TO DOCUMENTS

As an EU agency, ESMA is obliged to provide access to its documents on the basis of Article 15(3), first subparagraph, TFEU. In addition, Article 72(1) ESMA Regulation explicitly applies Regulation 1049/2001/EC on public access to documents.[11] Given the broad definition of a 'document' in Article

---

5 Craig 2012, p. 166.

6 Senden & Van den Brink 2012, p. 44.

7 Scott 2011, p. 336.

8 Senden & Van den Brink 2012, p. 44.

9 Craig 2012, p. 166.

10 Ibid.

11 ESMA Regulation, Art 72(1): 'Regulation (EC) No 1049/2001 shall apply to documents held by the Authority.' EU agency practices differ: some of them also have a reference to this regulation in their founding acts; others (often older) do not.

3(1) of the latter regulation,[12] this requirement equally concerns *all three categories of ESMA's soft law instruments.*

Pursuant to Articles 47(5) and 72(2) ESMA Regulation, the Management Board adopted by decision practical measures for applying the Regulation on access to documents.[13] This decision clarifies that ESMA has to deal promptly with an application for access to a document. Within 15 working days from the registration of such an application, the agency has to either grant access to the document requested or state the reasons for its total or partial refusal in a written reply.[14] In the latter case, ESMA has to inform the applicant of the remedies open to him or her. These include making a complaint to the Ombudsman or instituting proceedings before the ESA Board of Appeal and, where appropriate, to the CJEU in accordance with the conditions laid down in Articles 228 and 263 TFEU respectively.[15] As the General Court emphasised in *ClientEarth and International Chemical Secretariat v ECHA*, it follows from Articles 8(1) and (3) of Regulation 1049/2001/EC – which is a specific expression of the principle of judicial protection – that 'any refusal of access to the documents requested from the administration may be subject to challenge by way of court proceedings. That is so whatever the reason relied on to refuse access.'[16] The same applies to a failure on the part of ESMA to reply within the prescribed time limit. ESMA further enhances its transparency by annexing to its annual report the number of cases in which ESMA has refused to grant access to documents, the reasons for such refusals and the number of sensitive documents not recorded in the register.[17]

---

[12] 'Document' shall mean any content whatever its medium (written on paper or stored in electronic form or as a sound, visual or audiovisual recording) concerning a matter relating to the policies, activities and decisions falling within the institution's sphere of responsibility. See Chapter 2.

[13] ESMA Management Board, Decision, Access to documents (2011) ESMA/2011/MB/69.

[14] Access to Documents Regulation, Art 8(1).

[15] Ibid., Art 8(3) and ESMA Regulation, Art 72(3).

[16] Case T-245/11 *ClientEarth and International Chemical Secretariat v ECHA* [2015], para 107. Similarly, an EU agency has also been challenged for not disclosing certain documents in Case C-615/13 P *ClientEarth and PAN Europe v EFSA* [2015], para 56. In this case, the Court was of the opinion that EFSA had to disclose to ClientEarth and PAN Europe the names of the external experts who had submitted comments on a draft guidance document. It contended: 'The transparency of the process followed by a public authority for the adoption of a measure of that nature contributes to that authority acquiring greater legitimacy in the eyes of the persons to whom that measure is addressed and increasing their confidence in that authority.'

[17] Pursuant to the Access to Documents Regulation, Art 17(1). See for instance ESMA, Annual Report 2019, 65: 'In 2019, ESMA received 21 requests for access to documents pursuant to the Access to Documents Regulation. In eight different cases,

In accordance with the third subparagraph of Article 15(3) TFEU, both ESMA's Board of Supervisors and the Management Board have elaborated specific provisions regarding access to documents in their own Rules of Procedure. They state that the minutes of the meetings of both Boards and their decisions shall be subject to the provisions on access to documents in Article 72 ESMA Regulation and to the measures taken for its implementation.[18] Indeed, in practice, all summaries of conclusions and decisions are published on the ESMA website.[19] The Rules of Procedure of the ESA Board of Appeal[20] also include a provision on access to documents which requires it to consider, as appropriate, the relevant provisions of the Regulation on public access to documents.[21] Hence, all important decision-making bodies within and relevant to the agency are bound by the access to documents requirement.

It is also important to note that the fact that ESMA is subject to the obligations stemming from the access to documents aspect of the principle of transparency is without prejudice to the requirements of professional secrecy pursuant to Article 339 TFEU. In accordance with Article 70(3) ESMA Regulation, the agency has laid down in its internal rules of procedure the practical arrangements for implementing the confidentiality rules.[22] These include, *inter alia*, a prohibition on disclosing confidential information and exceptions thereto. However, although there may be sound arguments for secrecy, individual interests have to be balanced against the public interests involved.[23] Not providing openness, and thus not setting aside the principle of transparency, can ultimately lead to ineffective enforcement.[24] This would ultimately undermine the effectiveness of the rules.

ESMA provided full access to the documents requested. In two cases, ESMA did not possess the document requested. In the remaining five cases, ESMA decided not to grant access to the documents, as the disclosure of certain documents would have been in breach of specific provisions of the Staff Regulations or EMIR or would have seriously undermined ESMA's decision-making process, legal advice, commercial interests of a natural or legal person, or international relations.'

[18] ESMA, Decision of the Board of Supervisors Rules of Procedure (2020) ESMA22-328-266, Art 6(4); ESMA, Management Board, Decision, Rules of Procedure (2020) ESMA22-328-275, Art 8(4).

[19] ESMA, 'ESMA Library' <www.esma.europa.eu/databases-library/esma-library> accessed 16 February 2021.

[20] See Chapter 10, Section 2 for an explanation of this Board.

[21] ESA Board of Appeal, Board of Appeal of the European Supervisory Authorities Rules of Procedure (2020) BoA 2020 01, Art 26(2).

[22] ESMA, Decision of the Management Board on adopting rules of procedure on professional secrecy for non-staff, and repealing Management Board decision on professional secrecy of 11 January 2011 (2017) ESMA40-1432018523-304.

[23] Ottow 2015, pp. 83–84 and De Vries 2016.

[24] Ottow 2015, p. 84.

4. THE REQUIREMENT TO GIVE REASONS

The principle of transparency also entails the possibility of knowing the reasons behind the adoption of a legal act as a result of the requirement to give reasons as laid down in the second subparagraph of Article 296 TFEU.[25] This provision obliges public authorities to communicate the reasons for their decisions.

The Union courts have held that the statement of reasons 'must disclose in a clear and unequivocal fashion the reasoning followed by the institution which adopted the measure in question in such a way as to enable the persons concerned to ascertain the reasons for the measure and to enable the competent Community Court to exercise its power of review'.[26] This means that both the legal basis and the factual and legal considerations which underpin the measure have to be set out.[27] However, public authorities do not need to address all relevant points of fact and law. Where the reasons for the decision are clear and understandable to the parties concerned, a sufficient level of transparency has been realised and the duty to give reasons has been met.[28] The Union courts have argued that 'the requirements to be satisfied by the statement of reasons depend on the circumstances of each case, in particular the content of the measure in question, the nature of the reasons given and the interest which the addressees of the measure, or other parties to whom it is of direct and individual concern, may have in obtaining explanations'.[29] It is thus clear that the extent of the reasoning often depends on the particular circumstances of the case[30] and on the nature of the measure in question.[31] Where the act is of general application it would be excessive 'to require a specific state-

---

25 Hofmann, Rowe & Türk 2011, pp. 170–72.

26 Case T-102/03 *CIS v Commission* [2005] ECR II-2357, para 47; Case T-245/03 R *FNSEA and Others v Commission* [2004] ECR II-271, para 48; C-304/01 *Spain v Commission* [2004] ECR I-7655, para 50. See also Türk 2009.

27 Türk 2009.

28 Buijze 2013, p. 275. See also Case T-317/02 *FICF and Others v Commission* [2004] ECR II-4325, para 129; Case C-76/01 P *Eurocoton and Others v Council* [2003] ECR I-10091, para 88. On the relevance of this dialogue function, see Shapiro 1992, pp. 203–04.

29 Case T-317/02 *FICF and Others v Commission* [2004] ECR II-4325, para 129; Case C-76/01 P *Eurocoton and Others v Council* [2003] ECR I-10091, para 88.

30 Türk 2009.

31 Case 5/67 *Beus GmbH v Hauptzollamt München* [1968] ECR 83, p. 95; Case T-213/00 *CMA DGM and Others v Commission* [2003] ECR II-913, para 80; Case T-251/00 *Lagardère and Canal+ v Commission* [2002] ECR II-4825, para 155; Joined Cases T-44, 119 and 126/01 *Vieira and Others v Commission* [2003] ECR II-1209, para 193; Case C-304/01 *Spain v Commission* [2004] ECR I-7655, para 51; Case T-245/03 R *FNSEA and Others v Commission* [2004] ECR II-271, para 48.

ment of reasons for each of the technical choices made by the institution'.[32] It is sufficient to indicate the general situation which led to its adoption and the general objectives which it intended to achieve.[33] In contrast, acts of individual application often have to contain a greater detail of reasoning.[34] The following subsections show that there is indeed a difference in the extent of the reasoning that ESMA offers with regard to its draft technical standards and guidelines, on the one hand, and its non-binding instruments, on the other.

4.1 Draft Regulatory and Implementing Technical Standards

Although Article 296 TFEU does not explicitly apply to EU agencies and soft law instruments,[35] it can be observed that ESMA scores highly on the requirement to give reasons with regard to its draft technical standards. The Final Reports of these instruments include the legislative mandate to develop technical standards; the cost–benefit analysis; the advice of the Securities and Markets Stakeholder Group (SMSG) when the Group has been consulted and has provided comments; the feedback received from stakeholders in ESMA's open consultation process and from the stakeholders in the SMSG; ESMA's elaborate responses thereto (a so-called feedback statement); and the actual draft technical standards themselves.[36] Although it had already been good practice, as part of the ESA review ESMA has now formally been put under a duty to give reasons with regard to its technical standards. Indeed, it has become mandatory for ESMA to publish a summary of the input received from stakeholders and an overview of how information and views gathered from the consultations were used in a draft regulatory or implementing technical standard. Besides, since the ESA review, ESMA also has to publish how advice and results of SMSG consultations have been taken into account (Article 37(7) ESMA Regulation). Whereas ESMA previously only had to make public the

---

[32] Case C-122/94 *Commission v Council* [1996] ECR I-881, para 29; Case C-110/97 *Netherlands v Council* [2001] ECR I-8763, para 166; Case T-189/00 R *'Invest' Import und Export and Invest Commerce v Commission* [2000] ECR II-2993, para 43; Case C-304/01 *Spain v Commission* [2004] ECR I-7655, para 51.

[33] Case 5/67 *Beus GmbH & Co. v Hauptzollamt München* [1968] ECR 83, p. 95; Case T-13/99 *Pfizer Animal Health v Council* [2002] ECR II-3305, para 510; Case T-70/99 *Alpharma v Council* [2002] ECR II-3495.

[34] See Case 24/62 *Germany v Commission* [1963] ECR 63; Case T-102/03, *CIS v Commission* [2005] ECR II-2357; Case T-251/00, *Lagardère v Commission* [2002] ECR II-4825, paras 155–158.

[35] See Chapter 2, Section 9.1.2.

[36] For an example, see ESMA, Final Report on Draft technical standards on the provision of investment services and activities in the Union by third-country firms under MiFID II and MiFIR (2020) ESMA35-43-2424.

advice of the SMSG, it thus has recently had imposed upon it a duty to give reasons with regard to this group as well.

Hence, ESMA states the reasons on which its legal acts are based and responds to the arguments that have been put forward by the stakeholders during the preparation of a particular act. For the record, the agency does not respond to each contribution individually, but provides a general response in which it highlights some stakeholder contributions that deserve specific attention. ESMA also indicates whether changes are envisaged as a result of the comments it has received. As the example in the following textbox demonstrates, this gives the Member States and the parties concerned a good understanding of the motives behind ESMA's decisions.[37]

According to the feedback statement belonging to the Final report on draft regulatory technical standards on types of Alternative Investment Fund Managers (AIFMs), ESMA received 27 responses to its consultation paper.[38] Responses came from asset managers (and their associations), banks (and their associations), an association of investors, law firms, a private equity fund administrator and public authorities. ESMA asked only seven questions; what follows relates to the fifth of these.

Q5: Do you agree with the proposed approach as regards the treatment of hybrid structures? If not, please explain why and, if possible, provide alternative proposals.

29. *A bank disagreed with the proposed approach* on hybrid structures and argued that a change in the redemption policy during the life cycle of a product from closed-ended to open-ended, or vice versa, should not entail a change in the applicable liquidity management and valuation regime.

30. *The large majority of the responses to this question were supportive of the approach* proposed in Article 1(4) of the draft RTS. However, a few of these respondents asked ESMA to limit the requirement to adapt the new rules when the type of AIF changes. Along the same lines, an asset manag-

[37] In contrast, the Commission has been criticised for its limited feedback on the contributions of stakeholders to its consultations, see Senden 2011, pp. 27–48.

[38] ESMA, Final report on Draft regulatory technical standards on types of AIFMs (2013) ESMA/2013/413. ESMA, Consultation paper on Draft regulatory technical standards on types of AIFMs (2012) ESMA/2012/844. See for an overview of the response of each stakeholder: ESMA, 'Consultation on draft regulatory technical standards on types of AIFMS' <www.esma.europa.eu/press-news/consultations/consultation-draft-regulatory-technical-standards-types-aifms> accessed 20 October 2020.

ers' association noted that the Level 1 provisions on liquidity management and valuation anticipate that the systems and procedures to be established by AIFMs are tailored to the specific AIFs (i.e. Level 1 says 'for each AIF they manage') and it is not required that the liquidity management and valuation procedures apply without further differentiation to all AIFs managed by an AIFM.

31. Two respondents asked ESMA to clarify that a modification of the redemption policy in an existing vehicle is solely relevant for the application of liquidity management and valuation rules under the AIFMD.

ESMA's response: *Given the support received, ESMA did not change its approach,* but decided to clarify that, as requested by certain respondents, the requirement to adapt to the new rules is limited to the particular AIF that has changed type.[39]

Even those who are unfamiliar with the technical background and content of ESMA's question will understand that it was answered in a predominantly positive way by its stakeholders. Only one bank disagreed and some respondents asked for clarifications. The ensuing response from ESMA makes it clear that the agency did not change its approach, because the agency found that it received enough support.

It is debatable whether the requirement to give reasons has a dialogue dimension alongside its transparency dimension.[40] This would mean that the institutions are obliged to respond to all the arguments that have been put forward by the parties concerned during the preparation of a certain act. The Court has not been inclined to accept such an obligation, which would in fact create a participation *right*,[41] but Shapiro argues that 'participation in government, possibly through dialogue, is a precondition for full transparency'.[42]

Although the Court has been reluctant to recognise in its case-law a dialogue dimension to the requirement to give reasons, ESMA's practice comes close to the existence of such a dimension.[43] This is of course only to be welcomed, in

---

39 ESMA, Final report on Draft regulatory technical standards on types of AIFMs (2013) ESMA/2013/413, 10.

40 Shapiro 1992.

41 Joined cases 240–242, 261–262 and 268–269/82 *Stichting Sigarettenindustrie v Commission* [1985] ECR 3831.

42 Shapiro 1992.

43 This is a positive development, given the fact that parties which forwarded their opinions during Commission consultations do not have any right to be informed indi-

order to achieve the highest level of transparency possible. The agency deals with all arguments put forward by the stakeholders in the same way as set out in the example above, that is, by repeating the question, by summarising the stakeholder feedback thereto and by setting out its response to this feedback. ESMA's response includes the choice as to whether or not it will follow the feedback from the stakeholders. When the answers received are mostly positive, ESMA usually sticks to its approach. When the responses are more critical, the agency either changes its approach, provides clarifications, makes small amendments to the text or explains why it will nonetheless retain its own approach. This enables the addressees of a legal instrument to find out why certain choices have been made and whether the decisions were legitimate, which ultimately facilitates judicial review. It also contributes to meeting the requirement of Article 11(2) TEU for the institutions to 'maintain an open, transparent and regular dialogue with representative associations and civil society'. In addition, it ensures that the agency is really listening to the comments received.[44] Indeed, as follows from the following example, ESMA takes the responses from its stakeholders very seriously. In some cases, ESMA even goes as far as to reject the view of the European Commission and instead stick to the preferences expressed by the consulted stakeholders.[45]

With regard to ESMA's draft regulatory technical standards on types of Alternative Investment Fund Managers (AIFMs), the agency organised two rounds of consultations.[46] On the basis of the stakeholders' responses, it

vidually as to the extent to which their view has been embraced by relevant EU policy documents. The Commission does not find the idea of providing feedback on an individual basis (feedback statements) to be compatible with the requirement of *effectiveness* of the decision-making process: see Obradovic & Alonso Vizcaino 2006, p. 1061.

[44] In the US, the courts expanded the APA's notice and comment provisions into a dialogue requirement. They argued that it would mean little to require an agency to invite comments if the agency did not listen seriously to those comments it received. The only way judges could know whether the agencies were listening seriously was by requiring the agencies to reply to each and every argument offered by interested parties: see Shapiro 1992, p. 186.

[45] Another example may be found in ESMA, Opinion on Draft Regulatory Technical Standards on methodology for calculation and the application of position limits for commodity derivatives traded on trading venues and economically equivalent OTC contracts (2016) ESMA/2016/668, 38. ESMA retained its approach because it found wide support in ESMA's consultation and is also the one used in the US, where this approach appears to be working smoothly in practice.

[46] ESMA, Discussion paper on Key concepts of the Alternative Investment Fund Managers Directive and types of AIFM (2012) ESMA/2012/117; ESMA, Consultation paper on Draft regulatory technical standards on types of AIFMs (2012) ESMA/2012/844.

drafted a final report which it submitted to the Commission for endorsement.[47] However, the Commission rejected the draft technical standards on the basis of its analysis, which indicated a risk that Article 1(2)(a) may not be fully compatible with Directive 2011/61/EU (AIFMD).[48] Its concern related to the fact that Article 1(2)(a) suggested that the distinction between open and closed-end Alternative Investment Funds (AIF) was based on whether these funds offer redemptions and whether these redemptions are available at least once a year. The Commission had serious doubts as to whether the frequency of redemptions is a criterion that can be employed to distinguish the two categories. In accordance with Article 10(1) ESMA Regulation, the Commission invited ESMA to submit new draft regulatory technical standards. ESMA responded to this letter by means of an Opinion.[49] It reiterated that its approach to identification of closed-ended and open-ended AIFs was based on the frequency of redemptions.[50]

The agency referred to the fact that it had consulted twice on this approach and that the feedback received from a broad range of stakeholders, including consumer representatives, was broadly positive.[51] ESMA therefore reiterated that the approach followed under Article 1(2)(a) of the draft regulatory technical standards submitted to the Commission was appropriate and consistent with the level 1 text.[52] ESMA considered that the solution proposed by DG MARKT (now DG FISMA) in the Letter was not the only reasonable way of interpreting the AIFMD provisions.[53] Moreover, the agency stressed that draft technical standards submitted by ESMA should only be made subject to amendments by the Commission in very restricted and extraordinary circumstances.[54] However, in order to ensure a timely implementation of the AIFMD provisions and to move the process forward with the Commission, ESMA decided to submit an amended version of the draft technical standards for the Commission's consideration.[55] ESMA be-

---

[47] ESMA, Final report on Draft regulatory technical standards on types of AIFMs (2013) ESMA/2013/413.

[48] Commission, Letter to ESMA regarding draft RTS on types of AIFMD, 4 July 2015 <www.esma.europa.eu/sites/default/files/library/2015/11/ec_letter_to_esma_re_draft_rts_on_types_of_aifmd_4_july_2013.pdf> accessed 18 February 2021.

[49] ESMA, Opinion on Draft regulatory technical standards on types of AIFMs under Article 4(4) of Directive 2011/61/EU (2013) 2013/ESMA/1119.

[50] Ibid., para 10.

[51] Ibid., para 12.

[52] Ibid., para 25.

[53] Ibid., para 33.

[54] Ibid., and ESMA Regulation, recital 23.

[55] ESMA, Opinion on Draft regulatory technical standards on types of AIFMs under Article 4(4) of Directive 2011/61/EU (2013) 2013/ESMA/1119, para 34.

lieved that these revised regulatory technical standards fully addressed the concerns expressed in the Letter, while retaining some more flexibility to take account of existing market practice.[56]

4.2 Guidelines and Recommendations

ESMA scores equally high on the requirement to give reasons with regard to its guidelines, because the detail of the reasoning is similar to that of draft technical standards. However, contrary to the latter, there is no formal obligation for ESMA to publish a summary of the input received from stakeholders and an overview of how information and views gathered from the consultations were used in guidelines. The agency nonetheless does this in practice.

4.3 Non-binding Instruments

Previously, the legal basis for ESMA's non-binding instruments did not oblige the agency to consult.[57] Hence, hitherto ESMA's opinions only set out the legal basis on which the opinion is based, the background to it and the opinion itself.[58] Its supervisory briefings present the scope and status of the document, their purpose and the briefing itself. The agency's Q&As stick to the structure of explaining the background, the purpose and the status of the legal act, followed by the questions and answers themselves.[59] The agency has so far thus provided fewer reasons concerning its non-binding instruments than concerning its draft technical standards and guidelines.[60] However, as the extent of the reasoning is dependent on the particular circumstances of the case and the nature of the measure in question, this is rather normal. The difference can also be explained by the fact that ESMA did not carry out consultations with regard to its non-binding instruments. It was therefore quite logical that ESMA was not able to be as active in its reason-giving. There were simply fewer reasons

---

56 Ibid., para 35.

57 ESMA Regulation, Art 29.

58 ESMA, Opinion on Draft Implementing Technical Standards on main indices and recognised exchanges under the Capital Requirements Regulation (2016) ESMA/2016/163; ESMA, Opinion on the composition of CCP colleges under EMIR (2015) ESMA/2015/838.

59 ESMA, Questions and Answers on the Market Abuse Regulation (2016) ESMA/2016/1129; ESMA, Questions and Answers on the Application of the UCITS Directive (2016) 2016/ESMA/181.

60 See Chapter 1, Section 6.4 regarding the levels of 'bindingness': technical standards are more binding than guidelines; guidelines are more binding than ESMA's non-binding instruments.

to give reasons. Hence, a dialogue with stakeholders could not possibly take place. Nonetheless, the reasons for the decisions were clear and understandable for the parties concerned. Hence, although ESMA scored relatively low on the requirement to give reasons with regard to its non-binding instruments, a sufficient level of transparency had been realised. Now that ESMA is also required to conduct open public consultations in relation to its opinions and new practical instruments and convergence tools (Article 29(2), third paragraph, ESMA Regulation), and may be requested to do so by the Board of Supervisors in the case of Q&As (Article 16b(4) ESMA Regulation), this situation may change. It remains to be seen whether ESMA will follow the same approach to the duty to give reasons as it does with regard to draft technical standards and guidelines, or whether it will approach this in a different manner.

5. THE PUBLICATION AND TRANSLATION REQUIREMENTS

The third element of the principle of transparency encompasses the possibility of taking note of EU legislation.[61] This stems from the publication requirement as laid down in Article 297 TFEU. The Court has ruled that it is evident from the very wording of that provision that the legislative acts set out therein cannot produce legal effects unless they have been published in the Official Journal of the European Union (OJ).[62]

Article 297 TFEU does not require the publication of non-binding instruments in the OJ.[63] However, following the line of reasoning in the case-law, it could be maintained that soft law must be published *somewhere*.[64] Indeed, the addressees of soft law acts need to have an opportunity to at least make themselves acquainted with the acts before such acts can be enforced against them. Furthermore, the principle of legal certainty requires that those concerned know precisely the extent of the obligations which are imposed on them, since such acts may nevertheless entail legally binding effects. Not only is this

---

[61] See Chapter 2, Section 9.1.3.

[62] Case C-161/06 *Skoma-Lux* [2007] ECR I-10841, para 33; Case C-410/09 *Polska Telefonia Cyfrowa* [2011] I-3853, para 25.

[63] Looking at institutional practice, however, the Commission often publishes its interpretative and decisional acts in the 'C' series of the OJ. Recommendations of both the Commission and the Council are generally published in the 'L' series. Yet, it also occurs that certain acts are merely published as COM documents or are made accessible on the internet: see Senden 2013, p. 68.

[64] The 'L' series of the OJ is intended for the publication of legally binding measures, whereas the 'C' series is for information, recommendations and opinions concerning the EU: see Case C-410/09 *Polska Telefonia Cyfrowa* [2011] I-3853, para 35. Hence, publication on a website is certainly not for legally binding measures.

important from the perspective of safeguarding the legal certainty of those concerned, but it also contributes to ensuring a higher level of compliance and thus effectiveness.

The proper publication of an EU measure also entails the obligation to publish legal acts in all of the EU's official languages.[65] This also applies to soft law documents. Nevertheless, translation practices vary significantly among the different EU agencies; that is, not all of their soft law acts are available in all of the EU's official languages:[66] some are only available in English[67] and some in a handful of EU languages.[68] Only a minority are published in all the official languages, such as ECHA's guidance documents and ESMA's guidelines and recommendations.[69] However, in order to respect the publication and translation requirements stemming from the principle of transparency, it should be considered whether EU agencies' soft law acts should always be published in all of the EU languages. The need for publication should in any case not be hindered by practical translation issues, such as funding and agency staffing.[70]

Considering the above, there is no doubt about the need for ESMA to be subject to the publication and translation requirements. Indeed, national competent authorities and financial market participants should have an opportunity to at least acquaint themselves with the soft law acts issued by the agency.[71] They would otherwise have no idea about the extent of obligations imposed upon them. Under the revised ESMA Regulation, it has even become explicitly mandatory for ESMA to publish on its website all regulatory and implementing technical standards, guidelines, recommendations and questions and answers.[72] This requirement includes overviews that concern the state of play of ongoing work and the planned timing of the adoption of draft regulatory and implementing technical standards. This section shows that each category of ESMA's soft law instruments entails the publication of different types of documents and that translation practices also differ per category. The differences are visualised in Table 6.1 and explained in the following subsections.

---

65 Case C-361/01 P *Kik v OHIM* [2003] ECR I-8283, para 60.

66 Vaughan 2015b, p. 84.

67 For example, the CPVO Protocols.

68 For example, the ERA guidance.

69 See further on translation Case C-410/09 *Polska Telefonia Cyfrowa* [2011] I-3853. See also Stefan 2012b.

70 Vaughan 2015b, p. 84.

71 A measure adopted by the public authorities should not be enforceable against those concerned before they have had an opportunity to make themselves acquainted with it: see Case C-410/09 *Polska Telefonia Cyfrowa* [2011] I-3853, para 23.

72 ESMA Regulation, Art 8(ka). ESMA already did this in practice, though.

Table 6.1 Types of documents published per category of soft law instruments

	Draft technical standards	**Guidelines and recommendations**	**Non-binding instruments**
Preparation phase	- consultation paper - final report	- consultation paper - final report	- in the case of Q&As: publication of all questions received - other non-binding instruments: not clear yet*
Commission phase	- rejection letter - ESMA opinion proposing revised technical standards	n/a	n/a
Publication phase	- Official Journal of the EU - translations in all EU languages (Commission responsibility)	- ESMA website - translations in all EU languages (ESMA responsibility)	- ESMA website - no translations, i.e. only in English (ESMA responsibility)
Compliance phase	n/a	- compliance tables	n/a

Note: * Since there are no examples of consultations on ESMA's non-binding instruments as of yet, it remains to be seen which documents ESMA will publish throughout the process.

5.1 Draft Regulatory and Implementing Technical Standards

The transparency of ESMA's draft regulatory and implementing technical standards is rather high. In practice, any rule-making activity becomes visible to the public as soon as a *consultation paper* on the proposed draft technical standards is published on ESMA's website under the section entitled Consultations. In this document, the agency sets out the background to its proposals, includes the first draft of the technical standards and invites comments on all matters in the paper, particularly on the specific questions it asks throughout the paper.[73] This could lead to more than 100 questions being raised.[74] Each paper sets out, at the beginning, who should read it. For instance, the consultation paper on draft regulatory technical standards under the Benchmarks Regulation invites all interested stakeholders to respond to the

[73] For an example, see ESMA, Consultation Paper on Draft Regulatory Technical Standards under the Benchmarks Regulation (2020) ESMA70-156-1464.

[74] For an example, see ESMA, Discussion Paper on Draft RTS and ITS under SFTR (2016) ESMA/2016/356, 2. As ESMA's Consultation Paper on Draft Regulatory Technical Standards under the Benchmarks Regulation demonstrates, a Consultation Paper could also be relatively short, for example comprising 12 questions.

consultation, but particularly seeks input from administrators of benchmarks, contributors to benchmarks and any investor dealing with financial instruments and financial contracts whose value is determined by a benchmark or with investment funds whose performances are measured by means of a benchmark.[75] Those responding to the consultation paper differ per legal instrument. The interested stakeholders are invited to respond by means of filling in the reply form attached.

When the consultation period is over,[76] ESMA publishes all the responses it has received on its website. These are categorised on the basis of the respondent's activity, such as asset management, banking and regulated markets.[77] A stakeholder may object to such publication if it clearly and prominently requests (a part of) its submission not to be publicly disclosed. Nonetheless, a confidential response may be requested from ESMA in accordance with the rules on access to documents. ESMA will consult the stakeholder concerned if it receives such a request. Any decision the agency makes not to disclose the response is reviewable by the European Ombudsman, the ESA Board of Appeal and, where appropriate, the CJEU.[78]

The responses are processed by ESMA within the framework of the Standing Committee that is responsible for the drafting of the technical standards concerned.[79] The Standing Committee members meet each other for a discussion on the feedback in order to finalise the draft technical standards. Once ready, they are sent to the Board of Supervisors for approval with a qualified majority vote. As soon as they are adopted, a *final report* is published on ESMA's website and submitted to the Commission for approval.

The Commission then has three months to decide whether or not to approve the draft technical standards.[80] When it chooses to approve them in part only, or with amendments, the Commission sends a letter to ESMA and a copy of this letter to the European Parliament and Council. This letter will be published

---

75 ESMA, Consultation Paper on Draft Regulatory Technical Standards under the Benchmarks Regulation (2020) ESMA70-156-1464, 2.

76 Usually after two months. However, due to the Covid-19 crisis longer consultation periods have been offered to financial market participants, for instance four months for the Joint ESA consultation on ESG disclosures (2020) JC 2020 16.

77 See ESMA, 'Consultation Paper on Draft Regulatory Technical Standards under the Benchmarks Regulation' <www.esma.europa.eu/press-news/consultations/draft-regulatory-technical-standards-under-benchmarks-regulation> accessed 18 February 2021 for an overview of all stakeholder responses to this Consultation Paper.

78 See Section 3.

79 For instance, the draft regulatory technical standards under the Benchmarks Regulation were discussed by the Market Integrity Standing Committee.

80 ESMA Regulation, Arts 10(1) and 15(1).

on ESMA's website as well.[81] Within a period of six weeks, ESMA may amend its draft technical standards on the basis of the European Commission's proposed amendments and resubmit it in the form of a formal opinion to the Commission.[82] At the same time, ESMA sends a copy of its opinion to the European Parliament and Council. The opinion will also be published on ESMA's website.[83] After this six-week period, the Commission may either amend the draft technical standards on the basis of ESMA's proposed amendments or adopt them with such amendments as it considers relevant.[84] However, since the Commission agrees with ESMA most of the time, this so-called Commission phase is usually skipped.[85]

Finally, the regulatory or implementing technical standards are published as Commission delegated or implementing acts in the Official Journal and enter into force on the date stated therein.[86] The words 'regulatory technical standard' or 'implementing technical standard' have to appear in the title of such acts.[87] They are translated into all of the official languages of the EU by the Commission on the basis of Articles 4 and 5 of Regulation No. 1/58, as they are acts of general application.[88] ESMA provides links on its website to the translations published in the OJ.[89]

---

[81] For example, see the Commission's letter of 25 May 2016 informing ESMA that the Commission intends to endorse the draft ITS once certain amendments were introduced <www.esma.europa.eu/sites/default/files/library/esma70-151-1651_annex_1_-_letter_from_ec.pdf> accessed 18 February 2021.

[82] ESMA Regulation, Arts 10(1) and 15(1).

[83] See as a reply to the Commission's letter: ESMA, Opinion on Draft Implementing Technical Standards on the technical means for appropriate public disclosure of inside information and for delaying the public disclosure of inside information (2016) ESMA/2016/982.

[84] ESMA Regulation, Arts 10(3) and 15(3).

[85] This is in line with previous experience which shows that the Commission, with regard to older EU agencies, tends to opt for 'rubberstamping' the proposed standards instead of not endorsing, endorsing only in part or endorsing with amendments: see Senden & Van den Brink 2012, p. 43. See also Dehousse 2002, p. 223.

[86] ESMA Regulation, Arts 10(4) and 15(4). See for an example Commission Implementing Regulation (EU) 2016/1055.

[87] ESMA Regulation, Arts 10(4) and 15(4).

[88] EBA also confirmed that its technical standards are of general application within the meaning of Regulation 1/58, see European Ombudsman, 'Decision of the European Ombudsman closing his inquiry into complaint 1363/2012/BEH against the European Banking Authority' (19 February 2013).

[89] See for an overview of ESMA's technical standards <https://www.esma.europa.eu/convergence/guidelines-and-technical-standards> accessed 18 February 2021.

5.2 Guidelines and Recommendations

The transparency of ESMA's guidelines and recommendations is also very high. The public is first made aware of ESMA's guidelines and recommendations when a *consultation paper* is published on the website under the section entitled Consultations.[90] The consultation paper includes the first draft of the guidelines and specific questions for the stakeholders.[91] The stakeholders are invited to reply and their responses are then published on ESMA's website.[92] The Standing Committee discusses the feedback in order to finalise the draft guidelines. Once ready, they are sent to the Board of Supervisors for approval with a qualified majority vote. Once adopted, a *final report* is published on ESMA's website.[93] The actual guidelines are then translated into the Union's official languages and competent authorities to which these guidelines apply must notify ESMA of whether they (i) comply, (ii) do not comply but intend to comply, or (iii) do not comply and do not intend to comply with the guidelines within two months after the publication of the translations on ESMA's website.

The obligation to translate guidelines may be said to follow from Article 73 ESMA Regulation. This provision explicitly applies the language arrangements of Council Regulation No. 1/58 to the agency. Article 3 requires that 'documents which an institution of the Community sends to a Member State or to a person subject to the jurisdiction of a Member State shall be drafted in the language of such State'.[94] Since ESMA's guidelines are addressed to the national competent authorities of all of the Member States and also have consequences for the financial market participants operating within them, these documents have to be made available in all Union languages. An even stronger obligation follows from Article 4, which requires that 'Regulations and other documents of general application shall be drafted in the official languages'.[95] This article is not confined to binding acts, but encompasses any document of general application. It is not entirely clear whether 'other documents of general application' can be said to entail soft law documents, but given the fact that

---

[90] See for an example ESMA, Consultation Paper on the Guidelines on reporting obligations under Article 3 and Article 24 of the AIFMD (2013) ESMA/2013/592.

[91] ESMA, 'Consultations' <www.esma.europa.eu/press-news/consultations> accessed 18 February 2020.

[92] See for an example ESMA, 'Consultation on guidelines on AIFMD reporting obligations' <www.esma.europa.eu/press-news/consultations/consultation-guidelines-aifmd-reporting-obligations> accessed 18 February 2021.

[93] ESMA, Guidelines on reporting obligations under Articles 3(3)(d) and 24(1), (2) and (4) of the AIFMD (2014) ESMA/2014/869.

[94] Council Regulation No. 1, Art 3.

[95] Ibid., Art 4. There are currently 22 languages.

the Regulation dates from 1958, a logical explanation anno 2020 would be to apply it to soft law as well. ESMA's guidelines could then be said to fall within the scope of application of Article 4 too.[96] Even if they are not binding, they are followed by an indefinite number of national competent authorities and financial market participants. Although the Regulation only refers to the institutions of the European Union, most EU agencies' establishing regulations contain a provision that explicitly applies it to the agency at stake.[97]

It is thus only the actual guidelines that will be translated. The consultation paper, the cost–benefit analysis, the advice of the SMSG and the feedback statement pertaining to the guidelines are only available in English.[98] It is simply too expensive to translate them as well. However, we should be aware of the risk that consulting only in English 'excludes especially smaller associations and citizens that might in many cases not be used to express professional positions in English'.[99] This requires a balancing exercise between legitimacy and efficiency. The consultation process is either more efficient, but exclusive, when it focuses only on one language;[100] or it is fully inclusive to all stakeholders, but burdens the process with the incredible amount of administrative costs generated by translation of documents.[101]

In any case, the Court has rejected the existence of a general principle of EU law under which anything that might affect the interests of an EU citizen must be drawn up in his language in all circumstances.[102] Such a principle cannot be derived from the several references in the Treaty to the use of languages in the European Union.[103] In the context of the three ESAs, this issue has already been subject to a judgment by the CJEU, when *Mutuelle des Architectes Français assurances* challenged EIOPA.[104] The French mutual insurance company

---

96 EBA explicitly acknowledged that it considers its guidelines to be of general application within the meaning of Council Regulation No. 1: see European Ombudsman, 'Decision of the European Ombudsman closing his inquiry into complaint 1363/2012/BEH against the European Banking Authority' (19 February 2013), para 14.

97 See for instance ESMA Regulation, Art 73; EFCA Regulation, Art 41; EMSA Regulation, Art 9 and FRA Regulation, Art 25.

98 This is the same for the preparatory documents in relation to ESMA's draft technical standards.

99 Marxsen 2015, p. 274.

100 Ibid.

101 Ibid.

102 Case C-410/09 *Polska Telefonia Cyfrowa* [2011] I-3853, para 38.

103 Case C-361/01 P *Kik v OHIM* [2003] ECR I-8283, paras 82–83.

104 EBA has also been subject to an investigation by the European Ombudsman following a complaint from a German citizen claiming that, contrary to EBA Regulation, Art 73(1) and Council Regulation No. 1, Art 4, the agency's website provides information exclusively in the English language. The complainant considered this practice also to amount to an instance of language discrimination. The claim was rejected by

asked the General Court to annul EIOPA's decision to publish information on its website exclusively in English and asked specifically to annul EIOPA's Consultation Paper on the Proposal for Guidelines on Own Risk and Solvency Assessment.[105] EIOPA asked the Court to declare the appeal inadmissible, because it considered that a Consultation Paper is not a challengeable act as it is a preparatory work document and does not produce legal effects for individuals.[106] The Court agreed with the agency. It held that a Consultation Paper concerns an open public consultation with the aim of drafting guidelines on the basis of Article 16 EIOPA Regulation;[107] the final text will be adopted by EIOPA itself and thus constitutes a preparatory act.[108] As EIOPA is not obliged to organise an open public consultation, the Court concluded that the fact that the agency did not translate its Consultation Paper cannot produce legally binding effects which are capable of affecting the interests of the addressed public, or bring about a change in its legal position.[109]

It is therefore understandable that, given its tight budget, ESMA only translates the actual guidelines and not its preparatory documents. The latter are usually added to the Final report of the guidelines (which is only available in English).[110]

Since the Commission is not involved in the adoption of ESMA's guidelines, there is no possibility for it to (partially) reject them. Hence, there is no Commission phase, as is sometimes the case in relation to the adoption of draft

---

the Ombudsman. EBA had identified, and placed on a non-exhaustive list, documents which might be considered to be of general application, including its technical standards and guidelines. The fact remained that some documents were not available in all the official languages. However, given the short period of EBA's existence (less than two years at the time of the complaint) as well as the limited resources available to it, the Ombudsman understood well that not all documents covered by Article 4 could be available in all the official languages. The Ombudsman thus concluded that there was no maladministration in the EBA's activities with respect to the complainant's allegation and claim: see European Ombudsman, 'Decision of the European Ombudsman closing his inquiry into complaint 1363/2012/BEH against the European Banking Authority' (19 February 2013), paras 1, 13, 14, 15 and 27.

105 Case T-23/12 *MAF v EIOPA* [2013], para 22. See also EIOPA, Consultation Paper on the Proposal for Guidelines on Own Risk and Solvency Assessment (2011) EIOPA-CP-11/008.

106 Case T-23/12, *MAF v EIOPA* [2013], para 27.

107 EIOPA Regulation.

108 Case T-23/12, *MAF v EIOPA* [2013], paras 13 and 37.

109 Ibid., para 37.

110 ESMA, Guidelines on sound remuneration policies under the UCITS Directive and AIFMD (2016) ESMA/2016/411, 51–54.

technical standards, and, logically, there are no documents to be published in this regard.

In addition, in order to ensure transparency, ESMA publishes so-called guidelines compliance tables on its website.[111] Such tables could be seen as a form of 'naming and shaming' with a view to strengthening NCAs' compliance with the guidelines.[112] In this way, transparency may be regarded as an enforcement instrument,[113] and thus relates to effectiveness.

5.3 Non-binding Instruments

The transparency of ESMA's non-binding instruments was rather low. There were no consultation papers preceding the publication of a final document on ESMA's website for the simple reason that stakeholders were not consulted in the framework of adopting opinions, new convergence tools or Q&As. Likewise, since there were no requirements to carry out a cost–benefit analysis or to request the advice of the SMSG, such documents did not exist either.[114] In the same way, since the Commission is not involved in the adoption, no documents come from this Union institution. Hence, only the final acts were published on ESMA's website. As part of the ESA review, this has however changed, in two important ways.

First of all, as explained in Chapter 5, the Union legislator imposed upon ESMA an obligation to conduct open public consultations in relation to its opinions and new practical instruments and convergence tools, and it may be

---

[111] See more in Chapter 9, Section 3. ESMA Regulation, recital 26. For an example, see ESMA, Guidelines compliance table on the Guidelines for the assessment of knowledge and competence (2020) ESMA35-43-2183. See for an overview of all guidelines, including the corresponding compliance tables, <www.esma.europa.eu/convergence/guidelines-and-technical-standards> accessed 24 June 2020. The agency sometimes refrains from preparing such a table. This may be the case when guidelines apply to market participants and/or supervised entities, but not to national competent authorities: see for instance ESMA, Guidelines and Recommendations on the scope of the CRA Regulation (2013) ESMA/2013/720 and ESMA, Guidelines on periodic information to be submitted to ESMA by Credit Rating Agencies (2015) ESMA/2015/609. Even if consultations were carried out, a compliance table is then not required. The same applies where guidelines are directed at national competent authorities but implementation by the Member States is not required: see for instance ESMA, Guidelines on the application of the endorsement regime under Article 4(3) of the Credit Rating Agencies Regulation No 1060/2009 (2011) ESMA/2011/139, Annex I.

[112] Van Rijsbergen 2014, p. 124.

[113] Ottow 2015, p. 83.

[114] With the exception of some examples where ESMA decided to carry out a cost–benefit analysis anyway, such as ESMA, Technical Advice under the CSD Regulation (2015) ESMA/2015/1219.

requested to do so by the Board of Supervisors in the case of Q&As. It remains however to be seen whether ESMA will follow the same approach to the duty to give reasons as it does with regard to draft technical standards and guidelines, and whether it will also start publishing consultation papers, cost–benefit analyses and advice by the SMSG.

Second, whereas previously only the final Q&As were published, in the new situation ESMA is required to publish on its website all questions rejected and questions received, even when no answers are yet available. The agency has to establish and maintain a web-based tool for this purpose.[115] It will publish three types of questions: 'questions for which a Q&A will be put on the agenda of ESMA's relevant Standing Committee; rejected questions, i.e. questions that were tabled for discussions in an ESMA Standing Committee and to which ESMA does not intend to provide an answer; and questions forwarded to the Commission.'[116] This new development entails a movement towards more compliance with the publication requirement in the sense that Q&As are now published before an answer has been forthcoming. This means that the Union legislature has put more emphasis on the publication requirement of the principle of transparency when negotiating the new ESMA regulation.

Unlike regulatory and implementing technical standards and guidelines, ESMA's non-binding instruments are only available in English. The question is, however, whether these documents should be translated into all official languages of the Union. It could be said that they are followed by an indefinite number of national competent authorities and financial market participants. They therefore seem to be acts of general application. This would require them to be translated into all of the official languages of the EU by virtue of Article 4 of Regulation 1/58. However, in practice, the choice has been made to not qualify non-binding instruments as acts of general application. They are considered to have a different legal value than ESMA's guidelines given the fact that they lack the 'comply or explain' mechanism. This remains unchanged after the ESA review. This is not problematic for their applicability, though, since, owing to their content, they do not lay down any obligations capable of being imposed, directly or indirectly, on individuals.[117] Hence, in line with the argumentation of the CJEU in *Polska*

---

[115] ESMA Regulation, Art 16b(3).

[116] ESMA, 'ESMA starts publishing questions received through its Q&A process' <www.esma.europa.eu/press-news/esma-news/esma-starts-publishing-questions-received-through-its-qa-process> accessed 18 February 2021.

[117] With regard to the Commission's Guidelines on market analysis and the assessment of significant market power under the Community regulatory framework for electronic communications networks and services, the Court has held in *Polska Telefonia* that it is necessary to determine whether, owing to its content, the legal

Telefonia, a national authority can still rely upon non-binding instruments against financial market participants when performing its supervisory duties, notwithstanding the fact that they have not been translated into the language of the Member State in question.[118]

6. CONCLUSION AND ASSESSMENT ON TRANSPARENCY WITH REGARD TO ESMA'S SOFT LAW INSTRUMENTS

Generally speaking, ESMA aims at being an open and transparent agency when it comes to its rule-making activities. The three requirements of the principle of transparency – access to documents; giving reasons; publication and translation – all contribute to the legitimacy of ESMA's soft law. At the same time, they contribute to increasing and facilitating compliance and thus effectiveness. However, alongside these benefits, the requirements all pose hurdles in terms of time and money. They may consequently decrease the flexibility of the rule-making procedure, and with that the efficiency thereof. The following sections conclude this chapter and assess the areas in which ESMA's transparency obligations lead to tensions on the basis of legitimacy and effectiveness concerns.

6.1 Different Transparency Requirements Result in Different Levels of Legitimacy and Effectiveness

ESMA is bound by the principle of transparency. It provides *access to its documents* in relation to *all three categories of its soft law instruments*, unless the professional secrecy requirements of Article 70(3) ESMA Regulation and Article 339 TFEU dictate otherwise. However, the balance between openness and confidentiality is a delicate one.[119] Not providing openness, and thus setting aside the principle of transparency, can lead to ineffective enforce-

act concerned imposes obligations on individuals. With regard to the Guidelines, the Court argued that if that proved to be the case, it would only be possible for them to be relied upon against an individual if they were published in the language of that individual. After reviewing all sections of the Guidelines, the Court held that they did not lay down any obligation capable of being imposed, directly or indirectly, on individuals. Hence, in the case at hand, the Court concluded that the national regulatory authority of Poland was able to refer to the Guidelines in a decision addressed to an individual, even though they were not published in Polish in the OJ. See Case C-410/09 *Polska Telefonia Cyfrowa* [2011] I-3853, paras 30 and 34.

[118] Ibid., para 39.

[119] De Vries 2016.

ment.[120] This undermines the effectiveness of the rules. At the same time, while transparency safeguards a better position for individuals in the rule-making process by making it more accessible, it may have a negative impact on public trust in the Union itself[121] and, as a result, may be less instrumental in realising the Union's objectives.

ESMA scores very highly on the requirement of giving reasons with regard to its *draft technical standards* and *guidelines*. Indeed, ESMA states the reasoning on which its legal acts are based and responds to the arguments that have been put forward by the stakeholders during the preparation of a particular act. The agency also indicates whether changes are envisaged as a result of the comments received. This enables the addressees of a legal instrument to find out why certain choices have been made and whether the decisions were legitimate, which ultimately facilitates judicial review. ESMA's consultation practice thus not only contributes to the transparency of the decision-making process, but also entails a dialogue dimension. What this dialogue dimension seems to suggest is the existence of a participation right for external stakeholders in the decision-making process.[122] Hence, an impressive level of transparency has been realised. The fact that ESMA provides the reasons for its draft technical standards and guidelines contributes to democratic legitimacy, because it makes the decisions more accessible and acceptable to the citizens. However, it makes the decision-making process rather slow, as it poses a procedural hurdle that takes time and money and thus lowers the efficiency of the process. On the other hand, compliance is enhanced, and with that effectiveness. The dialogue dimension makes it easier for people to comply with the rules when the reasons for the adoption of a legal act are known, explained and justified to the addressees.

ESMA has a good track record in terms of publishing and translating its draft technical standards and guidelines, but less so regarding its non-binding instruments. The publication and translation of soft law instruments contributes to safeguarding the legal certainty of those concerned as it enables them to know precisely the extent of the obligations which are imposed on them. At the same time, it contributes to ensuring a higher level of compliance and thus effectiveness. With regard to *draft technical standards*, the ESMA website provides access to the preparatory documents (consultation paper and final report) and, if applicable, to the Commission rejection letter and ESMA's reaction thereto. All these documents are only available in English. Only the final acts are published in the OJ and translated into all official languages of

[120] Ottow 2015, p. 84.
[121] Frissen 2016.
[122] See Chapter 5, Sections 4.1 and 7.2.

the EU. It is striking that none of the preparatory documents are translated; for example, a consultation paper that invites private stakeholders to respond to proposals is only available in English. It could be said that this entails a benefit to financial market participants in Ireland and Malta, and is therefore not a legitimate practice. However, according to the relevant case-law, there is no need to offer such documents in all EU languages.[123] With regard to its *guidelines*, ESMA publishes the preparatory documents (consultation paper and final report) in English and the actual guidelines in all official Union languages on its website. In addition, it provides an extra transparency element by issuing so-called guidelines compliance tables. In this way, outsiders actually know who complies and how. These matters remain unclear with regard to ESMA's draft technical standards and other soft law instruments because this 'naming and shaming' practice does not exist in relation thereto. With regard to *ESMA's non-binding instruments*, only the final instruments are published on ESMA's website and they are only available in English. For the time being, they are not considered to be major normative sources whose translation is required in all official languages of the EU by virtue of Article 4 of Regulation 1/58. As a result of the ESA review, this situation has altered in relation to *Q&As*. Indeed, ESMA now publishes in English on its website all questions rejected and questions received, even when no answers are yet available. This ensures additional interaction with stakeholders regarding Q&As, which is to be welcomed from the perspective of legitimacy. Yet, both the possibility to involve stakeholders in the Q&A process and the publication of all Q&As, including those rejected, might also make the agency more prone to industry pressure. This seems to be especially the case when questions are rejected against stakeholders' will. Indeed, 'regulatory capture' is a risk of involving industry in the process.[124]

6.2 The New ESMA Regulation: Striving towards Equalisation in Relation to the Requirement to Give Reasons

Under the previous ESMA Regulation, ESMA scored relatively low on the requirement to give reasons with regard to its *non-binding instruments.* There were no consultation papers preceding the publication of a final document on ESMA's website, for the simple reason that stakeholders were not consulted in the framework of adopting such instruments. Likewise, since there were no requirements to carry out a cost–benefit analysis or to request the advice of the Stakeholder Group, no such documents existed. Hence, *only the final*

---

[123] Case C-410/09 *Polska Telefonia Cyfrowa* [2011] I-3853, para 38.

[124] See Chapter 5, Section 7.1.

acts were published on ESMA's website. The fact that the process regarding non-binding instruments was not transparent and did not impose upon ESMA any duty to give reasons had an impact on democratic legitimacy, though, in the sense that it was difficult for individuals to understand and accept the rules laid down therein. Addressing these issues has actually been one of the main drivers behind the changes to the new ESMA Regulation. Now that ESMA is also required to conduct open public consultations in relation to its opinions and new practical instruments and convergence tools, and may be requested to do so by the Board of Supervisors in the case of Q&As, it makes the instruments as such more legitimate, because it allows for an opportunity to include those being affected by the norms laid down therein. However, it does reduce the efficiency of the process as there are more procedural hurdles to overcome, whereas the non-binding instruments of ESMA are typically used as instruments to respond to market changes rather quickly. At the same time, ESMA will be able to increase the transparency of its instruments as it is under a duty to give reasons when it publishes the responses to the feedback it received from external stakeholders or the SMSG. Indeed, stakeholder feedback cannot be simply put aside. The recommendation is therefore for ESMA to set up an internal procedure similar to the one used for regulatory and implementing technical standards, as well as guidelines in order to fulfil its duty to give reasons. In this way, the financial institutions can understand the reasons and the factual and legal considerations behind the choices that have been made by ESMA, and therefore whether the decisions are legitimate. Besides, it is easier for addressees to comply with the rules when the reasons for the adoption of a legal act are known, explained and justified to them. This leads to a higher level of effectiveness. In the case of Q&As, the increase in legitimacy and effectiveness of course only applies when ESMA indeed conducts public consultations and/or requests advice from the SMSG.

All in all, with regard to draft technical standards and guidelines, the principle of transparency leads to a higher level of legitimacy and effectiveness, but potentially to a lower level of efficiency.[125] In the case of ESMA's non-binding instruments the conclusion used to be the other way around: there was a high level of efficiency, but a rather low level of legitimacy and effectiveness. Under the new ESMA Regulation, ESMA's non-binding instruments are now *de iure* at the same level of legitimacy and effectiveness. The only exception to this is the instrument of Q&As, where there is only a duty to give reasons when the Board requests ESMA to consult the public or the SMSG. Also, in practice, it still remains to be seen whether

---

[125] See, for comparative insights in US administrative law, Lubbers 2012, p. 53.

ESMA will follow the same approach to the duty to give reasons as it does with regard to draft technical standards and guidelines, or whether it will approach this in a different manner.

7. Transposition of ESMA's soft law instruments

When EU agencies have drafted and finally adopted a soft law act, their acts need to be effectuated. This demands that national authorities give proper follow-up to EU agencies' soft law instruments, which entails the fifth stage of the policy cycle. Interestingly, in this stage, a shift takes place from a 'collegiate inter-authority relationship' to a 'hierarchical EU–national level relationship'.[1] While the NCAs were involved in a horizontal manner in the previous stages, that is, on an equal footing with ESMA, they come into a vertical relationship once the soft law instruments have been adopted. This gives the cooperation between the agency and national authorities a completely new dynamic as it goes from centralised to decentralised governance.[2]

This chapter zooms in on the transposition of ESMA's soft law instruments. Transposition entails the translation of Union law into the domestic legal system. What concrete actions are required from Member States, and the extent to which they enjoy the freedom to choose the forms and methods necessary in order to obtain the objective of the Union act, depends on the act under consideration. In this respect, the institutional and procedural autonomy of the Member States needs to be taken into account.[3] The *principle of institutional autonomy* entails that it is up to the Member States to designate the national authorities that are responsible for the transposition of the relevant EU law. Procedural rules are also necessary for the transposition of EU law by national implementing bodies. To the extent that such rules are not enshrined in EU law itself or where EU law contains explicit references to national law, the application of such national procedural rules is a matter for the internal legal order of the Member State. This is referred to as the *principle of procedural autonomy*.

Given the importance of appropriate transposition for the legitimacy and effectiveness of ESMA's soft law-making powers, the aim of this chapter is primarily to establish whether there is a duty of transposition with regard to EU agencies' soft law for the Member States and their authorities, and, if so, on what (legal) basis. Section 1 demonstrates the practical relevance of trans-

1 In relation to networks, see De Visser 2009, p. 498.
2 Ibid., pp. 499–500 in relation to network-based governance.
3 Chapter 2, Section 10.1.

position for ESMA by presenting some exemplary considerations made by the agency. Sections 2–4 analyse the legal obligations (*de iure* level) and the factual expectations (*de facto* level) regarding transposition. Section 5 assesses the influence of ESMA's *de iure* transposition mechanisms and *de facto* practice on the legitimacy and effectiveness of the effectuation of ESMA's soft law-making activity. It concludes that transposition is not required for any of the three categories of ESMA's soft law; hence, problems arise due to the diverging practices throughout the European Union.

1. TRANSPOSITION CONCERNS IN RELATION TO ESMA'S SOFT LAW INSTRUMENTS IN PRACTICE

Concerns with regard to transposition are not merely of theoretical relevance. As follows from ESMA's practice, ESMA is faced with considerations on the transposition of its soft law acts. Transposition reflections or problems generally come to the fore during Board of Supervisors meetings. The practical example in the box that follows demonstrates that ESMA is concerned with the proper transposition of its guidelines into the national legal framework.

> During the meeting of the Board of Supervisors of 24 and 25 June 2015, the chair of the Corporate Reporting Standing Committee reported on the Guidelines on Alternative Performance Measures (APM). The Board discussed these guidelines, in particular *the need for national measures accompanying the Guidelines to ensure the enforceability of the Guidelines.*[4] At this meeting, the Board eventually approved the APM Guidelines.[5] Interestingly, at that time, the Swedish national competent authority objected. However, as follows from the related *compliance table*, Sweden is now also in compliance with the guidelines.[6]

This brief account shows the daily relevance of ESMA ensuring that its soft law instruments are properly transposed. We now turn to an investigation of the extent to which the national competent authorities are subjected *de iure* and *de facto* to the principles of institutional and procedural autonomy.

---

[4] ESMA, Board of Supervisors Summary of Conclusions of 24 and 25 September 2015 (ESMA/BS/140), 9.

[5] ESMA, Guidelines on alternative performance measures (2015) ESMA/2015/1057.

[6] ESMA, Guidelines compliance table on the Guidelines on alternative performance measures (2015) ESMA-32-67-184.

2. THE DUTY OF TRANSPOSITION OF ESMA'S SOFT LAW INSTRUMENTS: THE PRINCIPLES OF INSTITUTIONAL AND PROCEDURAL AUTONOMY

National competent authorities are responsible for the transposition of ESMA's soft law instruments once they are adopted. This section therefore focuses on what happens with these instruments at the national level. The argumentation is built along two main lines. It analyses whether the transposition of ESMA's soft law instruments is required, by looking at the ESMA Regulation and the soft law instruments themselves (*de iure* level), and investigates what the national authorities do with ESMA's soft law acts in order to integrate these acts into the national legal system (*de facto* level). It shows that transposition threatens coherence, because there is no *de iure* rule on the transposition of ESMA's guidelines and non-binding instruments in the national legal framework.

3. A *DE IURE* RULE ON THE TRANSPOSITION OF ESMA'S SOFT LAW INSTRUMENTS IN THE NATIONAL LEGAL FRAMEWORK?

There is no general rule on the transposition of EU agencies' soft law.[7] This section therefore first deals with the question of whether there is a duty or prohibition for the Member States to transpose EU soft law in general. After this more general starting point, it investigates whether transposition is required with regard to ESMA's soft law instruments.

It can be deduced *a contrario* from Article 291(1) TFEU that there is *no general obligation* to transpose EU soft law into national law. On the basis of this provision, the Member States are only required to take all measures of national law that are necessary to implement *legally binding Union acts*.[8] Neither can a general obligation be inferred for the Member States to transpose Union soft law instruments from the principle of sincere cooperation, although defined in broader terms than Article 291(1) TFEU.

While there is thus no duty to transpose imposed on the Member States, there is equally *no general prohibition* of such transposition laid down in

---

7 This is in line with the logic that the principles of procedural and institutional autonomy apply when EU law neither appoints specific existing national bodies nor sets out any procedural rules. Member States' authorities then have the freedom to decide upon the transposition of EU agencies' soft law themselves. See Chapter 2, Section 10.1.

8 Luijendijk & Senden 2011, p. 329.

EU law.[9] As decided by the Court of First Instance in the *Nefarma* case, the Member States are indeed allowed to transpose Union soft law into national law.[10] The consequence is, however, that national implementing bodies are bound by such acts on the basis of national law. The objection one could raise to this is that non-legally binding acts are in this way transformed into law. In any case, the transposition of Union soft law measures is thus a matter for the Member States themselves.[11] Indeed, according to the principles of institutional and procedural autonomy, Member States are free to determine by means of which institutions and which processes they want to incorporate Union law into the domestic legal order, as long as they are efficient and do not obstruct the European provision's implementation.[12]

Nevertheless, questions remain as to whether the procedural and institutional autonomy of the Member States may be curtailed – that is, could there be any restrictions on the ways and means by which Union soft law is to be transposed?[13] The starting point is that Union institutions adopting soft law cannot object as such to the transposition of Union soft law into national hard law. If they do not wish to see their soft law acts transposed in any way at all, they should make this unequivocally clear in the wording thereof. In this respect, it is important to consider *what the soft law act specifies* concerning the kind of transposition that is aimed at. Where discretion is left to the Member States, such as by the stipulation that they should take any 'appropriate' or 'necessary measures' or through the use of terms with a similar meaning, they in fact have *carte blanche* to transpose the act in any way they see fit, possibly also into legislation.[14] In such a case, the Member States retain their complete procedural and institutional autonomy. When soft law acts specify the transposition measures in detail, the adopting institution has clearly not wanted to leave the choice of the means of transposition to the Member States. Hence, when the form of transposition is specified, transposition in any way other than that prescribed must be deemed to have been excluded. In such a case, the procedural and institutional autonomy of the Member States is curtailed.

Since there is no general rule on the transposition of EU agencies' soft law, it is important to look at each of the founding regulations and/or the soft law acts themselves in order to see if anything is provided on the transposition of

---

[9] Senden 2004, p. 347.

[10] Case T-113/89 *Nefarma v Commission* [1990] ECR II-797.

[11] Luijendijk & Senden 2011, p. 329.

[12] See Case 33/76 *Rewe- v Landwirtschaftskammer für das Saarland* [1976] ECR I-1989. See also Lenaerts & Van Nuffel 2005, p. 608.

[13] Senden asks a similar question in the context of the Commission's soft law: see Senden 2004, p. 348.

[14] Ibid., p. 375.

the acts of each particular EU agency. The following subsections do so with regard to ESMA's three categories of soft law instruments. They demonstrate that the *de iure* expectations regarding transposition are different per category, but that the institutional and procedural autonomy of the Member States is not restricted in any of the three situations.

3.1 The Commission's Delegated and Implementing Acts[15]

The Commission has a choice between a regulation or a decision as the instrument used to adopt ESMA's draft technical standards. In practice, the Commission usually chooses the *regulation* instead of the decision. In fact, transposing regulations is prohibited, which means that transposition of the Commission's delegated and implementing acts is not allowed as a matter of principle.[16] Member States may however deem the adoption of implementing measures at the national level necessary in order to grant full effect to the regulations.[17] In any case, since a regulation brings about direct applicability by virtue of Article 288 TFEU, it does not entail a restriction on the institutional or procedural autonomy of the Member States.

3.2 Guidelines and Recommendations

When a national supervisory authority indicates that it complies or will in the future comply with a set of guidelines, it is expected that the guidelines are applied at the national level as well. The question is therefore whether and to what extent NCAs are required to transpose ESMA's guidelines into their national legal framework. Article 16(3) ESMA Regulation stipulates that they 'shall make every effort to comply'. This seems to give the Member States and their corresponding authorities broad discretion as to *how* they need to make this effort; that is, they maintain their entire institutional and procedural autonomy. At the outset, NCAs may decide for themselves whether they want to transpose the guidelines into their national legal framework at all. This means that not doing so is also an option. Yet, if NCAs choose transposition, Article

---

[15] As of this chapter, the book focuses primarily on the so-called final acts, that is, once the soft law acts have been adopted. This means that ESMA's draft technical standards have become, after endorsement by the Commission, Commission implementing and delegated regulations. The final act is therefore no longer an ESMA act.

[16] Prechal, Widdershoven & Jans 2015, p. 13.

[17] For instance, in the Netherlands, regulations in the area of the financial markets are implemented in the *Besluit uitvoering EU-verordeningen financiële markten*. In this national act, the appropriate organisation is assigned the necessary supervisory competences.

16 gives them *carte blanche* to transpose ESMA's guidelines in any way they see fit, possibly also into legislation. National authorities can thus use the form they consider desirable – be it by means of binding or non-binding national measures – as long as they have the competence to do so on the basis of their national law. In the case of binding national measures, NCAs may also have to work together with the national legislator when (parts of) ESMA's guidelines have to be implemented into national law. They may also use a combination of the two. In that case, it can be said that NCAs apply their own proportionality test at the national level, in the sense that they choose for themselves which instruments they will use for the transposition of ESMA's guidelines. For instance, they may choose the transposition instrument used with an eye to the guidelines' relevance to the national market. ESMA cannot object as such to the transposition of its guidelines into national binding measures. If there is a wish to see harmonisation with regard to the method of transposition of its acts, the Union legislature should make this unambiguously clear in the agency's founding regulation.[18]

3.3 Non-binding Instruments

Both Article 29 ESMA Regulation, which enables ESMA to provide opinions to national competent authorities and to develop new practical instruments and convergence tools, and Article 16b, which enables ESMA to issue Q&As, remain completely silent on transposition as such, and consequently also on the means to transpose these acts into the national legal framework. The soft law acts themselves do not prescribe or prohibit transposition either. Again, NCAs maintain their complete institutional and procedural autonomy.

4. *DE FACTO* EXPECTATIONS CONCERNING THE TRANSPOSITION OF ESMA'S SOFT LAW INSTRUMENTS

As follows from the following three subsections, the *de facto* expectations regarding transposition differ per category of ESMA's soft law instruments. In fact, there is little activity with regard to the Commission's delegated and implementing acts and ESMA's non-binding instruments. The focus of this section is therefore on ESMA's guidelines and recommendations. This is also where the main problem lies. Indeed, the lack of a *de iure* duty or prohibition as regards the transposition of guidelines leads to an incoherent system throughout the EU where the legal nature of the guidelines differs per Member

---

[18] See Section 5.1 and Chapter 11, Section 2.3.

State. As the following subsections show, this is evidenced by the fact that we can see in practice that the national authorities transpose ESMA's guidelines in three different ways.

4.1 The Commission's Delegated and Implementing Acts

The Commission's delegated and implementing acts cannot be transposed, because the Commission usually adopts them by means of a regulation and transposing regulations is prohibited.[19] With the exception of the potential adoption of national implementing measures, *de facto* nothing happens. This means that there are no relevant practical insights on this issue.

4.2 Guidelines and Recommendations

Since there is no *de iure* rule on the transposition of ESMA's guidelines and NCAs thus have *carte blanche* to do this in any way they see fit, transposition methods vary a great deal across the Member States. Such differences may also be partially explained by the fact that the legal nature of ESMA's guidelines is unclear and NCAs are thus not always sure what to do with the guidelines.[20] When we look at national practice, some NCAs directly apply ESMA's guidelines whereas others issue their own binding or non-binding instruments. In most Member States, NCAs also have the possibility to advise the national legislature to amend existing legislation or to adopt new laws in order to fully implement ESMA's guidelines and recommendations. Roughly speaking, this book identifies three different methods of transposition that appear to be used within the Member States. These methods may be visualised as in Table 7.1.

Table 7.1 Methods for the transposition of ESMA's guidelines into the national framework

Three different *de facto* methods of transposition
1) Direct application of ESMA's guidelines in the supervisory practices of the NCAs
2) Adoption of non-binding instruments by the NCAs
3) Adoption of binding instruments by the NCAs or implementation by the national legislature

[19] Prechal, Widdershoven & Jans 2015, p. 13.

[20] See Chapter 8.

4.2.1 Direct application of ESMA's guidelines in the supervisory practices of the NCAs

First of all, there are a number of Member States in which the national competent authority directly applies ESMA's guidelines in its own supervisory practices. The Dutch Authority for the Financial Markets (*Autoriteit Financiële markten*, AFM) is one of them. If the AFM decides to comply with a particular set of ESMA's guidelines, it publishes on its website a link to the Dutch translation of the guidelines in question to inform the financial market participants concerned.[21] In its publication, the AFM indicates which laws and regulations – both European and national – it will take account of ESMA's guidelines in relation to monitoring compliance. If applicable, the AFM also identifies the financial market participants to which the acts apply.[22] As such, the AFM does not integrate ESMA's soft law acts but rather applies them when monitoring compliance with national law – for example, the relevant rules of conduct of the Dutch Act on Financial Supervision (*Wet op het financieel toezicht*, Wft)[23] – or with Union law – for example, Regulation (EU) No. 36/2012 on short selling and certain aspects of credit default swaps.[24]

4.2.2 Adoption of non-binding instruments by the NCAs

Second, some national competent authorities choose to integrate ESMA's guidelines into the national framework by means of their own non-binding instruments.[25] The Federal Financial Supervisory Authority (*Bundesanstalt für Finanzdienstleistungsaufsicht*, BaFin) in Germany generally adopts guidelines issued by ESMA in its administrative practice.[26] For this purpose, it regularly adapts its non-binding *circulars* in order to reflect the implementation of ESMA's guidelines. For instance, on 9 January 2014 BaFin published the

---

[21] For the overview of all of ESMA's guidelines, see AFM, 'Richtsnoeren ESA' <www.afm.nl/nl-nl/professionals/onderwerpen/esa-richtsnoeren-bu> accessed 19 February 2021.

[22] For an example, see AFM, 'Richtsnoeren beloningsbeleid AIFMD (ESMA)' <www.afm.nl/nl-nl/professionals/onderwerpen/esa-richtsnoeren-bu/beloningsbeleid-aifmd-esma> accessed 19 February 2021.

[23] Ibid.

[24] AFM, 'AFM past ESMA Richtsnoeren met betrekking tot vrijstelling activiteiten market makers toe' (17 June 2013) <www.afm.nl/nl-nl/nieuws/2013/juni/esma-vrijstelling-activiteiten-market-makers> accessed 19 February 2021.

[25] Some NCAs may use a mix of binding and non-binding tools. This means they can also use non-binding instruments alone.

[26] BaFin, 'Guidelines and Q&As issued by the European Supervisory Authorities' <www.bafin.de/EN/RechtRegelungen/Leitlinien_und_Q_and_A_der_ESAs/Leitlinien_und_Q_and_A_der_ESAs_node_en.html> accessed 19 February 2021. See also Hartlapp & Hofmann 2020, p. 140.

fourth revised version of Circular 4/2010 (MaComp Circular).[27] This Circular was amended to reflect the implementation of ESMA's Guidelines on remuneration policies and practices (MiFID) in BaFin's administrative practice.[28] Circulars are very much adaptable to their legal environment, because BaFin may issue them without any outside intervention (such as from the Ministry of Finance) and may amend them whenever it wishes. Likewise, in France, the Financial Markets Authority (*Autorité des Marchés Financiers*, AMF) incorporates all ESMA's guidelines in its own legal framework by means of non-binding *positions.* These are presented on its website. For instance, as of 21 July 2018 for new funds, and from 21 January 2019 for existing funds, the AMF has applied ESMA's Guidelines on stress test scenarios under Article 28 of the MMF Regulation in practice.[29] The national authority has integrated these guidelines in its *position* DOC-2018-05.[30] Similarly, in Italy, the government authority responsible for regulating the Italian securities market (*Commissione Nazionale per le Società e la Borsa*, Consob) usually seeks to comply through *orientamenti* (Guidelines) or *comunicazioni* (Communications), which are equally non-binding acts.[31] It is however hard to see why NCAs transpose ESMA's guidelines into something that is non-binding, because ESMA's guidelines are already applicable as such.

In some Member States, NCAs have to carry out a consultation prior to the use of a non-binding instrument to integrate guidelines into their national framework.[32] Nowhere in the EU do NCAs have a *de iure* possibility to impose sanctions on financial market participants in case of non-compliance with their own non-binding acts.

---

27 BaFin, 'BaFin publishes revised MaComp Circular' (9 January 2014) <www.bafin.de/SharedDocs/Veroeffentlichungen/EN/Meldung/2014/meldung_140109_neufassung_macomp_en.html> accessed 19 February 2021. Note that there is already a new update of this Circular, but not for reasons relating to the implementation of ESA guidelines.

28 Ibid.

29 ESMA, Guidelines on stress tests scenarios under Article 28 of the MMF Regulation (ESMA34-49-115).

30 AMF, 'Position AMF – Requirements for stress test scenarios under Article 28 of the European Money Market Fund Regulation' (2020) <https://www.amf-france.org/en/news-publications/news/stress-testing-scenarios-money-market-funds-amf-complies-esma-guidelines> accessed 19 February 2021.

31 Alberti 2020, p. 309.

32 Ibid. This is also the case for Consob.

4.2.3 Adoption of binding instruments by the NCAs or implementation by the national legislature

Third, there are also some NCAs that have the possibility to adopt national binding instruments for the integration of ESMA's guidelines. In a similar vein, the national legislature in most of the Member States has a possibility to amend existing legislation or to adopt new laws in order to implement (parts of) ESMA's guidelines. This could be regarded as a benefit for ESMA. Indeed, it could be argued that from the perspective of the agency, there is nothing to be said against transposing guidelines into something that is stronger than the guidelines themselves, because that would obviously give them more impact. For instance, the Central Bank of Ireland (CBoI) can issue or update CBoI Regulations for this purpose, and its Central Bank UCITS Regulations[33] implement some concrete paragraphs of ESMA's guidelines on ETFs and other UCITS issues.[34] In a similar vein, BaFin can issue administrative acts in order to implement the provisions of ESMA's Guidelines.[35] An example may be found in BaFin's General Administrative Act pursuant to Article 42 of Regulation (EU) No. 600/2014 (MiFIR) regarding contracts for differences (CFDs),[36] which refers to the ESMA Guidelines on MiFID II product governance requirements.[37] In addition, Germany has for instance codified in national legislation[38] ESMA's guidelines on the Exemption for Market Making Activities and Primary Market Operations[39] and ESMA's guidelines on

---

[33] Irish Statute Book, S.I. No. 420/2015 – Central Bank (Supervision and Enforcement) Act 2013 (Section 48(1)) (Undertakings for Collective Investment in Transferable Securities) Regulations 2015 <www.irishstatutebook.ie/eli/2015/si/420/made/en/print> accessed 19 February 2021.

[34] ESMA, Guidelines on ETFs and other UCITS issues (2014) ESMA/2014/937.

[35] BaFin, 'General and collective administrative acts issued by BaFin' <www.bafin.de/EN/RechtRegelungen/Verfuegungen/liste_verfuegungen_node_en.html> accessed 19 February 2021.

[36] BaFin, 'General Administrative Act pursuant to Article 42 of Regulation (EU) No 600/2014 (MiFIR) regarding contracts for differences (CFDs)' <www.bafin.de/SharedDocs/Veroeffentlichungen/EN/Aufsichtsrecht/Verfuegung/vf_190801_allgvfg_Differenzgeschaefte_en.html?nn=8661832#doc13060548bodyText6> accessed 19 February 2021.

[37] ESMA, Guidelines on MiFID II product governance requirements (2018) ESMA35-43-620.

[38] Hartlapp & Hofmann 2020, p. 140. The government altered existing national legislation; see for example the adjustment of Verordnung zur Konkretisierung von Art, Umfang und Form der Mitteilungen und Benachrichtigungen (Leerverkaufs-Anzeigeverordnung) <www.gesetze-im-internet.de/lanzv_2014/LAnzV.pdf> accessed 19 February 2021.

[39] ESMA, Guidelines on the exemption for market making activities and primary market operations under Regulation (EU) 236/2012 of the European Parliament

Remuneration Policies and Practices.[40] Generally speaking, NCAs have a possibility to carry out a consultation prior to the use of a binding transposition instrument, although the consultation period differs in each Member State. It could however be argued that an additional consultation at the national level is not necessary when consultations have already taken place at the ESMA level. From the point of view of throughput legitimacy, it is nonetheless of interest that this possibility exists, because in the case that ESMA has not carried out consultations, the NCAs can add legitimacy to the guidelines by consulting at the national level instead. Additionally, the use of binding transposition measures is usually paired with a *de iure* possibility to impose sanctions – such as the withdrawal of a licence, corrective measures or fines – on financial market participants. This gives ESMA's guidelines, which are by their nature a soft law instrument, a very hard character at the national level.

4.3 Non-binding Instruments

There is no *de iure* expectation regarding the transposition of ESMA's non-binding instruments. In practice, most NCAs therefore take the view that they do not need to integrate such acts into their national legal framework. This could be explained by the fact that there is no 'comply or explain' mechanism that is applicable to such acts. Instead, NCAs merely publish the instruments on their websites and/or use them in their supervisory practices.[41] NCAs therefore do not have to carry out a consultation prior to the use of ESMA's non-binding instruments. Likewise, none of the NCAs can impose sanctions in case of non-compliance. Yet, there are several NCAs that may do so when not following a non-binding instrument leads to non-compliance with any underlying binding law. In this case, the sanction is based not on the breach of the non-binding instrument but on a breach of binding rules.

---

and the Council on short selling and certain aspects of Credit Default Swaps (2013) ESMA/2013/74.

[40] ESMA, Guidelines on Remuneration Policies and Practices MiFID (2013) ESMA/2013/606.

[41] See for instance

BaFin, 'ESA Q&As that have not been adopted in BaFin's administrative practice' <www.bafin.de/EN/RechtRegelungen/Leitlinien_und_Q_and_A_der_ESAs/Nicht_uebernommene_Q_and_A/nicht_uebernommene_Q_and_A_node_en.html> accessed 19 February 2021; AFM, 'Status Q&As van ESMA' <www.afm.nl/nl-nl/professionals/onderwerpen/esma-int> accessed 19 February 2021.

5. CONCLUSION AND ASSESSMENT ON THE TRANSPOSITION OF ESMA'S ACTS

The situation regarding the Commission's delegated and implementing acts is clear. Since these are mostly regulations, transposition is prohibited, although national implementing measures might be necessary in order to grant full effect to the rules laid down in the Regulation. The ESMA regulation is silent with regard to the transposition of non-binding instruments. In principle, NCAs do not transpose these acts at all. The situation regarding ESMA's guidelines is more ambiguous. The analysis above has shown that the agency's establishing regulation does not provide for any *de iure* rule on the transposition of guidelines. This means that NCAs have the freedom to choose whether they want to transpose them or not, and if so, by what means. Their institutional and procedural autonomy is thus not limited in any way.[42] The same applies regarding the Commission's delegated and implementing acts and ESMA's non-binding instruments.

In the current situation, some financial market participants are thus subject to national binding instruments and face serious consequences in the form of sanctions for not abiding by these rules, whereas others remain subject to non-binding instruments and do not necessarily face any consequences if they do not comply with such instruments. That cannot really be regarded as in the interest of ESMA. Depending on the national follow-up given to ESMA's guidelines, rights and obligations derived therefrom may thus vary from one Member State to another.[43] As a result, the rules may have different implications in different jurisdictions.

From a legal perspective, such differences may be explained by the principles of institutional and procedural autonomy that give the Member States discretion to deal with EU law in a way that fits their own legal system. The 'form' of transposition ultimately depends on the instruments available in the Member State concerned. From a policy perspective, however, this entails a problem for the creation of a single market where unity and convergence are of utmost importance. It also makes achievement of the Capital Markets Union (CMU) objectives more difficult. Such differences in transposition are not helpful for the effectiveness or the legitimacy of ESMA's guidelines.

The following subsections conclude this chapter and provide an assessment of areas where transposition leads to tensions on the basis of legitimacy and effectiveness concerns.

---

[42] See Section 3.2.

[43] Acceto & Zleptnig 2005, p. 380.

5.1 Differences in the Transposition of ESMA's Guidelines Negatively Affect Effectiveness

In practice, three different methods are used to integrate ESMA's guidelines into the national legal framework. These are: direct application; adopting non-binding instruments; and adopting binding instruments. The fact that ESMA's guidelines are transposed in different ways is interesting from the viewpoint of effectiveness. All of ESMA's soft law instruments apply to all Member States, meaning that the approach *at the Union level* is indeed coherent. However, the discretion for the NCAs and national legislature to deviate and transpose ESMA's guidelines in the way they see fit may result in incoherence *at the national level.* Besides, it harms the other trend in financial market regulation aiming at coherence *at the Union level*, that is, that of the Union legislature using more and more regulations instead of directives for the reason that regulations do not need to be transposed. The transposition of guidelines is again detrimental to this aim. In this sense, non-binding instruments are actually a better tool for the achievement of convergence, because they are not converted at all.

In such a system, are the objectives of the guidelines still met? After all, 'the common, uniform and consistent application of EU law' is one of the objectives for which guidelines are issued in the first place. Due to the different transposition methods used in practice, ESMA's guidelines cannot always guarantee such convergence throughout the Member States. This is also detrimental to the legal certainty of the system as a whole.[44] It is thus not inconceivable that, in this way, soft law achieves the opposite result of what it intends to realise.[45] Do guidelines then still contribute to effectiveness? The answer is no, not always. The fact that NCAs and the national legislature use different methods, and thus may give ESMA's guidelines a different legal nature at the national level, negatively affects the effectiveness of these acts, because it may not be possible for the objective of the guidelines to be attained. Likewise, transposition at the national level may also slow the policy process and the entry into force of ESMA's guidelines. In this way, the effectiveness of ESMA's guidelines is decreased by the unilateral actions of the NCAs. It is therefore recommended that only one common European approach towards transposition be selected – direct application, for example – so that all Member States are acting in the same manner.[46]

---

[44] The different methods of transposition also lead to differences in the extent of judicial protection at the national level: see Chapter 10, Section 5.2. This also harms the legal certainty of the system as a whole.

[45] Luijendijk & Senden 2011, p. 319.

[46] See Chapter 11, Section 2.3.

5.2 Transposition of Soft Law into Hard Law Negatively Affects Legitimacy and Effectiveness

The question is whether the transposition of ESMA's soft law into hard law at the national level should be allowed or prohibited. To begin with, the fact that in some Member States ESMA's guidelines are transposed by means of legally binding instruments is interesting from the viewpoint of legitimacy. Indeed, it could be argued that the transposition of ESMA's soft law into legally binding instruments at the national level is not desirable from the perspective of legitimacy, given the fact that its soft law mostly comes about without any involvement of the other Union institutions, and thus also without any democratic control.[47] Besides, the question could be raised as to whether such transposition is in fact a form of introducing *regulation by the backdoor*. Indeed, how do we know whether, for instance, Bulgarian national law correctly transposes a particular ESMA guideline if we do not speak this language?[48] Transposition thus makes it rather difficult for others to control the NCAs, because of language barriers. Both concerns impair the legitimacy of ESMA's guidelines.

In some Member States, however, NCAs have to carry out a consultation prior to the use of a non-binding instrument to integrate guidelines into their national framework. Likewise, most NCAs have the possibility to carry out a consultation prior to the use of a binding transposition instrument. The consultation period differs in each country. Where consultations take place (again) at the national level, it may be said that at least some legitimacy is given to the national measures implementing ESMA's guidelines. However, it follows from practice that stakeholders are essentially always consulted by ESMA regarding guidelines.[49] It is therefore questionable why consultations would take place again at the national level. This does not add much to the legitimacy of the guidelines. From the viewpoint of efficiency, such national consultations are not in fact considered desirable, because they erect an extra procedural hurdle and slow the process. As a result, guidelines might apply much later than is the case in Member States where guidelines are directly applied or are applied by means of national measures which can be adopted rather quickly without extra consultations. It is also quite disturbing from the perspective of effectiveness when a Member State turns ESMA's soft law into national hard law. Indeed, hardening ESMA's soft law goes against the agen-

---

47 See Chapter 5, Section 6. See also Luijendijk & Senden 2011, p. 341.

48 Peer reviews are a helpful tool in this regard, though: see Chapter 9, Section 4.

49 See Chapter 5, Section 4.3.

cy's preference for effectiveness, since soft law is often chosen on the basis of considerations such as flexibility and proportionality.[50]

5.3 NCAs Choose Transposition Methods on the Basis of Their Own Proportionality Test

In practice, some NCAs do use more than one of the three transposition methods, sometimes even combining binding and non-binding measures. They choose the instrument used to integrate the guidelines into the national framework on a case-by-case basis, with a view to choosing the instrument which best serves the goal of the specific guidelines. In this way, NCAs seem to make an effectiveness consideration by keeping the objective of the guidelines at the centre of their attention. What this means in practice, however, is that in some Member States one particular set of guidelines may be transposed by means of a national non-binding instrument whereas another set of guidelines may be transposed into a national binding instrument. This is not the most desirable scenario from the perspective of legal certainty, because the legal status of the guidelines may differ each time, in this way resulting in different possibilities for judicial review at the national courts.[51] Of course, this scenario only applies to those NCAs that have a choice between binding and non-binding instruments on the basis of their national law. In that case, it can be said that NCAs apply their own proportionality test at the national level, in the sense that they choose for themselves which instruments they use for the transposition of ESMA's guidelines.

NCAs and/or the national legislature consider which instrument to choose, that is, which instrument is best to achieve the guidelines' objective(s). It could however be argued that the transposition of this category of agency soft law instruments into binding measures or national hard law would run counter to efforts towards less intrusive regulation. By establishing rules in such a soft law instrument, ESMA chooses to alleviate the burden imposed by Union legislation. The transposition of soft law into binding measures or national legislation counteracts this effort. Hence, the principle of proportionality could be said to bring about an obligation for the Member States to try to transpose Union soft law through the most appropriate and least burdensome means.[52]

---

[50] This is especially true if ESMA is acting on the basis of a 'may' provision: see Chapter 3, Section 3 on conferral. It is important to recall the reasons behind the choice of the soft law instrument. As we have seen, ESMA takes several considerations into account when it needs to choose the most appropriate instrument during the proportionality test.

[51] See Chapter 10, Section 5.2.

[52] Senden 2004, p. 358.

Proportionality namely aims to limit government interference, not only at the Union but also at the national level. It is therefore all the more important, one could say, that the proportionality considerations are set out in the soft law acts of ESMA.

When NCAs choose to use a binding instrument on the basis of their own proportionality test, the question arises as to whether the proportionality choice of ESMA or that of the NCA should prevail. Indeed, when implementing Union law, Member States are likely to be torn between loyalty towards their own national interests and loyalty towards the European Union.[53] On the one hand, it could be argued that Member States have institutional and procedural autonomy and may thus act by means of the measures they deem most appropriate. On the other hand, the principle of sincere cooperation requires Member States' authorities to do whatever is necessary to implement and execute Union law within their jurisdiction.[54]

This in fact shows an apparent tension between the principles of autonomy and sincere cooperation. Too much emphasis on sincere cooperation highlights only the effectiveness of regulation and might encroach upon the sovereignty of the Member States. Yet, concentrating too much on the autonomy of the Member States might hinder the effectiveness of the Union's actions, because it might prevent the Union from achieving its objectives. Therefore, the legal framework should ideally pursue a balance between the two principles: NCAs should enjoy a sufficient degree of autonomy to give effect to ESMA's soft law but should respect their obligations under the principle of cooperation to the extent that they do not hamper the effectiveness of ESMA's rule-making powers. This is another reason to select only one common European approach towards transposition – direct application, for example – so that all NCAs are acting in the same manner, at the same pace and with the same degree of flexibility.

---

[53] Acceto & Zleptnig 2005, pp. 379 and 382.

[54] Ibid., pp. 379 and 387.

8. Compliance with ESMA's soft law instruments

In order to give further effect to EU agencies' soft law, national authorities have to comply with such instruments. This entails the sixth stage of the policy cycle. As in the case of transposition, in this stage a shift takes place from a 'collegiate inter-authority relationship' to a 'hierarchical EU–national level relationship'.[1]

This chapter zooms in on compliance with ESMA's soft law instruments. Indeed, in order to be fully effective, Union rules need to be complied with by those to whom they are addressed. In this stage, the principles of legitimate expectations and sincere cooperation need to be taken into account.[2] The first principle aims to protect individuals against arbitrary actions on the part of states or public authorities by requiring them, as far as is possible, to act in conformity with legitimate expectations to which they have given rise.[3] The second principle constitutes the basis for cooperation between the Member States and the Union institutions, and requires the Member States' authorities to do whatever is necessary to implement and execute Union law within their jurisdictions.[4] Given the importance of appropriate compliance for the legitimacy and effectiveness of ESMA's soft law-making powers, the aim of this chapter is primarily to establish whether there is a duty of compliance with EU agencies' soft law for the Member States and their authorities, and, if so, on what (legal) basis. Section 1 demonstrates the practical relevance of compliance for ESMA by presenting some exemplary considerations made by the Commission and the agency. Sections 2, 3 and 4 analyse the legal obligations (*de iure* level) and the factual expectations (*de facto* level) regarding compliance. Section 5 assesses the influence of ESMA's *de iure* compliance mechanisms and *de facto* practice on the legitimacy and effectiveness of the effectuation of ESMA's soft law-making activity. It also concludes that the duty of compliance with ESMA's guidelines and non-binding instruments is still dependent on clarification regarding the legal nature of ESMA's soft

[1] See Chapter 7. In relation to networks, see De Visser 2009, p. 498.
[2] See Chapter 2, Section 11.
[3] Van den Brink and others 2015, pp. 207–08.
[4] Van den Brink 2012, p. 147; Acceto & Zleptnig 2005, p. 385 and 387.

law instruments and that, specifically with regard to guidelines, differences in compliance at the national level hamper the instruments' effectiveness.

1. COMPLIANCE CONCERNS IN RELATION TO ESMA'S SOFT LAW INSTRUMENTS IN PRACTICE

Concerns with regard to compliance are not merely of theoretical relevance. As follows from ESMA's practice, the agency itself is faced with considerations on ensuring compliance with its soft law acts. To begin with, compliance reflections or problems may come to the fore during the Board of Supervisors meetings. In addition, it is clear that the European Commission also has a strong interest in this matter. The example in the box below indeed shows that divergence in compliance with guidelines is a matter of concern for the European Commission as well.

In a report on the evaluation of the Short Selling Regulation (SSR), the Commission expressed its concerns regarding the *non-compliance of the competent authorities of five Member States with ESMA's guidelines* on the exemption for market making activities and primary market operations under the SSR.[5] As follows from the guidelines compliance table, the authorities have explained their non-compliance with aspects of the guidelines by referring to their divergent views on a number of issues, such as the scope of the covered instruments and the conditions for granting the market maker exemption.[6] The Commission warned that 'the non-compliance by some competent authorities is bound to create a situation whereby the SSR is applied in a divergent manner', resulting in an unlevel playing field across the Union.[7] This could undermine the main objectives of the Regulation, that is, ensuring the proper functioning of the internal market for financial services and ensuring a high level of consumer and investor protection.

---

[5] ESMA, Guidelines on the exemption for market making activities and primary market operations under Regulation (EU) 236/2012 of the European Parliament and the Council on short selling and certain aspects of Credit Default Swaps (2013) ESMA/2013/74.

[6] ESMA, Guidelines compliance table on the Guidelines on the exemption for market making activities and primary market operations under Regulation (EU) 236/2012 of the European Parliament and the Council on short selling and certain aspects of Credit Default Swaps (2013) ESMA/2013/765.

[7] Commission, 'Report from the Commission to the European Parliament and the Council on the evaluation of the Regulation (EU) No 236/2012 on short selling and certain aspects of credit default swaps' COM(2013) 885 final, 6.

In addition, different criteria applied to the market maker exemption can also lead to a divergent application of that exemption. Yet, according to the Commission, a consistent application of the SSR framework and, in particular, of the market making exemption in all Member States is crucial in ensuring a level playing field and the consistency of market practices across the Union. 'Non-compliance with guidelines is therefore not desirable and may indicate an underlying breach of Union law.'[8] If the market making exemption is thus 'applied in a manner which is in breach of the SSR, the Commission will take appropriate follow-up measures'.[9]

During the meeting of ESMA's Board of Supervisors of 4 July 2013,[10] 'the Commission also indicated that it might ask ESMA to take action regarding the divergence in compliance with the guidelines by NCAs'. The topic was further discussed at the Board of Supervisors meeting in September,[11] but 'even today, the five NCAs still remain non-compliant' and 'a further three NCAs have changed their status to non-compliant in the meantime'.[12]

This brief account shows the daily relevance of ESMA ensuring that its soft law instruments are properly complied with. We now turn to an investigation of the extent to which the national competent authorities are subjected *de iure* and *de facto* to the principles of legitimate expectations and sincere cooperation.

---

[8] In relation to the reporting by a group of NCAs of their non-compliance with ESMA's guidelines on the exemption of market makers under the Short Selling Regulation, see Commission, 'Report from the Commission, the European Parliament and the Council on the evaluation of the Regulation (EU) No 236/2012 on short selling and certain aspects of credit default swaps' COM(2013) 885 final, 6. The Commission also indicated to ESMA that it might request that it take action: see ESMA, Board of Supervisors Summary of Conclusions of 4 July 2013 ESMA/2013/BS/125.

[9] Commission, 'Report from the Commission, the European Parliament and the Council on the evaluation of the Regulation (EU) No 236/2012 on short selling and certain aspects of credit default swaps' COM(2013) 885 final, 6.

[10] ESMA, Board of Supervisors Summary of Conclusions of 4 July 2013 (ESMA/2013/BS/125), 3.

[11] ESMA, Board of Supervisors Summary of Conclusions of 24 September 2013 (ESMA/2013/BS/155).

[12] ESMA, Guidelines compliance table on the Guidelines on the Exemption for market making activities and primary market operations under Regulation (EU) 236/2012 of the European Parliament and the Council on short selling and certain aspects of Credit Default Swaps (2021) ESMA70-21038340-46.

2. THE DUTY OF COMPLIANCE WITH ESMA'S SOFT LAW INSTRUMENTS: THE COURT'S TEST AND THE PRINCIPLES OF LEGITIMATE EXPECTATIONS AND SINCERE COOPERATION

Compliance is an important next step in the effectuation of EU law. This section therefore focuses on the question whether there is a duty of compliance with ESMA's three types of soft law instruments. The argumentation is built on two main lines. It first analyses the extent to which ESMA's soft law instruments are or are not binding, and whether compliance with ESMA's soft law instruments is required, by looking at the ESMA regulation and the soft law acts themselves (*de iure* level). Second, it investigates whether it can be established that these instruments (are intended to) produce legal effects on the basis of the Court's test as developed in the case-law or on the basis of the principles of legitimate expectations and sincere cooperation, and in this way entail any compliance expectations (*de facto* level).[13] It shows that the Commission's delegated and implementing acts are 'inherently' legally binding and compliance is mandatory; that guidelines may have 'incidental' and 'indirect' legal effects when NCAs indicate that they comply or will comply in the future; and that non-binding instruments merely produce *de facto* effects, which means that compliance is at most voluntary.

3. A *DE IURE* DUTY OF COMPLIANCE WITH ESMA'S SOFT LAW INSTRUMENTS?

There is no general rule on compliance with EU agencies' soft law. This subsection therefore first sets out what types of bindingness could exist with regard to EU soft law in general and whether they could lead to any compliance obligations. Indeed, the exact duty of compliance depends to a great extent on the legal nature of the Union act at hand. In fact, the more binding the instrument is, the stronger the compliance obligations are. After this more general starting point, the subsections which follow investigate whether compliance is required *de iure* with regard to ESMA's soft law instruments.

As follows from the Treaties, only the instruments that as such have been attributed legally binding force can have *general and 'inherent' legally binding force*.[14] In such a case, an act is in and of itself capable of creating or imposing rights and obligations. The instruments concerned constitute

---

13 Korkea-Aho 2009 also takes into account both components, that is, case-law and general principles.

14 See TFEU, Art 288. See also Senden 2004, p. 246.

a closed or exhaustive system which can only be extended by the legislature. Consequently, instruments that have been explicitly denied legally binding force in Article 288 TFEU – that is, recommendations and opinions – lack the capability to have 'inherent' legally binding force. The same holds true for all soft law instruments on which the Treaties are largely silent, including those emanating from EU agencies.

However, the way in which the Court has assessed appeals under Article 263 TFEU has clarified that the system is not closed as regards *individual Union acts*.[15] Indeed, on the basis of what one could call the 'particular or specific merits' of an individual act, the legally binding force of a Union act in its own right could also be established.[16] If certain conditions are fulfilled, an act that does not have 'inherent' legally binding force can nonetheless obtain *'incidental' legally binding force*.[17] In order to determine whether an act is capable of having such legal effects,[18] it is necessary to examine (i) its wording, (ii) its context, (iii) its substance and (iv) the intention of its author.[19] It will usually be found that soft law instruments lack 'incidental' legally binding force, as they are not intended to have legal effects. Union law does however offer still other ways and means whereby a Union act can influence a person's legal position. In this regard, the Court has adhered to a broader concept of legal effect than legally binding force alone. Indeed, the fact that an act does not (intend to) have legal effects does not mean that it has no legal effect at all. Another way to establish such effects is on the basis of the act in combination with other legal 'mechanisms'.[20] In this case, one could say that legal effect does not ensue directly from the nature of the act itself, but indirectly from the operation of other legal methods and principles.[21] Such *indirect legal effects* can occur as a result of interpretation by the national court[22] and, most importantly for this

---

15 Senden 2004, p. 265.

16 Ibid.

17 Ibid.

18 Korkea-Aho 2009, p. 275: 'At the core of the legal conception of soft law lies the difference between legal bindingness and legal effects. The simple way to differentiate between them is to say that legally binding force means that a regulatory instrument could be ultimately enforced by means of legal sanctions. (…) By contrast, legal effects of soft law refer to the potential of soft law instruments to create legitimate expectations for individuals and businesses, or to clarify and specify the terms of hard law.'

19 These four criteria are dealt with in various cases, such as Case T-671/15 *E-Control v ACER* [2016], para 21 and Case T-496/11 *United Kingdom v ECB* [2015], para 31.

20 Senden 2004, p. 240.

21 Ibid., and Stefan 2008, p. 772.

22 The Court established that the recommendations could gain legal effect by way of the national court taking them into account in its interpretation of Union law or

analysis, via the intermediary use of general principles of EU law such as the principles of legitimate expectations and sincere cooperation.[23]

Finally, when there is voluntary compliance with a soft law instrument, that is, not compliance imposed by the law itself, we may speak of a purely *de facto* effect.[24] The essential point for the distinction between legal effect and *de facto* effect is thus whether or not there is a legal obligation to give effect to or to comply with the rights and obligations contained in a Union act.

In conclusion, if there is no explicit *de iure* obligation to comply laid down in the Union act itself, a *de facto* duty of compliance could be established on the basis of the 'inherent' or 'incidental' legally binding force of the act or on the basis of the 'indirect' legal effects thereof.[25] Compliance obligations cannot derive from acts with purely *de facto* effects. The following three subsections analyse whether there is a *de iure* duty of compliance for each of the three categories of ESMA's soft law instruments. They demonstrate that the expectations regarding compliance are different per category.

3.1 Draft Regulatory and Implementing Technical Standards and the Commission's Delegated and Implementing Acts

In order to establish whether there is a *de iure* duty of compliance, we need to make a distinction between the *preparatory* ESMA draft technical standards and the Commission's *final* delegated or implementing acts. The former are not legally binding,[26] because they are preparatory measures. Hence, a duty of compliance regarding the drafts does not exist.[27] The latter are adopted by the

---

national law: see C-322/88 *Grimaldi v Fonds des maladies professionnelles* [1989] ECR 4407, paras. 12 and 16.

[23] Georgieva 2015, p. 237 points to the fact that '[t]he creation of indirect legal effects, or the ability of soft law to produce legal effects via the intermediary use of general principles of EU law, is a thesis purported in several scholarly accounts on soft law'. See also Senden 2004, p. 240; Stefan 2012a, pp. 142–54; Wellens & Borchardt 1989, pp. 288–89.

[24] Senden 2004, pp. 246–47.

[25] Stefan's research on competition and state aid case law has found more than 600 judgments, orders and opinions which have acknowledged the binding legal effects of soft law instruments: see Stefan 2012a, p. 57.

[26] See also Chapter 10 on the possibilities for judicial review of draft technical standards and the Commission's delegated and implementing acts: preparatory measures are not judicially reviewable.

[27] This is also in line with the case-law of the Court in which it has been decided on multiple occasions that a person may not plead a breach of the principle of protection of legitimate expectations unless he has been given precise assurances; see Case T-264/07 *CSL Behring v Commission and EMA* (2010) ECR II-4469, para 117. Such assurances cannot be said to have been given when the process is still under way.

Commission by means of a *regulation* or a *decision*.[28] These instruments have been attributed legally binding force as an inherent feature by virtue of Article 288 TFEU. Consequently, there is an irrefutable presumption that they 'are intended to' have legally binding force, unless of course they are annulled or declared invalid by the Court of Justice.[29] There is no need to demonstrate this intention on the basis of their actual contents, nor will the Court test whether they do indeed aim at being legally binding.[30] Indeed, as follows from Article 288 TFEU, a *regulation* has general application, is binding in its entirety and is directly applicable in all Member States. A *decision* is binding in its entirety as well, unless it specifies those to whom it is addressed – in such a case, the decision is only binding on them. As said before, in practice the Commission has so far only used the regulation.[31]

Based on the 'inherent' legally binding force of the Commission's delegated or implementing regulations, there is thus a clear *de iure* duty of compliance for both NCAs *and* financial market participants. It is axiomatic that a public body must follow formal legal rules.[32] A failure on the part of the NCAs to abide by hard law might therefore result in a breach of Union law procedure by ESMA or sanctions in the form of infringement proceedings by the Commission.[33] If financial market participants do not comply, it is for the NCAs to take appropriate action.

3.2 Guidelines and Recommendations

In order to establish whether there is a *de iure* duty of compliance, we need to first emphasise that ESMA's guidelines and recommendations have not been attributed 'inherent' legally binding force by the Treaties. However, the agency has a different kind of compliance mechanism regarding its guidelines and recommendations, namely the so-called comply or explain mechanism.

---

28 ESMA Regulation, Arts 10(4) and 15(4).

29 Senden 2004, pp. 246–47. If their adoption or their contents are not in conformity with the requirements imposed by the law, their annulment or invalidity may be requested in a TFEU Arts 263 or 267 procedure, respectively.

30 Ibid., p. 246.

31 This is analysed on the basis of the overview of all technical standards ESMA has issued: see <https://www.esma.europa.eu/convergence/guidelines-and-technical-standards> accessed 24 February 2021. The Commission has not used a decision as of the time of writing (24 February 2021).

32 Craig 2012, p. 578.

33 See Chapter 9 on enforcement for other mechanisms to be used for tackling non-compliance by national authorities.

Article 16(3) ESMA Regulation provides:

> The competent authorities and financial market participants ***shall make every effort to comply*** with [ESMA's] guidelines and recommendations.
>
> Within 2 months of the issuance of a guideline or recommendation, each competent authority shall confirm whether it complies or intends to comply with that guideline or recommendation. In the event that a competent authority does not comply or does not intend to comply, it shall inform the Authority, stating its reasons.
>
> The Authority shall publish the fact that a competent authority does not comply or does not intend to comply with that guideline or recommendation. The Authority may also decide, on a case by case basis, to publish the reasons provided by the competent authority for not complying with that guideline or recommendation. The competent authority shall receive advanced notice of such publication.
>
> If required by that guideline or recommendation, financial market participants shall report, in a clear and detailed way, whether they comply with that guideline or recommendation.

On the basis of this *de iure* compliance mechanism, each national competent authority has to notify ESMA of whether it complies or intends to comply with the agency's guidelines and recommendations within two months of the issuance of those guidelines and recommendations. A template for such notification is available from the ESMA website. In the absence of a response by this deadline, ESMA will publish the fact that it did not receive a response from that competent authority within the legislative time period provided. In the event that a national authority does not comply or does not intend to comply, it has to inform ESMA, stating its reasons. ESMA will publish this fact in a so-called guidelines compliance table and it may also decide, on a case-by-case basis, to publish the reasons provided by the competent authority for not complying with the guidelines.[34] The NCA receives advance notice of such publication.

3.3 Non-binding Instruments

In order to establish whether there is a *de iure* duty of compliance, we need to first emphasise that ESMA's non-binding instruments have not been attributed 'inherent' legally binding force by means of the Treaties. There is no 'comply or explain' mechanism or any other *de iure* obligation imposed by the law itself to give effect to or to comply with this type of soft law instrument. In the case of Q&As, the ESMA Regulation even states explicitly that ESMA's answers are non-binding.[35] In a similar vein, supervisory briefings – which are

---

[34] See more on ESMA's guidelines compliance tables and how they work as a soft enforcement mechanism in Chapter 9, Section 3.

[35] ESMA Regulation, Art 16b(2).

a type of new practical instrument and convergence tool as meant in Article 29(2) ESMA Regulation – also explicitly set out they are not binding.[36] As a result, NCAs only comply on a voluntary basis. This means that non-binding instruments merely have *de facto* effects.

4. *DE FACTO* EXPECTATIONS CONCERNING COMPLIANCE WITH ESMA'S SOFT LAW INSTRUMENTS

Since the Commission's delegated and implementing regulations have 'inherent' legally binding force, there is always a *de iure* duty to comply.[37] However, the 'comply or explain' mechanism still leaves room to deviate from ESMA's guidelines, and non-binding instruments have no *de iure* compliance obligations at all. The question is therefore whether there are any other ways in which a more stringent duty of compliance could be established in practice. We should pay further attention to the issue of whether and to what extent they (are intended to) produce legal effects and may on this basis entail *de facto* compliance obligations.[38] For this purpose, it is important to look at the Court's test in order to determine whether ESMA's guidelines and non-binding instruments are capable of having 'incidental' legally binding force and to see whether in this particular context 'indirect' legal effects could be established on the basis of the principles of the protection of legitimate expectations and sincere cooperation. The following subsections demonstrate that both the Court's test and the principles could lead to the conclusion that ESMA's guidelines (are intended to) produce legal effects, and may thus generate *de facto* compliance expectations. The contrary applies in the case of non-binding instruments: neither the Court's test nor the general principles generate *de facto* compliance expectations.

4.1 The Commission's Delegated and Implementing Acts

Since the Commission's delegated and implementing acts have been attributed inherent legally binding force, it is clear that they 'are intended to' have legally

---

36 ESMA, MiFID II Supervisory briefing on appropriateness and execution-only (2019) ESMA35-36-1640, para 7.

37 See Chapter 7, Section 3.1. This *de iure* duty of compliance applies to both NCAs *and* financial market participants.

38 Acceto & Zleptnig 2005, p. 380. This concern has also been raised in Commission, 'Report from the Commission to the European Parliament and the Council on the operation of the European Supervisory Authorities (ESAs) and the European System of Financial Supervision (ESFS)' COM(2014) 509 final, 5–6.

binding force. There is therefore no need for the Court to test whether they aim at being legally binding. The principles of legitimate expectations and sincere cooperation strengthen the conclusion that there is a clear *de iure* duty of compliance with these acts for NCAs. Legitimate expectations may indeed be created by legislation.[39] Based on the principle of legitimate expectations, financial market participants may thus legitimately expect NCAs to act in conformity with the Commission's delegated or implementing regulations. This is further reinforced by the facts that experts of the NCAs themselves were responsible for the drafting of the technical standards and that their heads, as members of ESMA's Board of Supervisors, took the decision to approve these drafts before they were submitted to the Commission for adoption. The principle of sincere cooperation also brings about the expectation that one abides by binding law. This follows from Article 4(3), second paragraph, TEU, which requires Member States to take 'any appropriate measure, general or particular, to ensure fulfilment of the obligations arising out of the Treaties or resulting from the acts of the institutions of the Union'.

4.2 Guidelines and Recommendations: 'Incidental' Legally Binding Force Based on the Court's Test

At the moment, there is still very limited case law on the legal nature of EU agencies' soft law acts.[40] Where an Advocate General or the Court encounters a soft law act of an EU agency, it usually concerns a procedure in which the Commission is responsible for the adoption of the final legally binding act. *E-Control v ACER* is one of the few interesting judgments that concern the legal nature of a soft law act emanating from an EU agency which is directly addressed to national authorities and third parties.[41] This case concerns an opinion of the Agency for the Cooperation of Energy Regulators (ACER). The Court followed the four conditions as established in the case-law in order to determine whether an act is capable of having legal effects, that is, (i) its wording, (ii) its context, (iii) its substance and (iv) the intention of its author.[42] This section explains and applies these four conditions with regard to ESMA's guidelines and recommendations in order to analyse whether these acts could

---

[39] See Chapter 2, Section 11.1.

[40] This follows from an investigation into the case law on EU agencies' soft law. The following search terms were used: binding, legal, nature, effect, intend*, intent*.

[41] Case T-671/15 *E-Control v ACER* [2016].

[42] Ibid., para 21: the Court concluded that it is apparent from the wording and the substance of the contested opinion as well as from its context and ACER's intention that it constituted an opinion without legally binding force. See also Case T-496/11 *United Kingdom v ECB* [2015], para 31.

produce 'incidental' legally binding force and thus entail any *de facto* compliance obligations. It shows that the context and intention of the agency are decisive if we are to accept that ESMA intends to ensure compliance with its guidelines, which should thus be regarded as an intention to produce legally binding effects. It is doubtful how successful an argument based on the wording and substance of ESMA's guidelines would be. Clarification on the legal nature of the guidelines would in any case be very welcome.[43]

4.2.1 Wording

In order to determine whether or not a soft law act is capable of having legal effect, it is first of all necessary to examine its wording.[44] For instance, in *France v Commission*, the French Republic maintained essentially that the Commission Communication in question[45] was a binding act on the ground that it was clear from the precision of its wording that it imposed new obligations on Member States.[46] The Court agreed by considering as decisive the fact that the provisions of the act were characterised by imperative wording (*shall*) and were thus of a binding nature.[47] Indeed, if the terms of a soft law act are of an obligatory nature, 'it will be difficult to maintain that the act does not intend to impose any obligations'.[48] In contrast, in *Belgium v Commission*,[49] the General Court observed that the Commission Recommendation in question[50] is worded mainly in non-mandatory terms.[51] It looked at the different language versions for support and concluded that the wording used is a clear and specific indication that the content of the contested recommendation is not intended to provide legally binding effects.[52] The General Court pointed out that both the recitals and the paragraphs of the Commission recommendation on principles for the protection of consumers and players of online gambling services and for the prevention of minors from gambling online are mostly drafted in the conditional.[53] This is shown in particular by the use of the French terms *devrait/*

---

43 See Chapter 10, Section 6.2 and Chapter 11, Section 2.4.

44 Case T-671/15 *E-Control v ACER* [2016], para 29.

45 Commission, 'Communication on an Internal Market for Pension Funds' (1994) OJ 94/C 360/08.

46 Case C-57/95 *France v Commission* [1997] ECR I-1627, para 12.

47 Ibid., paras 16–18 and 22.

48 Ibid. See also Senden 2004, p. 253.

49 Case T-721/14 *Belgium v Commission* [2015], para 21.

50 Commission, 'Recommendation 2014/478/EU on principles for the protection of consumers and players of online gambling services and for the prevention of minors from gambling online' (2014) OJ L214/38.

51 Case T-721/14 *Belgium v Commission* [2015], para 21.

52 Ibid., para 24.

53 Ibid., para 22.

devraient (in Danish 'bør', in German 'sollte/sollten', in Estonian 'peaks/peaksid', in Spanish 'debería/deberían', in Italian 'dovrebbe/dovrebbero', in Dutch 'zou moeten/zouden moeten', in Polish 'powinien/powinno/powinny', in Swedish 'bör' and in English 'should')[54] and the French expressions *il est recommandé aux États membres de* (in Danish 'Medlemsstaterne anbefales', in Estonian 'Liikmesriikidel soovitatakse', in Italian 'si raccomanda agli Stati membri', in Polish 'zaleca się', in Portuguese 'recomenda-se aos Estados-Membros', in Swedish 'Medlemsstaterna rekommenderas', in English 'Member States are recommended to'), *les États membres sont encouragés à* (in Italian 'gli Stati membri sono incoraggiati', in Polish 'zachęca się', in Portuguese 'os Estados-Membros são incentivados/encorajados', in English 'Member States are encouraged to') and *les États membres sont invités à* (in Danish 'Medlemsstaterne opfordres', in Estonian 'Liikmesriike kutsutakse üles', in Italian 'gli Stati membri sono invitati', in Portuguese 'os Estados-Membros são convidados', in Swedish 'Medlemsstaterna uppmanas', in English 'Member States are invited to').[55]

It may be observed that some paragraphs are, at least to some extent, drafted in more mandatory terms in other language versions, particularly the German, Spanish and Dutch versions. Nonetheless, the General Court established that those divergences are small, because most of the language versions are drafted in mainly non-binding terms.[56] Besides, it pointed at the settled case-law which provides that 'for the purposes of ensuring a uniform application and interpretation of the same text, the version of which in one European Union language diverges from those in other languages, the provision in question must be interpreted by reference to the *purpose* and *general scheme* of the rules of which it forms part' [emphasis added MvR].[57] It therefore concluded that the recommendation does not have and is not intended to have binding legal effects.[58] The Court of Justice later confirmed this in the appeal case by reiterating that the wording used in one of the language versions of an act cannot serve as the sole basis for the interpretation of that act, or be made to override the other language versions in that regard.[59] Such an approach would be incompatible with the requirement of the uniform application of EU law.

The provisions of ESMA's guidelines are worded mainly in non-mandatory terms (*should*). If we follow the lines of the case-law as set out above, the wording of the guidelines alone thus cannot lead to the conclusion that there

---

54 Ibid.
55 Ibid., para 23.
56 Ibid., para 27.
57 Ibid., para 28.
58 Ibid., para 37.
59 Case C-16/16 P *Belgium v Commission* [2018], para 50.

is 'incidental' legally binding force.[60] Since ESMA's guidelines are translated into all the official languages of the EU, the wording of the different language versions may also play an important role with regard to the establishment of 'incidental' legally binding force.[61] Indeed, confusion can arise from different expressions in different language versions.[62] However, those divergences that may be observed should be interpreted by reference to the purpose and general scheme of the guidelines, and are thus too trivial to change the conclusion that legal effects cannot be established on the basis of the guidelines' wording alone.[63]

4.2.2 Context

The context in which a soft law act is developed is the second crucially important condition regarding the establishment of 'incidental' legally binding effects. In the case of ESMA's guidelines, the so-called comply or explain mechanism and the interaction between the agency and the national supervisors play a key role in this regard.

The 'comply or explain' mechanism is unique: it applies neither to ESMA's technical standards and non-binding instruments nor to the soft law instruments of other EU agencies.[64] As follows from the legislative history, the mechanism did not exist during CESR times.[65] In the first proposal of the Commission on the establishment of the ESAs, the 'comply or explain' requirement was introduced, but it had not been formalised.[66] It was the European Parliament

---

[60] Ibid., para 21.

[61] In the context of EU agencies' soft law, one example of looking at different language versions is to be found in Joined Cases C-439 and 454/05 P *Land Oberösterreich v Commission* [2007] ECR I-7141, Opinion of AG Sharpston. However, this case was not so much about whether the opinion at stake was intended to produce binding legal effects, but rather about the meaning of a certain term. The AG looked at the German and French language versions of the summary of EFSA's opinion of 4 July 2003, of which the authentic language is English, to assess the meaning of the term 'unique'. She argued that the French and German versions of Commission Decision 2003/653/EC, which was contested in this case and which quoted a statement of the EFSA opinion, diverge somewhat from the authentic English of the original.

[62] See two examples at Van Rijsbergen 2014, p. 126.

[63] This is similar to what the Court concluded in Case T-721/14 *Belgium v Commission* [2015], para 28.

[64] Except of course to EBA and EIOPA guidelines, since the three ESAs have a similar founding regulation.

[65] By the end of the CESR era, CESR members had formalised their commitment to this principle in the 2008 CESR Charter, but it was not required as a matter of EU law: see Moloney 2014, p. 930.

[66] Commission, Proposal for a Regulation of the European Parliament and of the Council establishing a European Securities and Markets Authority COM(2009) 503

that presented the more formal 'comply or explain' mechanism that made it, with some minor amendments, to the current version of Article 16(3) ESMA Regulation.[67] In this sense, specifically at the instigation of the European Parliament, the nature of the guidelines hardened when CESR as a network developed into ESMA as an EU agency. Under the revised ESMA Regulation, this remained the same. To determine whether ESMA's guidelines are capable of having legal effects, *the indication of compliance (or not)* by the national authorities during the 'comply or explain' period may therefore be very relevant.[68]

The interaction between the NCAs and ESMA is another unique characteristic in this particular soft law-making context. Their cooperation is completely institutionalised and goes much further than, for instance, the interaction between national authorities and the Commission in the case of network governance.[69] Experts of the NCAs intensively work together with ESMA staff members – that is, in a horizontal manner – when they are drafting the guidelines in the Standing Committees and Working Groups.[70] It is during those meetings that NCAs may raise concerns if they disagree with what is proposed to be in the guidelines. The heads of the NCAs, as members of the ESMA Board of Supervisors, are subsequently responsible for taking decisions concerning the approval of the acts.[71] It is during those meetings that NCAs can vote against the adoption of the guidelines. Guidelines need a qualified majority vote,[72] which means that they can even be adopted if some NCAs disagree. To determine whether ESMA's guidelines are capable of having legal effect, *the voting behaviour* of NCAs may therefore also be of relevance.

The above leads to two possible scenarios, which may be visualised as in Figure 8.1.

final. Article 8 merely stated that '[t]he competent authorities shall make every effort to comply with those guidelines and recommendations' and that '[w]here the competent authority does not apply those guidelines or recommendations it shall inform the Authority of its reasons'.

67 See for the amendments by the European Parliament to the Commission proposal <www.europarl.europa.eu/sides/getDoc.do?type=TA&language=EN&reference=P7-TA-2010-270> accessed 19 February 2021.

68 It could be argued that guidelines have 'incidental' legally binding force when an NCA has indicated that it complies or will comply in the future with the guidelines during the 'comply or explain' period. This will of course be more difficult to uphold when an NCA informed ESMA of its non-compliance.

69 De Visser 2009, p. 278.

70 See Chapter 3.

71 Ibid.

72 ESMA Regulation, Art 44(1).

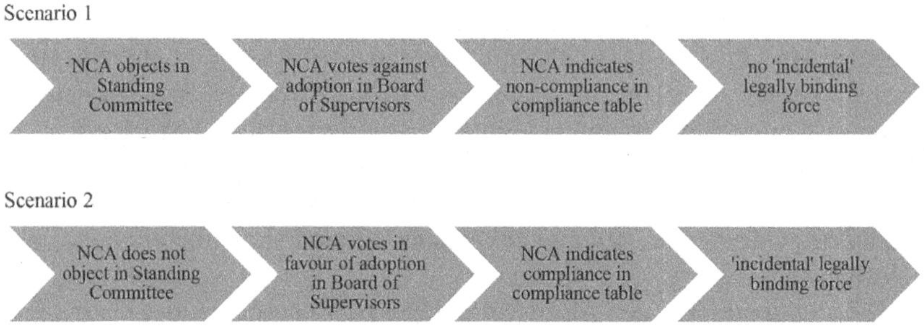

Figure 8.1 *Two possible compliance scenarios affecting the legal nature of ESMA's guidelines and recommendations*

On the one hand, if an NCA has already informed ESMA at the Standing Committee meetings of its disapproval of the guidelines, voted against their adoption at the Board of Supervisors meeting and indicated that it will not comply with the guidelines during the 'comply or explain' period, the guidelines cannot be considered to have 'incidental' legally binding force for this particular NCA. On the other hand, if an NCA has not raised major objections during the Standing Committee meetings, has voted in favour of adoption and has committed to complying with the guidelines, the guidelines do have 'incidental' legally binding force for this particular NCA. This therefore leads to a situation in which guidelines have legally binding force in some Member States, but not in others.[73]

Interestingly, the EU Court has already determined on a number of occasions in State aid cases that Commission guidelines that are not accepted by Member States cannot bind them.[74] Likewise, once these instruments are accepted by the Member States, they can impose binding obligations.[75] It is

[73] Although the so-called guidelines compliance tables clarify which NCAs indicated to comply, it is not known which NCAs voted in favour or against the adoption of a particular set of guidelines at the Board of Supervisors of ESMA. This issue could however easily be solved by adding this information to the minutes of the meetings of the Board. This solution is in line with the Proposal for a Regulation of the European Parliament and of the Council amending Regulation (EU) No 182/2011 laying down the rules and general principles concerning mechanisms for control by Member States of the Commission's exercise of implementing powers COM(2017) 85 final.

[74] Case C-242/00 *Germany v Commission* [2002] ECR I-5603, para 35 and Case T-176/01 *Ferriere Nord v Commission* [2004] ECR II-3931, para 134. See also Stefan 2017, p. 11.

[75] Case C-313/90 *CIRFS and Others v Commission* [1993] ECR I-1125 and Case C-311/94 *Ijssel-Vliet v Minister van Economische Zaken* [1996] ECR I-5023. See also Stefan 2017, p. 11.

therefore not unlikely that the Court would also agree with the establishment of the 'incidental' legally binding force of ESMA's guidelines in the way presented in this book.

4.2.3 Substance

A third way to ascertain whether or not a soft law act is capable of having legal effect is by looking at the content.[76] The key test for the Court to ascertain whether a measure produces such effects is to look at the *substance* of the act and the intention of those who drafted it, irrespective of the *form* it takes or the title it receives, as long as it is capable of affecting an applicant by bringing about a distinct change in its legal position.[77] The Court has thus taken a non-formalistic approach when deciding upon the binding nature of EU acts.[78] The form in which an act is cast is, in principle, immaterial.[79] Therefore, the fact that a measure is packaged in a legal form that is not recognised by the Treaties will not deter the Court from exercising its powers of review.[80] In this way, the Court guards against the danger that new legal obligations might be smuggled in by disguising them in a non-binding form.[81]

As a consequence, the mere fact that ESMA's guidelines are formally designated as guidelines cannot automatically rule out that they are not intended to have legally binding effects.[82] They could still have 'incidental' legally binding effects on the basis of their content. It is however for the Court to

---

[76] Case C-147/96 *Netherlands v Commission* (2000) ECR I-4723, para 27; Case 60/81 *IBM v Commission* [1981] ECR 2639, para 9; Case T-671/15, *E-Control v ACER* [2016], para 29.

[77] For a clear statement from the Court on the prevalence of substance over form when deciding the binding nature of an act, see Case 60/81 *IBM v Commission* [1981] ECR 2639, para 9.

[78] Barnard & Peers 2014, p. 266.

[79] Scott 2011, p. 339. Case C-521/06 P*Athinaïki Techniki v Commission* [2008] ECR I-05829, para 41; Case 60/81 *IBM v Commission* [1981] ECR 2639, para 9; Case C-208/03 P *Le Pen v Parliament* [2005] ECR I-6051, para 46; Case T-397/06 *Dow AgroSciences Ltd v EFSA* [2008] ECR II-90, para 42; Case T-334/12 *Plantavis and NEM v Commission and EFSA* [2015], para 56; Case T-456/07 *Commission v CdT* [2010] ECR II-183, para 53; Case C-160/03 *Spain v Eurojust* [2005] ECR I-2077, Opinion of AG Maduro, para 21; Case T-675/13 *K Chimica v ECHA* [2016], para 24; Case T-673/13 *European Coalition to End Animal Experiments v ECHA* [2015], para 21; Case T-96/10 *Rütgers Germany and Others v ECHA* [2013], para 29; Case T-1/10, *PPG and SNF v ECHA* [2011] II-6576, para 39. The Court already took this approach in its early case-law: see Joined Cases 1 and 14/57 *Usines à tubes de la Sarre v High Authority* [1957] ECR 105 and Senden 2004, p. 249.

[80] Scott 2011, p. 339.

[81] Ibid., p. 344.

[82] Case T-721/14 *Belgium v Commission* [2015], para 20.

decide this on a case-by-case basis by ascertaining whether the substance of the guidelines is 'wholly consistent with the form attributed to it'.[83]

4.2.4 Intention of the author

A final parameter for determining whether an act is capable of having legal effect is the *intention of its author*. As follows from the relevant case-law, it is in principle those measures which definitively determine the position of the author upon the conclusion of an administrative procedure which are intended to have legal effects capable of affecting the interests of third parties. This means that intermediate measures, whose purpose is to prepare for the final decision, do not have those effects.[84] Since ESMA's guidelines lay down the agency's final position, this is a first indication that such acts could be capable of having legal effects.

Besides, in most of the guidelines' documents, ESMA states in rather strong terms under the heading 'Status of the guidelines' that in accordance with Article 16(3) ESMA Regulation, 'competent authorities *must make every effort to comply* with the guidelines'[85] and that 'competent authorities to whom the guidelines apply *should comply* by incorporating them into their supervisory practices'.[86] Together with ESMA's other contextual characteristics, such as qualified majority voting and the 'comply or explain' mechanism, this type of wording gives the impression that ESMA has the *intention to ensure compliance*. Such intention could be regarded to be decisive for the establishment of an *intention to produce legally binding effects*.[87] Put differently: how could an authority possibly have the intention to ensure compliance without having the intention to generate legal effects?

---

[83] C-322/88 *Grimaldi v Fonds des maladies professionnelles* [1989] ECR 4407, para 14.

[84] Case C-521/06 P *Athinaïki Techniki v Commission* [2008] ECR I-5829, paras 41 and 42; Case C-362/08 P *Internationaler Hilfsfonds v Commission* [2010] ECR I-669, para. 52.

[85] For an example, see ESMA, Guidelines on reporting obligations under Articles 3(3)(d) and 24(1), (2) and (4) of the AIFMD (2014) ESMA/2014/869, para. 5.

[86] Ibid., para 6.

[87] This would also make them reviewable under TFEU, Art 263 which enables the Court to review the legality of acts 'intended to produce legal effects vis-à-vis third parties'.

4.3 Guidelines and Recommendations: 'Indirect' Legal Effects Based on the Principles of Legitimate Expectations and Sincere Cooperation

The above sections showed that the Court's test would probably result in a positive answer to the question of whether or not guidelines and recommendations may produce 'incidental' legal effects. 'Indirect' legal effects could potentially also be established on the basis of a general principle of EU law.

The first question to ask here is whether the *principle of legitimate expectations* could be successfully invoked in order to establish 'indirect' legal effects of the agency's guidelines. As a starting point, the Court's case-law brings with it that soft law too could potentially give rise to a legitimate expectation.[88] In my view, legitimate expectations could indeed arise from ESMA itself as well as from those NCAs that have committed themselves to compliance with the guidelines within the two-month 'comply or explain' period, especially when we take into account the fact that the latter have themselves written the guidelines and approved them as members of the Board of Supervisors. This is even more so when NCAs have used (binding) measures for the integration of ESMA's guidelines or when the national legislature has implemented ESMA's guidelines into the national legal framework.[89] In such a case the NCAs limit their own discretion, which means that one may legitimately assume that they cannot and will not suddenly depart from ESMA's guidelines, their national transposition measures or the national legislation.[90] In this way, with the indication of compliance, an NCA imposes upon itself a *de facto* duty to comply.[91]

It is much more difficult, if not impossible, to successfully invoke this principle when an NCA has indicated non-compliance or is expected to indicate non-compliance with the guidelines, especially if it even voted against their adoption during the Board of Supervisors meeting.[92] Indeed, if legitimate expectations arise from the Hungarian NCA, Magyar Nemzeti Bank (MNB), the principle can only be invoked against this authority. It cannot be relied on against the Greek NCA, Ελληνική Επιτροπή Κεφαλαιαγοράς (HCMC),

---

88 Section 2, Section 11.1.

89 See Chapter 7, Section 4.2.

90 See in comparison Case C-526/14 *Kotnik and Others* [2016], para 40: 'In accordance with settled case-law, in adopting such guidelines and announcing by publishing them that they will apply to the cases to which they relate, the Commission imposes a limit on the exercise of that discretion and cannot, as a general rule, depart from those guidelines, at the risk of being found to be in breach of general principles of law, such as equal treatment or the protection of legitimate expectations.'

91 This is in line with the argumentation in Sections 4.2.2 and 4.2.4.

92 Ibid.

if that national authority does not want to comply with ESMA's guidelines and acts completely differently from the Hungarian NCA.[93] An interesting practice may be found on the website of the German NCA, Bundesanstalt für Finanzdienstleistungsaufsicht (BaFin): it publishes here the ESA guidelines that have not been adopted in BaFin's administrative practice or have not been adopted in full.[94] In this case, it will be very difficult for a financial market participant to argue that ESMA's guidelines gave rise to legitimate expectations. In any case, it should be noted that, at the time of writing, applicants have not (yet) been successful in invoking the principle of the protection of legitimate expectations in relation to EU agencies' soft law or the national authorities responsible for the implementation of such acts.[95] This is in line with the fact that the CJEU has rarely accepted arguments in relation to legitimate expectations in other cases.[96] It thus remains to be seen what the Court will determine when a party invokes this principle in a case concerning ESMA's guidelines and recommendations.

The second question is whether the *principle of sincere cooperation* could be successfully invoked in order to establish 'indirect' legal effects of

---

[93] See for a similar reasoning C-585/13 P *Europäisch-Iranische Handelsbank v Council* [2015], Opinion of AG Mengozzi, para 79: 'if the conduct of the Bundesbank is indeed capable of supporting a legitimate expectation on the part of the appellant, the appellant could rely on such expectation only against the national authority in question. In other words, the hypothetical legitimate expectation arising from the conduct of the Bundesbank cannot be relied on against the Council when the latter decides to impose restrictive measures on EIH.'

[94] BaFin, 'ESA Q&As that have not been adopted in BaFin's administrative practice' <www.bafin.de/EN/RechtRegelungen/Leitlinien_und_Q_and_A_der_ESAs/Nicht_uebernommene_Q_and_A/nicht_uebernommene_Q_and_A_node_en.html> accessed 19 February 2021.

[95] This finding follows from an investigation into the case-law on EU agencies' soft law. The search was carried out on the basis of the terms *'legitimate expectation*' agencies* and *'legitimate expectation*' agency.* It gave more than 500 results, of which only a few appeared to be relevant for this book as we can distil some relevant lessons from them with regard to the principle of protection of legitimate expectations concerning EU agencies in general: see for instance Case T-309/03 *Camós Grau v Commission* [2006] ECR II-1173; Case T-264/07 *CSL Behring v Commission and EMA* [2010] ECR II-4469; Case T-326/07 *Cheminova and Others v Commission* [2009] ECR II-2685; Case T-36/09 *dm-drogerie markt v OHIM* [2011] ECR II-6079; Case T-487/11 *Banco Privado Português and Massa Insolvente do Banco Privado Português v Commission* [2014]; Case T-483/13 *Oikonomopoulos v Commission* [2016]; Joined Cases C-630-633/11 P *HGA and Others v Commission* [2013]; Case C-585/13 P *Europäisch-Iranische Handelsbank v Council* [2015]; Case C-106/14 FCD and FMB [2015]; Case C-526/14 *Kotnik and Others* [2016].

[96] See Chapter 2, Section 11.1. See also Hofmann, Rowe & Türk 2011, p. 181 and Craig 2012, p. 577.

ESMA's guidelines. Article 4(3) TEU cannot *itself* create, independently of other (binding) Union law provisions, any enforceable rights and obligations as regards compliance with soft law.[97] Consequently, a general obligation for Member States and national authorities to act in accordance with Union soft law on the basis of the principle of sincere cooperation does not exist. It could however be argued that it is in the spirit and scheme of sincere cooperation to take account of soft law acts insofar as they contribute to compliance with the underlying Union law obligations. Such an obligation could be said to *derive* from Article 4(3), third paragraph, TEU, which requires the Member States to 'facilitate the achievement of the Union's tasks and refrain from any measure which could jeopardise the attainment of the Union's objectives'. Yet, the Court's case-law clarifies that the provisions of soft law acts have to be taken into due account by the Member States' authorities by virtue of the duty of sincere cooperation, but that 'that duty cannot be understood as making those rules binding – not even *de facto* – on pain of eluding the legislative procedure set out in the TFEU'.[98] It is clear from this proposition of the Court that by virtue of the principle of sincere cooperation, soft law's 'soft' legal obligation begins to harden, but not to the extent that it is either *de facto* or formally binding.[99] Nevertheless, a new, yet more up-to-date interpretation of the principle of sincere cooperation could also be supported. As follows from the practical example in Section 1, non-compliance with ESMA's guidelines 'may indicate an underlying breach of Union law'.[100] That is to say, if non-compliance with EU agencies' soft law leads to non-compliance with underlying Union obligations, one should definitely comply with the soft law act of the EU agency. Hence, if an NCA indicates that it complies or will in the future comply with ESMA's guidelines and recommendations, compliance is indeed mandatory if it would otherwise breach the underlying Union law. In particular, a combination in which an NCA has indicated that it is compliant, but in practice does not comply, leads to a breach, because such indication makes compliance mandatory.[101] This may then be regarded as a violation of the duty of sincere cooperation. In this sense, sincere cooperation has therefore further developed.

---

[97] Senden 2004, p. 352.

[98] Case C-311/94 *Ijssel-Vliet v Minister van Economische Zaken* [1996] ECR I-5023, para 211.

[99] Stefan & others 2018, p. 28.

[100] Commission, Report from the Commission, the European Parliament and the Council on the evaluation of the Regulation (EU) No 236/2012 on short selling and certain aspects of credit default swaps COM(2013) 885 final, 6. The Commission also indicated to ESMA that it might request it to take action: see ESMA, Board of Supervisors Summary of Conclusions of 4 July 2013 (ESMA/2013/BS/125).

[101] In accordance with the change from an effort obligation to a result obligation: see Section 5.1.

ESMA's soft law has been established in a different context in which the parts (NCAs) of the whole (ESMA) may even be considered to be more important than the whole itself. Likewise, given the context in which ESMA's guidelines have been developed and the intention to ensure compliance on the part of the agency,[102] it would be illogical for NCAs not to follow up on these acts. All in all, both principles are capable of establishing 'indirect' legal effects in relation to ESMA's guidelines.

4.4 Non-binding Instruments: 'Incidental' Legally Binding Force Based on the Court's Test

In order to determine whether ESMA's non-binding instruments could produce 'incidental' legally binding force and thus entail any *de facto* compliance obligations, it is insightful to also apply the aforementioned four criteria of the Court's test: (i) wording; (ii) context; (iii) substance; and (iv) the intention of the author. This section shows that on the basis of the wording, context and intention of ESMA, it is difficult to successfully maintain that non-binding instruments produce legal effects.[103] Not following up on the interpretations laid down in a non-binding instrument might at most eventually entail a breach of the underlying legislation, but never a breach of the non-binding instrument itself.

4.4.1 Wording

Although a comparison of different language versions is normally useful for the determination of the legal nature of a soft law act,[104] this does not make any sense in the case of ESMA's non-binding instruments. Indeed, these acts are only published in English and are not translated into the other languages of the EU.[105] Therefore, in view of their wording, it must be held that ESMA's non-binding instruments are not intended to have legal effects.

4.4.2 Context

The context in which non-binding instruments are developed does not allow for the conclusion that they would be intended to have legally binding effects either. Unlike ESMA's guidelines, the non-binding documents are not paired with a 'comply or explain' mechanism. Compliance is therefore entirely voluntary. Additionally, although the interaction between the NCAs and ESMA

---

[102] See Sections 4.2.2 and 4.2.4.

[103] For the sake of clarity, the focus of this section is on Q&As. Yet, a similar exercise can be done in relation to opinions or other (new) soft law instruments.

[104] See Section 4.2.1 on ESMA's guidelines.

[105] See Chapter 6, Section 5.3.

in the drafting and decision-making process is similar to that of ESMA's guidelines, the content of the non-binding instruments can still change rather easily. This is especially true in the case of Q&As, because there are in principle no procedural guarantees, such as consultations and cost–benefit analyses. Hence, if ESMA wants to update its Q&As, it can easily do that, and on its own initiative. Besides, the adoption of non-binding instruments by the Board of Supervisors only requires a simple majority.[106] Those who have cast votes in favour of or against such instruments' adoption are however not known to the public; hence, it cannot be determined towards which NCAs a non-binding instrument could have 'incidental' legally binding force. In this respect, BaFin's practice of also publishing the Q&As that have not been adopted in its administrative practice or that have not been adopted in full removes any potential doubt.[107]

4.4.3 Substance

Although the form in which an act is cast is in principle immaterial to ascertaining whether or not a soft law act is capable of having legal effect, it is unlikely that ESMA's non-binding instruments will be regarded as such. It could be argued that there is a strong incentive for NCAs and financial market participants to follow up on the substance of non-binding instruments, though, because they entail the interpretation considered best throughout Europe according to ESMA and the NCAs. The addressees know that they will not breach any underlying binding legislation when they follow the EU interpretation as laid down in non-binding instruments. This is why most NCAs are compliant anyway, even though such compliance is only voluntary.

4.4.4 Intention of the author

ESMA clearly does not have the intention to give its non-binding instruments legal effect. This can best be explained by taking Q&As as an example. There is an explicit statement on ESMA's website that Q&As are not legally binding.[108] Instead, the content of a Q&A document is aimed at the national competent authorities in order to ensure that in their supervisory activities their actions are converging along the lines of the interpretations adopted by ESMA. The answers are also intended to help third parties by providing clarity as to

---

106 ESMA Regulation, Art 44(1).

107 BaFin, 'ESA Q&As that have not been adopted in BaFin's administrative practice' <www.bafin.de/EN/RechtRegelungen/Leitlinien_und_Q_and_A_der_ESAs/Nicht_uebernommene_Q_and_A/nicht_uebernommene_Q_and_A_node_en.html> accessed 19 February 2021.

108 ESMA, 'Questions and Answers' <www.esma.europa.eu/questions-and-answers> accessed 17 February 2021.

the content of the level one, two or three measures, *rather than creating an extra layer of requirements*.[109] ESMA sets out in the Q&A document itself that it does not constitute new policy. Instead, as the textbox below shows through the concrete example of the Guidelines on Alternative Performance Measures (APMs), the aim of Q&As is only to provide clarification on the practical application of the relevant level 1, 2 or 3 measures.[110]

> **Question:** Do the APMs Guidelines apply to interim financial reporting?
> **Answer:** The APMs Guidelines apply to interim financial reporting if it falls under the definition of regulated information set out in the [Transparency Directive]. Therefore, the APMs Guidelines apply to: (i) additional periodic financial information, when this information is published in accordance with Article 3(1a) of the [Transparency Directive]; (ii) half yearly financial reports, as required by Article 5 of the [Transparency Directive]; or (iii) any financial information published in accordance with Article 17 of the [Market Abuse Regulation] (such as ad-hoc disclosures).
>
> Where interim financial reports or the additional periodic financial information are regulated information, the APMs Guidelines only apply to the information accompanying financial statements (e.g. interim management report) as the APMs Guidelines exclude financial statements from their scope (paragraph 4).

In the Q&A documents themselves, ESMA makes clear that it periodically reviews questions and answers to identify whether there is, in a certain area, a need to convert some of the material into ESMA guidelines.[111] If that were to happen, the procedures foreseen under Article 16 ESMA Regulation would be followed.[112] In this way, Q&As may be regarded as a primary step in the development of 'harder' types of legal instruments. In any case, it demonstrates that ESMA considers its Q&As to be less binding than its guidelines. They cannot be considered as acts having the intention to produce legal effects or as acts being able to have 'incidental' legally binding force. This means that Q&As merely have *de facto* effects.

---

[109] ESMA, Questions and Answers on the application of the AIFMD (2017) ESMA34-32-352, 6.

[110] ESMA, Questions and Answers on the Guidelines on Alternative Performance Measures (2017) ESMA32-51-370.

[111] Ibid., para 10. ESMA, Questions and Answers on the application of the UCITS Directive (2017) ESMA34-43-392, para 9. This is again a proportionality consideration in the sense of Chapter 4.

[112] See Chapter 5.

4.5 Non-binding Instruments: 'Indirect' Legal Effects Based on the Principles of Legitimate Expectations and Sincere Cooperation

Although the Court's test results in a negative answer to the question whether or not ESMA's non-binding instruments may produce 'incidental' legal effects, 'indirect' legal effects could potentially be established on the basis of a general principle of EU law. The first question is whether *the principle of legitimate expectations* could be successfully invoked in order to establish such 'indirect' legal effects. In any case, since the Court has argued that 'the form is immaterial',[113] the non-binding instruments by themselves are capable of giving rise to legitimate expectations, even in the absence of legislation.

To begin with, there is no duty of compliance with regard to ESMA's non-binding instruments, because they merely produce *de facto* effects.[114] As a consequence, it will be very difficult for financial market participants to argue on the basis of legal grounds that they could legitimately expect NCAs to be bound by the interpretations laid down in ESMA's non-binding instruments. Besides, as the Court has previously held, economic operators are not justified in having a legitimate expectation that an existing situation, which is capable of being altered by the EU institutions in the exercise of their discretion, will be maintained.[115] This is particularly so in a field such as financial market supervision, which involves constant adjustment to reflect changes.[116] Furthermore, most NCAs do not use any national measures in order to integrate ESMA's non-binding instruments in the national framework. Hence, legitimate expectations cannot arise from national practices either. It is therefore unlikely that 'indirect' legal effects of non-binding instruments could be established based on the principle of the protection of legitimate expectations.

This does not mean that legitimate expectations could never arise. Although there is as yet no relevant case-law from the CJEU on legitimate expectations with regard to EU agencies' soft law, the case of *N.V. Elektriciteits* at the Board of Appeal of the European Chemicals Agency (ECHA) is an interesting comparative example.[117] In this case, the ECHA Board of Appeal accepted that the ECHA's Frequently Asked Questions (FAQs) created legitimate

[113] For a clear statement from the Court on the prevalence of substance over form when deciding the binding nature of an act, see Case 60/81 *IBM v Commission* [1981] ECR 2639.

[114] See Section 3.3.

[115] See, for a similar argument with regard to state aid in the banking sector, Case C-526/14 *Kotnik and Others* [2016].

[116] Ibid.

[117] ECHA Board of Appeal case A-001-2010, 10 November 2011.

expectations for applicants.[118] It referred to the *Holland Malt* case,[119] in which the CJEU held that

> [i]n adopting rules of conduct and announcing by publishing them that they will apply to the cases to which they relate, the Commission imposes a limit on the exercise of its aforementioned discretion and cannot depart from those rules under pain of being found, where appropriate, to be in breach of general principles of law, such as equal treatment or the protection of legitimate expectations.[120]

On the basis of this case-law, the ECHA Board of Appeal came to the conclusion that while administrative guidance does not constitute a source of law which would be comparable to legislation, such administrative guidance can nevertheless bind the administrative body in question if it is published.[121] Hence, it concluded that where ECHA has decided to publish guidance, the agency's conduct can be confined by such guidance.[122]

Vaughan has posed a relevant follow-up question: are the other types of guidance documents that ECHA or other EU agencies produce also capable of giving rise to legitimate expectations? In other words, 'is there a point at which guidance stops creating legitimate expectations, or is everything that an agency puts out which impacts on the operation of underlying legislation capable of creating expectations that are legitimate'?[123] At the time of writing, there is no clear answer to this question in the existing case-law.

The second question is whether the *principle of sincere cooperation* could be successfully invoked in a case against ESMA in order to establish 'indirect' legal effects of the agency's non-binding instruments. There is no general obligation for Member States to act in accordance with Union soft law on the basis of this principle alone.[124] It could however be argued that it is in the spirit and scheme of sincere cooperation to take account of soft law acts insofar as they contribute to compliance with the underlying Union law obligations.[125] This however seems a rather far-fetched interpretation in the case of non-binding instruments, because they are not meant to create an extra layer of requirements. In practice, though, NCAs like to use ESMA's non-binding instruments because they help with the interpretation of EU law. There is thus

118 Ibid., paras 40, 88–94 and 168.
119 Case C-464/09 P *Holland Malt v Commission* [2010] I-12443, para 46.
120 ECHA Board of Appeal case A-001-2010, 10 November 2011, para 58.
121 Ibid., para 59.
122 Ibid., para 60.
123 Vaughan 2015b.
124 See Section 4.3.
125 Ibid.

not necessarily a duty of sincere cooperation *de iure*, but NCAs nonetheless comply because they see the benefits for themselves in practice.

All in all, the principles of legitimate expectations and sincere cooperation are not able to establish 'indirect' legal effects in relation to ESMA's non-binding instruments.

5. CONCLUSION AND ASSESSMENT ON COMPLIANCE WITH ESMA'S ACTS

As follows from the analysis in this chapter, both the *de iure* and *de facto* expectations regarding compliance differ per category of ESMA's soft law instruments. The situation regarding the Commission's delegated and implementing acts is clear. Such acts are 'inherently' legally binding by virtue of Article 288 TFEU, which means that the *de iure* compliance obligation for Member States and third parties derives from this. This means that compliance is mandatory. With regard to ESMA's non-binding instruments, there is no *de iure* obligation to comply. They thus merely have *de facto* effects, which means that compliance occurs on a voluntary basis. The compliance obligations with respect to ESMA's guidelines are however more ambiguous.

ESMA's guidelines are not 'inherently' legally binding, nor do they produce *de facto* effects only. They are therefore rather to be regarded as hybrid or quasi-binding instruments. Article 16(3) ESMA Regulation namely lays down a different type of *de iure* compliance duty, that is, the 'comply or explain' mechanism. This means that the national competent authorities have to indicate compliance to the agency within two months, unless they do not wish to comply. In the latter case, they have to explain to ESMA their reasons for non-compliance. Non-compliance is thus still an option. The analysis in Sections 4.2 and 4.3 however shows that ESMA's guidelines are non-binding as an instrument, but each act may separately produce 'incidental' legally binding effects and 'indirect' legal effects on the basis of the Court's test or the principles of legitimate expectations and sincere cooperation, respectively. In this way, a *de facto* compliance duty may be established. As follows from the analysis in Sections 4.4 and 4.5, it is difficult to maintain that ESMA's non-binding instruments have 'incidental' legally binding effects or 'indirect' effects. Therefore, a *de facto* compliance duty cannot be established. Table 8.1 sets out the legal nature of the three types of instrument.

The following section concludes this chapter and provides an assessment of areas where compliance leads to tensions on the basis of effectiveness concerns.

Table 8.1 *Legal nature of the three types of ESMA's soft law instrument including* de iure *compliance obligations*

Type of instrument	Legal nature	*De iure* compliance obligations
Commission implementing and delegated acts	'Inherently' legally binding	Mandatory compliance
ESMA guidelines	'Incidental' legally binding effects or 'indirect' legal effects	'Comply or explain'
Non-binding instruments	*De facto* effects	Voluntary compliance

5.1 Differences in Compliance at the National Level Hamper the Effectiveness of ESMA's Guidelines

As follows from the wording of Article 16(3) ESMA Regulation, national competent authorities and financial market participants *shall make every effort to comply* with ESMA's guidelines and recommendations. The ESMA Regulation thus presupposes *a de iure effort obligation.* This could be regarded as a concrete expression of the principle of sincere cooperation. It is linked to the requirement for Member States to 'take any appropriate measure, general or particular, to ensure fulfilment of the obligations arising out of the Treaties or resulting from the acts of the institutions of the Union'.[126] However, in practice, NCAs may not be aware of the fact that this effort obligation is converted into *a* de facto *result obligation* as soon as an NCA indicates that it is compliant with ESMA's guidelines. In this way, the guidelines give rise to strong legal effects and NCAs curtail their own autonomy with an indication to comply. Legal effects are further reinforced by the regulatory context in which guidelines are developed; that is, ESMA clearly has the intention to ensure compliance with its guidelines, and thus the intention to produce legally binding effects.[127] In this manner the agency attaches great importance to the effectuation of its guidelines. This means that the focus on effectiveness, in the sense of compliance with the rules, is very high.

In a context in which NCAs may choose for themselves whether they want to be compliant or not, differences may arise among the Union's Member States with respect to the binding effects of ESMA's guidelines at the national level. Again, this undermines the legal certainty of the system as a whole and makes the creation of a level playing field across the Union very difficult. Differences in compliance could also hamper the effectiveness of the rules if, as a result,

[126] TEU, Art 4(3) para 2.

[127] See the analysis on 'incidental' legally binding force in Section 4.4.

the goal of the underlying legislation is not achieved.[128] This is precisely due to the fact that the legal nature of and compliance obligations regarding these acts are not clearly specified. The solution is thus to provide clarification on the legal nature of ESMA's guidelines.[129] In the meantime, clear analysis of this from the Court of Justice would be very welcome.[130]

---

[128] In the example given in Section 1, the Commission warned that the non-compliance with ESMA's Guidelines on the Exemption for market making activities and primary market operations under Regulation (EU) 236/2012 of the European Parliament and the Council on short selling and certain aspects of Credit Default Swaps (2013) ESMA/2013/74 by some of the NCAs could undermine the main objective of the Short Selling Regulation.

[129] See the recommendation in Chapter 11, Section 2.4.

[130] As it did with regard to private European standardisation bodies in Case C-613/14 *James Elliott Construction* [2016].

9. Enforcing ESMA's soft law instruments vis-à-vis national authorities

As follows from the previous chapter, compliance is an important next step in the effectuation of EU law. The ideal picture is therefore that Member States and national authorities always comply with EU agencies' soft law instruments. However, in practice this is not always the case. In the *ex post* dimension of the policy cycle, it is therefore also required that appropriate (indirect) enforcement mechanisms are in place in order to enhance compliance with EU agencies' soft law instruments. This entails the seventh stage of the policy cycle. In this stage, the principle of proportionality is also relevant.[1] Article 5(4) TEU is broadly formulated in the sense that the principle requires that the content and form of Union *action* shall not exceed what is necessary to achieve the objectives of the Treaties. This means that (indirect) enforcement mechanisms should be used on the basis of proportionality considerations.

Indirect enforcement entails 'the supervision of the application of the law by public authorities – and foremost of the Member States – but not directly over whether citizens as such obey it'.[2] It concerns the protection of the *public* interest through *general* enforcement mechanisms, such as peer reviews and the Commission's infringement procedure. Given the importance of appropriate enforcement mechanisms vis-à-vis national authorities for the legitimacy and effectiveness of ESMA's (soft) rule-making powers, the aim of this chapter is to establish if, how and by whom ESMA's soft law instruments can be enforced in the case of non-compliance by national authorities.

Section 1 demonstrates the practical relevance of enforcement for ESMA by presenting some exemplary considerations made by the agency itself. Sections 2–6 investigate the extent to which enforcement mechanisms have already been put into place, and for whom (*de iure* level), and analyse if and how such mechanisms are being used in practice (*de facto* level). In Section 7 the chapter

1 See Chapter 2, Section 12.1.

2 Hofmann & Türk 2009, p. 188. Indirect enforcement is the opposite of direct enforcement. The latter concerns enforcement action taken by Union or Member State authorities and aimed directly at Union citizens and economic actors. For a complete study of direct enforcement by EU authorities, see Scholten & Luchtman 2017.

concludes that ESMA has a mix of soft and hard enforcement mechanisms at its disposal and therefore needs to choose which mechanism to use on the basis of the demands stemming from the principle of proportionality.

1. ENFORCEMENT CONCERNS IN RELATION TO ESMA'S SOFT LAW INSTRUMENTS IN PRACTICE

Concerns of enforcement are not merely of theoretical relevance. As follows from ESMA's practice, ESMA is faced with considerations concerning the enforcement of its soft law instruments vis-à-vis national authorities. This section provides some examples of instances in which indirect enforcement reflections or problems generally come to the fore. These are mostly observed during the meetings of the Board of Supervisors.[3] The first example shows that ESMA is committed to monitoring follow-up actions taken by national competent authorities to address the findings of peer reviews.[4]

On 18 May 2017, ESMA published a Follow-up Report providing an update on the actions undertaken by ten national competent authorities further to the deficiencies defined in the 2014 Peer Review on MiFID Conduct of Business rules relating to fair, clear and not misleading information,[5] which focused on NCAs' supervision of information and marketing communications under MiFID.[6]

The 2014 Peer Review concluded that there was overall a high degree of

---

[3] For instance, the Board discussed the proposed on-site visits in the framework of the ESMA peer review on the Guidelines on certain aspects of the MiFID compliance function: see ESMA, Board of Supervisors, Summary of Conclusions of 26 January 2017 (ESMA22-247440098-103). In addition, the Board discussed the peer review on prospectus approval, in particular whether, in addition to the proposed changes to EU legislation, further ESMA activities could contribute to supervisory convergence in relation to the prospectus approval: see ESMA, Board of Supervisors Summary of Conclusions of 25 May 2016 (ESMA/2016/BS/151rev1). Furthermore, the Board took note of the legal changes introduced by the Parliament of the Republic of Poland since the Follow-up on Peer Review on Market Abuse Directive and adopted the Follow-up Report: see ESMA, Board of Supervisors Summary of Conclusions of 24 and 25 September 2015 (ESMA/BS/140).

[4] See more on peer reviews in Section 4.

[5] ESMA, Peer Review Report on MiFID Conduct of Business rules relating to fair, clear and not misleading information (2014) ESMA/2014/1485.

[6] ESMA, Follow-up Report to the Peer Review on MiFID Conduct of Business rules relating to fair, clear and not misleading information (2017) ESMA42-113-627, para 1.

compliance amongst the NCAs with the identified ESMA good practices.[7] However, it was found that ten of the NCAs (Cyprus, Denmark, Estonia, Greece, Lithuania, Latvia, Malta, Poland, Portugal and Romania) were not fully applying certain good practices considered essential for effectively ensuring the application of MiFID rules, that is, concerning organisation, supervision, monitoring activities, thematic work or the handling of complaints.[8]

As follows from the 2017 Follow-up Report, the NCAs from Lithuania, Latvia, Malta, Poland, Portugal and Romania have addressed all of the deficiencies previously identified.[9] For the remaining four NCAs, one (Denmark, Estonia, Greece) or more (Cyprus) deficiencies remain, although the significant efforts that have been made by Cyprus and Greece have been noted.[10] However, ESMA expressed its confidence that the NCAs in which deficiencies remain would address those as soon as possible, and at the very latest with the new MiFID II/MiFIR regime that entered into force on 3 January 2018.[11] The agency also emphasised that it would continue to check on the progress made by NCAs in implementing recommendations of peer reviews and to foster supervisory dialogue on MiFID rules on fair, clear and not misleading information provided to clients as well as on conduct of business rules in general.[12]

The example in the following box shows that the Breach of Union Law procedure is also of practical interest to ESMA and the NCAs.[13]

At the Board of Supervisors meeting of 27 January 2016, the Head of the Legal, Convergence and Enforcement Department presented the annual update on the Breach of Union Law cases.[14] The Board discussed the report and in particular the exchanges taking place between national competent authorities and ESMA as part of the Breach of Union Law cases.

The brief account just provided shows that ESMA has been given an array of instruments for the purpose of enforcement vis-à-vis national authorities.

---

7 Ibid., para 2.
8 Ibid.
9 Ibid., para 3.
10 Ibid.
11 Ibid., para 5.
12 Ibid.
13 See Section 5 on the Breach of Union Law procedure.
14 ESMA Board of Supervisors, Summary of Conclusions of 27 January 2016 (ESMA/2016/BS/61).

We now turn to an investigation of the *de iure* and *de facto* possibilities for enforcement by the Commission and by ESMA itself. The aim is to find out what kind of obligations the principle of proportionality contains for the enforcement of ESMA's soft law instruments.

2. SOFT AND HARD ENFORCEMENT MECHANISMS REGARDING ESMA'S SOFT LAW INSTRUMENTS

This section focuses on who does what in terms of enforcement with a view to enhancing compliance with ESMA's soft law instruments (*de iure* level), and analyses if and how such mechanisms are being used in practice (*de facto* level). It shows that both the Commission and ESMA itself may be involved in the enforcement of the Commission's delegated and implementing acts, mainly by means of hard enforcement mechanisms. It also demonstrates that with regard to its guidelines, ESMA can only use enforcement mechanisms of a soft kind, whereas regarding its non-binding instruments it cannot use any mechanisms at all.

Indeed, the workings of the enforcement mechanisms are explained in the order of soft to hard so as to propose that ESMA prefers to start with its softest enforcement mechanisms where possible and uses its harder enforcement mechanisms only when necessary,[15] but this is not a requirement. Likewise, it is also possible to use more than one mechanism at the same time. For this purpose, the distinction between hard enforcement, soft enforcement and the absence of any enforcement mechanism proposed by Terpan is helpful.[16] *Hard enforcement* relates to those situations where rules are submitted to judicial control or to a very constraining form of non-judicial control.[17] In the case of an international organisation this would materialise in a binding decision taken by a supranational institution.[18] *Soft enforcement* is about procedures aimed at ensuring compliance without necessarily resorting to coercion or constraint.[19] Finally, *the absence of enforcement mechanisms* refers to situations where compliance only depends on the actors' political will.[20]

---

15 Ayres & Braithwaite 1992.

16 Terpan 2015, p. 73.

17 Ibid. Although judicial review may be regarded as a hard enforcement mechanism (see Terpan 2015, p. 73), it will be dealt with in a separate chapter in this book, namely Chapter 10.

18 Ibid.

19 Ibid., p. 74.

20 Ibid.

3. COMPLIANCE TABLES

A first way for ESMA to enhance compliance with its legal instruments is by publishing so-called compliance tables on its website. Since guidelines form the only category of soft law instruments that are subject to a 'comply or explain' mechanism, ESMA only has a *de iure* duty, with regard to its guidelines, to publish the fact that an NCA does not comply or does not intend to comply.[21] It does so in a 'guidelines compliance table' set out on its website. It may also decide, on a case-by-case basis, to publish in such a table the reasons provided by the NCA for not complying with the guidelines.[22]

3.1 Draft Regulatory and Implementing Technical Standards

There are no compliance tables with regard to ESMA's technical standards, because there is no 'comply or explain' mechanism in relation to such standards. Indeed, compliance with ESMA's technical standards is mandatory, because they become binding EU law after endorsement by the Commission.[23] This excludes the possibility to 'explain' non-compliance and therewith the need to publish compliance tables, because non-complying national competent authorities are automatically in breach of EU law.

3.2 Guidelines and Recommendations

As follows from the previous chapter, ESMA's guidelines come with a 'comply or explain' mechanism.[24] Following up on this mechanism, the agency stimulates compliance with, and the coherent application of, its guidelines by publishing so-called *guidelines compliance tables* on its website.[25] As the example in Table 9.1 demonstrates, such tables literally state which competent authorities of which Member States comply with ESMA's guidelines by indicating a 'Yes' in green or a 'No' in red.[26] In addition, competent authorities that have the intention to comply will be marked in light green with the words 'Intends to comply'. In line with the most recent approach taken by ESMA, in their compliance notification form they have to provide a date by which they will comply and must regularly update ESMA on the progress that has been

---

[21] ESMA Regulation, Art 16(3).
[22] Ibid.
[23] Ibid.
[24] See Chapter 8, Section 3.2.
[25] For a more general account on implementation tasks of EU agencies, see Kaeding & Versluis 2014, pp. 73–86.
[26] Van Rijsbergen 2014.

Table 9.1 *Guidelines compliance table with possible responses of NCAs to ESMA's 'comply or explain' mechanism*

Member State	Competent authority	Complies	Comments
[ ]	[ ]	Yes	[A link to the national measures taken to comply will be published here]
[ ]	[ ]	Intends to comply	Intends to comply by[insert date]
[ ]	[ ]	No	[Both the reasons for non-compliance and the extent of non-compliance will be published here].

made in terms of compliance. In the absence of a competent authority's notification of its compliance position by the compliance reporting deadline, ESMA will publish the fact that it did not receive a response from that authority within the legislative time period provided.

In the interests of transparency and legal certainty, it is no longer possible for competent authorities to maintain an intention to comply after the guidelines' application date has passed. After this period they will automatically be considered to be non-compliant, 'unless (A) the Guidelines relate to a type of institution or instruments which do not currently exist in the jurisdiction concerned; or (B) legislative or regulatory proceedings have been initiated to bring any national measures necessary to comply with the Guidelines in force in the jurisdiction concerned'.[27]

The practice of labelling NCAs red or (light) green raises doubt with regard to the non-binding character of the guidelines. Indeed, the compliance tables entail a type of 'naming and shaming' mechanism, even more so when ESMA also publishes the NCAs' reasons for non-compliance.[28] Such publication could lead to press reports which may have some impact on Member States. The use of such tables may thus typically be regarded as a soft enforcement mechanism, because it aims at 'ensuring compliance without necessarily resorting to coercion or constraint'.[29] Clearly, no national authority is likely to be happy with being marked in red.[30] The mandatory publication of

[27] ESMA, Guidelines compliance table on Guidelines on the calibration of circuit breakers and publication of trading halts under MiFID II (2017) ESMA70-156-177, 4.

[28] Van Rijsbergen 2014.

[29] In conformity with the definition of 'soft enforcement' used by Terpan 2015, p. 74.

[30] Van Rijsbergen 2014.

non-compliance is therefore described as one of the core features that significantly increases application of the guidelines.[31]

Indeed, analysis of all of the compliance tables shows that Member States' authorities in general seem to be willing to comply with ESMA's guidelines and recommendations, notwithstanding doubts as to whether this occurs voluntarily or rather as a result of peer pressure caused by 'naming and shaming'. In any case, the high compliance level is mainly fostered by the relevant actors' determined political commitment to achieve the goal of a harmonised financial markets law.[32] Another reason for compliance is related to the agency's governance structure. The heads of the national supervisory authorities, as members of the Board of Supervisors and in this capacity being responsible for the ultimate decision, of course know exactly what is politically feasible in their respective Member States.[33] At the same time, peer pressure among Board members is likely to serve as another factor inducing compliance. They might fear for their credibility and will therefore not deviate from guidelines once they have been agreed to.[34]

At the time of writing, non-compliance has been indicated only to a very limited extent. There has been one rather controversial set of guidelines, though.[35] The corresponding compliance table shows that seven competent authorities (Denmark, Germany, Ireland, Spain, France, Italy and Sweden) did not confirm their compliance or their intention to comply.[36] In general, the seven non-compliant Member States intend to comply with the majority of the guidelines, yet they have no such intention regarding certain parts or provisions of the guidelines. ESMA published their reasons for non-compliance in the compliance table. The textbox below demonstrates an interesting example of how a number of NCAs – in this case the Central Bank of Ireland (CBoI) and the French *Autorité des Marchés Financiers* (AMF) – may deal with the 'explain' part of the 'comply or explain' mechanism in order to deviate from their compliance obligations: The CBoI deems that the level playing field is significantly undermined by the fact that a significant number of National

---

31 Schemmel 2016, p. 470.

32 Ibid., p. 464.

33 Ibid., p. 494.

34 Ibid.

35 ESMA, Guidelines on the Exemption for market making activities and primary market operations under Regulation (EU) 236/2012 of the European Parliament and the Council on short selling and certain aspects of Credit Default Swaps (2013) ESMA/2013/74.

36 ESMA, Guidelines compliance table on the Guidelines on the Exemption for market making activities and primary market operations under Regulation (EU) 236/2012 of the European Parliament and the Council on short selling and certain aspects of Credit Default Swaps (2021) ESMA70-21038340-46.

Competent Authorities do not apply the Guidelines in full. The CBoI believes that, to the extent the Guidelines are not applied they are not effective, and their implementation has become problematic.

> Until the lack of convergence is remedied, the CBoI will comply with the Guidelines save for the provisions relating to:
> - membership requirements (paragraphs 19–22; 35–36; 43 first bullet and last bullet), and
> - product scope (paragraphs 30; 32).
>
> The CBoI clarified that it is its intention to fully comply with these Guidelines when they are effective, i.e. when all National Competent Authorities have notified their full compliance with them.[37]
>
> The AMF declared to ESMA that it intends to comply with the full provisions of the guidelines although the said guidelines shall only enter into force as soon as they are fully applied by all National Competent Authorities throughout the EU. This is in order to avoid competition distortion between the French financial industry and that of any EU Member States partially or not applying the Guidelines. Hence, a common level playing field based on converging supervisory and market practices across the EU shall be achieved.[38]

With this statement, the Irish and French authorities express their fear that the guidelines do not create a level playing field when not everyone is compliant, and indicate a desire for consistent, efficient and effective supervisory practices as well as a common, uniform and consistent application of ESMA's guidelines within the EU from the perspective of the Member States. The Italian and Spanish authorities follow a similar line of reasoning.[39] They thus indirectly refer to the objectives of the use of guidelines as set out in Article 16(1) ESMA Regulation.[40]

Yet, NCAs cannot provide just any explanation. For instance, if they disregard ESMA's guidelines and explain their non-compliance by reference to local market conditions or a difference of interpretation, this is more likely to be accepted than if they explain their non-compliance on the basis of narrow

37 Ibid., p. 7.
38 Ibid., pp. 7–8.
39 Ibid., p. 8.
40 Van Rijsbergen 2014, p. 122.

national interest grounds.[41] The explanation requirement thus leads to a certain degree of reasoned decision-making, 'as insufficient explanations run the risk of being published along with the noncompliance notice and might turn into an embarrassment or an undesired market signal that undermines a supervisor's reputation'.[42]

3.3 Non-binding Instruments

There is no 'comply or explain' mechanism or any other duty of compliance in relation to ESMA's non-binding instruments.[43] Hence, the agency does not ask NCAs to report on their compliance with these acts. Logically, a compliance table is not published either.

4. PEER REVIEWS

Another way for ESMA to enhance compliance with its legal instruments is by periodically organising and conducting so-called *peer reviews* of some or all of the activities of national competent authorities.[44] When conducting a peer review, ESMA objectively assesses and compares the competent authorities reviewed and considers existing information and evaluations already made regarding the competent authority concerned. Peer reviews portray the extent of compliance in the Member States and identify good or best practices at the level of the NCAs. In the case of non-compliance, ESMA provides suggestions for improvement in order to enhance compliance. Peer reviews may thus be used to gently encourage compliance with the law. With the publication of good or best practices, enforcement is established via positive incentives to comply. In this way, ESMA's ad hoc peer review committees – which are responsible for the peer reviews – may be regarded as a peer pressure group which could exercise peer pressure by reviewing national authorities against certain benchmarks. Peer reviews may thus be regarded as a *soft enforcement mechanism*, because it is clear that they aim at 'ensuring compliance without necessarily

---

[41] Moloney 2014, p. 930.

[42] Schemmel 2016, p. 470. The fact that insufficient explanations are a real problem follows from a study in the area of corporate governance where a 'comply or explain' mechanism, although more modest and applicable to private actors rather than to national public authorities, also exists. This study showed that the informative quality of explanations published by companies departing from the corporate governance code's recommendation is – in the majority of cases – not satisfactory: see Commission, Green Paper on the EU corporate governance framework, COM(2011) 164 final 3.

[43] See Chapter 8.

[44] ESMA Regulation, Art 30(1).

resorting to coercion or constraint'.[45] Article 30(3) ESMA Regulation provides that a peer review includes, but is not limited to, an assessment of:

(a) the adequacy of resources, the degree of independence, and governance arrangements of the competent authority, with particular regard to the effective application of regulatory and implementing technical standards and of the acts referred to in Article 1(2) and the capacity to respond to market developments;
(b) the effectiveness and the degree of convergence reached in the application of Union law and in supervisory practice, including regulatory technical standards and implementing technical standards, guidelines and recommendations adopted pursuant to Articles 10 to 16, and the extent to which the supervisory practice achieves the objectives set out in Union law;
(c) the application of best practices developed by competent authorities whose adoption might be of benefit for other competent authorities; and
(d) the effectiveness and the degree of convergence reached with regard to the enforcement of the provisions adopted in the implementation of Union law, including the administrative sanctions and other administrative measures imposed against persons responsible where those provisions have not been complied with.

4.1 The Peer Review Procedure

In line with ESMA's Peer Review Methodology,[46] the Management Board proposes a strategy, over a two-year period, for determining in which areas national competent authorities are to be analysed and their activities subjected to peer review.[47] Beyond the topics listed in the so-called Peer Review Work Plan and in cases of urgency or unforeseen events, it may also propose a topic for a fast-track peer review.[48] The focus of each peer review is different. For instance, if it concentrates on the legal framework, the Peer Review Committee is required to ascertain that Union law, including regulatory and implementing technical standards, is uniformly implemented and enforceable, and that the implementation of guidelines and recommendations fully respects the 'comply or explain' mechanism.[49] It is not always at the discretion of ESMA to select

---

45 In conformity with the definition of 'soft enforcement' used by Terpan 2015, p. 74.

46 This work was previously done by the Review Panel. However, in line with the ESMA 2016–2020 Strategic Orientation, the shift towards more convergence activities is reflected by the establishment of the Supervisory Convergence Standing Committee and the repeal of the Review Panel: see ESMA, Annual Report 2015 (2016) ESMA/2016/960, 11–12.

47 Ibid., para 12.

48 ESMA Regulation, Art 30(8).

49 ESMA, Peer Review Methodology (2020) ESMA42-111-4966, para 28.

the scope, topic and duration of peer reviews, though. Several sectoral legislative acts explicitly require ESMA to undertake peer reviews and specify these matters.[50] These so-called mandatory peer reviews therefore have different characteristics. For instance, under Article 21(6)(a) EMIR, the agency has been entrusted with a specific role to enhance supervisory convergence, and the scope of peer reviews is defined and their frequency established as annual.[51]

For each peer review, ESMA sets up a Peer Review Committee which is chaired by a member of ESMA staff and composed of experts from ESMA staff and members of the national competent authorities.[52] As the following subsections explain, the peer review procedure that follows consists of different steps. To begin with, ESMA sends out questionnaires to all NCAs. On the basis of the input received, the agency then selects the NCAs to be visited. Next, it actually carries out these on-site visits. Finally, ESMA publishes the peer review reports and, if necessary, deals with the follow-up to the peer reviews (Figure 9.1).

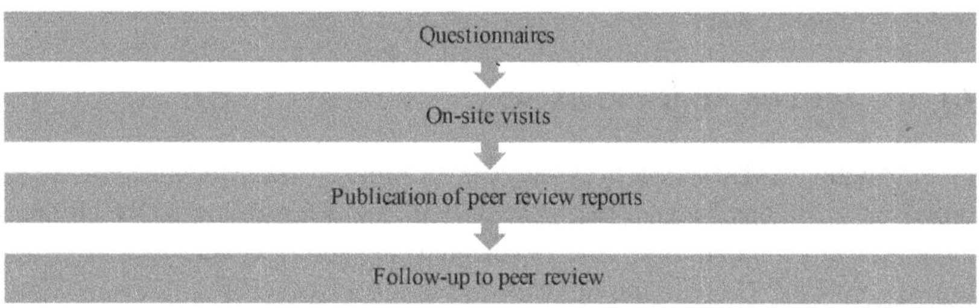

Figure 9.1 The peer review procedure

4.2 The Questionnaire

The actual peer review starts with a questionnaire of around 40 items which is sent to the national competent authorities of all EU Member States to identify

[50] CSDR, AIFMD and EMIR.

[51] EMIR, Art 21(6)(a) reads 'ESMA shall, at least annually (a) conduct a peer review analysis of the supervisory activities of all competent authorities in relation to the authorisation and the supervision of CCPs in accordance with Article 30 of Regulation (EU) No 1095/2010'. For this specific type of mandatory peer review, ESMA has prepared the Methodology for Mandatory Peer Reviews in relation to CCPs' authorisation and supervision under EMIR: see ESMA, Methodology for Mandatory Peer Reviews in relation to CCPs' authorisation and supervision under EMIR (2017) ESMA71-1154262120-155.

[52] ESMA, Peer Review Methodology (2020) ESMA42-111-4966, paras 19–26.

possible issues or gaps.[53] The questions are usually open. When NCAs answer such questions, they often refer to internal documents, procedures and decisions. The Peer Review Committee usually asks the NCAs to provide ESMA with such supporting documents.[54] The evidence is to be provided in English if available. When an English version of the evidence is not available, the answer – to the extent that this is practicable – describes the relevant evidence in English.[55] In practice it is often the case that an NCA offers a summary in English or agrees to provide the Peer Review Committee with a full translation, for example when the document is not long, when only a part of the document is relevant, or when the document really describes the main procedure.

4.3 On-site Visits

Once ESMA receives the outcomes of the questionnaire, the Peer Review Committee starts to analyse them with a view to drafting its peer review report.[56] When a peer review includes on-site visits, the Board of Supervisors, upon a proposal by the Peer Review Committee and following consultation of the relevant Standing Committee(s) and thereafter the Management Board, designates the NCAs to be visited.[57] Since this is quite a costly affair, the Peer Review Committee has to select the most representative authorities for on-site visits on the basis of objective criteria.[58] This includes, for instance, NCAs' relative significance as regards the topic under review and whether there is an indication of insufficient implementation or insufficient level of supervision by NCAs.

For instance, regarding the market making peer review in relation to the Short Selling Regulation, one of the criteria was the number of market makers in a Member State.[59] Therefore, the selection was made on the basis of the countries where the number of market makers was the highest. This resulted in on-site visits to the national competent authorities of Germany (BaFin), Italy (Consob), the United Kingdom (FCA), Sweden (FI) and Hungary (MNB). In addition, three of the five Member State authorities visited did not comply with the Guidelines on the Exemption for market

---

53 Ibid., para 39.
54 Ibid., paras 34–43.
55 Ibid., para 39.
56 Ibid., para 42.
57 Ibid., para 47.
58 Ibid., paras 44–45.
59 ESMA, Peer Review Report on Compliance with SSR as regards Market Making activities (2016) ESMA/2015/1791. See also Chapter 8, Section 1.

making activities and primary market operations under the Short Selling Regulation.[60]

ESMA tries to incorporate both bigger and smaller markets in its choice, because all markets have to apply the same rules. Even in the smallest markets, it is important to learn whether or not NCAs are at the right level of understanding, and to see what they are doing in practice. In order to prevent the peer review process becoming excessively burdensome for some Member States, ESMA also takes into account the fact that a big player such as France – even though it has a lot of interesting cases and many types of financial instruments – may not be visited on every occasion. The selection is therefore not random. In fact, the Board of Supervisors needs to ensure that over several peer reviews all NCAs are subject to on-site visits.[61] With this in mind, ESMA staff maintains an overview of all on-site visits that have taken place, including the number and timing of on-site visits to each NCA. Such balance is necessary, because a peer review visit – even though it takes only one to three days – represents a substantial amount of work within a very short period of time. This means that all NCAs will eventually have to undergo on-site visits, and none will be excluded.

4.4 The Peer Review Report

Based on analysis of the responses to the questionnaire and the findings from the on-site visits and engagement with stakeholders, the Peer Review Committee produces a general peer review report.[62] The NCAs are given time to check the accuracy of the report. After that, it is submitted for consultation to the relevant Standing Committee(s) and thereafter the Management Board.[63] Following discussion at a meeting, the final peer review report is adopted by the Board of Supervisors through written procedure. The report is published on the ESMA website in full on a named basis to encourage compliance and increase transparency.[64] The peer review reports often serve as a basis for NCAs to learn from the different *good practices* in other Member States. In

[60] Guidelines compliance table on the Guidelines on the Exemption for market making activities and primary market operations under Regulation (EU) 236/2012 of the European Parliament and the Council on short selling and certain aspects of Credit Default Swaps (2013) ESMA/2013/765.

[61] ESMA, Peer Review Methodology (2020) ESMA42-111-4966, para 44.

[62] Ibid., para 51.

[63] Ibid., para 56.

[64] The individual responses to the assessment questionnaire are not published: see ESMA, Peer Review Methodology (2020) ESMA42-111-4966, para 61.

no way are good practices intended to disqualify other practices, or forms of implementation, that may be more suitable for a specific jurisdiction. Good practices do not have any normative or binding character and the 'comply or explain' procedure does not apply to them. NCAs may choose to apply a similar practice themselves, but there are also NCAs that ask for technical assistance from the biggest markets or those with the greatest level of experience.

For example, during the market making peer review,[65] the Hungarian authority (MNB) asked the Italian authority (Consob) to provide advice on how to deal with the exemption process, because they knew that Italy has a bigger market and had already heard through meetings that the Italian authority has a good knowledge of this field and the appropriate procedures in place. NCAs may contact each other directly for such purposes.

The peer review report also explains and indicates the follow-up measures that are deemed appropriate, proportionate and necessary as a result of the peer review. Those follow-up measures may be adopted in the form of guidelines and recommendations pursuant to Article 16 and opinions to national competent authorities pursuant to Article 29(1)(a) ESMA Regulation.[66]

4.5 Follow-up to ESMA's Peer Review Reports

A peer review may lead to a variety of results, such as findings of potential breaches of Union law, findings that may lead ESMA to recommend changes to Union law, findings of the incomplete implementation of non-binding instruments and identification of good practices. Concretely, if the outcome of a peer review leads ESMA to consider that further harmonisation of Union rules applicable to financial market participants or competent authorities would be necessary from the Union's perspective, it can submit an opinion to the Commission.[67] ESMA may also issue guidelines and recommendations on the basis of a peer review and it must take the outcome of peer reviews into account when developing its draft regulatory or implementing technical standards.[68] In this sense, the peer review process is very much linked to ESMA's quasi-rulemaking activities.[69]

---

[65] ESMA, Peer Review Report on Compliance with SSR as regards market making activities (2016) ESMA/2015/1791.

[66] ESMA Regulation, Art 30(4).

[67] Ibid., Art 30(5).

[68] Ibid., Art 30(4).

[69] Moloney 2012, p. 102.

In order to enhance the effectiveness of the peer review procedure, ESMA also monitors follow-up actions taken by national competent authorities to address the findings of any peer review. The Peer Review Committee is therefore entrusted to undertake and prepare a follow-up report two years after the publication of the peer review report.[70]

For instance, ESMA's 2017 follow-up report on the best execution peer review provides an update of the actions that national authorities have undertaken further to the 2015 peer review on best execution under MiFID.[71] During the peer review, it was found that 15 NCAs did not apply or only partly applied criteria that are considered essential for ensuring an effective best execution under MiFID. As follows from the follow-up report, five of them (Cyprus, Hungary, Lithuania, Malta, Poland) have reported that they have taken action to address the deficiencies identified by the 2015 peer review. In one Member State (Poland) the national law has been reviewed and the exemption from best execution requirements for firms in certain situations has been removed. However, ESMA also identified that for the remaining ten NCAs (Bulgaria, Denmark, Estonia, Greece, Liechtenstein, Latvia, Romania, Sweden, Slovenia, Slovakia) some of the deficiencies still remain.[72]

The Peer Review Committee sends individual letters to the relevant members of the Board of Supervisors requesting NCAs to provide a status update on the work performed to address the findings and recommendations, including supporting evidence.[73] A focused on-site visit to those NCAs with serious findings may occur, subject to the follow-up report.[74] The follow-up report includes an assessment of the adequacy and effectiveness of the actions undertaken by the NCAs in response to the findings and recommendations of the peer review report and suggests suitable responses in case of possible delays in implementation.[75] Following consultation of the relevant Standing Committee(s), the report is submitted to the Management Board for consultation, discussed at a meeting of the Board of Supervisors and adopted by the latter by means of written procedure.[76]

---

70 ESMA Regulation, Art 30(6).

71 ESMA, Follow-up Report to the Peer Review on Best Execution (2017) ESMA42-1643088512-2962, para 2.

72 Ibid., para 9.

73 ESMA, Peer Review Methodology (2020) ESMA42-111-4966, para 65.

74 Ibid., para 66.

75 Ibid., para 67.

76 Ibid., paras 68–69.

Interestingly, the publication of a follow-up peer review report was already good practice during the first years of ESMA's operations. Under the ESA review, it has been integrated as a formal step in the peer review process. The fact that ESMA is checking upon the NCAs, potentially with a focused on-site visit to those NCAs with serious findings subject to the follow-up, emphasises the use of the peer review tool as an enforcement mechanism.

4.5.1 Draft regulatory and implementing technical standards

As follows from Articles 30(3)(a) and (b) ESMA Regulation, it is certainly possible to carry out a peer review with regard to regulatory and implementing technical standards. The objective is to ascertain that such standards are uniformly implemented and enforceable.[77]

For instance, the peer review on Central Counterparties (CCPs)[78] aimed to assess the effectiveness of supervisory practices put in place by authorities in order to assess CCPs' compliance with the provisions of Articles 41 (Margin requirements) and 46 (Collateral requirements) of EMIR and the related regulatory technical standards, namely Articles 24–28 and Articles 37–42 of Commission Delegated Regulation (EU) No 153/2013 on requirements for CCPs.[79]

4.5.2 Guidelines and recommendations

As follows from Article 30(3)(b) ESMA Regulation, it is also possible to carry out a peer review with regard to guidelines and recommendations. ESMA regularly makes use of this possibility in practice: see, for instance, the peer review on the Guidelines on ETFs and other UCITS issues[80] or the peer review on Guidelines on Enforcement of Financial Information.[81] The objective is then to ascertain that the implementation of this type of soft law instrument fully respects the 'comply or explain' mechanism.[82] Peer reviews are particularly helpful for ESMA to research the follow-up on guidelines at the national

---

[77] Ibid., para 28.

[78] EMIR, Art 2(1): 'CCP' means a legal person that interposes itself between the counterparties to the contracts traded on one or more financial markets, becoming the buyer to every seller and the seller to every buyer.

[79] ESMA, Peer Review under EMIR Art. 21 Supervisory activities on CCPs' margin and collateral requirements (2016) ESMA/2016/1683, 4.

[80] ESMA, Peer Review Report on the Guidelines on ETFs and other UCITS issues (2018) ESMA42-111-4479.

[81] ESMA, Peer Review Report on the Guidelines on enforcement of financial information (2017) ESMA42-111-4138.

[82] ESMA, Peer Review Methodology (2020) ESMA42-111-4966, para 28.

level and to see whether Member States which say they comply do indeed do so. The reviews may urge lagging national supervisory authorities to perform better.[83]

4.5.3 Non-binding instruments

ESMA does not undertake peer reviews with regard to its non-binding instruments. There is no legal basis for this in Article 30 ESMA Regulation.

5. BREACH OF UNION LAW

Yet another way in which ESMA could try to ensure compliance with its acts is through the so-called Breach of Union Law (BUL) procedure, according to which ESMA is entitled to proceed against a national competent authority if the latter has not applied or has not correctly applied Union law.[84] This provision aims to solve what was considered as one of the most significant weaknesses in the regulatory system before ESMA's establishment, that is, the actual implementation of the Union rules by the Member States.[85] Only the Commission was in charge of ensuring compliance with Union law by the Member States by virtue of Article 258 TFEU, but this procedure was particularly heavy-handed and only worked with regard to significant violations of level 1 instruments.[86]

5.1 The Breach of Union Law Procedure

The three-step mechanism of the BUL procedure starts with an ESMA recommendation to the NCA, which might then be reinforced by a formal opinion of the Commission to the NCA,[87] and might eventually conclude with a binding ESMA decision directly addressed to a financial market participant.[88] Since the

---

83 Wymeersch 2012, pp. 280–81.

84 ESMA Regulation, Art 17.

85 Wymeersch 2012, p. 255.

86 Ibid., p. 256.

87 This three-step mechanism is to be understood as an attempt to facilitate a gradual decision-making process, in which ESMA's expertise is combined with the Commission's political legitimacy: see Weismann 2012, p. 497. The legislator might have deemed the involvement of the Commission to be mandatory in light of the delegation case-law of the CJEU: see Joined Cases T-369 and T-85/95 *DIR International Film and Others v Commission* [1998] ECR II-357, para 52 with reference to the *Meroni* decision.

88 ESMA follows its own rules of procedure: see ESMA, Decision of the Board of Supervisors Rules of procedure on breach of Union law investigations (2020) ESMA43-318-5630.

output becomes more and more authoritative[89] – a recommendation, a formal opinion and, finally, a binding decision – the Breach of Union Law procedure may be regarded as a *hard enforcement mechanism*, as the rules are submitted to 'a very constraining form of non-judicial control'.[90] The procedure may be visualised as in Figure 9.2.

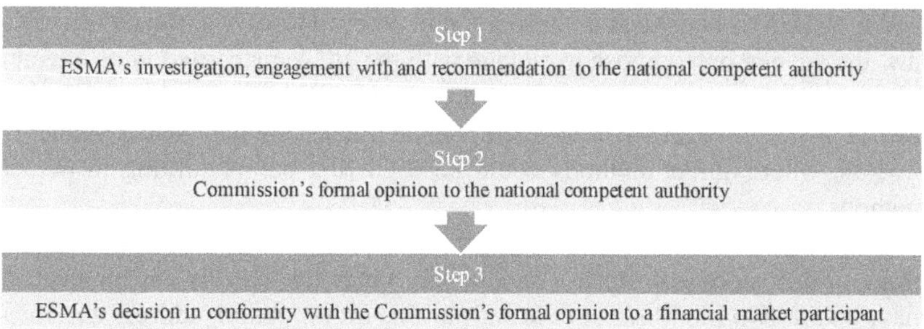

Source: Based on Scholten & Ottow 2014, p. 83.

Figure 9.2 *Stages in the Breach of Union Law procedure under Article 17 ESMA Regulation*

5.1.1 ESMA's investigation, engagement with and recommendation to the national competent authority

As a first step, ESMA may investigate an alleged breach or non-application of Union law upon a request[91] from one or more national supervisory authorities, the European Parliament, the Council, the Commission or the Securities and Markets Stakeholder Group or on its own initiative, including when this is based on well-substantiated information from natural or legal persons. Yet, individual plaintiffs have no right to request that ESMA investigate a specific case.[92] In the event of an investigation, the NCA concerned has to provide ESMA, without delay, with all information which the agency considers neces-

---

[89] Weismann 2012, p. 497.

[90] In conformity with the definition of 'hard enforcement' used by Terpan 2015, p. 73.

[91] ESMA is not, however, obliged to start an investigation even if it has received a request from one of the bodies mentioned: see Wymeersch 2012, p. 258.

[92] Schammo argues in favour of improving the procedural position of 'ordinary' complainants under Article 17 who ask an ESA to investigate an (alleged) breach of Union law by a competent authority, especially a right of access to the ESA Board of Appeal, if an ESA declines to investigate an alleged breach of Union law: see Schammo 2018.

sary for its investigation.[93] When the requested information is, however, insufficient for the purpose of investigating the alleged breach of non-application of Union law, ESMA may address a duly justified and reasoned request for information directly to other NCAs. It has to inform the NCA concerned thereof.[94] This possibility is introduced as a result of the ESA review to ease, and speed up, ESMA's access to information.[95]

Where ESMA considers it appropriate in order to resolve a breach of Union law, the agency may choose to engage with the NCA concerned in an attempt to reach agreement on actions necessary for the NCA to comply with Union law. This may be regarded as an attempt to facilitate a gradual decision-making process, where softer methods could be used first before turning to harder methods.

If ESMA does not consider engagement with the NCA concerned appropriate or if it does not reach a satisfactory outcome with its engagement, it may, within two months from the start of this investigation, address a *recommendation* to the NCA concerned setting out the action necessary to comply with Union law.[96] The NCA must inform ESMA of the steps it has taken or intends to take to ensure compliance with Union law within ten working days of receipt of the recommendation.[97]

5.1.2 The Commission's formal opinion to the national competent authority

As a second step, if the NCA concerned does not comply with Union law within one month of receipt of ESMA's recommendation, the Commission may issue a *formal opinion* requiring the NCA to take the action necessary to comply with Union law.[98] It may do so after having been informed by ESMA or on its own initiative.[99] The Commission's formal opinion has to take into account ESMA's recommendation and must be issued no later than three months after the adoption of that recommendation.[100] The Commission may extend this period by one month.[101] The NCA has to inform the Commission and ESMA of the steps it has taken or intends to take to comply with the

93 ESMA Regulation, Art 17(2).
94 Ibid., Art 17(2a).
95 Ibid., recital 23.
96 Ibid., Art 17(3).
97 Ibid.
98 Ibid., Art 17(4).
99 Ibid.
100 Ibid.
101 Ibid.

Commission's formal opinion within ten working days of receipt of that formal opinion.[102]

5.1.3 ESMA's decision in conformity with the Commission's formal opinion to a financial market participant

As a third step and without prejudice to the powers of the Commission pursuant to Article 258 TFEU, ESMA may, as a last resort, adopt an *individually binding decision* addressed to a financial market participant, requiring it to take all necessary action to comply with its obligations under Union law, including the cessation of any practice.[103] This power aims to overcome exceptional situations of persistent inaction by the NCA concerned when the latter does not comply with the Commission's formal opinion within the period of time specified therein. The power is limited to exceptional circumstances: (a) where it is necessary to remedy, in a timely manner, such non-compliance in order to maintain or restore neutral conditions of competition in the market or to ensure the orderly functioning and integrity of the financial system and (b) where the relevant requirements of the legislative acts referred to in Article 1(2) are directly applicable to financial market participants.[104] ESMA's decision has to be in conformity with the formal opinion issued by the Commission[105] and prevails over any previous decision adopted by the national competent authorities on the same matter.[106] When it was first introduced in 2010, this individual decision-making power represented a *novum* in the field of financial market supervisory law.[107] Its purpose is to ensure that the financial market participant in question complies with its EU law obligations, notwithstanding the failings of the competent authority.[108] In this case, the consequence of *indirect* enforcement by an EU authority vis-à-vis a national authority is thus *direct* enforcement by an EU authority against a financial market participant.[109]

ESMA lists in its annual report the national competent authorities and financial market participants which have not complied with the formal opinions of the Commission and the decisions of ESMA.[110] It does not set out how it intends to ensure compliance in the future. Nonetheless, this could be regarded

---

[102] Ibid., Art 17(5).
[103] Ibid., Art 17(6).
[104] Ibid.
[105] Ibid.
[106] Ibid., Art 17(7).
[107] Ottow 2011.
[108] Schammo 2011, p. 1886.
[109] See for a complete study on direct enforcement by EU authorities, Scholten & Luchtman 2017.
[110] ESMA Regulation, Art 17(8).

as a practice of naming and shaming, because details of which NCAs and market parties are non-compliant are still publicly known to others.

5.2 Draft Regulatory and Implementing Technical Standards and the Commission's Implementing and Delegated Acts

In principle, a Breach of Union Law procedure can only be initiated by ESMA if an NCA has not applied or has not correctly applied the acts referred to in Article 1(2) ESMA Regulation, including the regulatory and implementing technical standards established in accordance with Articles 10 to 15 ESMA Regulation. The possibility to start this procedure on the basis of an alleged breach of technical standards is thus explicitly laid down in Article 17(1) ESMA Regulation itself.

5.3 Guidelines and Recommendations

As follows from the above, ESMA can only pull the trigger to start a Breach of Union Law procedure with regard to non-compliance with binding legislation, that is, level 1 legislation and level 2 technical standards. A disadvantage regarding the enforcement of guidelines via a Breach of Union Law procedure is therefore that, considering the lack of 'inherent' legally binding force, a case cannot be initiated on the basis of non-compliance with the guidelines alone. This has been discussed and recognised at the level of ESMA's Board of Supervisors. The Commission has however suggested that non-compliance with guidelines could indicate an underlying breach of EU law.[111] This might particularly be the case if guidelines have 'incidental' legally binding force by virtue of an NCA's indication of compliance.[112] Consequently, ESMA has to prove that if an NCA does not comply with the guidelines, it is infringing the underlying legislation.

---

[111] In relation to the reporting by a group of NCAs of their non-compliance with ESMA's guidelines on the exemption of market-makers under the Short Selling Regulation, see Commission, 'Report from the Commission the European Parliament and the Council on the evaluation of the Regulation (EU) No 236/2012 on short selling and certain aspects of Credit Default Swaps' COM(2013) 885 final, 6. The Commission also indicated to ESMA that it might request it to take action: see ESMA, Board of Supervisors Summary of Conclusions of 4 July 2013 (ESMA/2013/BS/125).

[112] See the argumentation in Chapter 8, Section 4.2.2.

5.4 Non-binding Instruments

Since ESMA's non-binding instruments merely produce *de facto* effects and therefore lack a *de iure* and *de facto* compliance obligation,[113] it is impossible to start an investigation of an alleged breach of Union law on the basis of non-compliance with such an instrument. Non-compliance with the interpretation of ESMA as laid down in non-binding instruments may lead to an infringement of the underlying binding legislation, but a breach certainly cannot be proven on the basis of non-compliance with such instruments alone.

6. INFRINGEMENT PROCEDURES BY THE EUROPEAN COMMISSION

The Commission may also play a role in ensuring compliance with ESMA's acts. Indeed, Article 258 TFEU enables the Commission to initiate a so-called infringement procedure if it considers that a Member State has failed to fulfil an obligation under the Treaties, even though ESMA now also has the possibility to ensure compliance with Union law with a Breach of Union Law procedure. This means that either procedure can be initiated regardless of the other, and also at the same time,[114] because the addressees of both procedures are different: Article 258 TFEU addresses the *Member State* with respect to its legislative or administrative action or inaction, whereas Article 17 ESMA Regulation addresses the action of the *national supervisory authority* in its capacity as a rule-making body or its administrative action as a supervisor.[115] If the Breach of Union Law procedure however ends with an ESMA decision addressed to the financial market participant concerned and the national competent authority executes it accordingly, the infringement is remedied and the Commission will not be successful before the CJEU.[116]

6.1 The Infringement Procedure

In the first stage of this procedure, the so-called administrative or preliminary stage, the Commission sends the Member State a *letter of formal notice* inviting it to submit its observations within two months. This exchange of views is not normally publicised. Where the observations submitted by the Member State fail to persuade the Commission to change its point of view or where the

---

[113] See Chapter 8, Section 3.3.
[114] Weismann 2012, p. 497.
[115] Wymeersch 2012, p. 257.
[116] Weismann 2012, p. 497.

Member State fails to respond to the request, the Commission may issue a *reasoned opinion*, allowing the Member State an additional two-month period within which to comply. At this stage, the Commission issues a press release informing the EU's citizens of the purpose of the procedure.

In the second stage, the so-called litigation or judicial stage, the Commission may bring the matter before the CJEU if the Member State concerned does not comply with the reasoned opinion within the period laid down by the Commission.[117] If the Member State also fails to comply with the Court's judgment, the Commission may bring the matter before the Court a second time in order to seek the imposition of a lump sum or penalty payment by virtue of Article 260 TFEU.

The Commission's infringement procedure may thus be regarded as a *hard enforcement mechanism*, since the rules are submitted to 'a very constraining form of non-judicial control' in the first stage and to 'judicial control' in the second stage.[118]

6.2 The Commission's Delegated and Implementing Acts

Article 258 TFEU explicitly enables the Commission to initiate infringement proceedings if 'a Member State has failed to fulfil *an obligation* under the Treaties'. This means that the Commission can only take enforcement action against alleged non-compliant behaviour with respect to *hard legal obligations*.[119] This includes non-compliance with the Commission's delegated and implementing acts.

6.3 Guidelines and Recommendations

As follows from the subsection above, the obligations that are relevant for the application of the infringement procedures are necessarily of a hard character.[120] Consequently, as a general rule, it is not possible for the Commission to initiate infringement proceedings when a soft law act has not been complied with, using the argument that a Member State has failed to fulfil an obligation

---

117 In practice, only a small number of all infringement procedures makes it to the judicial phase. All other cases are closed before a referral to the Court of Justice of the EU. Each year, the Commission publishes its annual reports on monitoring the application of EU law at <https://ec.europa.eu/info/publications/annual-reports-monitoring-application-eu-law_en> accessed 25 February 2021.

118 In conformity with the definition of 'hard enforcement' used by Terpan 2015, p. 73.

119 Koops 2014, p. 146.

120 Ibid.

under the Treaties as required by Article 258 TFEU.[121] This is so, in short, because such acts are not legally binding. This excludes the *de iure* possibility for the Commission to start such a procedure on the basis of non-compliance with ESMA's guidelines alone. The Court will thus base a breach of an obligation under the Treaty not on a soft law instrument, but primarily on the underlying secondary law or Treaty norm.[122] In this way, the 'Commission can constrain the recalcitrant Member State to agree to a certain soft law instrument by threatening to issue a hard law decision'.[123]

6.4 Non-binding Instruments

For the same reasons as set out in the subsection above, the Commission cannot start an infringement procedure regarding non-compliance with ESMA's non-binding instruments either.

7. CONCLUSION AND ASSESSMENT ON THE ENFORCEMENT OF ESMA'S INSTRUMENTS VIS-À-VIS NATIONAL AUTHORITIES

Both soft and hard enforcement mechanisms exist in the context of ESMA's soft law-making. The softer the legal instruments, the softer the enforcement mechanisms, and vice versa. The enforcement mechanisms in relation to ESMA's soft law instruments can be visualised as in Table 9.2.

ESMA can use a mix of enforcement mechanisms with regard to ensuring compliance with *the Commission's implementing or delegated acts*. It is therefore rather powerful. To begin with, it has one soft enforcement mechanism at its disposal, namely *peer reviews*. If that does not work, ESMA can also use a hard enforcement mechanism. This is quite logical, because implementing and delegated acts are legally binding once they are endorsed by the Commission.[124] Hence, when an NCA has not applied such acts or has applied them in a way which appears to be a breach of Union law, ESMA can start

---

[121] Senden 2004, p. 352.

[122] Luijendijk & Senden 2011, p. 321. See, as an illustrative example, Case T-258/06 *Germany v Commission* [2010] ECR-2027, para 151. See also Case C-69/05 *Commission v Luxemburg* [2006] ECR I-7, para 9, where the Commission started a TFEU, Art 258 action against the Grand Duchy of Luxembourg for a failure to notify its annual reports on state aid in the agriculture sector for the period 2000–01 within the deadline, as it should have done in accordance with the Commission guidelines for state aid in the agriculture sector. The Court considered the action brought by the Commission well founded. This example has been taken from Stefan 2017, p. 11.

[123] Stefan 2017, p. 11.

[124] See Chapter 8, Section 3.1.

Table 9.2 *ESMA's soft law instruments and related enforcement mechanisms*

	Enforcement mechanism	**Nature of the enforcement mechanism**	**Enforcement mechanism used by...**	**Hard, soft, no enforcement**
The Commission's delegated or implementing acts	Peer review	Good/best practices	ESMA	Soft enforcement
	Infringement procedure	Hard sanctions (via Member States)	Commission	Hard enforcement
	Breach of Union law procedure	Hard sanctions	ESMA	Hard enforcement
Guidelines	Compliance tables	Naming and shaming	ESMA	Soft enforcement
	Peer review	Good/best practices	ESMA	Soft enforcement
Non-binding instruments	Not applicable	Not applicable	Not applicable	No enforcement

a *Breach of Union Law procedure.* If ESMA's soft or hard enforcement does not work, the Commission may step in by starting an *infringement procedure* against a Member State in order to ensure compliance with its implementing or delegated acts. This procedure may run simultaneously with a Breach of Union Law procedure undertaken by ESMA, because Member States are addressed in the first procedure whereas NCAs are addressed in the latter.

Since *ESMA's guidelines and recommendations* are, formally speaking, not enforceable through conventional judicial mechanisms – due to their legal nature – ensuring compliance is mainly a responsibility for ESMA. The ESMA regulation establishes several soft enforcement tools that, up to now, have worked mostly efficiently. First of all, ESMA fills in so-called *guidelines compliance tables* on the basis of the self-assessment and self-declaration from each NCA as to whether it complies with the agency's guidelines or not.[125] If non-compliance persists, ESMA then prefers to interact with the various NCAs in order to gain an insight into why they have difficulties in implementing certain parts or paragraphs of the guidelines. The agency aims to solve misunderstandings in an informal way by carrying out *peer reviews* in order to investigate certain cases of non-compliance, with the aim being to turn non-complying authorities into compliant ones. ESMA therefore has no hard enforcement mechanisms. Indeed, it is remarkable that ESMA

[125] See Section 3.2.

adopts a compliance-based approach to its enforcement task in the sense that it uses non-punitive measures in order to promote conformity with its soft law instruments.[126] As a result, it mostly aims to ensure compliance before an infringement has taken place.[127] The Commission cannot start an infringement procedure either and it remains to be seen whether a case of non-compliance with guidelines alone will ever be judicially reviewed by the Court.[128]

However, as follows from practice, all in all ESMA's soft enforcement mechanisms appear to be very effective. Naming and shaming by means of publishing compliance tables, as well as using peer reviews as a 'carrot' to steer NCAs towards compliance, greatly contributes to the very high level of *de facto* compliance with ESMA's guidelines. In addition, this high level of compliance may be explained by the fact that NCAs are politically committed to achieving the goal of a harmonised financial markets law, that they know exactly what is politically feasible in their respective Member States and that they fear losing credibility as a supervisor as a result of peer pressure from Board members.[129] For the moment, there is thus no pressing need to give ESMA any hard enforcement mechanisms in order to ensure compliance with its guidelines. The *de facto* level of effectiveness is already very high.

ESMA is powerless with regard to its *non-binding instruments*. This is in line with the finding in the previous chapter that non-binding instruments merely produce *de facto* effects and compliance is thus in no way required. It is however regrettable that even naming and shaming is not possible, because the lack of enforcement mechanisms affects the effectiveness of the instruments as such. If there is no voluntary compliance, there is no way that their objectives can be achieved.[130]

The following sections conclude this chapter and assess the areas where enforcement vis-à-vis national authorities leads to tensions on the basis of legitimacy and effectiveness concerns.

---

[126] Lachnit 2016, pp. 77–78.

[127] Ibid., p. 76: this is contrary to a deterrence-based approach to enforcement which focuses on punishing offenders by means of sanctions or a fine.

[128] See Chapter 10, Section 4.2.

[129] Schemmel 2016, pp. 464 and 494.

[130] Nonetheless, ESMA periodically reviews questions and answers to identify if, in a certain area, there is a need to convert some of the material into ESMA guidelines. Guidelines are then enforceable by means of soft enforcement mechanisms.

7.1 Enforcement Mechanisms Need to Be Selected on the Basis of the Principle of Proportionality

The principle of proportionality is also relevant for enforcement. Indeed, Article 5(4) TEU is broadly formulated in the sense that the principle requires that the content and form of Union *action* shall not exceed what is necessary to achieve the objectives of the Treaties. Proportionality thus entails that every exercise of competence by the Union has to be performed with reservation. This implies that 'whenever equally effective options are available, the EU must choose the forms of action and measures which leave the Member States, individuals and businesses the greatest degree of freedom'.[131] The importance of the principle of proportionality is now explicitly emphasised in the preamble of the amended ESMA Regulation. The agency should not exceed what is necessary to achieve the objectives of the ESMA Regulation and should act proportionately to the nature, scale and complexity of the risks inherent in the financial activity or business of the affected financial institution or undertaking.[132]

The Union legislature has already applied a proportionality test by laying down that ESMA can take enforcement action with regard to its guidelines by means of soft enforcement mechanisms only (compliance tables and peer reviews). In the case of non-compliance with the Commission's delegated and implementing acts, ESMA (the Breach of Union Law procedure) and the Commission (the infringement procedure) may use hard enforcement mechanisms, although ESMA has one soft method at its disposal (peer reviews). The fact that, to put it simply, soft law is paired with soft enforcement mechanisms whereas hard law is paired with hard enforcement mechanisms could thus be regarded as an expression of the principle of proportionality.

Subsequently, ESMA has to consider proportionality when deciding *if* it wants to take enforcement action and *how* it might do this. In order to ensure the effectiveness of its rule-making powers, the agency therefore has the discretion to choose, based on proportionality considerations, the most appropriate enforcement mechanism for achieving compliance with the soft law act concerned. The choice of either a hard or soft enforcement instrument is decisive for the obligations being imposed on the NCAs. This therefore affects legitimacy in the sense of the vertical division of powers. It would therefore be desirable for ESMA to try to use its softest enforcement mechanisms first so as to alleviate the burden for NCAs as much as possible, gradually building up to hard(er) ones. However, ESMA may also skip soft enforcement or use

[131] Senden 2004, p. 90.

[132] Amended ESMA Regulation, recital 5.

more than one mechanism at the same time if this is necessary to tackle the problem of non-compliance. In any case, ESMA should itself strike a balance between legitimacy and effectiveness each time it intends to use an enforcement mechanism.

With regard to guidelines, it should be noted, though, that ESMA has no choice with regard to publishing compliance tables, because it is legally obliged to do so on the basis of the ESMA Regulation. It may however decide for itself, subject to approval by the Management Board, whether it wants to carry out a peer review or not and in which Member States it wants to carry out inspections on-site. With regard to the Commission's delegated and implementing acts, it has the possibility to use a soft or a hard enforcement mechanism. In a situation of perceived non-compliance, it may thus be more proportionate to use a soft enforcement mechanism first (peer review), before taking hard enforcement action (starting a Breach of Union Law procedure). In terms of time and resources, soft enforcement mechanisms are easier to use, whereas hard enforcement mechanisms may be much more difficult to use successfully in practice.

7.2 *De Facto* Effectiveness of the Breach of Union Law Procedure

The question remains as to what extent the aforementioned enforcement mechanisms actually contribute to effectiveness in practice. Of course, any use of such mechanisms costs time, money and staff resources. It should therefore logically be ensured that sufficient resources are available to ESMA for its indirect enforcement tasks. It has long been maintained that ESMA's *governance structure* might hamper the effective use of enforcement mechanisms vis-à-vis national authorities, especially in relation to the Breach of Union Law procedure. Indeed, this procedure has so far not been successful.[133] The threat

---

[133] The same applies to EIOPA. EBA has been successful in two cases. On 17 October 2014, EBA adopted a formal recommendation addressed to the Bulgarian National Bank (BNB) and the Bulgarian Deposit Insurance Fund (BDIF) notifying that they were breaching Articles 1(3)(i) and 10 of Directive 94/19/EC (the Deposit Guarantee Schemes Directive – DGSD). EBA also informed the two national authorities of the actions that they needed to follow in order to comply with their obligations under EU legislation, see EBA, Recommendation to the Bulgarian National Bank and Bulgarian Deposit Insurance Fund on action necessary to comply with Directive 94/19/EC, EBA/REC/2014/02, 17 Oct 2014. On 11 October 2018, EBA issued a recommendation addressed to the Maltese Financial Intelligence Analysis Unit (FIAU) after establishing that it had breached Union law in relation to its supervision of Pilatus Bank. The EBA Recommendation aims at remedying the particular failings identified by the EBA by encouraging the FIAU to take all the necessary actions to comply with the Anti-Money Laundering and Countering Terrorism Financing Directive: see

of Article 17 ESMA Regulation is an extremely political and sensitive issue for the members of the Board of Supervisors. Whereas the Board is a very collegiate body in which the members gladly cooperate, a Breach of Union law case changes the entire dynamic of a Board meeting, with members initially sitting as colleagues and suddenly finding themselves talking about just one national authority.

This is regarded as a problem, because if governance issues mean this procedure cannot be effectively used, compliance cannot be enhanced in this way. This would in fact be contrary to the objective of the Breach of Union Law procedure, because this mechanism is in place exactly to be used as a strategy to influence NCAs' incentives to comply with the level 1 and 2 legislation. As a result, this factor has negatively affected the effectiveness of the legal acts.[134]

Hence, during the public consultation on the operations of the European Supervisory Authorities (ESA review), the Commission posed the following question: 'Is there a need to adjust the tasks and powers of the ESAs in order to facilitate their actions as regards breach of Union law by individual entities? For example, changes to the governance structure? Please elaborate and provide specific examples.'[135] The respondents merely made suggestions of a procedural kind through, for example, including an obligation for the ESAs to duly motivate and publish any decision not to launch a breach of Union law investigation. Yet, in the amended ESA Regulations, each ESA Chair has been tasked with a duty to convene an independent panel for the purposes of the Breach of Union Law procedure (Article 17).[136] The panel consists of the Chair and six other members of the Board of Supervisors. The latter neither may be representatives of nor may have any direct links to the competent authority alleged to have breached Union law. Likewise, they are not allowed to have any interest in the matter. The panel proposes the decisions under Article 17 for final adoption by the Board of Supervisors.[137] This should take the edge off the sensitivity that Board members experienced before the establishment

---

EBA, Recommendation to the Maltese Financial Intelligence Analysis Unit (FIAU) on action necessary to comply with the Anti-Money Laundering and Countering Terrorism Financing Directive, EBA/REC/2018/02, 11 July 2018. See also Schammo 2018, p. 1424.

[134] See Chapter 2: effectiveness focuses on compliance with the rules.

[135] Commission, 'Public consultation on the operations of the European Supervisory Authorities' <https://ec.europa.eu/info/sites/info/files/2017-esas-operations-consultation-document_en.pdf> accessed 16 February 2021.

[136] ESMA Regulation, Art 41(2).

[137] ESMA Regulation, Art 41(5). See also ESMA, Decision of the Board of Supervisors Rules of procedure on breach of Union law investigations (2020) ESMA43-318-5630.

of such panels. The extent to which this amendment to ESMA's governance structure *de facto* enhances the effectiveness of the process, and whether the number of Breach of Union Law cases will increase, remains to be seen.

10. Reviewing ESMA's soft law instruments

Chapter 9 showed that ESMA and the European Commission have several *general* enforcement mechanisms for the protection of the *public* interest at their disposal in order to enhance compliance with ESMA's soft law instruments. The *ex post* dimension of the policy cycle however also entails that third parties are offered the appropriate extent of judicial protection by ensuring that such acts can be judicially challenged. There should therefore also be a possibility for individual plaintiffs to go to court. This entails the eighth stage of the policy cycle. Judicial review as addressed in this chapter is therefore about the extent of *individual* judicial protection.[1]

Judicial review is of an *ex post facto* nature in the sense that the legality of a certain measure or decision is under scrutiny by the EU or the national courts. It concerns the possibility to enforce *private* interests through mechanisms for *individual* judicial protection. Effective judicial protection concerns the opportunity for individuals to enforce all rights conferred on them by Union law before a court.[2] Given the importance of appropriate judicial review for the legitimacy and effectiveness of ESMA's (soft) rule-making powers, the aim of this chapter is to establish the possibilities for judicial review at both the Union and national level with regard to ESMA's soft law instruments.

Section 1 demonstrates the practical relevance of judicial review for ESMA by presenting some exemplary considerations made by the European Commission and market parties. Sections 2–5 investigate the extent to which the Commission's delegated or implementing acts, ESMA's guidelines and recommendations and the agency's non-binding instruments may be subject to judicial review at the ESA Board of Appeal, at the Court of Justice of the EU and at the national courts, and the extent to which individuals may seek legal remedies at the European Commission (*de iure* level). Besides, these sections analyse what has occurred so far in practice and what kind of problems could be faced in the context of judicial review (*de facto* level). The chapter shows that the differences in the legal nature of ESMA's three categories of soft law

---

[1] For two elaborate studies of soft law and courts, see Stefan 2012a and Georgieva 2017.

[2] Chapter 2, Section 13.1. See also Ortlep & Widdershoven 2015, p. 333.

instruments bring about different possibilities for judicial review. It concludes, in Section 6, that there is a high level of judicial protection with regard to the Commission's final delegated and implementing acts, that ESMA's guidelines can only be reviewed if the CJEU can be convinced of an intention to produce legal effects vis-à-vis third parties on the part of the agency and that ESMA's non-binding instruments escape all forms of judicial review.

1. JUDICIAL REVIEW CONCERNS IN RELATION TO ESMA'S SOFT LAW INSTRUMENTS IN PRACTICE

Concerns regarding judicial review are not merely of theoretical relevance. As follows from ESMA's practice, ESMA is faced with considerations concerning the judicial review of its soft law instruments. This section provides some examples of instances in which judicial review reflections or problems generally come to the fore.

With regard to judicial review, it is not necessarily the agency itself which considers the justiciability of its soft law instruments. This is quite logical, because ESMA itself is not affected by a possible lack of judicial protection. Instead, national competent authorities, public authorities such as national ministries, financial market participants and the European Commission are more concerned with this matter. Indeed, the example in the textbox below shows that the lack of clarity on the possibility to challenge guidelines and recommendations under EU law is a matter of concern for both ESMA's stakeholders and the European Commission. The latter received 94 contributions from registered organisations, public authorities and individuals to its consultation on the review of the European System of Financial Supervision in 2014.

During the Commission's review of the operation of the three European Supervisory Authorities and the European System of Financial Supervision, stakeholders asked for further clarification on the possibility to challenge guidelines and recommendations under EU law.[3] The Commission expressed the view that an appeal at the ESA Board of Appeal on the basis of Article 60 of the founding Regulations of the ESAs is limited to decisions and thus does not provide a legal basis for challenging guidelines and recommendations.[4] It further argued that guidelines and recommendations

---

[3] Commission, 'Report from the Commission to the European Parliament and the Council on the operation of the European Supervisory Authorities (ESAs) and the European System of Financial Supervision (ESFS)' COM(2014) 509 final, 5–6.

[4] Ibid.

should be subject to review under Article 263(1) TFEU to the extent that they are intended to produce legal effects vis-à-vis third parties, but at the same time emphasized that the Court of Justice had not yet had the opportunity to judge this particular aspect of the ESAs' Regulations.[5] For the time being, stakeholders, NCAs and the ESAs themselves will thus be faced with uncertainty regarding the extent of judicial protection in relation to guidelines and recommendations at the Union level.

ESMA's Board of Supervisors discussed the review report by the European Commission during its meetings on 25 September 2014 and 6–7 November 2014, but did not as such focus on the issue of justiciability of its guidelines.[6]

This brief account demonstrates the practical relevance of providing clarity on the reviewability of ESMA's soft law instruments. We now turn to an investigation of the *de iure* and *de facto* possibilities for judicial review by the ESA Board of Appeal, the Court of Justice of the EU and the courts at the national level, as well as the possibilities to seek legal remedies at the European Commission. The aim is to find out what kind of obligations the principle of effective judicial protection contains for the judicial review of ESMA's soft law instruments.

2. JUDICIAL REVIEW OF ESMA'S SOFT LAW INSTRUMENTS AT THE BOARD OF APPEAL[7]

Any natural or legal person, including competent authorities, may appeal to the ESA Board of Appeal. The Board of Appeal is a joint body of the ESAs and is empowered to review their decisions referred to in Articles 17 (breach of Union law), 18 (action in emergency situations) and 19 (settlement of disagreements between NCAs) and any other decision taken by the agencies in accordance with the Union acts referred to in Article 1(2) which is addressed to that person.[8] An appeal can also be launched by other persons when the

[5] Ibid.

[6] ESMA Board of Supervisors, Summary of Conclusions of 25 September 2014 (ESMA/2014/BS/159), 6; ESMA, Board of Supervisors, Summary of Conclusions of 6–7 November 2014 (ESMA/BS/201), 7.

[7] EU authorities with Boards of Appeal include the EU Intellectual Property Office (EUIPO), EU Chemicals Agency (ECHA), Community Plant Variety Office (CPVO), European Aviation Safety Agency (EASA), Single Resolution Board (SRB), Agency for the Cooperation of Energy Regulators (ACER) and EU Agency for Railways (ERA).

[8] ESA Regulations, Art 60(1).

decision is of direct and individual concern to that person.[9] This means that the EU institutions and Member States are excluded from the right to appeal to the ESA Board of Appeal.[10]

No appeal can be brought against a preparatory decision, such as a draft technical standard or a recommendation about a breach of Union law.[11] Only the final, legal act can be subject to review. The Board of Appeal may confirm the decision taken by ESMA or consider the appealed decision to be objectionable. In the latter situation, it will remand the case to ESMA without annulling the decision. ESMA is not entitled to derogate from the decision of the Board of Appeal and for that reason has to adopt an amended decision after re-analysing the facts and the legal context.[12]

A decision taken by the Board of Appeal may be contested by bringing a proceeding before the CJEU in accordance with Article 263 TFEU.[13] This is why some authors regard the review by the Board of Appeal as quasi-judicial or administrative review.[14] In any case, the right to appeal to the CJEU is available to Member States and the Union institutions, as well as to any natural or legal persons provided that they fulfil the standing requirements. ESMA itself cannot do much against a decision of the Board of Appeal that it does not agree with; that is, it can neither go to the CJEU nor appeal to the Board of Appeal itself. Since the latter is a part of the three ESAs, including ESMA, acting against it would harm the reputation of the agency. As can be seen from the three subsections that follow, none of the categories of ESMA's soft law instruments is appealable at the ESA Board of Appeal.

2.1 The Commission's Delegated or Implementing Acts

Given the fact that an appeal can only be instituted against decisions by ESMA as referred to in Article 60 ESMA Regulation, it will be impossible to bring a matter before the ESA Board of Appeal against a delegated or implementing act of the Commission. Such acts are not ESMA decisions, since the agency

9 Ibid.

10 Wymeersch 2012, p. 293.

11 Ibid.

12 Ibid., 295.

13 This is evidenced by ESA Board of Appeal, Decision of the Board of Appeal of 24 June 2013, *SV Capital OÜ v EBA* (BoA 2013 008). This case has been brought to the General Court – see Case T-660/14 *SV Capital v EBA* [2015] – and was even appealed to the CJEU: see Case C-577/15 P *SV Capital v EBA* [2016].

14 Some call this quasi-judicial: see Van Cleynenbreugel 2014a, p. 147. Others call this administrative review, see Kanninen 2017. This book will not deal with this issue any further, since none of the three categories of ESMA's soft law instruments can be reviewed by the ESA Board of Appeal anyway.

is only responsible for the draft technical standards and the Commission takes the ultimate decision as regards the endorsement of such standards. The ESA Board of Appeal therefore does not play any role at all in the justiciability of the Commission's delegated or implementing acts.

2.2 Guidelines and Recommendations

It is also impossible to appeal to the ESA Board of Appeal against ESMA's guidelines or the decision by which ESMA's Board of Supervisors adopted the guidelines. Neither the guidelines themselves (which are not decisions anyway) nor the decisions on their adoption fall within the scope of the decisions mentioned in Article 60 ESMA Regulation. Individual judicial protection with regard to ESMA's guidelines therefore cannot be sought at the Board of Appeal. This does not mean that guidelines have no relevance at all for the Board of Appeal. Interestingly, it has acknowledged the 'hard' quality of ESA guidelines.

In its first decision, the Board of Appeal relied on the EBA Guidelines[15] for the interpretation of the (now repealed) 2006 Capital Requirements Directive I (CRD I) as potentially requiring NCAs to impose management suitability requirements on the management of a bank branch.[16] The EBA had argued that such an obligation was not required under EU law under CRD I and that its guidelines were not binding and could not extend the scope of EU law.[17] The Board of Appeal nonetheless relied on the guidelines and a wider interpretation of CRD I to find that a breach of EU law would have taken place. It argued that even if the EBA guidelines were not binding, they addressed the matter in question from a practical perspective and assisted in the interpretation of CRD I.[18] In a later case, the Board of Appeal merely referred to the EBA Guidelines on key function holders on a few occasions, but did not say anything regarding the legal nature of such an act.[19] This was the same with regard to ESMA's Guidelines on the validation and review of credit rating agencies' methodologies in the Board of Appeal's

[15] EBA, Guidelines on the assessment of the suitability of members of the management body and key function holders (2012) EBA/GL/2012/06.

[16] ESA Board of Appeal, Decision of the Board of Appeal of 24 June 2013, *SV Capital OÜ v EBA* (BoA 2013 008)

[17] Ibid., para 54.

[18] Ibid., 56.

[19] ESA Board of Appeal, Decision of the Board of Appeal of 14 July 2014, *SV Capital OÜ v EBA* (BoA 2014-C1-02).

most recent case.[20] None of the guidelines of any of the three ESAs have played a role in the Board of Appeal's other cases.

2.3 Non-binding Instruments

Given the fact that only the decisions referred to in Articles 17, 18 and 19, and any other decisions taken by the agency in accordance with the Union acts referred to in Article 1(2) ESMA Regulation, are appealable, the Board of Appeal cannot review ESMA's non-binding instruments either. Indeed, such acts do not fall within the scope of any of the provisions mentioned in Article 60 ESMA Regulation.

3. REMEDIES AT THE EUROPEAN COMMISSION

The above section demonstrates that an appeal at the ESA Board of Appeal on the basis of Article 60 ESMA Regulation is limited to decisions and thus does not provide a legal basis for challenging ESMA's soft law instruments. Yet, during the Commission's ESA review, stakeholders asked for further clarification on the possibility to challenge guidelines and recommendations under EU law.[21] The Commission expressed the view that an appeal at the ESA Board of Appeal on the basis of Article 60 of the founding Regulations of the ESAs is limited to decisions and thus does not provide a legal basis for challenging guidelines and recommendations.[22] It further argued that guidelines and recommendations should be subject to review under Article 263(1) TFEU to the extent that they are intended to produce legal effects vis-à-vis third parties, but at the same time emphasised that the Court of Justice had not yet had the opportunity to judge this particular aspect of the ESA's Regulations.[23]

In its legal proposal for a revised ESMA Regulation, the Commission therefore originally foresaw review of guidelines and recommendations by the Commission at the request of a majority of the Securities and Markets Stakeholder Group.[24] If the Commission were to agree with the Group's view that ESMA had exceeded its competences, it could require the agency to with-

---

20 ESA Board of Appeal, Decision of the Board of Appeal of 28 December 2020, *Scope Ratings GmbH v ESMA* (BoA 2020-D-03).

21 Commission, 'Report from the Commission to the European Parliament and the Council on the operation of the European Supervisory Authorities (ESAs) and the European System of Financial Supervision (ESFS)' COM(2014) 509 final, 5–6.

22 Ibid.

23 Ibid.

24 Commission, 'Proposal for a Regulation amending the ESA Regulations' COM (2017) 536 final.

draw the soft law act concerned. The European Parliament further proposed to allow guidelines, recommendations and opinions to be challengeable before the ESA Board of Appeal. Yet, neither of the two proposals were accepted. Therefore, during the formal trilogues' negotiations, Article 60a was put on the table, and it made it into the final revised ESMA Regulation. It provides any natural or legal person that is directly and individually concerned with the opportunity to send reasoned advice to the Commission if that person is of the opinion that ESMA has exceeded its competence when acting under Article 16. This entails another mechanism of control on ESMA's use of its power to issue guidelines and recommendations, and is also applicable to Q&As.

4. JUDICIAL REVIEW OF ESMA'S SOFT LAW INSTRUMENTS AT THE COURT OF JUSTICE OF THE EU

The focus of this section is on whether or not the EU Courts are under any obligation to review soft law instruments emanating from EU agencies. Not every Union act is judicially reviewable by the Court of Justice of the EU. Indeed, by virtue of Article 263 TFEU the Court can only

> review the legality of legislative acts, of acts of the Council, of the Commission and of the European Central Bank, other than recommendations and opinions, and of acts of the European Parliament and of the European Council intended to produce legal effects vis-à-vis third parties. It shall also review the legality of acts of bodies, offices or agencies of the Union intended to produce legal effects vis-à-vis third parties.

There are two primary hurdles standing in the way of those seeking to challenge soft law instruments before the European courts. These concern the authorship of the putative act and the measure's capacity to generate relevant legal effects.[25] To begin with, legal review is only possible when a measure constitutes an act adopted by an institution of the EU.[26] As is now confirmed in Article 263 TFEU, the general scheme of the Treaty is to make a direct action available against all measures adopted by the institutions, bodies, offices or *agencies* of the Union which are intended to have legal effects vis-à-vis third parties.[27] Acts adopted by EU agencies thus fall within the scope of this pro-

---

[25] Scott 2011, p. 337. Concerning the relevant legal effects, see the distinction between 'inherent' legally binding force, 'incidental' legally binding force, indirect legal effects and *de facto* effects: see Chapter 8, Section 3.

[26] Ibid.

[27] On this basis, the Court of Justice concluded in Case 294/83 *Parti écologiste 'Les Verts' v European Parliament* [1986] ECR 1339 that an action for annulment could be

vision.[28] However, the Court is only able to review the legality of legislative acts or acts giving rise to relevant legal effects.[29] With regard to EU agencies, it may thus only review acts that are intended to produce legal effects vis-à-vis third parties. It is submitted, nevertheless, that this provision is of rather limited effect, given that most agencies do not produce acts with 'legal effects' as understood in the case-law of the Union Courts[30] and, by its very nature, soft law lacks the intent of legal effects. Indeed, the wording 'intended to produce legal effects' excludes judicial review of acts that *de facto* produce legal effects but without an explicit intention on the part of the actor to achieve this effect.[31] Although many of the political, moral or even social effects of soft law might have important consequences, they are considered extra-legal by the Courts.[32] Hence, soft law instruments do not automatically fall within the scope of acts which are legally reviewable by the CJEU pursuant to Article 263 TFEU. If the first paragraph of this provision is interpreted narrowly, some intent of legal effect has to be demonstrated. If it is interpreted more broadly, an action for annulment could also be initiated if one demonstrates that such an act produces legal effects.[33] A broader interpretation allows for more legal protection than

---

brought against measures of the European Parliament intended to have legal effects vis-à-vis third parties, even though the provision of the Treaty on actions for annulment, in the version then in force, referred only to acts of the Council and the Commission. See in the context of EU agencies C-160/03 *Spain v Eurojust* [2005] ECR I-2077, Opinion of AG Poiares Maduro and Case T-70/05 *Evropaïki Dynamiki v EMSA* [2010] ECR II-313, para 64.

[28] This has not always been the case. Before the Treaty of Lisbon entered into force, Article 230 EC (now 263 TFEU) did not contain any reference to acts of EU agencies. As a result, in older case-law, the Courts often had to deal with the question whether an application concerning an act of an EU agency was admissible in the first place. The Courts did not instantly reject this possibility, but always based their assessment on the general principle to be elicited from *Les Verts*: see Case 294/83 *Parti écologiste 'Les Verts' v European Parliament* [1986] ECR 1339 and Case T-411/06 *Sogelma v AER* [2008] ECR II-2771, para 37. This entails that in a Union governed by the rule of law, any act adopted by a Union body such as an EU agency which is intended to have legal effects vis-à-vis third parties must be amenable to review by the Courts: see for instance Case T-331/06 *Evropaïki Dynamiki v AEE* [2010] II-136, para 33. The *Les Verts* principle can thus be said to be extended to EU agencies and TFEU, Art 263 could be regarded as a codification of this principle. By explicitly mentioning them in the Treaties, the legislature has sought to enhance the protection of individuals regarding actions on the part of EU bodies, offices and agencies.

[29] Scott 2011, p. 339.

[30] Hofmann, Rowe & Türk 2011, p. 303.

[31] Such as 'incidental' legally binding force or 'indirect' effects: see Section 5.7. See also Senden & Van den Brink 2012, p. 49.

[32] Stefan & Petri 2018, p. 533.

[33] Ibid.

a narrow one. In practice, the Court considers on a case-by-case basis whether there is an intention to produce legally binding effects on the part of the agency and thus whether the act is amenable to judicial review.

Previous judgments do not provide us with a great deal of guidance on the reviewability of EU agencies' soft law, because their acts, being hard or soft law, have not often been the subject of the European Courts' case-law thus far.[34] Even though the Advocates General (AG) have often commented on the binding nature of an act, on a few occasions the Court has missed the opportunity to rule on this aspect of EU agencies' soft law.[35] This is particularly striking with regard to the opinion of AG Bobek in which he suggested revising the test for the reviewability of soft law measures.[36] He argued that the requirement of an act being 'intended to produce legal effects' should be reconsidered in light of its unclear connotation, the restrictive subsequent case-law of the Court of Justice and the proliferation of soft law instruments in the past decades.[37] In this light, the AG proposed that the test for admissibility should be whether the challenged measure is capable of producing legal effects.[38] Such approach would arguably remove the uncertainty surrounding the 'intention' of the drafter of the rule and the need for a measure to produce 'binding' legal effects.[39] In essence, the AG pleaded for a much lower admissibility threshold for soft law measures, but this was not followed by the Court of Justice, which applied the orthodox criterion of a measure's intention to produce binding legal effects.[40]

In some cases the Court has casually mentioned a particular EU agency soft law act, or just regarded it as applicable law without saying anything on the legal nature of the act;[41] in others, it has looked at the legal nature of an EU agency act in order to deal with the admissibility question. Nevertheless, in

---

[34] Others have similarly concluded that – outside the EU agency context – there are only a small number of cases on the specific use of post-legislative soft norms by the EU courts on which to draw: see Korkea-Aho 2013, p. 379; Scott 2011; Vaughan 2015a, p. 91.

[35] For instance, Case C-324/15 P *Hitachi Chemical Europe and Polynt v ECHA* [2017], Opinion of AG Mengozzi, para 103 and the judgment itself. The CJEU did not say anything on the nature of the ECHA's guidance.

[36] C-16/16 P *Belgium v Commission* [2018], Opinion of AG Bobek.

[37] Eliantonio & Stefan 2018, p. 466.

[38] Ibid.

[39] Ibid.

[40] Case C-16/16 P *Belgium v Commission* [2018].

[41] For instance, see Case C-546/12 P *Schräder v CPVO* [2015], in which CPVO guidelines were mentioned ten times and a CPVO protocol three times, but nothing whatsoever was said about their legal nature. See also Case T-100/15 *Dextro Energy v Commission* [2016]: EFSA's opinion is mentioned 50 times, but nothing is said about its legal nature or the possibilities of judicial review.

most of its judgments so far, the Court has been very reluctant to recognise an intention to produce legally binding effects on the part of EU agencies. Although the final decisions of EU agencies have mostly been considered to produce legally binding effects –the decisions of the EEA and EMSA in tendering procedures, for example[42] – the Courts have usually not found such an intention with regard to real soft law acts emanating from EU agencies, such as the opinions provided to the Commission by EFSA and the CdT.[43] It is therefore still unknown what the standard of review would be, for instance whether the soft law acts would be upheld or overturned, and so on.[44]

The Court has also not yet ruled elaborately on the soft law instruments of ESMA, or of the other two ESAs, for that matter.[45] Altogether only 33 cases

---

[42] Case T-70/05 *Evropaïki Dynamiki v EMSA* [2010] ECR II-313, para 67.

[43] For instance, in Case T-397/06 *Dow AgroSciences v EFSA* [2008] ECR II-90, para 53, the Court concluded that *EFSA's opinions to the Commission* on the basis of Article 8(7) of Regulation No. 451/2000 did not produce binding legal effects such as to affect the interests of the applicants by bringing about a distinct change in their legal position and were therefore not amenable to judicial review. In addition, in Case T-456/07 *Commission v CdT* [2010] ECR II-183, paras 64 and 66, the Court determined that the *opinion of the CdT's Board of Management addressed to the Commission* does not constitute a definitive taking of a position and could not entail binding legal effects capable of affecting the interests of third parties by bringing a distinct change in their legal position. It thus concluded that the CdT opinion was not amenable to judicial review under Article 230 EC (now TFEU, Art 263). Moreover, in Case T-675/13 *K Chimica v ECHA* [2016], para 25, the Court regarded *ECHA invoices* as confirmatory measures implementing an ECHA MB decision and concluded that those are not open to challenge. Lastly, in Case T-1/10 *PPG and SNF v ECHA* [2011] II-6576, para 46, the Court argued that *the decision of ECHA* identifying acrylamide (EC No. 201-173-7) as a substance of very high concern, resulting from the procedure set out in Article 59 of Regulation (EC) No 1907/2006, was not intended to produce legal effects vis-à-vis third parties.

[44] In any case, on questions of law, Craig has pointed out that the CJEU has the monopoly on legal interpretation and may accordingly substitute the legal interpretation of the proceeding authority, whereas it tends not to substitute its judgments for that of the initial decision-maker on issues of fact and discretion. See Craig 2012, p. 405 and Simoncini 2018, pp. 169–73.

[45] Their soft law instruments are similar to those of ESMA. Therefore, whatever the Courts have said on one of the ESAs' acts is relevant for the other two ESAs as well.

regarding EBA,[46] EIOPA[47] and ESMA[48] have been brought to the attention of the Court. In only four of them is there any reference *at all* to the ESAs' soft law instruments,[49] but the Courts and Advocates General did not make any observations about their legal nature.[50] Given that this book exposes the many uncertainties concerning ESMA's soft law instruments, this lack of any reference in the case law is striking. It is not known why the EU Courts have been so silent on soft law instruments in their ESA rulings. As Vaughan also wonders in relation to the thinness of the CJEU's jurisprudence on ECHA's guidance, does this mean that the conditions and practices of the ESA's soft law are actually *not* problematic?[51] Or is it that only the 'wrong' sorts of cases (that is, those not really about the ESA's soft law instruments) have so far reached the Court?[52] The three subsections that follow analyse the extent to which the Commission's delegated or implementing acts, draft technical

---

46 The search term 'EBA' provided 14 results, of which eight were relevant: Case T-712/15 *Crédit Mutuel Arkéa v ECB* [2017]; Case T-52/16 *Crédit Mutuel Arkéa v ECB* [2017]; Case C-577/15 P *SV Capital v EBA* [2016]; Case T-660/14 *SV Capital v EBA* [2015]; Case C-127/14 *Surmačs* [2015], Opinion of AG Mengozzi; C-507/13 *United Kingdom v Parliament and Council* [2014], Opinion of AG Jääskinen; Case T-229/15 *European Dynamics Luxembourg and Others v EBA* [2017]; Case T-321/13 *Adorisio and Others v Commission* [2014].

47 The search term 'EIOPA' provided eight results, of which five were staff cases and three were on the substance: Case C-559/15 *Onix Asigurări v Istituto per la Vigilanza Sulle Assicurazioni (IVASS)* [2017], Opinion of AG Bot; Case T-590/15 *Onix Asigurări v EIOPA* [2016]; Case T-23/12 *MAF v EIOPA* [2013].

48 The search term 'ESMA' gave 11 results, of which ten were staff cases and only one was substantive, namely the well-known Case C-270/12 *United Kingdom v Parliament and Council* [2014].

49 Case T-52/16 *Crédit Mutuel Arkéa v ECB* [2017]; Case T-712/15 *Crédit Mutuel Arkéa v ECB* [2017]; C-127/14 *Surmačs* [2015], Opinion of AG Mengozzi; Case T-23/12 *MAF v EIOPA* [2013]. See Chapter 6, Section 5.2 for further details on this case.

50 Note that two of these cases deal with the question to what extent the Court may take into account the CEBS guidelines on revised Article 3 of Directive 2006/48/EC, given the fact that they were adopted by the competent body at that time (CEBS is the predecessor of the EBA) and at the request of the EU legislature. The Court argued that the interpretation of the relevant legislation by an administrative authority cannot bind the EU Courts which have exclusive jurisdiction to interpret EU law under Article 19 TEU. It therefore concluded that, although the CEBS guidelines are an aspect which might be taken into account by the EU Courts, they cannot be accorded any particular weight: see Case T-52/16 *Crédit Mutuel Arkéa v ECB* [2017], paras 73, 74 and 77; Case T-712/15 *Crédit Mutuel Arkéa v ECB* [2017], paras 74, 75 and 78. Yet, the comply-or-explain mechanism did not yet exist during CEBS times; hence, the Court's conclusion cannot apply mutatis mutandis to the EBA guidelines.

51 Vaughan 2015a, p. 96.

52 Ibid.

standards and guidelines and recommendations, and ESMA's non-binding instruments, are reviewable by the Court.

4.1 Draft Regulatory and Implementing Technical Standards and the Commission's Delegated and Implementing Acts

To begin with, ESMA's draft technical standards cannot be judicially challenged. Indeed, a specific strand of case-law of the General Court – in which EU agencies' soft law also plays a role – continuously emphasises that 'only measures the legal effects of which are binding on the applicant and capable of affecting his interests by bringing about a distinct change in his legal position are acts or decisions against which proceedings for annulment may be brought'.[53] As a consequence, in a procedure involving several stages, only measures definitively laying down the position of the institution, body, office or agency of the Union on the conclusion of that procedure are, in principle, open to judicial review by the CJEU. This means that preliminary measures, measures of a purely preparatory nature or provisional measures intended to pave the way for the final decision are not amenable to judicial review.

In the context of ESMA, it can be inferred from Articles 10 to 15 ESMA Regulation that the procedure for regulatory and implementing technical standards is made up of successive stages. At every stage, the agency and the Commission are each assigned a specific role.[54] Whereas the drawing up of the draft technical standards is an intermediary step in the procedure that is undertaken at the ESMA level,[55] it is the Commission that has the final responsibility to adopt the technical standards by means of delegated or implementing acts under Articles 290–291 TFEU. The Commission is thus regarded as the institution having the authorship, which means that this type of act falls within the scope of Article 263 TFEU. The fact remains that this provision explicitly mentions the Commission as an author of which the acts can be reviewed.[56]

---

[53] Case T-312/06 *FMC Chemical v EFSA* [2008] ECR II-89; Case T-311/06 *FMC Chemical v EFSA* [2008] ECR II-88, para 43; Case T-397/06 *Dow AgroSciences v EFSA* [2008] ECR II-90, para 40; Case T-456/07 *Commission v CdT* [2010] ECR II-183, para. 52.

[54] Case T-312/06 *FMC Chemical v EFSA* [2008] ECR II-89; Case T-311/06 *FMC Chemical v EFSA* [2008] ECR II-88, para. 45; Case T-397/06 *Dow AgroSciences v EFSA* [2008] ECR II-90, para 42 for an example in which the Court made a similar analysis regarding an opinion delivered by EFSA pursuant to Commission Regulation (EC) No. 451/2000, Art 8(7).

[55] This view is confirmed by the ESA Board of Appeal in its Decision of 13 September 2019, *Creditreform Rating AG v EBA* (BoA-2019-D-05), paras 55–72.

[56] It should be noted that, in principle, an application for annulment must be made against the author of the contested measure. However, in certain cases, the General

The question whether this type of act has the capacity to generate relevant 'legal effects' is also to be answered in the positive. Indeed, the Commission's delegated and implementing acts are inherently legally binding acts and are thus judicially reviewable. This means that any natural or legal person can start an action for annulment at the Court of Justice of the EU as long as the act is of direct and individual concern to that person.[57]

4.2 Guidelines and Recommendations

Written by experts of the national competent authorities and approved by the Board of Supervisors of the agency, guidelines and recommendations are officially regarded as ESMA acts. In terms of authorship, this type of act could therefore potentially fall within the scope of Article 263 TFEU, since this provision explicitly empowers the Court to review the legality of acts of EU agencies. However, it is not yet clear whether ESMA's guidelines produce the relevant 'legal effects' – that is, can they be regarded as acts having the intention to produce legal effects vis-à-vis third parties?

According to Scott, there are three situations in which post-legislative guidance may have legal effects for the purposes of Article 263 TFEU and thus may be amenable to judicial review by the EU courts.[58] The first is where guidance is construed as introducing new obligations and adding to the relevant EU legislation; the second situation is where guidance sets out how an EU institution will exercise its discretionary and supervisory powers; and the third is where certain measures, through express statement in legislation or via implication, may be binding on Member States.[59] While many guidance documents do not clearly state that they are simply guidance and not legally binding, 'non-binding should not be equated with an absence of (legal) effects and careful, contextual analysis is required to assess and evaluate their nature and extent'.[60] ESMA's guidelines seem to fall within the first category, because the level 1 legislation often requests that the agency issues guidelines in order to clarify or interpret certain matters. In this way, guidelines introduce

Court has held that measures adopted pursuant to delegated powers were ascribable to the delegating institution, to which it fell to defend the measure in question. That is in particular the case when the author of the measure exercises a merely advisory competence or the measure whose annulment is sought was conditional upon the prior agreement of the delegating institution: see Case T-578/13 *Luxembourg Pamol (Cyprus) and Luxembourg Industries v Commission* [2015], para 53.

[57] TFEU, Art 263(4).

[58] Scott 2011, pp. 340–42 and Vaughan 2015a, p. 90.

[59] Scott 2011, pp. 340–42.

[60] Ibid., p. 331.

new obligations and add to the relevant EU legislation. Besides, numerous other factors support the view that guidelines are intended to produce legal effects vis-à-vis third parties.[61]

To begin with, there is always a legal basis for the guidelines: either the general one in the ESMA Regulation (Article 16), or a specific one in the level 1 legislation. Furthermore, guidelines are elaborated on the basis of a legitimated procedure which places high value on transparency and stakeholder participation. This is not automatically the case with regard to ESMA's non-binding instruments. Next, guidelines are translated into all the official Union languages and published on the ESMA website. By contrast, ESMA's non-binding instruments are merely issued in English. In addition, guidelines include the 'comply or explain' mechanism whereas the non-binding instruments do not. Why would it be desirable for national competent authorities and financial market participants to 'make every effort to comply' if there is no intention at all on the part of ESMA to produce legal effects? ESMA's soft enforcement mechanisms put further peer pressure on national competent authorities to comply. This is for instance the case for compliance tables, which provide a first public instance of naming and shaming. Finally, ESMA may carry out peer reviews in order to stimulate compliance. This raises the question why the Union legislature and ESMA would be so concerned with compliance if there is no intention to produce legal effects vis-à-vis third parties.[62]

All in all, when considering all the characteristics of ESMA's guidelines together, it appears that the guidelines are rather close to its ultimately binding technical standards. This would make judicial review a very logical next step.

4.3 Non-binding Instruments

ESMA's non-binding instruments are also officially regarded as ESMA acts. In terms of authorship, they could therefore potentially fall within the scope of Article 263 TFEU, since this provision mentions EU agencies explicitly. However, Q&As, opinions and the like cannot be regarded as acts having the intention to produce legal effects.[63] Hence, justiciability is very difficult to ensure. The Court has also pointed out in *Sepracor Pharmaceuticals (Ireland) v Commission* that a rather broad range of acts fall outside the scope of judicial

---

[61] See Chapter 8, Section 4.4.

[62] Ibid., Section 4.4.4: ESMA has the *intention to ensure compliance*. Such intention could be regarded as being decisive for the establishment of an *intention to produce legally binding effects*.

[63] They do not fall within any of the three categories defined in Scott 2011, p. 331.

review provided for in Article 263 TFEU.[64] Not only preparatory acts, but any act not producing legal effects which are binding on and capable of affecting the interests of the individual – such as confirmatory measures and implementing measures, mere recommendations and opinions and internal instructions – are excluded.[65] Article 263 TFEU even expressly excludes the opinions and recommendations of the EU institutions from its scope, which means that they cannot therefore be the subject of an action for annulment.[66] Given the above, since ESMA's non-binding instruments merely produce *de facto* effects without having the intention to produce legal effects,[67] it is not likely that they will ever be reviewable.

5. JUDICIAL REVIEW OF ESMA'S SOFT LAW ACTS AT THE NATIONAL COURT

The focus of this section is the question of the extent to which the national courts are required to take into account EU agencies' soft law instruments or the national instruments transposing them. Not unsurprisingly, the Treaties remain silent as regards the reviewability of EU agencies' soft law at the national level. The Court has not yet said very much concerning the relationship between EU agencies and the national courts within the context of soft law, either.[68] The three subsections that follow therefore consider the possibilities for judicial review at the national level with regard to the Commission's delegated or implementing acts, and ESMA's guidelines and recommendations and its non-binding instruments.

5.1 The Commission's Delegated or Implementing Acts

Since technical standards ultimately become legally binding Commission delegated or implementing acts in the form of regulations or decisions, they may be subject to a judicial procedure at the national level.[69] As follows from

---

[64] Case C-477/11 P *Sepracor Pharmaceuticals v Commission* [2012], para 52.

[65] Ibid.

[66] Ibid.

[67] See Chapter 8, Sections 3.3, 4.4 and 4.5.

[68] One relevant judgment is Joined Cases C-211/03, C-299/03 and C-316/03 to C-318/03 *HLH Warenvertriebs and Orthica* [2005] ECR I-5141, para 89, see Section 5.2.1.

[69] For more on the application of EU law and remedies in national courts, see Craig & De Búrca 2011, p. 225.

Foto-Frost, national courts can investigate the validity of a Union act, but they have no jurisdiction themselves to declare that the act is invalid.[70]

Therefore, in the case that a national court, having undertaken its own investigation, is unable to rule that an action is valid, it will have to submit questions to the Court of Justice of the EU, since only the latter is competent to declare acts of the Union institutions invalid. Indeed, Article 267 TFEU confers jurisdiction on the Court to give preliminary rulings on (a) the interpretation of the Treaties and (b) the validity and interpretation of acts of the institutions, bodies, offices or agencies of the EU. A national court may choose to refer such a question to the CJEU if it considers that a decision on the question is necessary to enable it to deliver a judgment. Where such a question is raised in a case before the final courts in any Member State, those courts are obliged to bring the matter to the attention of the CJEU. The rationale behind this division of jurisdiction is based on a teleological interpretation of Union law; that is, if any national court is allowed to annul a Union act, Union law loses its uniformity.

The only possibility at the national level therefore seems to be the triggering of a preliminary reference, although in practice preliminary references occur infrequently for a variety of reasons.[71] It is not always easy to start such proceedings, because only the courts of final appeal are bound to refer a question of EU law when one is addressed. What is more, an exception to this obligation applies when there is no doubt about the correct interpretation of the act (*acte clair*) or when the EU Court has already ruled on that act (*acte éclairé*).[72] But such a procedure is likely to take years and, even if successful, to be only of limited assistance, because it is restricted to the questions presented to the CJEU and the latter does not publicly denounce a certain act as legally invalid. Instead, it merely answers a legal question *inter partes*. It thus seems more fruitful to bring an action for annulment by virtue of Article 263 TFEU in order to challenge a Commission's delegated or implementing act, provided that the standing requirements are met.

5.2 Guidelines and Recommendations

An extensive inquiry into the possibilities for judicial review at the national courts of the Member States is beyond the scope of this book.[73] Nonetheless,

---

[70] Case 314/85 *Foto-Frost v Hauptzollamt Lübeck-Ost* [1987] ECR 4199, para 20.

[71] Vaughan 2015a, p. 86. For an overview of why this is so, see Heyvaert, Thornton & Drabble 2014.

[72] Case 283/81 *CILFIT v Ministero della Sanità* [1982] ECR 3415.

[73] See Stefan 2012a, Georgieva 2017 and Van Dam 2020 on Union soft law at the national courts.

Table 10.1 Obligations for the national courts depending on the national methods chosen for the transposition of ESMA's guidelines into the national framework

Methods of transposition	Obligations for the national courts
Direct application of ESMA's guidelines in the supervisory practices of the NCAs	Duty to take into consideration, and possibly a preliminary procedure
Adoption of non-binding instruments by the NCAs	Differs per jurisdiction, that is, depending on the national view regarding the reviewability of soft law
Adoption of binding instruments by the NCAs or implementation by the national legislature	Reviewable

it is important to link the observations of Chapter 7 on the transposition of ESMA's guidelines into the national legal framework with the possibilities for judicial review at the national level. This interconnection makes the situation with regard to ESMA's guidelines rather complex.

As follows from Section 4.2, three different transposition methods may be distinguished within the EU. These include: (1) the direct application of ESMA's guidelines in the supervisory practices of the NCA; (2) the adoption of non-binding instruments by the NCA; and (3) the adoption of binding instruments by the NCA or implementation by the national legislature. The subsections that follow show that the obligations for the national courts differ per national transposition method chosen at the national level. These obligations may be visualised as in Table 10.1.

5.2.1 Direct application of ESMA's guidelines in the supervisory practices of the NCAs

When an NCA does not transpose ESMA's guidelines into the national framework, but rather applies such acts directly, the question is whether a national court may review this type of soft law instrument or not. It depends in principle on the national court's level of willingness to use such documents in order to support its argumentation in its judgments and to follow the interpretation laid down therein.[74] There is neither a duty nor a prohibition in Union law

[74] Ibid. In general, the administrative judges in the Netherlands refer to EU soft law instruments as non-legally binding, but they nevertheless assign them legal effects as they have few problems with the use of such documents in their judgments: see Van den Brink & Van Dam 2014, pp. 26–27. They also point at the problem that the referral to EU soft law is generally not or only very briefly reasoned by the judges. For example, it does not follow from the judgments whether the administrative judge questions the legally binding force of the soft law at all. Only the *College van Beroep voor het bedrijfsleven (CBb)*, which is the highest administrative court in the Netherlands in the field of socio-economic administrative law, seems to be inclined to take a critical stance

for national courts to take account of such acts. This is different with regard to (legally binding) directives, because the Court unambiguously held in *Von Colson* that national courts are required to interpret their national law in the light of the wording and purpose of relevant directives.[75] It thereby established an unequivocal obligation of consistent interpretation of national legislation with directives. Later, in *Grimaldi*, the Court urged national courts to 'take into consideration' Commission recommendations whenever deciding on cases, 'in particular where they cast light on the interpretation of national measures adopted in order to implement them or where they are designed to supplement binding Community provisions'.[76] The question, however, is whether such an obligation only applies to Commission recommendations or if it also exists with regard to EU agencies' soft law instruments, such as ESMA's guidelines.[77] There are two possible views on this.

To begin with, the recommendation is one of the formal legal instruments of the Union and it is therefore only logical, also given the duty of sincere cooperation laid down in Article 4(3) TEU, that Member States' authorities, including the courts,[78] have to take these into account in their interpretation of related Union and national law.[79] In contrast, EU agencies' soft law instruments are not recognised as formal legal instruments in the hierarchy of norms in the Treaties and there is no general obligation for Member States to act in accordance with Union soft law on the basis of the principle of sincere cooperation, so this logic cannot simply be extended to EU agencies' soft law instruments. This is confirmed by the fact that the Court has never referred to 'instruments' or 'acts' more generally, but has only ever spoken of 'recommendations'. Furthermore, since Union soft law has no primacy over national law and no direct effect in the national legal order, it is difficult to argue that national courts are under an obligation to take Union soft law instruments into account, including those emanating from EU agencies. In addition, national courts are

---

sometimes. This tribunal puts aside a soft law document fairly easily by explicitly referring to its non-binding character.

[75] Case 14/83 *Von Colson and Kamann v Land Nordrhein-Westfalen* [1984] ECR 1891. National courts are required to do so 'as far as possible': see Case C-106/89 *Marleasing v Comercial Internacional de Alimentación SA* [1990] ECR I-4135.

[76] Case C-322/88 *Grimaldi v Fonds des maladies professionnelles* [1989] ECR 4407, para 18.

[77] Senden has asked a similar question with regard to other soft law instruments: see Senden 2004, p. 387. See also on this topic Van Dam 2017 and Korkea-Aho 2018, p. 493.

[78] The obligations stemming from the duty of sincere cooperation apply to all authorities applying Union law within a Member State, that is, the legislative, executive and judicial authorities: see Prechal 2015, p. 41. See also Chapter 2, Section 11.2.

[79] Senden 2004, p. 393.

subordinated to the CJEU, which means that they are obliged to follow the interpretations given to Union law by the Court. Yet, there is no hierarchical relationship between EU agencies and national courts. The latter therefore cannot be obliged to follow the interpretations given by EU agencies in their soft law acts. Moreover, the Court itself is not very willing to take soft law acts, including those emanating from EU agencies, into account,[80] so it seems rather arbitrary to impose a more onerous burden upon the national courts than upon itself.[81] Following this argumentation, the question whether a similar obligation to the one formulated in *Grimaldi*, that is, the duty for national courts to take Commission recommendations into account, also applies to EU agencies' soft law instruments must be answered in the negative.[82] Such an obligation would in fact clash with the principles of conferral and proportionality, because the decision to use soft law may be made precisely because legally enforceable rights and obligations are not desirable (proportionality), or because there is no legal basis for them (conferral).[83] Indeed, a duty for national courts to take EU agencies' soft law into account would indirectly 'approve regulation through the back door', even though such acts are not legally binding and not always adopted pursuant to a predetermined decision-making procedure.[84] Hence, although a flexible attitude on the part of the national judge enhances the effective implementation of soft law at the national level, courts and tribunals may not lose sight of the lack of legitimacy of such instruments.

The second view, however, entails that it would be arbitrary to focus on the name of a soft law act to the exclusion of its intended effects. This is particularly so given that the Court itself has always practiced an effect-based case law. Therefore, if we follow the 'supplement' rationale of the Court of Justice in *Grimaldi* – the national courts are bound to take Commission recommendations into consideration, especially *where they are designed to supplement*

---

[80] See Case C-127/14 *Surmačs* [2015], in which the Court did not even mention the EBA Guidelines on the assessment of the suitability of members of the management body and key function holders, whereas the AG in his opinion regarded them as relevant EU law, see C-127/14 *Surmačs* [2015], Opinion of AG Mengozzi.

[81] Eliantonio shows, however, that, even if the Court relies on soft law to a certain extent when interpreting environmental hard law, it is not a significantly authoritative interpretation source. This limited use of soft law suggests that the Court indeed applies double standards – while it does not consider itself bound by soft law, it urges national courts to take soft law into consideration when judging cases: see Eliantonio 2018 and Eliantonio & Stefan 2018.

[82] Senden already came to a similar conclusion with regard to other soft law instruments: see Senden 2004, pp. 408–09.

[83] See further in Chapters 4 and 3 on the principles of proportionality and conferral.

[84] Senden 2004, p. 390.

binding Community provisions[85] – then an extension of the obligation to types of soft law other than recommendations must follow.[86] EU agencies' soft law fulfils an identical function.[87] Indeed, ESMA's level 3 guidelines are used for the interpretation of the underlying level 1 and 2 legislation, and in this way the former supplement the latter.

Furthermore, it seems that the Court of Justice of the EU has extended the line of reasoning in *Grimaldi* to the context of EU agencies' soft law. In the *Orthica* case,[88] the Oberverwaltungsgericht für das Land Nordrhein-Westfalen – which is a German national court – asked whether a national court may refer questions on the classification of products to the European Food Safety Authority (EFSA) and, if so, what the binding force of the opinions of that agency vis-à-vis the court concerned will be.[89] The Court ruled that national courts may not refer such questions to EFSA,[90] but added that an opinion delivered by this agency, possibly in a matter forming the subject-matter of a dispute pending before a national court, may constitute evidence that that court should *take into consideration* in the context of that dispute.[91] EFSA's opinions are thus not binding on the national courts, but these courts do have a duty to take such soft law acts into consideration. Similar to the question that arises after reading the *Grimaldi* case, the question here is whether this duty is a general one, that is, are national courts also obliged to *take into consideration* the soft law instruments of other EU agencies? In a more recent judgment, dealing with guidance prepared by the European Chemicals Agency (ECHA), the Court concluded that guidance 'may be one of the factors to be taken into account' by the national court in deciding the case.[92] This would suggest that

---

[85] C-322/88 *Grimaldi v Fonds des maladies professionnelles* [1989] ECR 4407, paras 16 and 18. See also De Visser 2009, p. 261.

[86] AG Ruiz-Jarabo Colomer has held that there are no serious impediments to extending the *Grimaldi* case-law to other forms of soft law, such as guidelines. See Case C-415/07 *Lodato Gennaro & C. SpA v Istituto nazionale della previdenza sociale (INPS) and SCCI* [2008] ECR I-2599, Opinion of AG Ruiz-Jarabo Colomer. See also De Visser 2009, p. 262 and Van Dam 2017.

[87] ESMA's guidelines fulfil a *post-law* function, because they are adopted subsequent to existing Union law in order to supplement and support secondary Union law as well as to ensure proper implementation thereof in the Member States: see Chapter 1, Section 6.4.

[88] Joined Cases C-211, 299 and 316 to C-318/03 *HLH Warenvertriebs and Orthica* [2005] ECR I-5141.

[89] Ibid., para 89.

[90] Ibid., paras 90–92.

[91] Ibid., para 94. This is in line with Joined Cases C-211, 299 and 316 to C-318/03, *Warenvertriebs and Orthica* [2005] ECR I-5141, Opinion of AG Geelhoed, para 102.

[92] Case C-106/14 *FCD and FMB* [2015], para 28.

as far as ECHA's guidance is concerned, national judiciaries can, but are not obliged to, consider non-binding rules.[93]

In my view, there is nothing wrong with a general obligation for the national courts to consider soft law.[94] It is not any more than that – the Court implicitly recognises that national courts also possess an inherent competence to deviate from soft law instruments when adjudicating.[95] Indeed, to consider something means that one must take it into account, and arguably justify the choice for a different course of action, yet it cannot be taken to mean that the discretion to arrive at another conclusion is negated.[96] In any case, in order to contest the content of ESMA's guidelines, financial market participants must bring an action for annulment in a national court and pursue this action up to the point at which the national court of last resort is legally obliged to bring the matter before the CJEU as a preliminary ruling under Article 267 TFEU.

5.2.2 Adoption of Non-binding Instruments by the NCAs

If a competent authority transposes ESMA's guidelines into its own non-binding measures, it is in principle within the national court's competence to decide whether or not it will review this national soft law act. It is not a given that national judges will engage with national soft law. For instance, only on 21 March 2016 did the highest administrative court in France (the *Conseil d'État*) agree for the first time to judge actions for the annulment of soft law acts, subject to certain conditions.[97] This is a positive development from the viewpoint of effective judicial protection, because such acts were hitherto unlikely to be subject to judicial remedies provided they had no legal effect.[98] The first case concerned press releases (*communiqués*) issued by the French financial markets supervisor, that is, the *Autorité des Marchés Financiers* (AMF), which cautioned investors against certain real estate investments.[99] The second

---

93 Korkea-Aho 2018, p. 493.

94 Georgieva proposes a 'comply or explain' mechanism for national courts: see Georgieva 2017.

95 Ibid and De Visser 2009, p. 262.

96 Ibid.

97 Conseil d'État, 'Droit souple' (21 March 2016) <www.conseil-etat.fr/actualites/actualites/droit-souple> accessed 21 February 2021.

98 Ibid. This issue raised a great deal of academic interest. For case notes, see Deumier 2016; Dutheillet de Lamothe & Odinet 2016; Melleray 2016a; Melleray 2016b; Von Coester 2016.

99 Conseil d'État, 'Société Fairvesta International GMBH et autres' (21 March 2016) <www.conseil-etat.fr/ressources/decisions-contentieuses/les-grandes-decisions-du-conseil-d-etat/conseil-d-etat-21-mars-2016-societe-fairvesta-international-gmbh-et-autres-conseil-d-etat-assemblee-21-mars-2016-societe-nc-numericable> accessed 21 February 2021.

concerned a statement (*prise de position*) by the French competition authority, that is, the *Autorité de la concurrence*, on the application of an injunction formulated in its previous decision of 23 July 2012 authorising the takeover of TPS and CanalSatellite by Vivendi and the Canal Plus Group.[100] In these two cases, neither the press releases issued by the *Autorité des Marchés Financiers* nor the statement by the *Autorité de la concurrence* created any legal right or obligation for any person.[101] These acts strongly influence market players through the publicity they attract and the standing of their authors, but from a legal point of view, market players are in no way bound to follow the position of these public authorities.[102] Interestingly, the *Conseil d'État* considered that such acts are subject to an action for annulment at the national level in two cases: first, in accordance with previous case law, when it concerns opinions, recommendations, warnings and statements which could subsequently justify sanctions on the part of the authorities; second, and innovatively, where the contested measure is likely to produce significant effects, in particular of an economic nature, or where its purpose is to have a significant effect on the behaviour of the persons to whom it is addressed.[103] This means that, even though the French *Conseil d'État* took a big step forward with regard to the justiciability of national soft law acts, not all such acts are susceptible to judicial review. Whether or not national courts are willing to review national soft law thus differs per Member State.[104] Consequently, the extent of effective judicial protection is also dependent on Member State willingness.

5.2.3 Adoption of binding instruments by the NCAs or implementation by the national legislature

If an NCA transposes ESMA's guidelines into its own binding measures or if the national legislature implements them into national law, judicial review at the national court will certainly be possible. Financial market participants will thus have access to the court at the national level, where they will effectively enjoy judicial protection, as the courts will be competent to review the binding national measures of the NCAs and the national law adopted by the legislature.

---

100 Ibid.

101 Conseil d'État, 'Droit souple' (21 March 2016) <www.conseil-etat.fr/actualites/actualites/droit-souple> accessed 21 February 2021.

102 Ibid.

103 Ibid.

104 This conclusion is also drawn by Avbelj and others 2018 who analysed the judicial application of EU financial regulation soft law in Finland, France, Germany, Italy, the Netherlands, Slovenia and the UK.

However, as a further example in Germany demonstrates,[105] the fact that a national court is receptive to requests to review an NCA's national binding transposition measure does not necessarily lead to a satisfactory situation. EIOPA's Guidelines on Complaints-Handling by Insurance Undertakings, applying certain very broad compliance requirements of the Solvency II Directive, provided that insurers were obliged to establish an internal complaint-management process.[106] German insurance firms were convinced that this constituted regulatory overreach by EIOPA. The German supervisory authority BaFin did not agree, but instead complied with the Guidelines and published a legally binding collective decree (*Sammelverfügung*) addressed to German insurers that required them to implement the internal process.[107] While it is possible to contest the collective decree in a German court, the situation is regarded as inadequate, especially when considered against the fact that ESA Guidelines enjoy a presumption of lawfulness in German courts.[108]

5.3 Non-binding Instruments

It is not possible to directly challenge ESMA's non-binding instruments at the national level and, as already pointed out in Section 5.2 of this chapter, it is still questionable whether there exists a general obligation or prohibition for national courts to *take into consideration* all soft law instruments emanating from EU agencies. As long as this matter remains unresolved, it is for the national courts to decide whether or not to take account of ESMA's non-binding instruments. Similar to challenging ESMA's guidelines, financial market participants must bring an annulment action against ESMA's non-binding instruments in a national court and pursue this action until the national court of last resort is legally obliged to bring the matter before the CJEU as a preliminary ruling under Article 267 TFEU.

---

105 This example is taken from Schemmel 2016, p. 495.

106 EIOPA, Guidelines on Complaints-Handling by Insurance Undertakings (2012) EIOPABoS-12/069, para 11.

107 In Germany, the Federal Financial Supervisory Authority (BaFin) recently published parts of an EIOPA Guideline as a legally binding *Sammelverfügung* (collective decree). For an English translation, see BaFin, Collective Decree: Complaints Management Function and Complaints-Handling of Insurance Undertakings (20 September 2013) <www.bafin.de/SharedDocs/Veroeffentlichungen/EN/Aufsichtsrecht/Verfuegung/vf_130920_beschwerdebearbeitung_va_en.html> accessed 21 February 2021.

108 Schemmel 2016, p. 495.

6. CONCLUSION AND ASSESSMENT ON THE JUDICIAL REVIEW OF ESMA'S ACTS

The principle of effective judicial protection plays a large role in the eighth stage of the policy cycle. As follows from the analysis above, there are no possibilities to challenge any of the three categories of ESMA's soft law instruments at the ESA Board of Appeal, because the latter may only review the decisions referred to in Articles 17, 18 and 19 ESMA Regulation and any other decisions taken by the agency in accordance with the Union acts referred to in Article 1(2) ESMA Regulation. ESMA's soft law instruments cannot be considered to be such decisions. Furthermore, the extent of effective judicial protection at the Union and national courts differs per category of ESMA's soft law instruments. It can be concluded that, all in all, there is a high level of judicial protection for individuals with regard to the Commission's final delegated and implementing acts. In contracts, individual plaintiffs are powerless when it comes to ESMA's non-binding instruments, as there is hardly any effective judicial protection. An overview of the possibilities for judicial review per category of ESMA's soft law instruments can be visualised as in Table 10.2.

Table 10.2 Possibilities for judicial review per category of ESMA's soft law instruments

Type of review body / **Type of instrument**	**European Commission**	**ESA Board of Appeal**	**Court of Justice of the EU**	**National courts**
Commission's delegated or implementing acts	No	No	Yes	Yes
Guidelines and recommen-dations	Only in cases of individual and direct concern	No	Only if the CJEU recognises an intention to produce legally binding effects on the part of ESMA	- If guidelines are not transposed: only expected to be 'taken into account', or a preliminary procedure - If guidelines are transposed into non-binding national instruments: only if the national court is willing to review soft law instruments, or a preliminary procedure - If guidelines are transposed into binding national instruments or implemented into national law: yes
Non-binding instruments	Only in case of individual and direct concern	No	No	Only expected to 'take into account', or a preliminary procedure

The following sections conclude this chapter and provide an assessment of where judicial review leads to tensions on the basis of legitimacy and effectiveness concerns.

6.1 Concerns Regarding *De Facto* Effectiveness of Legal Remedies at the European Commission

A new Article 60a was introduced in the ESMA Regulation as part of the ESA Review. It provides any natural or legal person that is directly and individually concerned with the opportunity to send reasoned advice to the Commission if that person is of the opinion that ESMA has exceeded its competence to issue guidelines, recommendations and Q&As. There are however two questions that come to mind when reflecting upon how this new mechanism would effectively work in practice. The first relates to the uncertainty around the legal remedies. A natural or individual person may send a reasoned advice to the Commission and under the original proposal the Commission would be able to require ESMA to withdraw the soft law act concerned. However, it is not made explicit what the Commission can do when it receives a reasoned advice now. The second question relates to how one is supposed to prove direct and individual concern in the case of guidelines and Q&As. Does this have to be interpreted in line with Article 263 TFEU? In that context, the test of direct concern has been construed as satisfied when the act in question directly affects the legal situation of the individual[109] and leaves no discretion to its addressees who are entrusted with the task of implementing it.[110] Yet, how can soft law affect the legal situation of the individual, and does soft law not by definition leave discretion to the addressees on whether or not to follow up? The test of individual concern is even more difficult to satisfy. The applicant has to be a member of a 'closed category' of people, that is, a category the membership of which is already formally fixed and ascertained when the act in question enters into force.[111] Carrying out a particular economic activity affected by the measure does not suffice, even where the applicant is gravely affected by the measure[112] or when, at the time the measure was enacted, the applicant was effectively one of very few – or even the only one – carrying out that activity, as long as others could decide to undertake that activity in

---

[109] Joined Cases 41 to 44/70 *International Fruit Co v Commission* [1971] ECR 411, paras 23–28.

[110] Case 294/83 *Parti écologiste 'Les Verts' v European Parliament* [1986] ECR 1339.

[111] Case 25/62 *Plaumann v Commission* [1962] ECR 95.

[112] Case T-173/98 *Agricultores Unión de Pequeños Agricultores v Council* [1999] ECR II-3357, para 50.

the future (that is, after the adoption of the act).[113] Given the fact that they are by definition addressed to all competent authorities and/or all financial market participants, this seems a very high threshold for guidelines and Q&As. The amended ESMA Regulation clarifies explicitly that recommendations may be issued to one or more competent authorities or to one or more financial market participants. Hence, it may be easier to satisfy the test of individual concern in relation to recommendations.

Since the Article 60a mechanism has, to my knowledge, not yet been invoked, the extent to which these two questions *de facto* result in any issues, or whether they are merely of theoretical concern, remains to be seen.

6.2 Clarification Needed on the Reviewability of ESMA's Guidelines by the CJEU

The CJEU is entitled to review the Commission's delegated and implementing acts as they are 'inherently' legally binding and thus automatically fall within the scope of Article 263 TFEU. ESMA's non-binding instruments merely produce *de facto* effects and are thus not amenable to judicial review under Article 263 TFEU. The real uncertainty mainly concerns the agency's guidelines and recommendations, however. These are not 'inherently' legally binding, but may have 'incidental' legally binding force or may produce 'indirect' legal effects. The CJEU could potentially review ESMA's guidelines if they are challenged via a direct action under Article 263 TFEU, since this provision explicitly empowers the Court to review the legality of EU agencies' acts that are 'intended to produce legal effects vis-à-vis third parties'. The possibility for judicial review is thus completely dependent on whether the Court can be convinced of an intention to produce legal effects vis-à-vis third parties on the part of ESMA. The question is however whether the Court would accept such an intention and, if so, whether or not it would then be willing to review the guidelines.[114] It could be argued that the rules laid down therein are highly technical and that the Court generally lacks the knowledge to really say anything about them. However, when a case is clearly about the fact that ESMA is issuing guidelines in an area where it has no competence at all and it is thus 'missing a legal hook' (conferral),[115] the Court could certainly intervene

[113] See e.g. Case 1/64 *Glucoseries réunies v Commission* [1964] ECR 413 and Case C-290/94 P *Buralux v Council* [1996] ECR I-615, paras 28 and 29.

[114] As follows from an investigation by Stefan and Petri on ACER's soft law instruments, in the absence of binding effects, most of the agency's soft law instruments are not justiciable, see Stefan & Petri 2018, p. 549.

[115] See Chapter 3, Section 3.2.

– even more so when national competent authorities have an obligation arising therefrom.

In my view, guidelines should be reviewable under Article 263 TFEU, because they risk ending up in a legal vacuum and otherwise escaping all judicial review.[116] Such a situation should always be avoided, since the CJEU has repeatedly stressed that the European Union 'is a Community based on the rule of law, inasmuch as neither its Member States nor its institutions can avoid a review of the question whether the measures adopted by them are in conformity with the basic constitutional charter, the Treaty'.[117] Besides, one important component of the *Meroni* doctrine, as developed in *Romano*, is judicial review of delegated powers, with the Court also reinstating this point in the *Short Selling* case.[118] Hence, when guidelines issued by ESMA are not justiciable, this undermines another tenet of the doctrine, which is accountability, and more generally the balance of powers.[119] Therefore, some sort of judicial review should always be possible. As Scott has argued, there is a strong argument for enabling judicial review of post-legislative guidance documents, because 'guidance of this kind is intended to interpret a binding legal obligation and to shape the manner in which this binding legal obligation is interpreted, enforced and applied'.[120] She further notes that 'by acknowledging the normative force of guidance of this kind, and by accepting that it may in principle be subject to judicial review, the legitimacy of guidance documents would be enhanced', even if judicial oversight of the development of guidance would only rarely be required.[121] It should however also be noted that the case-law of the CJEU as such can only contribute to the correct and

---

[116] Scott calls this 'in legal limbo', see Scott 2011. Besides, in Case T-70/05 *Evropaïki Dynamiki v EMSA* [2010] ECR II-313, paras 64, 65, 67 and 75, the Court pointed out that 'the general scheme of the Treaty is to make a direct action available against all measures adopted by the institutions which are intended to have legal effects'. Hence, any act adopted by a body such as EMSA, which is intended to have legal effects vis-à-vis third parties, must be amenable to review by the Courts. The Court argued that it is not in line with the spirit and general scheme of the Treaty that, in this case, decisions which are adopted by EMSA in public procurement procedures – which are indeed intended to produce legal effects vis-à-vis third parties – would end up in a 'legal vacuum' and escape all judicial review. Hence, such decisions are acts open to challenge.

[117] Case 294/83 *Parti écologiste 'Les Verts' v European Parliament* [1986] ECR 1339, para 23. See in the context of EU agencies, Case C-160/03 *Spain v Eurojust* [2005] ECR I-2077, Opinion of AG Poiares Maduro, para 17 and the judgment itself at para 41.

[118] Stefan & Petri 2018, p. 532.

[119] Ibid.

[120] Scott 2011, p. 350.

[121] Ibid.

uniform implementation of Union law in the Member States to a limited extent, because it can only give a retrospective interpretation of Union law, often after a lengthy judicial procedure.[122]

For the time being, the Court has not (yet) ruled on the reviewability of ESMA's guidelines, so we have to await its judgment. In the short term, if guidelines are not sufficiently clear or if there are inconsistencies between the guidelines and the level 1 legislation, instead of trying to take the guidelines to court, the best way for NCAs to handle the matter would probably be to ask ESMA to revise them. Guidelines are anyway written during an interactive process with a great deal of discussion and preparatory work (such as consultation papers), so it is much simpler to build on this contact and find a common approach and mutual understanding at the ESMA level, for instance in a Standing Committee. For the time being, the best way for a natural or legal person is to use the Article 60a route to the Commission, with reasoned advice when one is of the opinion that the agency has exceeded its competence. In the long term, however, it would be very desirable from the point of view of legal certainty for the Union legislature or the Court to provide clarification on this matter. The Court has already done this in the *Elliott* case with regard to European harmonised technical standards issued by organisations governed by private law (private European standardisation bodies);[123] indeed, the Court's judgment in *Elliott* can be seen as 'a landmark decision insofar as it provides for the long-desired clarification on the legal nature of European harmonised technical standards and the question whether or not they are subject to the Court's jurisdiction'.[124] In this case, the Court arguably established an assessment framework that is pertinent to the general question of whether or when private regulatory acts may be considered as acts of EU law having legal effects,[125] thus being amenable to judicial review. Such a clarification of the legal nature of ESMA's guidelines is also very necessary.

---

[122] Luijendijk & Senden 2011, p. 318.

[123] Case C-613/14 *James Elliott Construction Limited* [2016]. In this regard, it should be noted that the judicial scrutiny of harmonised standards has long been controversial. The Treaties have never mentioned them among the reviewable acts. 'Given the voluntary application and the lack of binding legal effects, a harmonized standard was deemed unsuitable for judicial review, especially under Article 263 TFEU. Against this background, although this case concerns only the jurisdiction of the Court under Article 267 TFEU, the outcome of this case stands out': see Volpato 2017, p. 579.

[124] Klinger & Senden 2017.

[125] Ibid.

6.3 Different Interpretations by National Courts Negatively Affect Effectiveness of ESMA's Guidelines

The Commission's delegated and implementing acts may be subject to a judicial procedure at the national level.[126] National courts can investigate the validity of a Union act, but must refer questions for preliminary rulings to the CJEU if they want an act to be declared invalid.[127] The national judge is expected to take into consideration ESMA's non-binding instruments, but there is no possibility at the national level to declare them invalid. With regard to guidelines, however, the level of effective judicial protection at the national level is dependent on external factors, such as the transposition methods used by the NCAs and the willingness of the courts.

Indeed, judicial review by the national court is only guaranteed in case a national competent authority has integrated ESMA's guidelines into the national framework by means of a binding instruments or where the national legislature has implemented the guidelines into national law (method 3),[128] that is, 'when soft law is transformed into hard law'. In such cases, proceedings may be brought at the national court against the national binding measure of the NCA or the national legally binding provision. Interestingly, in such cases, the national court has to rule on national transposition acts whose origins might not even be known to it. When an NCA transposes guidelines into a non-binding national instrument (method 2), the latter might only be challenged at the national level if the national court is willing to review soft law. This will differ from Member State to Member State. Where ESMA's guidelines are directly applied by the national supervisor and are thus not transposed at all (method 1) it is for the national court to decide whether or not it will take account of ESMA's guidelines in its judgments. Analysis on EU financial regulation soft law in Finland, France, Germany, Italy, the Netherlands, Slovenia and the UK undertaken by a group of scholars shows there have been no cases involving ESMA soft law in Slovenia, Germany, Finland and Italy.[129] On the other hand, ESMA soft law has been at least mentioned or (indirectly) relied upon by the parties in the Netherlands, France and the UK.[130] A private party may also invoke soft law as a 'sword' in a national court with recourse to the CJEU by means of Article 267 TFEU,[131] that is, preliminary references

---

[126] For more on the application of EU law and remedies in national courts, see Craig & De Búrca 2011, p. 225.

[127] Case 314/85 *Foto-Frost v Hauptzollamt Lübeck-Ost* [1987] ECR 4199, para 20.

[128] For more on the three methods, see Chapter 7, Section 4.2.

[129] Avbelj and others 2018, p. 19.

[130] Ibid.

[131] De Visser 2009, p. 425.

made to the EU courts by Member State courts. The choice of tools to be used to integrate ESMA's guidelines into the national framework thus affects, to a large extent, the level of judicial protection at the national level. The consequence of such differences is that the system will be more legitimised in one Member State than in another; that is, in some Member States judicial review is possible, whereas in others it is not. On the one hand, a financial market participant in a Member State where the NCA transposes ESMA's guidelines into a non-binding national measure may remain empty-handed if the national court does not consider itself competent to review soft law instruments. On the other hand, a financial market participant in a Member State where the NCA transposes ESMA's guidelines into its own binding national measures or where the national legislature implements them into national law can at least resort to the national court to challenge the national act. The national court then assesses whether the action of the national supervisor or legislature is lawful and, in this way, plays an important role in enhancing legitimacy.[132]

A positive result of the transposition of soft law into hard law is in some Member States thus a higher level of legitimacy *ex post*, that is, it enhances the possibilities for judicial review and effective judicial protection. This refers to the fact that the Union is based on the rule of law in which its institutions are subject to a judicial review of the compatibility of their acts with the Treaty and with the general principles of law.[133] Individuals are therefore entitled to effective judicial protection of the rights they derive from the Union legal order.[134] A major disadvantage, however, is that this type of legitimacy is not ensured in all the Member States. Besides, judicial review by a national court could once again lead to diverging interpretations of Union law if the court finds that the interpretation laid down in ESMA's guidelines violates the Member State's law.[135] This would in fact be contrary to the central aim of the guidelines: harmonisation.[136] Since ensuring the common, uniform and consistent application of Union law is one of the objectives of ESMA's guidelines as provided for in Article 16(1) ESMA Regulation, this also means that judicial review's contribution to this goal is fairly limited. A low degree of effectiveness is the unfortunate result.

In order to answer the question of whether a judicial review of ESMA's guidelines should be possible at the national level, it is important to strike a balance between the fact that an increase in the possibilities for judicial

---

[132] Aelen 2014, p. 380.

[133] C-50/00 P *Unión de Pequeños Agricultores v Council* [2002] ECR I-6677, para 38.

[134] Case 222/84 *Johnston* [1986] ECR 1651, para 18.

[135] Schemmel 2016, p. 495.

[136] Ibid.

review leads to a lower level of effectiveness due to the differences in interpretations by the different national courts, but at the same time leads to a greater extent of legitimacy. Indeed, if we would accept the existence of a general obligation for courts to *take into consideration* the soft law instruments of EU agencies, the national court may deviate from soft law tools in adjudicating only when it justifies the choice of a different course of action.[137] In this way, it is ascertained that guidelines and non-binding instruments do not end up in a legal vacuum[138] – especially when they cannot be challenged at the CJEU. As a result, an individual has a greater chance of effective judicial protection when he/she knows that the national court takes the soft law act into account. Furthermore, judicial review contributes to the effectiveness of the system as a whole, because it relates to the ways in which regulation is effectuated and is of crucial importance for the achievement of regulatory objectives.

Yet, in the current situation, it is thus conceivable that judicial review is possible in some Member States and not in others. This is a serious implication of the fact that ESMA's guidelines are transposed differently at the national level. Indeed, the differences in transposition result in differences in judicial review at the national level. This affects the legal certainty of the system as a whole. Besides, it does not live up to the expectations of the CJEU as they are laid down in the *UPA* case.[139] The Court considers it important for individuals to be able to rely on their rights and to question the acts of the Union institutions if they consider that such acts are not in accordance with EU law.[140] The Treaty has therefore established a complete system of legal remedies and procedures designed to ensure judicial review of the legality of acts of the institutions, and has entrusted such a review to the Union Courts.[141] It is however not required that each act is reviewable at the Union level, as long as one can challenge it before the national court. Therefore, it is for the Member States to establish a system of legal remedies and procedures which ensure respect for the right to effective judicial protection.[142] This is however not realistically attainable in current practice. The differences in transposition hence make the availability of judicial review at the Union level very important in order to ensure that an equal level of effective judicial protection is offered throughout the entire European Union.

---

137 This proposal is in line with the suggestion by Georgieva to introduce a 'comply or explain' mechanism for national courts: see Georgieva 2017.

138 At the moment, there is no duty for national courts to take account of EU agencies' soft law acts. It is therefore at their own discretion whether they do so.

139 C-50/00 P *Unión de Pequeños Agricultores v Council* [2002] ECR I-6677.

140 Ibid.

141 Ibid., para 40.

142 Ibid., para 41.

11. Conclusions and recommendations

EU agencies and soft law are two constitutional anomalies in EU law and governance. Despite their close relationship, these two modes of governance are usually studied separately. This book has addressed the gap in the literature and contributed to the scholarly works on EU agencies and soft law by bringing the two subjects together in relation to ESMA. It has shown that legitimacy and effectiveness concerns arise not only in theory but also in practice, because both developments are barely regulated in the EU Treaties and the legal nature of EU agencies' soft law instruments is not at all clear. This chapter brings together the findings and conclusions of this book. It addresses the question: *What procedural and institutional safeguards regarding ESMA's soft law measures would reflect an adequate balancing of both legitimacy and effectiveness concerns?*

The following sections provide a step-by-step answer to this question, emphasising the main findings and recommendations made in the individual chapters. The first section provides the conclusions per category of ESMA's soft law instruments, that is, draft technical standards, and the Commission's delegated and implementing acts (1.1), guidelines and recommendations (1.2) and non-binding instruments (1.3). Section 2 provides the recommendations for ESMA. These might be useful for the purposes of further revision of the European Supervisory Authorities' operations as well. Section 3 sets out the position of EU agencies' soft law-making in the bigger picture of Union rule-making practices. Section 4 presents the rules of the game for the Union legislator in setting up EU agencies with soft law-making powers, and for other authorities and institutions with similar powers to that of ESMA. Section 5 ends with some final thoughts.

1. CONCLUSIONS ON THE LEGITIMACY AND EFFECTIVENESS OF ESMA'S SOFT LAW INSTRUMENTS

ESMA has been established in order to tackle the lack of effectiveness of its predecessor CESR and has for this reason been entrusted with stronger rule-making powers. The aim of this book was to investigate whether ESMA's soft law instruments are effective in achieving the Union's objectives and whether a sufficient level of legitimacy is provided for at the same time. An assessment framework was developed in Chapter 2 and has been applied to ESMA throughout the book. This enabled a comprehensive investigation of legitimacy and effectiveness in the context of soft law-making by ESMA. This book has made it very clear that theoretical concerns in relation to legitimacy and effectiveness also play a significant role in practice for ESMA and other parties, such as stakeholders and Union institutions. The conclusions in the three subsections below highlight the many good practices with regard to each category of ESMA's soft law instruments, but also show that ESMA still faces its own dilemmas in terms of legitimacy and effectiveness.

1.1 ESMA's Draft Technical Standards and the Commission's Delegated or Implementing Acts

This section concludes that legitimacy and effectiveness concerns are limited in the case of ESMA's draft technical standards and the Commission's implementing and delegated acts. Considering the findings across the eight stages, one can conclude that they have a low level of efficiency, but a high level of legitimacy and effectiveness.[1]

With regard to draft technical standards, ESMA fulfils the legitimacy requirements. It can only act upon a specific legal basis allocated by the Union legislator in specific sectoral legislation, that is, level one legislation (conferral). Hence, with regard to draft technical standards, *specific* competence allocation takes place. Standards can be developed on an obligatory or a discretionary legal basis. In the case of a 'shall' provision, a subsidiarity check by ESMA is not required, because the choice of the appropriate level has already been made by the Union legislature. Indeed, the competence is undoubtedly ESMA's. In the case of a 'may' provision, ESMA may choose whether or not to use its rule-making power. In principle, this gives the agency the opportunity to apply a subsidiarity test, but it in no way engages with the question of whether action at either the Union or national level is desirable in practice.

The Union legislature has also made the so-called instrument choice already, because the specific *form* in which ESMA should act is prescribed: draft technical standards. In the case of a 'shall' provision, ESMA cannot make

---

[1] The levels of legitimacy and effectiveness are assessed as follows. Legitimacy: there is a high level if there are many guarantees, a medium level if there are few guarantees and a low level if there are no guarantees. Efficiency: there is a high level if there are very little procedural steps, a medium level if there are some procedural steps and a low level if there are many procedural steps. Effectiveness: there is a high level if there are many ways to effectuate compliance, a medium level if there are only a few ways to effectuate compliance and a low level if there are no ways to effectuate compliance.

any proportionality assessment itself; in the case of a 'may' provision, it does apply an extra proportionality check by considering whether or not to develop the technical standards. The agency cannot choose a different instrument to regulate the same matter instead. The *contents* of draft technical standards always have to remain within the substantive scope of their legal basis, because they can only be developed pursuant to an empowerment in the level one legislation and not on ESMA's own initiative. The drafts may not imply strategic decisions or policy choices.[2] The Commission undertakes a final check as to whether ESMA remains within the substantive scope of the legal basis upon which it acts.

The level of efficiency of draft technical standards is low, because there are many procedural hurdles to be addressed before such acts see the light of day. Yet, they result in a high level of legitimacy. Decision-making starts with the actual drafting of the technical standards by experts from the NCAs in the Standing Committees or Working Groups of ESMA. They are in a position to exert considerable influence on the content, and may even be regarded as the *de facto* regulators. At its own discretion, the Standing Committee or Working Group may seek input from the private stakeholders in the Consultative Working Groups, but it is not bound by their input. These closed consultations do not entail a mandatory step in the rule-making procedure, but are a form of institutional practice. ESMA is obliged to consult external stakeholders by conducting open public consultations[3] and is required to consult the private stakeholders sitting in the Securities and Markets Stakeholder Group (closed consultation). Both consultation processes are formalised as a mandatory step in the adoption procedure,[4] although ESMA is not strictly bound by the stakeholders' responses. With regard to open public consultations, the duty to give reasons entails that the agency cannot just ignore the feedback either.

Next, the decision whether to adopt the draft technical standards and to submit them to the Commission for endorsement is taken by the heads of the NCAs as members of ESMA's Board of Supervisors. They may be regarded as the ones with the *true decision-making power*.

ESMA is required to grant public access to its documents in relation to its draft technical standards.[5] It scores highly on the requirement of giving reasons,

---

[2] ESMA Regulation, Arts 10(1) and 15(1).

[3] Ibid. The agency may only refrain from such consultations when they are disproportionate in relation to the scope and impact of the draft technical standards concerned or in relation to the particular urgency of the matter.

[4] This might entail a participation right: see the assessment in Chapter 5, Section 7.2.

[5] Based on TFEU, Art 15(3); ESMA Regulation, Art 72(1); Access to Documents Regulation. This obligation is without prejudice to the requirements of professional secrecy pursuant to TFEU, Art 339 and ESMA Regulation, Art 70(3).

because it states the reasons on which its legal acts are based and responds to the arguments that have been put forward by the stakeholders during the consultations.[6] It also justifies why it came to a different conclusion (if this is the case). Although the Court in its case-law has been reluctant to recognise *a dialogue dimension* to the giving reasons requirement, ESMA's practice comes close to the existence of such a dimension. The final Commission delegated or implementing acts are published in the Official Journal of the European Union in all official Union languages.

In the case of Commission implementing and delegated acts, there is a high level of effectiveness.[7] There are many ways to effectuate technical standards, because compliance is mandatory via their confirmation in hard EU law. They are usually adopted by regulation, which means that they have general and 'inherent' legally binding force by virtue of Article 288 TFEU. As a consequence, NCAs may not transpose the Commission's acts into their national legal framework, although national implementing measures might be necessary in order to grant full effect to the rules laid down in the regulations. Furthermore, ESMA has a mix of soft and hard enforcement mechanisms at its disposal. It may carry out a *peer review* (a soft enforcement mechanism)[8] or start a *Breach of Union Law procedure* (a hard enforcement mechanism) which may result in hard sanctions for NCAs.[9] The Commission may also become involved by starting an *infringement procedure* (a hard enforcement mechanism). This may also result in hard sanctions, although via the Member States.[10] Finally, the CJEU is entitled to review the final Commission delegated and implementing acts as they are 'inherently' legally binding and thus automatically fall within the scope of Article 263 TFEU. Such acts may also be subject to a judicial procedure at the national level, because national courts can investigate the validity of Union acts. If they are however unable to rule that such an act is valid, Article 267 TFEU requires them to refer questions to the CJEU, because only the latter is competent to declare acts of Union law invalid.[11] The only possibility at the national level is therefore the triggering of a preliminary reference procedure.

---

6 The Final Reports of its draft technical standards include the legislative mandate to develop technical standards, the cost–benefit analysis, the advice of the SMSG if the group was consulted, the feedback received from stakeholders in ESMA's open consultation process as well as ESMA's elaborate responses thereto (a so-called feedback statement), and the actual draft technical standards themselves.

7 This is the conclusion of Chapters 7 to 10 together.

8 ESMA Regulation, Arts 30(2)(a) and 30(2)(b).

9 Ibid., Art 17(1).

10 TFEU, Art 258.

11 Case 314/85 *Foto-Frost v Hauptzollamt Lübeck-Ost* [1987] ECR 4199, para 20.

1.2 ESMA's Guidelines and Recommendations

This section shows that there are multiple legitimacy and effectiveness concerns in relation to the second type of ESMA's soft law, that is, guidelines. Considering the findings across the eight stages of the policy cycle, one can conclude that they have a medium level of legitimacy, a low level of efficiency and a medium level of effectiveness.

With regard to guidelines, ESMA only partly fulfils the rule of law requirements. Article 16(1) ESMA Regulation directly empowers ESMA to issue guidelines on its own initiative, but the agency may also act upon a mandatory or discretionary legal basis in the level one legislation (conferral). Hence, *general* competence allocation takes place. The situation with regard to a 'shall' or 'may' provision is the same as for technical standards as set out previously, that is, no subsidiarity test. ESMA does not carry out such a test when it issues guidelines on its own initiative either. The choice for ESMA is limited to whether or not to issue the guidelines. This makes it a proportionality test rather than a subsidiarity test.

The situation regarding a 'shall' or 'may' provision is the same as it is for technical standards as set out above, that is, no proportionality test. The Union legislature has already made the so-called instrument choice, because the specific *form* in which ESMA should act is prescribed, that is, guidelines. If ESMA acts upon its own initiative, though, it has discretion to select one type of instrument over another. The choice of form is then a matter for ESMA to decide. It is however not possible to choose technical standards without an empowerment in level one or level two legislation. When guidelines have been issued on the basis of a 'shall' or 'may' provision, their *contents* have to remain within the substantive scope of their legal basis. Yet, ESMA has a much broader scope when it acts on its own initiative. This does not mean that the agency has *carte blanche*, though, because the guidelines should address the objectives as set out in Article 16 ESMA Regulation, that is, establishing consistent, efficient and effective supervisory practices *and* ensuring common, uniform and consistent application of Union law. This provision does not explicitly exclude strategic decisions or policy choices. However, a new paragraph 2a to Article 16 imposes a further limit to the substantive scope of guidelines and recommendations: they shall not merely refer to, or reproduce, elements of legislative acts. Before issuing a new guideline or recommendation, ESMA therefore first has to review existing guidelines and recommendations, in order to avoid any duplication. In the case that a natural or legal person is still of the opinion that ESMA has exceeded its competence, including by failing to respect the principle of proportionality, when acting under Article 16 and that is of direct and individual concern to that person, it may send reasoned advice to the Commission.[12] In this way, the Commission has been given a possibility to reject the adoption of ESMA's guidelines and recommendations. There is no formal role for the other Union institutions.

The level of efficiency of ESMA's guidelines is low, because there are many procedural hurdles before such acts see the light of day. Yet, they result in a medium level of legitimacy. Decision-making also starts with the actual drafting of the guidelines by experts of the NCAs in the Standing Committees and Working Groups of ESMA. At their own discretion, they may also seek input from the private stakeholders in the Consultative Working Groups. They are requested to ask the advice of the Securities and Markets Stakeholder Group and, where appropriate, to carry out open public consultations.[13] In practice, ESMA almost always conducts open public consultations. Next, the decision whether or not to adopt the guidelines is also taken by the heads of the NCAs as members of ESMA's Board of Supervisors. Guidelines do not need to be sent to the Commission for endorsement.

ESMA is required to grant access to its documents in relation to its guidelines, without prejudice to the requirements of professional secrecy. ESMA scores equally highly on the requirement to give reasons with regard to its guidelines, since the level of detail in its reasoning is similar to that of draft technical standards. The final guidelines are published in all official Union languages on ESMA's website. In addition, ESMA publishes so-called guidelines compliance tables on its website in order to enhance transparency.

In the case of ESMA's guidelines, there is a medium level of effectiveness.[14] Because of their rather ambiguous legal nature, there are not many ways to effectuate guidelines. ESMA's guidelines and recommendations have not been attributed 'inherent' legally binding force by means of the Treaties, but include the so-called comply or explain mechanism which requires each NCA to notify ESMA of whether it complies or intends to comply. ESMA thus has the *intention to ensure compliance*. Such intention could be regarded as being decisive for the establishment of an *intention to produce legally binding effects*.[15] In this context, guidelines have *'incidental' legally binding*

---

[12] ESMA Regulation, Art 60a.

[13] Ibid., Art 16(2). In contrast to draft technical standards, ESMA thus has a little more leeway with respect to its guidelines, as consultations are to be conducted 'where appropriate'. 'The difference seems to be due to the different procedural outcome; that is, whereas the former result in the adoption of binding rules, the latter amount to the adoption of guidelines and recommendations. However, given the 'strong' nature of these guidelines and recommendations as outlined above, one could question whether such a differentiation is indeed warranted': see Busuioc 2013b, p. 119.

[14] This is the conclusion of Chapters 7 to 10 together.

[15] This would also make them reviewable under TFEU, Art 263. This provision empowers the Court to review the legality of acts 'intended to produce legal effects vis-à-vis third parties'.

force for the NCAs indicating that they do comply with the guidelines; they do not have such force for those that have indicated that they do not comply. Guidelines may also have *'indirect' legal effects* based on the principles of sincere cooperation and the protection of legitimate expectations, except in a situation in which an NCA has indicated that it does not comply with the guidelines. Yet, Article 16 remains completely silent on transposition. NCAs are thus free to decide whether and how they want to transpose ESMA's guidelines into their national legal framework, if at all. In practice, this results in three different transposition methods across the Member States: the direct application of ESMA's guidelines in the supervisory practices of the NCAs; the adoption of non-binding instruments by the NCAs; and the adoption of binding instruments by the NCAs or implementation by the national legislature. Furthermore, ESMA may undertake enforcement action by means of soft mechanisms only, that is, *guidelines compliance tables* and *peer reviews*.[16] These appear to be very effective, because *de facto* compliance with guidelines is, generally speaking, very high. It remains questionable whether ESMA or the Commission could successfully use hard enforcement mechanisms as well. In any case, neither a Breach of Union Law procedure nor an infringement procedure may be based on non-compliance with guidelines alone. Nevertheless, non-compliance with guidelines could potentially indicate an underlying breach of EU law. Finally, judicial review by the CJEU is only possible when an *intention* to produce legal effects vis-à-vis third parties can be proven. By taking all the characteristics of ESMA's guidelines together, this book argues that there is such an intention on the part of the agency. This makes judicial review a logical next step. Yet, this possibility remains fully dependent on whether the Court follows this argumentation. Reviewability by the national courts completely depends on the transposition methods used by the NCAs.[17] There is no general obligation for national courts to *take into consideration* the soft law instruments of EU agencies, including ESMA's guidelines.

---

[16] ESMA Regulation, Arts 16(3), 16(4) and 30(2)(b).

[17] When NCAs directly apply ESMA's guidelines in their supervisory practices, individuals must bring an action for annulment in a national court and pursue this action until the national court of last instance is legally obliged to bring the matter before the CJEU as a preliminary ruling under Article 267 TFEU. When NCAs transpose ESMA's guidelines by means of non-binding instruments, it differs per jurisdiction whether or not national courts are willing to review national soft law instruments. When NCAs use binding instruments for the transposition of ESMA's guidelines and/or in case of implementation into national law by the national legislature, such national instruments or national laws are certainly reviewable by the court.

1.3 ESMA's Non-binding Instruments

This third section shows that there are legitimacy and effectiveness concerns in relation to ESMA's third category of soft law, that is, non-binding instruments. On the other hand, however, it demonstrates that a number of important improvements were made as a result of the ESA review. Considering the findings across the eight stages, one can conclude that ESMA's *opinions and new practical instruments and convergence tools* by now have a medium level of legitimacy, a low level of efficiency and a medium level of effectiveness, while the agency's Q&As in principle have a very high level of efficiency, but a low level of legitimacy and effectiveness. Yet, the amended ESMA Regulation includes possibilities for the Board of Supervisors to request the addition of one or more procedural steps, and thus to compromise efficiency in order to increase the level of legitimacy from low to medium.

With regard to non-binding instruments, ESMA only partly fulfils the rule of law requirements. The Union legislature does not establish any express mandatory or discretionary legal bases in the level one legislation, thereby in fact giving the agency *carte blanche*. Indeed, *general* competence allocation takes place by means of Articles 16b, 29(1)(b) and 29(2) ESMA Regulation (conferral). The acts are always developed at ESMA's own initiative. The Union legislature has not yet prescribed the specific *form* in which ESMA should act. It is thus allowed to make a proportionality assessment itself, that is, the agency has the freedom whether or not to act, and subsequently has the choice as to the nature and extent of its action. ESMA does not apply a subsidiarity test in such situations, though. Regarding its non-binding instruments, the agency is not so limited as to what it may regulate in terms of *contents.* The general empowerments provide for a rather broad substantive scope and do not exclude strategic decisions or policy choices.[18] Yet, a new Article 60a provides any natural or legal person that is directly and individually concerned with the opportunity to send reasoned advice to the Commission if that person is of the opinion that ESMA has exceeded its competence when acting under Article 16b (that is, Q&As). There is no formal role for any of the other Union institutions.

The level of efficiency of ESMA's *opinions and new practical instruments and convergence tools* is low, because there are many procedural hurdles before such acts see the light of day. Yet, they result in a medium level of legit-

[18] ESMA Regulation, Art 29(1): 'building a common Union supervisory culture and consistent supervisory practices, as well as ensuring uniform procedures and consistent approaches throughout the Union' and ESMA Regulation, Art 29(2): 'to promote common supervisory approaches and practices.'

imacy. Decision-making starts with the actual drafting of these non-binding instruments. This is also done by experts from the NCAs in the Standing Committees and Working Groups of ESMA. At their own discretion, they may also seek input from the private stakeholders in the Consultative Working Groups (CWGs). They are requested to ask the advice of the Securities and Markets Stakeholder Group and, where appropriate, to carry out open public consultations.[19] Next, the decision whether or not to adopt opinions and new practical instruments and convergence tools is also taken by the heads of the NCAs as members of ESMA's Board of Supervisors. They do not need to be sent to the Commission for endorsement. There is no formal role for any of the other Union institutions either.

In principle, there are limited procedural hurdles before ESMA's *Q&As* see the light of day. The level of efficiency of such acts is therefore very high. Although this leads to a low level of legitimacy, a supervisory authority does need a flexible instrument in order not to become completely cramped. It should be able to respond to market developments promptly by offering clarification to market participants at short notice. The legal basis for ESMA's Q&As does not request that the agency carries out open public consultations or requests the advice of the Securities and Markets Stakeholder Group. Except for the small group of *a priori* selected private stakeholders in the CWGs, other parties thus have no possibility to participate in the decision-making process of ESMA's Q&As. This has, however, changed under the revised ESMA Regulation. Indeed, under the amended ESMA Regulation, efficiency may sometimes be compromised in order to increase the level of legitimacy from low to medium. Upon the instigation of three voting members of the Board of Supervisors, the Board may decide to request that ESMA seeks advice from the SMSG, conducts open public consultations or analyses costs and benefits.[20] For instance, legitimacy is considered to be more important when ESMA is requested to consult on Q&As, whereas effectiveness is assigned more weight when there is no such request. In such cases, it is thus the Board of Supervisors that performs a 'balancing exercise' between legitimacy and effectiveness.

ESMA is obliged to grant access to its documents in relation to its non-binding instruments as well. This obligation is also without prejudice to the requirements of professional secrecy. The agency is supposed to score equally highly on the requirement to give reasons with regard to its opinions and new practical instruments and convergence tools, since the procedural steps it has to follow are similar to those for guidelines. This would mean that the level of detail in its reasoning is also comparable. It remains however to

---

[19] ESMA Regulation, Art 29(2).

[20] Ibid., Art 16b(4).

be seen whether ESMA will follow the same approach, because as yet there are no examples in practice. With regard to Q&As, ESMA in principle scores relatively low on the requirement of giving reasons, but this is understandable given that it does not carry out consultations. A dialogue with stakeholders therefore cannot possibly take place. This is only different when ESMA is requested to consult by the Board of Supervisors. ESMA publishes the final Q&As, opinions and other practical instruments and convergence tools, which are only available in English, on its website. It is required to publish all questions rejected and questions received, even when no answers are yet available. ESMA is still in the process of establishing a web-based tool for this purpose.[21]

In the case of ESMA's non-binding instruments, there is a low level of effectiveness.[22] There are no ways to effectuate such acts, because they merely have *de facto* effects. Indeed, they have not been attributed 'inherent' legally binding force by means of the Treaties or secondary legislation, and there is no 'comply or explain' mechanism. It is not possible to successfully maintain that non-binding instruments could have *'incidental' legally binding force*[23] and they cannot produce *'indirect' legal effects* on the basis of the principles of the protection of legitimate expectations and sincere cooperation either. Compliance is thus voluntary. Articles 16b and 29 ESMA Regulation also remain completely silent on transposition, and the soft law acts themselves do not prescribe or prohibit transposition either. Yet, most NCAs take the view that they do not need to integrate such acts into their national framework. Instead, they merely publish them on their websites and/or use them in their supervisory practices. Furthermore, neither ESMA nor the Commission can undertake enforcement action. If there is no voluntary compliance, there is thus no way that their objectives can be achieved.[24] And finally, the CJEU cannot review ESMA's non-binding instruments. Justiciability on the basis of Article 263 TFEU is impossible, because the instruments merely produce *de facto* effects.

Additionally, it is not possible to directly challenge ESMA's non-binding instruments at the national level and there is no general obligation for national courts to *take into consideration* all soft law instruments emanating from EU

---

21 Ibid., Art 16b(3).

22 This is the conclusion of Chapters 7 to 10 together.

23 They are indeed not intended to create an extra layer of requirements. See, for instance, ESMA, Questions and Answers on the Guidelines on Alternative Performance Measures (2017) ESMA32-51-370, para 7; ESMA, Questions and Answers on the Application of the AIFMD (2017) ESMA34-32-352, 6.

24 Nonetheless, ESMA periodically reviews questions and answers to identify if, in a certain area, there is a need to convert some of the material into ESMA guidelines. Guidelines are then enforceable by means of soft enforcement mechanisms.

agencies. Similar to challenging ESMA's guidelines, financial market participants must bring an annulment action against ESMA's non-binding instruments in a national court and pursue this action until the national court of last instance is legally obliged to bring the matter before the CJEU as a preliminary ruling under Article 267 TFEU.

2. RECOMMENDATIONS FOR ESMA

The conclusions presented above show that the legitimacy and effectiveness considerations are different for each category of ESMA's soft law instruments in each of the eight stages of the entire policy cycle. None of the instruments is perfect. The soft law instruments thus each require different solutions which, taken together, would greatly benefit the legal certainty of the system as a whole. Even though many things are going well in the context of ESMA, there are still some matters that could be improved. The subsections below present the recommendations that can be made based on the analysis conducted in this book and offer proposals for change with a view to ESMA's soft law being used in a manner that actually contributes to the legitimacy and effectiveness of Union action. These include the requirements that the proportionality and subsidiarity tests should be made explicit in ESMA's soft law acts, that participation rights should be acknowledged with regard to draft technical standards and ESMA's guidelines, that the transposition method as regards the guidelines should be harmonised and that the legal nature and therewith the possibilities for judicial review of ESMA's soft law instruments should be clarified.

2.1 Proportionality and Subsidiarity Considerations Should Be Made Explicit in ESMA's Soft Law Acts

The first recommendation entails that ESMA should apply the subsidiarity and proportionality tests and explicate the considerations and outcomes of the two tests in each soft law act itself when it takes rule-making action. This includes the deliberations on the question of whether the Union or national level is the appropriate level to act (subsidiarity) and the justification of the instrument choice that has been made (proportionality). This recommendation addresses the problem of abuse of power so as to prevent ESMA from using a non-binding instrument instead of guidelines with the sole purpose of circumventing the adoption procedure, or for third parties to make a point when they consider an issue should be regulated at the national level. It is necessary for enhancing legitimacy, because it would ensure that ESMA acts within the boundaries of the law. Besides, this recommendation enhances effectiveness as it involves the choice of the most appropriate type of rule-making action for achieving the intended regulatory objectives.

For instance, when ESMA needs to respond to market developments very promptly, it may not have the time to request the views of external stakeholders through open public consultations. At this point, ESMA needs to make 'an instrument choice' between a less legitimate but more efficient softer tool *with fewer* procedural safeguards (such as Q&As) and a 'comply or explain' tool which is more legitimate but less efficient *with* procedural safeguards (such as guidelines). Both are own-initiative tools; hence a proportionality test needs to be applied by the agency itself. In such a case, ESMA needs to justify explicitly in the soft law act itself why it opts for a softer instrument with less procedural guarantees. The Union legislature should impose these requirements with regard to all three categories of ESMA's soft law instruments. This enables an *ex post* evaluation of the adequacy thereof.[25]

2.2 Participation Rights for External Stakeholders Should Be Recognised

The second recommendation entails that participation *rights* for stakeholders should be acknowledged for the stakeholders participating in the open public consultations and the stakeholders sitting in the Securities and Markets Stakeholder Group (SMSG) in relation to draft technical standards, guidelines, opinions and new practical instruments and convergence tools. This recommendation addresses the risk that the duty to consult remains a purely formal way of legitimising decisions. In this way, it enhances the opportunities for third parties to seek effective judicial protection at the CJEU. Indeed, judicial review would be an option if participation rights are not respected, for instance when ESMA does not consult in the case of guidelines, opinions or other practical instruments and convergence tools, or chooses Q&As in order to circumvent consultations. It is of course possible that the Board of Supervisors will then request consultations, but this is not a given. Recognising participation rights is necessary for enhancing legitimacy, because it enables critique, public debate and control over EU bodies' activities.[26] It is also necessary for enhancing effectiveness, because consultations increase the chances of compliance

[25] The recommendation to apply the subsidiarity and proportionality test and explicate the considerations and outcomes of the two tests in each soft law act itself is of relevance to all EU agencies with soft law-making powers: see Section 4.2.

[26] This is in line with the ways in which legitimacy of the Commission's decision is increased according to Marxsen 2015, p. 261.

with the legal instrument at hand and the external expertise of stakeholders contributes to the quality of legal acts.[27]

ESMA's current practice already approaches the existence of participation rights for private stakeholders. The open public consultations and the SMSG consultations are formalised as mandatory steps in the decision-making process, so the agency does not have much discretion with regard to the choice of whether to consult or not. Recognising participation rights implies that it is possible to challenge the final Commission delegated and implementing acts, ESMA's guidelines and opinions, and other practical instruments and convergence tools for an alleged lack of consultation of interested parties. Judicial review of the procedural requirements laid down in Articles 10, 15, 16 and 29(2) ESMA Regulation may be envisaged when a Union Court, called upon to review the legality of the final act within the context of an Article 263 or 267 TFEU procedure, has to examine an alleged violation of a procedural requirement. A claimant could then argue that the soft law act at stake is not legitimate, because a procedural step has been skipped.[28] In such a case, judicial review is used in order to effectuate the right to participation.[29] Participation rights do not have to be recognised in relation to ESMA's Q&As, because the consultation of stakeholders is not a standardised part of the decision-making process. When ESMA does not follow the request by the Board of Supervisors to organise public consultations or to ask for advice from the SMSG, it should also be possible to challenge ESMA's failure to do so at the Court.

2.3 The Transposition of ESMA's Guidelines Should Be Harmonised

The third recommendation entails that the transposition method as regards ESMA's guidelines should be explicitly harmonised in Article 16 ESMA Regulation.[30] This recommendation addresses the problem of a lack of conver-

---

[27] Buijze 2013, p. 46; Craig 2012, p. 231; Marxsen 2015, p. 261. See also Commission, 'European governance: A White Paper' COM(2001) 428 final, 10 and 15.

[28] Alemanno argued that '[t]o be successful, the plaintiff will have to prove that a consultation represents a binding step in the decision-making process, whose omission, or incorrect application, might affect the legality of the final act': see Alemanno 2009, p. 396. In this regard, it is very helpful that ESMA conforms to the giving reasons requirement of the principle of transparency, because that allows the addressees to review whether the decision was legitimate and to decide whether they want to challenge it: see Chapter 6, Section 4.

[29] See Chapter 10 on judicial review.

[30] A restriction as regards the transposition of non-binding instruments is not necessary. They are not considered to add an extra layer of requirements and are therefore not transposed by most NCAs anyway.

gence throughout the Member States. Indeed, different transposition methods hinder the achievement of one of the guidelines' objectives, that is, common, uniform and consistent application of Union law. Harmonising transposition is necessary for enhancing effectiveness, in the sense that the guidelines' objective to achieve convergence and a level playing field throughout the EU cannot be obstructed by NCAs that use different methods of transposition. It is also necessary for improving the legal certainty of the system as a whole, so that the legal nature of the guidelines themselves remains the same in every Member State.[31]

In the current legal framework, there is neither a *de iure* prohibition or requirement to transpose ESMA's guidelines nor any specification as to how this may or may not take place. The Member States thus retain their complete autonomy and convert ESMA's guidelines in the way they deem most appropriate, that is, by applying the guidelines directly, by transposing them into a non-binding instrument or by transposing them into a binding instrument or implementing them into national law.[32] The current differences lead to a situation where in some Member States the interpretations laid down in the guidelines are legally binding, whereas in others the same interpretations are not. ESMA's soft law thus ends up having different legal status in different Member States. This, in turn, also has an impact on the possibilities for judicial protection.[33] Indeed, in one Member State the transposition measure could be challenged, whereas in another that directly applies ESMA's guidelines this would not be possible.

The preferred solution based on the analysis in this book is therefore to lay down in Article 16 ESMA Regulation that transposition is not allowed.[34] Such an amendment would limit the institutional and procedural autonomy of the Member States. Yet, that autonomy may be limited as soon as rules are provided at the Union level. Based on the principle of sincere cooperation, Member States may then be expected to refrain from transposing ESMA's guidelines if Union law so requires. This would ensure that guidelines are applied everywhere in the same way, as it would mean that national competent authorities do not take any action and just refer to ESMA's guidelines as a tool. Consequently, NCAs should directly apply ESMA's guidelines. In this way, the legal nature of the guidelines remains the same in all the Member States, which ensures a much higher level of policy consistency and legal

---

[31] Third parties will then also have the same level of effective judicial protection. See Chapter 10 for the link between the legal nature and judicial review.

[32] See Chapter 7.

[33] See the analysis in Chapter 10, Section 5.

[34] Implementing measures would still be allowed, but they may not change the nature of the guidelines in the way that it happens in the current legal framework.

consequences, including a more equal level of effective judicial protection throughout the Member States.

2.4 The Legal Nature and the Possibilities for Judicial Review of ESMA's Soft Law Instruments Should Be Clarified

The fourth recommendation entails that the Union legislature should establish the legal nature and the possibilities for judicial review of the agency's soft law instruments in the ESMA Regulation. This recommendation addresses the problem of the unequal level of judicial protection for third parties throughout the EU. It is necessary for enhancing legitimacy, in the sense of democratic legitimacy, because judicial review increases the control of financial market participants over the decision-making process and prevents the abuse of public powers.[35] Judicial review would also enhance effectiveness, since it relates to the ways in which regulation is effectuated and is of crucial importance for the achievement of regulatory objectives. Moreover, the adequacy of judicial protection influences the attitude of the market towards compliance with the relevant legal rules and, also in that manner, has a direct relation with the effectiveness of these rules.[36]

In order to establish the duties for NCAs and third parties to comply with ESMA's soft law instruments, it is important to establish the legal nature of the instruments. The analysis in Chapter 8 has shown that the Commission's delegated and implementing acts are 'inherently' legally binding, and that ESMA's non-binding instruments merely produce *de facto* effects. The situation for guidelines is more uncertain. This book has argued that they may have 'incidental' legally binding force based on the Court's test or 'indirect' legal effects based on the workings of general principles of EU law, such as legitimate expectations and sincere cooperation. This point of view is not yet generally accepted, so we need to await the CJEU's determination of the legal nature and reviewability of such acts.[37]

It would first and foremost be desirable for the Court to accept an intention on the part of ESMA to produce legal effects for the reason that the agency intends to ensure compliance with its guidelines, but only when an NCA has indeed indicated that it is compliant. This would then also make it clear that guidelines fall within the scope of Article 263 TFEU and that judicial review at the CJEU is thus possible. This would enhance effective judicial protection.

---

[35] Bovens 2010, p. 955.

[36] De Visser 2009, p. 329.

[37] The Court has already done so with regard to private standards in Case C-613/14 *James Elliott Construction* [2016].

In such a case, third parties would be better protected, because there is *ex ante* participation at the agency level and *ex post* judicial protection at the Court.

The question remains, however, whether the opportunities for stakeholders to participate in the decision-making process regarding ESMA's guidelines may in fact justify a lack of judicial review. It could be argued that this is the case for NCAs, because they are drafting the soft law acts themselves, they may raise objections during the meetings of the Standing Committees, they take the decisions themselves as members of the Board of Supervisors and they may decide for themselves whether they are compliant or not. However, this is clearly not the case for financial market participants. They are only involved in the decision-making process, albeit in different ways (Consultative Working Groups, Securities and Markets Stakeholder Group and open public consultations). Yet, they do not have any influence on the NCAs' choice as to whether or not to comply. Hence, even if financial market participants have signalled their disagreements during the consultations, ESMA can choose to neglect them. As a result, NCAs will still apply the guidelines in their supervisory practices. A financial market participant can then no longer deviate and thus should be able to go to court to challenge the guidelines if it really disagrees with them. The addition of a new Article 60a partly solves the issue, because it enables any natural or legal person that is directly and individually concerned with the opportunity to send reasoned advice to the Commission if that person is of the opinion that ESMA has exceeded its competence, including by failing to respect the principle of proportionality, when acting under Article 16.[38]

3. THE POSITION OF EU AGENCIES' RULE-MAKING IN THE BIGGER PICTURE OF UNION RULE-MAKING PRACTICES

The investigation in this book has shown that soft law-making by EU agencies as it emerges in the Union's daily practice has an odd position within the overall system of the delegation of regulatory powers. Indeed, the formal hierarchy of norms as contained in Articles 288–291 TFEU only contains part of the picture. The Treaty of Lisbon brought notable changes with regard to the purposes for which the instruments as set out in Article 288 TFEU can be used. The new Articles 289, 290 and 291 TFEU make a distinction between, respectively, legislative acts, delegated acts and implementing acts, and Union directives, regulations and decisions taking any one of these forms. In this manner, the EU regulatory system is framed in a formal way. The Treaties lay down when the Commission may exercise its executive rule-making powers,

[38] The same applies to Q&As.

under which circumstances, and the nature of the role of the other Union institutions and the Member States. Such safeguards are necessary to prevent an abuse of power.

Yet, the set of legal instruments in Articles 288 to 291 TFEU is not exhaustive, since the functioning of the Union system clearly relies on other types of regulation operating in the shadow of the Treaties, such as soft law instruments of EU agencies, as well.[39] In the current legal framework, it is thus possible to entirely circumvent the system and requirements that apply to the Commission by deploying EU agencies to which such requirements do not apply. This type of soft law-making should however be understood as a form of subdelegation to EU agencies. Consequently, the latter should be tied to the same conditions as the delegating authority, that is, the Commission. EU agencies' soft law-making is however regulated in a very limited, fragmented way. This book has shown that many gaps can be identified, raising concerns of legitimacy and effectiveness in all eight stages of the policy cycle. These gaps need to be addressed. The below recommendations are proposed in order to compensate.

4. EU AGENCIES' SOFT LAW-MAKING: RULES OF THE GAME

The analysis of ESMA showed that the agency has many strengths, but it also pointed us to problems that might arise. This book therefore provides the rules of the game that the EU legislature has to take into account when it establishes new agencies with similar powers or when it wants to revise the legal framework of existing EU agencies with soft law-making powers. It should categorise the soft law instrument of the EU agency into one of the three categories of EU agencies' soft law instruments, that is, quasi-binding preparatory acts, 'comply or explain' guidelines and non-binding instruments. This helps the legislature to consider which legitimacy and effectiveness concerns may arise with regard to each instrument and to what extent the requirements stemming from the general principles of EU law do apply. For instance, participation requirements for quasi-binding preparatory acts are not the same as those for non-binding instruments. The legislature can then apply the assessment framework to decide which procedural and institutional safeguards need to be introduced in order to balance between legitimacy and effectiveness in each of the eight stages of the entire policy cycle for each type of soft law instrument.

---

[39] See, for other types of regulation operating in the shadow of the Treaties, Senden 2015.

To begin with, various scholars have already argued for the necessity of a legal basis in the Treaties as regards the establishment of EU agencies.[40] This argument has attracted the attention of the political institutions.[41] This book adds to the recommendation to include such a legal basis that *EU agencies may have soft law-making powers delegated to them*. The normative framework within which an agency may act should also be specified.[42] Alternatively, each relevant provision in the EU Treaties could be amended so as to reflect the practice of EU agencies' soft law-making and therewith the reality of the Union's institutional practice. For instance, where the relevant Treaty provisions only refer to 'the institutions of the Union', the text should be changed to '*the institutions, bodies, offices and agencies of the Union*'.[43] A horizontal solution would also be possible. This could mean that Articles 288–291 TFEU – which lay down the formal hierarchy of norms – recognise the existence of the three categories of EU agencies' soft law instruments used throughout the European Union. Finally, the rules of the game could also be laid down in a general secondary act on EU agencies' soft law-making.

Although Treaty amendments would greatly enhance the legitimacy and effectiveness of EU agencies' soft law-making, such revisions are not realistic in practice and will certainly not deliver a quick solution. Hence, for as long as the Treaty framework remains outdated or while political agreement cannot be reached on such proposals, it is recommended that the Union legislature adds to the establishing regulation of each EU agency the procedural and institutional safeguards that need to be taken into account in order to reflect concerns of both legitimacy and effectiveness in each of the eight stages of the entire policy cycle for each type of soft law instrument. These are set out below.

---

[40] See Chamon 2016 and Scholten 2014a on the proposal to introduce a legal basis for the establishment of EU agencies.

[41] For instance, the Commission stated in its Blueprint that 'a Treaty change creating a special status for Agencies in the field of financial regulation, strengthening the supranational character of these Agencies, and their democratic accountability could also be considered. [This would] very significantly enhance the effectiveness of the ESAs': see Commission, Communication, 'A blueprint for a deep and genuine economic and monetary union. Launching a European Debate' COM(2012) 777 final 2.

[42] This means that it needs to reflect the demands stemming from the principles of conferral, subsidiarity, proportionality, transparency, participation, institutional and procedural autonomy, the protection of legitimate expectations, sincere cooperation and effective judicial protection.

[43] This is the case for the principles of sincere cooperation in Article 4(3) TEU, conferral in Article 5(1) TEU, subsidiarity in Article 5(2) TEU, proportionality in Article 5(3) TEU, openness and transparency in Articles 15, 296 and 297 TFEU, and consultation and participation in Articles 11(1), 11(2) and 11(3) TEU.

4.1 Defining a Legal Basis for EU Agencies' Soft Law-making Powers

If the Union legislature wants to establish new EU agencies, it needs to identify a legal basis in the Treaties upon which the agency may be established and may have delegated to them soft law-making powers.[44] It also needs to lay down one or more specific legal bases for the exercise of such soft law-making powers in the establishing regulation of the agency. The first question for an EU agency is *if* it is competent to act in general. This entails the first stage of the policy cycle. As a result, in practice, each EU agency first needs to find *a legal basis* which gives it the power to undertake regulatory action (conferral). It needs to state in each specific soft law act which legal basis it has used.

4.2 Initiating EU Agencies' Soft Law-making Powers

The Union legislature also needs to ensure in the establishing regulation that the EU agency applies a subsidiarity and proportionality test. Indeed, when it has been established that the agency that has been allocated (soft) rule-making powers is competent to act in general, it needs to establish *whether* it may exercise its competence *in a given instance* (subsidiarity) and *how* it should exercise its competence in terms of form and content (proportionality). This entails the second stage of the policy cycle. In line with the recommendation for ESMA, this means that the EU agency has to apply the subsidiarity and proportionality tests.[45] The considerations and outcomes of the two tests have to be reflected in each soft law act in order to enable an *ex post* evaluation of the adequacy thereof. This includes deliberations on the question whether the Union or national level is the appropriate level to act (subsidiarity) and justification of the instrument choice that has been made (proportionality).

4.3 The Decision-making Process Concerning EU Agencies' Soft Law

Once an EU agency has established that it is competent to act in a given instance and how it is going to act, the decision-making process begins. Decision-making starts with the actual drafting of the soft law acts. This entails the third stage of the policy cycle. Since there is no electoral connection in EU agencies' general rule-making procedure, the Union legislature

---

[44] This could also be a new Treaty basis.

[45] Except for situations in which it acts on the basis of a mandatory competence, that is, a 'shall' provision.

needs to ensure sufficient procedural safeguards regarding participation in the decision-making process of the soft law instruments of the agency.[46] This means that it needs to lay down the relevant requirements in the agency's establishing regulation. In this respect, the legislature has to consider the legal nature of the different types of soft law instruments that an agency may have, because that is decisive for the types of procedural guarantees that should be provided. Indeed, quasi-binding preparatory acts (category 1) and 'comply or explain' guidelines (category 2) need more safeguards than non-binding instruments (category 3).

With regard to the demands stemming from the principle of participation, the legislature could either require or request that the agency carries out a cost–benefit analysis and opens public consultations, or create a possibility for a decision-making body of the agency to request that such procedural steps are taken. It may also consider the establishment of an institutionalised stakeholder group in which, among others, consumers and end-users are permanently reflected. In this way, citizens are nevertheless represented and a formal role for the European Parliament is not necessary. Citizens' participation is not necessary when the democratic input legitimacy gaps are addressed by means of stakeholder consultations aiming at bringing external expertise into the decision-making process, that is, with throughput legitimacy. When stakeholder consultations are a mandatory step in the decision-making process, it is necessary to recognise participation as a *right*. This enhances the opportunities for third parties to receive judicial protection at the CJEU. In practice, EU agencies should, as a general starting point, always carry out consultations to engage with stakeholders in order to give full effect to their participation rights.

4.4 Transparency with Regard to EU Agencies' Soft Law Instruments

Closely related to participation is the importance of transparency regarding EU agencies' soft law, because it is also a significant attribute of public decision-making processes of the European Union. Hence, the legislature also needs to consider the requirements stemming from the principle of transparency, that is, access to documents, giving reasons, and publication and translation. This entails the fourth stage of the policy cycle. To begin with, each EU

---

[46] Since a common framework is lacking, there is currently a wide variety regarding the extent to which procedural participation is provided for. Only in relation to the newer EU agencies do the establishing regulations provide for some procedural protection in relation to soft law-making by imposing the duty to consult. Most EU agencies are thus still far from the desired level of protection in this regard.

agency should provide access to its documents based on Article 15(3) TFEU.[47] As an extra safeguard, the legislature may explicitly declare the Regulation on public access to documents to be applicable in the establishing regulation of the agency itself. This is what has been done in relation to most EU agencies so far. In practice, EU agencies should thus provide access to all their relevant documents in relation to their soft law instruments.

The legislature should also keep in mind that EU agencies should communicate the reasons for their decisions. This requirement also applies to their soft law instruments. The legislature should therefore establish a duty to give reasons in the agency's founding regulation. The EU agency may decide for itself, by adopting its own internal procedures, how it fulfils its duty to give reasons.[48] It could publish the feedback from stakeholders that it has received during the open public consultations and its own answers thereto. In this way, the addressees can understand the reasons and the factual and legal considerations behind the choices that have been made by the agency, and therefore whether the decisions are legitimate. Besides, in this way, the agency also respects the dialogue dimension of the principle of transparency in Article 11(2) TEU.

The legislature also needs to lay down the publication and translation requirements per type of soft law instrument in the establishing regulation of each EU agency. Publication in the Official Journal of the European Union is not required. It is however mandatory to publish the requirements on the agency website, in a very clear manner, preferably in one place, providing an overview of all the relevant related documents. If appropriate, the EU agency also needs to publish translations of its soft law acts on its website.[49] This is required in case of acts of general application, that is, quasi-binding preparatory acts (category 1) and 'comply or explain' guidelines (category 2), but such obligation does not apply to non-binding instruments (category 3). The EU agency should in any case have sufficient resources to provide translations.

---

[47] The developments of EU agencies and soft law are already reflected in TFEU, Art 15(3), so this provision does not require any amendments.

[48] However, the extent of the reasoning depends 'on the circumstances of each case, in particular the content of the measure in question, the nature of the reasons given and the interest which the addressees of the measure, or other parties to whom it is of direct and individual concern, may have in obtaining explanations': see Case T-317/02 *FICF and Others v Commission* [2004] ECR II-4325, para 129 and Case C-76/01 P *Eurocoton and Others v Council* [2003] ECR I-10091, para 88.

[49] This is indeed required in the case of acts of general application.

4.5 Transposition of EU Agencies' Soft Law

When a soft law act has been drafted and finally then adopted, it is in the interest of the agency that it is effectuated. This entails the fifth stage of the policy cycle. It relates to the question as to whether the transposition of the soft law instruments by national authorities should be allowed or prohibited.

There is no general rule on the transposition of EU agencies' soft law. Hence, as long as EU law does not regulate anything concerning this matter, the principles of institutional and procedural autonomy give the national authorities a great deal of freedom. Their autonomy may only be limited when rules are provided at the Union level. If there is a wish to see harmonisation with regard to the method of transposition, the Union legislature should therefore make the *de iure* expectations as regards transposition of each category of soft law instrument unambiguously clear in the agency's founding regulation. For this purpose, the legislature needs to balance the institutional and procedural autonomy of the Member States with their duties of sincere cooperation. This does not however apply to the first category of soft law instruments, that is, quasi-binding preparatory acts, as this is a matter of concern for the Commission which adopts such acts by means of a legally binding act.

With regard to the second category, that is, 'comply or explain' guidelines, there is a danger that each Member State may react differently in seeking to provide a follow-up to the 'comply or explain' duty.[50] As the analysis of ESMA shows, national authorities indeed use different methods in practice for the transposition of the agency's guidelines. This hinders the achievement of their objectives.[51] It is therefore recommended that the Union legislature establishes a clear rule on the transposition of 'comply or explain' guidelines in the founding regulation of each EU agency. This preferably entails that transposing EU agencies' soft law instruments is not allowed, because direct effect is to be preferred over transposition. Regarding the transposition of category 2 soft law instruments, the balance should thus be tipped towards sincere cooperation. Such a restriction would limit the autonomy of the Member States, but this book shows that this would be justified for several reasons. It would greatly enhance the effectiveness of such soft law instruments and the legal certainty of the system as a whole. Besides, it would prevent Member States from giving general legally binding effect to such soft law instruments.

There is no duty to comply with the third category of soft law instruments, that is, non-binding instruments. This means that in principle it is not necessary

---

[50] This book has shown that this is the case with regard to ESMA's 'comply or explain' guidelines: see Chapter 7.

[51] ESMA Regulation, Art 16(1).

for the Union legislature to regulate whether transposition should be required or prohibited. In any case, were the Member States obliged to transpose non-binding instruments, this would interfere with their autonomy and constitute excessive interference.

4.6 Compliance with EU Agencies' Soft Law

In order to give further effect to EU agencies' soft law, national authorities have to comply with such instruments. This entails the sixth stage of the policy cycle. Another recommendation for the Union legislature is therefore to provide as much clarification as possible on the legal nature of the soft law instruments of the EU agency and on the compliance duties for national authorities and third parties. It should lay this down in the establishing regulation of each agency. This book has shown that the first category of EU agencies' soft law instruments, that is, quasi-binding preparatory acts, are non-binding until they are adopted by the Commission. The latter action gives them 'inherent' legally binding force. Compliance is thus mandatory. The second category of EU agencies' soft law instruments, that is, 'comply or explain' guidelines, may have 'incidental' legally binding force based on the Court's test or 'indirect' effects based on the working of general principles of EU law such as legitimate expectations and sincere cooperation. In any case, compliance is the starting point, unless explanations for non-compliance are provided by national authorities. The third category of EU agencies' soft law instruments, that is, non-binding instruments, merely produce *de facto* effects. Compliance is thus voluntary.

4.7 Enforcement of EU Agencies' Soft Law vis-à-vis National Authorities

Where national authorities try to escape their compliance duties, an EU agency needs appropriate enforcement mechanisms vis-à-vis national authorities in order to enhance compliance with its soft law instruments. This entails the seventh stage of the policy cycle.

A recommendation for the Union legislature is therefore to provide in the EU agency's establishing regulation possibilities for enforcement by the EU agency itself. Depending on the category of soft law instruments, it needs enforcement mechanisms of a soft and/or a hard nature. In the case of the first category, a combination of such mechanisms is best, because it enables the EU agency to choose between the softest mechanism and stronger mechanisms to the extent necessary. For the second category, soft enforcement mechanisms are in principle sufficient, but there should be a possibility to use a hard enforcement mechanism when non-compliance leads to a breach of the underlying binding legislation. In the case of the third category, a soft enforcement mechanism would be desirable so as to at least be able to encourage national authorities and third parties to comply. Where possible, the EU agency thus has to apply a proportionality test[52] itself by choosing between soft and hard enforcement. Preferably it will start with its softest enforcement mechanisms, where possible, and use its harder enforcement mechanisms only where necessary, but this is not required. This means that soft enforcement may be skipped as well. It is also possible to use more than one mechanism at the same time. It should in any case be ensured that an appropriate governance structure is put in place and that sufficient resources are available to the EU agency for its indirect enforcement tasks.

4.8 Judicial Review of EU Agencies' Soft Law

Finally, in order to provide third parties with effective judicial protection and to ensure legal certainty of the system as a whole, there might be a need, depending on their legal nature, to establish opportunities for the acts to be judicially challenged. This entails the eighth stage of the policy cycle.

The Courts need to ensure that this form of rule-making is not motivated by the wrong reasons, that is, the circumvention of the more formal procedures contained in the founding regulation of the EU agency concerned. Now that the principles of conferral, proportionality, subsidiarity, transparency and participation also apply in the context of EU agencies' soft law-making, the CJEU should not be so reticent as regards the grounds for review.[53] The creation of a participation right and the recognition of the duty of consultation and participation as an essential procedural requirement whose infringement might lead to the annulment of the act in question are important means to further enhance the judicial protection for third parties.

National courts should be under a general obligation to *take into consideration* the soft law instruments of EU agencies. The national court may then deviate from soft law tools in adjudicating only when it justifies the choice for a different course of action.[54] This is another way to ensure that category 2 and 3 acts do not end up in a legal vacuum. Indeed, third parties have a greater

---

[52] This is possible on the basis of the proportionality principle, because the provision is broadly formulated by referring to 'Union action'. Indeed, the principle does not merely apply to rule-making, but may also be said to encompass enforcement.

[53] Senden 2013, p. 73.

[54] At the moment, there is no duty for national courts to take account of EU agencies' soft law acts. Whether they do so is therefore a matter of their own discretion. Georgieva proposes a 'comply or explain' mechanism for national courts: see Georgieva 2017.

chance of finding effective judicial protection when they know that the national court takes soft law acts into account.

5. FINAL THOUGHTS

This book has developed and tested an assessment framework for a balancing act between legitimacy and effectiveness concerns of ESMA's soft law. It has identified eight stages of the policy cycle: defining a legal basis; initiation; decision-making; transparency; transposition; compliance; enforcement; and judicial review. It has categorised the many different types of soft law instruments being enacted by agencies throughout the EU into three distinct categories: quasi-binding preparatory acts; 'comply or explain' guidelines; and non-binding instruments. It has investigated, for each category of ESMA's soft law instruments in each of the eight stages of the policy cycle, what the legitimacy and effectiveness concerns are. The analysis has shown that legitimacy and effectiveness concerns are not only of theoretical relevance. Indeed, EU agencies such as ESMA deal with such issues on a daily basis. It is the hope of the author that the Union legislature will draw lessons from this book and follow its recommendations when establishing new EU agencies, authorities and institutions with similar powers, or when revising their establishing regulations. Following the proposed rules of the game will ensure that the game we are playing is fair and equitable.

Bibliography

Acceto, M and S Zleptnig, 'The Principle of Effectiveness: Rethinking Its Role in Community Law' (2005) 11 *European Public Law* 375.

Aelen, M, *Beginselen van goed markttoezicht. Gedefinieerd, verklaard en uitgewerkt voor het toezicht op de financiële markten* (Boom juridische uitgevers 2014).

Alberti, J, 'L'utilisation d'actes de soft law par les agences de l'Union européenne' (2014) 567 *Revue de l'union Européenne* 161.

Alberti, J, 'The Unbearable Lightness of European Securities and Markets Authority's Soft Law: An Italian Perspective' in M Buscemi, N Lazzerini, L Magi and D Russo (eds), *Legal Sources in Business and Human Rights: Evolving Dynamics in International and European Law* (Brill 2020) 302.

Alemanno, A, 'The Better Regulation Initiative at the Judicial Gate: a Trojan Horse within the Commission's Walls or the Way Forward?' (2009) 15 *European Law Journal* 382.

Alemanno, A, 'Unpacking the Principle of Openness in EU Law: Transparency, Participation and Democracy' (2014) 39 *European Law Review* 72.

Allott, A, 'The Effectiveness of Laws' (1981) 15 *Valparaiso University Law Review* 229.

Armstrong, K, 'New Governance and the European Union: An Empirical and Conceptual Critique' in G de Búrca, C Kilpatrick and J Scott (eds), *Critical Legal Perspectives on Global Governance* (Hart Publishing 2014) 249.

Arras, S and C Braun, 'Stakeholders Wanted! Why and How European Union Agencies Involve Non-state Stakeholders' (2017) 24 *Journal of European Public Policy* 1.

Avbelj, M, J Alberti, C Caufmann, M Hartlapp, E Korkea-Aho, P Leino-Sandbert, E Oliva, S Post and A Schwerdtfeger, 'EU Financial Regulation Soft Law in the Member States: Finland, France, Germany, Italy, the Netherlands, Slovenia and the UK', SOLAR, 2018, available at SoLaR-Working-Paper-Financial-Regulation.pdf (solar-network.eu), accessed 15 February 2021.

Ayres, I and J Braithwaite, *Responsive Regulation: Transcending the Deregulation Debate* (Oxford University Press 1992).

Barents, R, 'The Internal Market Unlimited: Some Observations on the Legal Basis of Community Legislation' (1993) 30 *Common Market Law Review* 85.

Barents, R, 'The Court of Justice after the Treaty of Lisbon' (2010) 47 *Common Market Law Review* 709.

Barnard, C and S Peers, *European Union Law* (1st edn, Oxford University Press 2014).

Beetham, D, *The Legitimation of Power* (Palgrave 2013).

Bergström, C, 'Shaping the New System for Delegation of Powers to EU Agencies: *United Kingdom v European Parliament and Council (Short Selling)*' (2015) 52 *Common Market Law Review* 219.

Blanc, F, 'Tools for Effective Regulation: Is "More" Always "Better"?' (2018) 9 *European Journal of Risk Regulation* 465.

Bovens, M, 'Two Concepts of Accountability: Accountability as a Virtue and as a Mechanism' (2010) 33 *West European Politics* 946.

Bovens, M, D Curtin and P 't Hart, 'The Quest for Legitimacy and Accountability in EU Governance' in M Bovens, D Curtin and P 't Hart (eds), *The Real World of EU Accountability: What Deficit?* (Oxford University Press 2010) 9.

Brandsma, GJ, *Backstage Europe: Comitology, Accountability and Democracy in the European Union* (Drukkerij Roos en Roos 2010).

Buijze, A, *The Principle of Transparency in EU Law* (Uitgeverij BOXPress 2013).

Burkens, M, H Kummeling, B Vermeulen and R Widdershoven, *Beginselen van de democatische rechtsstaat: inleiding tot de grondslagen van het Nederlandse staats- en bestuursrecht* (WEJ Tjeenk Willink 2001).

Busuioc, M, *European Agencies: Law and Practices of Accountability* (Oxford University Press 2013a).

Busuioc, M, 'Rule-making by the European Financial Supervisory Authorities: Walking a Tight Rope' (2013b) 19 *European Law Journal* 111.

Chamon, M, 'EU Agencies: Between *Meroni* and *Romano* or the Devil and the Deep Blue Sea' (2011) 48 *Common Market Law Review* 1055.

Chamon, M, 'The Influence of "Regulatory Agencies" on Pluralism in European Administrative Law' (2012) 5 *Review of European Administrative Law* 61.

Chamon, M, 'Le recours à la soft law comme moyen d'éluder les obstacles constitutionnels au développement des agences de l'UE' (2013) 567 *Revue de l'Union Européenne* 152.

Chamon, M, 'The Empowerment of Agencies under the *Meroni* Doctrine and Article 114 TFEU: Comment on *United Kingdom v Parliament and Council (Short-selling)* and the Proposed Single Resolution Mechanism' (2014) 39 *European Law Review* 380.

Chamon, M, *EU Agencies: Legal and Political Limits to the Transformation of the EU Administration* (Oxford University Press 2016).

Chiti, E, 'An Important Part of the EU's Institutional Machinery: Features, Problems and Perspectives of European Agencies' (2009) 46 *Common Market Law Review* 1395.

Chiti, E, 'European Agencies' Rule-making: Powers, Procedures, and Assessment' (2013) 19 *European Law Journal* 93.

Cengiz, F, 'The EU Policymaking Paradox: Citizen Participation Is a Must, but the Shaping of Policies Has Become Too Technical' (*EUROPP* 22 January 2016) accessed 15 February 2021.

Craig, C, 'Democracy and Rule-making within the EC: An Empirical and Normative Assessment' (1997a) 3 *European Law Journal* 105.

Craig, C, 'Formal and Substantive Conceptions of the Rule of Law: An Analytical Framework' (1997b) 21 *Public Law* 467.

Craig, P, *EU Administrative Law* (2nd edn, Oxford University Press 2012).

Craig, P and G de Búrca, *EU Law: Texts, Cases and Materials* (2nd edn, Oxford University Press 1998).

Craig, P and G de Búrca, *EU Law: Texts, Cases and Materials* (4th edn, Oxford University Press 2009).

Craig, P and G de Búrca, *EU Law: Texts, Cases and Materials* (5th edn, Oxford University Press 2011).

Curtin, D, *Executive Power of the European Union: Law, Practices, and the Living Constitution* (Oxford University Press 2009).

Curtin, D and I Dekker, 'Good Governance: The Concept and Its Application by the European Union' in D Curtin and R Wessel (eds), *Good Governance and the*

European Union: Reflections on Concepts, Institutions and Substance (Intersentia 2005) 3.

Curtin, D, H Hofmann and J Mendes, 'Constitutionalising EU Executive Rule-making Procedures: A Research Agenda' (2013) 19 *European Law Journal* 1.

De Benedetto, M, 'Effective Law from a Regulatory and Administrative Law Perspective' (2018) 9 *European Journal of Risk Regulation* 391.

de Búrca, G, 'The Quest for Legitimacy in the European Union' (1996) 59 *Modern Law Review* 3.

de Visser, M, *Network-based Governance in EC Law: The Example of EC Competition and EC Communications Law* (Wolf Legal Publishers 2009).

de Vries, F, *Leidt transparantie tot meer vertrouwen in de toezichthouder?* (inaugural lecture Rijksuniversiteit Groningen) 29 March 2016 available at https://www.afm.nl/~/profmedia/files/publicaties/2016/femke-de-vries/oratie-leidt-transparantie-tot-meer-vertrouwen.ashx, accessed 15 February 2021.

Dehousse, R, 'Misfits: EU Law and the Transformation of European Governance' in C Joerges and R Dehousse (eds), *Good Governance in Europe's Integrated Market* (Oxford University Press 2002) 223.

Dehousse, R, 'Delegation of Powers in the European Union: The Need for a Multi-Principals Model' (2008) 31 *West European Politics* 789.

Deumier, P, 'Quand le droit souple rencontre le juge dur' (2016) *RTD Civ* 571.

di Noia, C and M C Furlo, 'The New Structure of Financial Supervision in Europe: What's Next?' in E Wymeersch, K J Hopt and G Ferrarini (eds), *Financial Regulation and Supervision: A Post-crisis Analysis* (Oxford University Press 2012) 172.

Dutheillet, L, de Lamothe and G Odinet, 'Un recours souple pour le droit souple' (2016) 13 *L'Actualité Juridique Droit Administratif* 717.

Ehnert, T, 'The Legitimacy of New Risk Governance – A Critical View in Light of the EU's Approach to Nanotechnologies in Food' (2015) 21 *European Law Journal* 44.

Eliantonia, E and O Stefan, 'Soft Law before the European Courts: Discovering a "Common Pattern"?' 37 *Yearbook of European Law* 457.

Emiliou, N, *The Principle of Proportionality in European Law: A Comparative Study* (Kluwer Law International 1996).

Ferran, E, 'Understanding the New Institutional Architecture of EU Financial Market Supervision' in E Wymeersch, K J Hopt and G Ferrarini (eds), *Financial Regulation and Supervision: A Post-crisis Analysis* (Oxford University Press 2012) 134.

Fischer-Appelt, D, 'The European Securities and Markets Authority: The Beginnings of a Powerful European Securities Authority?' (2011) 5 *Law and Financial Markets Review* 21.

Frissen, P, *Het geheim van de laatste staat. Kritiek van de transparantie* (Boom uitgevers 2016).

Galetta, DU, H Hofmann, O Mir Puigpelat and J Ziller, 'The General Principles of EU Administrative Procedural Law' (PE 519/224 2015), available at www.europarl.europa.eu/RegData/etudes/IDAN/2015/519224/IPOL_IDA%282015%29519224_EN.pdf, accessed 15 February 2021.

Georgieva, Z, 'Soft Law in EU Competition Law and Its Judicial Reception in Member States: A Theoretical Perspective' (2015) 16 *German Law Journal* 223.

Georgieva, Z, *Soft Law in EU Competition Law and Its Reception in Member States' Courts* (dissertation Tilburg University 2017).

Gehring, T and S Krapohl, 'Supranational Regulatory Agencies between Independence and Control: The EMEA and the Authorization of Pharmaceuticals in the European Single Market' (2007) 14 *Journal of European Public Policy* 208.

Griller, S and A Orator, 'Everything under Control? The "Way Forward" for European Agencies in the footsteps of the *Meroni* Doctrine' (2010) 35 *European Law Review* 3.

Groenleer, M, *The Autonomy of European Union Agencies: A Comparative Study of Institutional Development* (Eburon 2009).

Harlow, C and R Rawlings, 'Promoting Accountability in Multilevel Governance: A Network Approach (2007) 13 *European Law Journal* 542.

Hartlapp, M and A Hofmann, 'The Use of EU Soft Law by National Courts and Bureaucrats: How Relation to Hard Law and Policy Maturity Matter' (2020) *West European Politics* 134.

Hartley, T, *The Foundations of European Community Law: An Introduction to the Constitutional and Administrative Law of the European Community* (4th edn, Oxford University Press 1998) 124.

Héritier, A, 'Composite Democracy in Europe: The Role of Transparency and Access to Information' (2003) 10 *Journal of European Public Policy* 814.

Heyvaert, V, J Thornton and R Drabble, 'With Reference to the Environment: The Preliminary Reference Procedure, Environmental Decisions and the Domestic Jury' (2014) 130 *Law Quarterly Review* 413.

Hofmann, H and A Türk, *Legal Challenges in EU Administrative Law: Towards an Integrated Administration* (Edward Elgar Publishing 2009).

Hofmann, H, G Rowe and A Türk, *Administrative Law and Policy of the European Union* (Oxford University Press 2011).

Howell, E, 'EU Agencification and the Rise of ESMA: Are Its Governance Arrangements Fit for Purpose?' (2019) 78 *Cambridge Law Journal* 324.

Jans, J, S Prechal and R Widdershoven, *Inleiding tot het Europees bestuursrecht* (Ars Aequi 2011).

Kaeding, M and E Versluis, 'EU Agencies as a Solution to Pan-European Implementation Problems' in M Everson, C Monda and E Vos (eds), *European Agencies in between Institutions and Member States* (Wolters Kluwer 2014) 73.

Kanninen, H, 'Litigation before the EU General Court and the Board of Appeal: Similarities and Differences' (24 May 2017) .

Kilpatrick, C, 'On the Rule of Law and Economic Emergency: The Degradation of Basic Legal Values in Europe's Bailouts' (2015) 35 *Oxford Journal of Legal Studies* 325.

Klamert, M, *The Principle of Loyalty in EU Law* (Oxford University Press 2014).

Klinger, K and L Senden, 'How Failing Aggregates Brought About a Landmark Decision of the CJEU' (*Renforce Blog* 3 January 2017) available at http://blog.renforce.eu/index.php/nl/2017/01/03/how-failing-aggregates-brought-about-a-landmark-decision-of-the-cjeu/, accessed 15 February 2021.

Koops, C, *Contemplating Compliance: European Compliance Mechanisms in International Perspective* (Digital Academic Repository 2014).

Korkea-Aho, E, 'EU Soft Law in Domestic Legal Systems: Flexibility and Diversity Guaranteed' (2009) 16 *Maastricht Journal of European and Comparative Law* 271.

Korkea-Aho, E, 'Laws in Progress: Reconceptualizing Accountability Strategies in the Era of Framework Norms' (2013) 2 *Transnational Environmental Law* 363.

Korkea-Aho, 'E, National Courts and European Soft Law: Is Grimaldi Still Good Law?' (2018) 37 *Yearbook of European Law* 470.

Kost de Sevres, N and L Sasso, 'The New European Financial Markets Legal Framework: A Real Improvement? An Analysis of Financial Law and Governance in European Capital Markets from a Micro- and Macro-economic Perspective' (2011) 7 *Capital Markets Law Journal* 30.

Lachnit, E, *Alternative Enforcement of Competition Law* (Eleven International Publishing 2016).

Lenaerts, K and P van Nuffel, *Constitutional Law of the European Union* (Sweet & Maxwell 2005).

Lindgren, K and T Persson, 'Input and Output Legitimacy: Synergy or Trade-off? Empirical Evidence from an EU Survey' (2010) 17 *Journal of European Public Policy* 449.

Lubbers, J, *A Guide to Federal Agency Rulemaking* (5th edn, American Bar Association 2012).

Luijendijk, H and L Senden, 'Preadvies NVER: De gelaagde doorwerking van Europese administratieve soft law in de nationale rechtsorde' (2011) 7/8 *SEW Tijdschrift voor Europees en economisch recht* 312.

Majone, G, *Regulating Europe* (Routledge 1996).

Majone, G, 'The Regulatory State and Its Legitimacy Problems' (1999) 22 *West European Politics* 1.

Majone, G, 'Legitimacy and Effectiveness: A Response to Professor Michael Dougan's Review Article on Dilemmas of European Integration' (2007) 32 *European Law Review* 70.

Marjosola, H, 'Bridging the Constitutional Gap in EU Executive Rule-making: The Court of Justice Approves Legislative Conferral of Intervention Powers to European Securities and Markets Authority' (2014) 10 *European Constitutional Law Review* 500.

Marxsen, C, 'Open Stakeholder Consultations at the European Level – Voice of the Citizens?' (2015) 21 *European Law Journal* 257.

Melleray, F, 'Le contrôle juridictionnel des actes de droit souple' (2016a) *Revue Française de Droit Administratif* 679.

Melleray, F, 'Précisions sur les modalités de contestation d'un acte de droit souple' (2016b) *L'Actualité Juridique Droit Administratif* 2119.

Mendes, J, *Participation in EU Rule-making: A Rights-based Approach* (Oxford University Press 2011).

Meuwese, A, *Impact Assessment in EU Lawmaking* (Kluwer Law International 2008).

Mitnick, B, 'Capturing "Capture": Definition and Mechanisms' in D Levi-Faur (ed), *Handbook on the Politics of Regulation* (Edward Elgar Publishing 2011) 35.

Moloney, N, 'The ESMA and Institutional Design for the EU Financial Market – A Tale of Two Competences: Part (1) Rule-Making' (2011a) 12 *European Business Organization Law Review* 41.

Moloney, N, 'Reform or Revolution? The Financial Crisis, EU Financial Markets Law and the European Securities and Markets Authority' (2011b) 60 *International and Comparative Law Quarterly* 521.

Moloney, N, 'Supervision in the Wake of the Financial Crisis: Achieving "Effective Law in Action" – A Challenge for the EU' in E Wymeersch, K J Hopt and G Ferrarini (eds), *Financial Regulation and Supervision: A Post-crisis Analysis* (Oxford University Press 2012) 102.

Moloney, N, 'The European Securities and Markets Authority: A Perspective from One Year On' (2013) 68 *Zeitschrif für öffentliches Recht* 59.

Moloney, N, *EU Securities and Financial Markets Regulation* (Oxford University Press 2014).

Mousmouti, M, 'Making Legislative Effectiveness an Operational Concept: Unfolding the Effectiveness Test as a Conceptual Tool for Lawmaking' (2018) 9 *European Journal of Risk Regulation* 445.

Neyer, J, 'Explaining the Unexpected: Efficiency and Effectiveness in European Decision-making' (2004) 11 *Journal of European Public Policy* 19.

Novak, S, 'The Silence of Ministers: Consensus and Blame Avoidance in the Council of the European Union' (2013) 51 *Journal of Common Market Studies* 1091.

Obradovic, D and J M Alonso Vizcaino, 'Good Governance Requirements Concerning the Participation of Interest Groups in the EU Consultations' (2006) 43 *Common Market Law Review* 1049.

Ortlep, R and R Widdershoven, 'Judicial Protection' in J Jans, S Prechal and R Widdershoven (eds), *Europeanisation of Public Law* (2nd edn, Europa Law Publishing 2015) 333.

Ossege, C, *European Regulatory Agencies in EU Decision-making: Between Expertise and Influence* (Springer 2016).

Ottow, A, *Telecommunicatietoezicht. De invloed van het Europese en Nederlandse bestuurs(proces)recht* (Sdu Uitgevers 2006).

Ottow, A, *De markt meester? De zoektocht naar nieuwe vormen van toezicht* (Boom Juridische uitgevers 2009).

Ottow, A, 'European Supervision of the Financial Markets' (2011) Working Paper 02/11 *Europa Institute Utrecht* 1.

Ottow, A, 'Europeanization of the Supervision of Competitive Markets' (2012) 18 *European Public Law* 191.

Ottow, A, *Market and Competition Authorities: Good Agency Principles* (Oxford University Press 2015).

Piris, J C, 'After Maastricht, Are the Community Institutions More Efficacious, More Democratic and More Transparent?' (1994) 19 *European Law Review* 449.

Polak, J, *What Works to Make EU Law Work? An Analysis of the Usefulness of National, Transnational, and Supranational Compliance Instruments* (dissertation Maastricht University 2015).

Prechal, S, *Directives in EC Law* (2nd edn, Oxford University Press 2005).

Prechal, S, 'Competence Creep and General Principles of Law' (2009) 3 *Review of European Administrative Law* 5.

Prechal, S, 'Europeanisation of National Administrative Law' in J Jans, S Prechal and R Widdershoven (eds), *Europeanisation of Public Law* (Europa Law Publishing 2015) 39.

Prechal, S, R Widdershoven and J Jans, 'Introduction' in J Jans, S Prechal and R Widdershoven (eds), *Europeanisation of Public Law* (Europa Law Publishing 2015) 1.

Rangone, N, 'Making Law Effective: Behavioural Insights into Compliance' (2018) 9 *European Journal of Risk Regulation* 483.

Schammo, P, 'The European Securities and Markets Authority: Lifting the Veil on the Allocation of Powers' (2011) 48 *Common Market Law Review* 1879.

Schammo, P, 'Actions and Inactions in the Investigation of Breaches of Union Law by the European Supervisory Authorities' (2018) 55 *Common Market Law Review* 1423.

Scharpf, F, *Governing in Europe: Effective and Democratic* (Oxford University Press 1999).

Scharpf, F, 'De-constitutionalisation and Majority Rule: A Democratic Vision for Europe' (2017) 23 *European Law Journal* 315.

Schemmel, J, 'The ESA Guidelines: Soft Law and Subjectivity in the European Financial Market – Capturing the Administrative Influence' (2016) 23 *Indiana Journal of Global Legal* 455.

Schmidt, V A, 'Democracy and Legitimacy in the European Union Revisited: Input, Output and "Throughput"' (2013) 61 *Political Studies* 2.

Schmidt, V and M Wood, 'Conceptualizing Throughput Legitimacy: Procedural Mechanisms of Accountability, Transparency, Inclusiveness and Openness in EU Governance' (2019) 97 *Public Administration* 727.

Scholten, M, 'Independent, Hence Unaccountable? The Need for a Broader Debate on the Accountability of the Executive' (2011) 4 *Review of European Administrative Law* 5.

Scholten, M, *The Political Accountability of EU and US Independent Regulatory Agencies* (Brill 2014a).

Scholten, M, 'Independence vs. Accountability: Proving the Negative Correlation' (2014b) 21 *Maastricht Journal of European and Comparative Law* 197.

Scholten, M and M Luchtman (eds), *Law Enforcement by EU Authorities: Implications for Political and Judicial Accountability* (Edward Elgar Publishing 2017).

Scholten, M, M Luchtman and E Schmidt, 'The Proliferation of EU Enforcement Authorities: A New Development in Law Enforcement in the EU' in M Scholten and M Luchtman (eds), *Law Enforcement by EU Authorities: Implications for Political and Judicial Accountability* (Edward Elgar Publishing 2017) 1.

Scholten, M and A Ottow, 'Institutional Design of Enforcement in the EU: The Case of Financial Markets' (2014) 10 *Utrecht Law Review* 80.

Scholten, M and M Van Rijsbergen, 'The ESMA-Short Selling Case: Erecting a New Delegation Doctrine in the EU upon the *Meroni–Romano* Remnants' (2014a) 41 *Legal Issues of Economic Integration* 389.

Scholten, M and M van Rijsbergen, 'The Limits of Agencification in the European Union' (2014b) 15 *German Law Journal* 1223.

Schütze, R, *From Dual to Cooperative Federalism: The Changing Structure of European Law* (Oxford University Press 2009).

Schwarze, J, *European Administrative Law* (Sweet & Maxwell 2006).

Scott, C, 'Accountability in the Regulatory State' (2000) 27 *Journal of Law and Society* 38.

Scott, J, 'Law, Legitimacy and EC Governance: Prospects for Partnership' (1998) 36 *Journal of Common Market Studies* 175.

Scott, J, 'In Legal Limbo: Post Legislative Guidance as a Challenge for European Administrative Law' (2011) 48 *Common Market Law Review* 329.

Scott, J and S Sturm, 'Courts as Catalysts: Rethinking the Judicial Role in New Governance' (2007) 13 *Columbia Journal of European Law* 565.

Senden, L, *Soft Law in European Community Law* (Hart Publishing 2004).

Senden, L, 'Gelijke behandeling, participatie en effectiviteit als fundamenten van het Unieburgerschap' in T van den Brink, S de Vries and M DeKoninck (eds), *Beginselen bouwen burgerschap* (Boom Juridische Uitgevers 2011) 27.

Senden, L, 'Soft Post-legislative Rulemaking in the EU: A Time for More Stringent Control' (2013) 19 *European Law Journal* 57.

Senden, L, 'Schaduwgebieden van Europese regulering' (2015) 5 *RegelMaat* 338.

Senden, L and C Scott, *The Onward March of Soft Law in the EU: From Core Institutions to Network and Private Governance Regimes*, EUSA Conference 2015: Boston.

Senden, L and A van den Brink, 'Checks and Balances of Soft EU Rule-making' (PE 462/433 2012) available at www.europarl.europa.eu/thinktank/en/document.html?reference=IPOL-JURI_ET(2012)462433, accessed 15 February 2021.

Shapiro, M, 'The Giving Reasons Requirement' [1992] *University of Chicago Legal Forum* 179.

Shapiro, M, 'Independent Agencies' in P Craig and G de Búrca (eds), *The Evolution of EU Law* (Oxford University Press 2011) 111.

Simoncini, M, 'Legal Boundaries of European Supervisory Authorities in the Financial Markets: Tensions in the Development of True Regulatory Agencies' (2015a) 34 *Yearbook of European Law* 319.

Simoncini, M, 'The Erosion of the *Meroni* Doctrine: The Case of the European Aviation Safety Agency' (2015b) 21 *European Public Law* 309.

Simoncini, M, *Administrative Regulation beyond the Non-delegation Doctrine: A Study on EU Agencies* (Hart Publishing 2018).

Simoncini, M and M Van Rijsbergen, 'Controlling ESMA's Enforcement Powers' in M Scholten and A Brenninkmeijer (eds), *Controlling EU Agencies: The Rule of Law in a Multi-jurisdictional Legal Order* (Edward Elgar Publishing 2020) 272.

Snyder, F, 'The Effectiveness of European Community Law: Institutions, Processes, Tools and Techniques' (1993) 56 *The Modern Law Review* 19.

Stefan, O, 'European Competition Soft Law in European Courts: A Matter of Hard Principles?' (2008) 14 *European Law Journal* 753.

Stefan, O, *Soft Law in Court: Competition Law, State Aid and the Court of Justice of the European Union* (Kluwer Law International 2012a).

Stefan, O, 'European Union Soft Law: New Developments Concerning the Divide between Legally Binding Force and Legal Effects' (2012b) 75 *Modern Law Review* 879.

Stefan, O, 'Soft Law and the Enforcement of EU Law' in A Jakab and D Kochenov (eds), *The Enforcement of EU Law and Values: Ensuring Member States' Compliance* (Oxford University Press 2017) 200.

Stefan, O and M Petri, 'Too Weak to Be Controlled: Judicial Review of ACER Soft Law' (2018) 37 *Yearbook of European Law* 525.

Stefan, O, M Avbelj, M Eliantonio, M Hartlapp, E Korka-Aho and N Rubio, 'EU Soft Law in the EU Legal Order: A Literature Review', SOLAR, 2018, available at www.solar-network.eu/publications/solar-working-papers/, accessed 26 February 2021.

Terpan, F 'Soft Law in the European Union: The Changing Nature of EU Law' (2015) 21 *European Law Journal* 68.

Tridimas, T, *The General Principles of EU Law* (Oxford University Press 2007).

Tridimas, T, 'EU Financial Regulation: Federalization, Crisis Management, and Law Reform' in P Craig and G de Búrca (eds), *The Evolution of EU Law* (Oxford University Press 2011) 783.

Türk, A, *Judicial Review in EU Law* (Edward Elgar Publishing 2009).

van Cleynenbreugel, P, *Market Supervision in the European Union: Integrated Administration in Constitutional Context* (Brill 2014a).

van Cleynenbrueguel, P, '*Meroni* Circumvented? Article 114 TFEU and EU Regulatory Agencies' (2014b) 21 *Maastricht Journal of International Law* 64.

van Dam, C, 'Het Hof van Justitie spreekt zich uit over de bindende werking van een aanbeveling van de Europese Commissie' (2017) 4 *Nederlands Tijdschrift voor Europees Recht* 84.
van Dam, C, *Guidance Documents of the European Commission in the Dutch Legal Order* (dissertation Leiden University 2020).
van den Brink, J, *De uitvoering van Europese subsidieregelingen in Nederland: juridische knelpunten en uitdagingen* (Kluwer 2012).
van den Brink, J, W den Ouden, S Prechal, R Widdershoven and J Jans, 'General Principles of Law' in J Jans, S Prechal and R Widdershoven (eds), *Europeanisation of Public Law* (2nd edn, Europa Law Publishing 2015) 133.
van den Brink, J and C van Dam, 'Nederlandse bestuursrechters en unierechtelijke "beleidsregels"' (2014) *JB Plus* 3, 26.
van den Broek, M, *Preventing Money Laundering: A Legal Study on the Effectiveness of Supervision in the European Union* (Eleven International Publishing 2015).
van Gestel, R, 'European Regulatory Agencies Adrift?' (2014) 21 *Maastricht Journal of European and Comparative Law* 188.
van Ooijk, R, *De keuze der rechtsgrondslag voor besluiten van de Europese Unie* (Kluwer 1999).
van Rijsbergen, M, 'On the Enforceability of EU Soft Law at the National Level: The Case of the European Securities and Markets Authority' (2014) 10 *Utrecht Law Review* 116.
van Rijsbergen, M and J Foster, '"Rating" ESMA's Accountability: "AAA" Status' in M Scholten and M Luchtman (eds), *Law Enforcement by EU Authorities: Implications for Political and Judicial Accountability* (Edward Elgar Publishing 2017) 53.
van Rijsbergen, M and E Rogge, 'Changes to the European Financial Supervisory Agencies' Soft Law Powers: Legitimacy Problems Solved or New Puzzles Created? (submitted for publication).
van Rijsbergen, M and M Scholten, 'ESMA Inspecting: The Implications for Judicial Control under Shared Enforcement' (2016) 7 *European Journal of Risk Regulation* 569.
Vaughan, S, *EU Chemicals Regulation: New Governance, Hybridity and REACH* (Edward Elgar Publishing 2015a).
Vaughan, S, 'Differentiation and Dysfunction: An Exploration of Post-legislative Guidance Practices in 14 EU Agencies' (2015b) 17 *Cambridge Yearbook of European Legal Studies* 66.
Verhoeven, M, 'Bestuursorganen en legaliteit in communautair perspectief' in M Verhoeven, J van den Brink and A Drahmann (eds), *Europees offensief tegen nationalerechtsbeginselen? Overlegaliteit, rechtszekerheid, vertrouwenentransparantie* (Boom Juridische uitgevers 2010) 15.
Verhoeven, M and R Widdershoven, 'National Legality and European Obligations' in L Besselink, F Pennings and S Prechal (eds), *The Eclipse of the Legality Principle in the European Union* (Wolters Kluwer 2010) 55.
Vervaele, J, *Compliance and Enforcement of European Community Law* (Wolters Kluwer 1999).
Volpato, A, 'The Harmonized Standards before the ECJ: James Elliott Construction' (2017) 54 *Common Market Law Review* 591.
von Coester, S, 'Les communiqués, Conclusions sur Conseil d'État, assemblée, 21 mars 2016, n° 368082, Société Fairvesta International GmbH et autres, au Lebon' [2016] *Revue Française de Droit Administratif* 497.

Vos, E, 'Independence, Accountability and Transparency of European Regulatory Agencies' in D Geradin, R Muñoz and N Petit (eds), *Regulation through Agencies in the EU: A New Paradigm of European Governance* (Edward Elgar Publishing 2005) 120.

Weber, A, 'Principles on the Distribution and Limits of Competences' in H J Blanke and S Mangiameli (eds), *The Treaty on European Union (TEU): A Commentary* (Springer 2010) 262.

Weismann, P, 'The European Financial Market Supervisory Authorities and Their Power to Issue Binding Decisions' (2012) 27 *Journal of International Banking Law and Regulation* 495.

Wellens, K and G Borchardt, 'Soft Law in European Community Law' (1989) 14 *European Law Review* 267.

Wiener, J and B Richman, 'Mechanism Choice' in D Farber and A O'Connell (eds), *Research Handbook on Public Choice and Public Law* (Edward Elgar Publishing 2010) 369.

Wymeersch, E, 'The European Financial Supervisory Authorities or ESAs' in E Wymeersch, K J Hopt and G Ferrarini (eds), *Financial Regulation and Supervision: A Post-crisis Analysis* (Oxford University Press 2012) 232.

Xanthaki, H, 'An Enlightened Approach to Legislative Scrutiny: Focusing on Effectiveness' (2018) 9 *European Journal of Risk Regulation* 431.

Zamboni, M, 'Legislative Policy and Effectiveness: A (Small) Contribution from Legal Theory (2018) 9 *European Journal of Risk Regulation* 416.

Index